DISCARD

AN UNOFFICIAL GUIDE TO BATTLE ROYALE

EXPERT SNIPER STRATEGIES FOR FORTNITERS

MASTER COMBAT SERIES #1

JASON R. RICH

Sky Pony Press
New York

Sky Pony Press books may be purchased in bulk at special discounts for sales promotion, corporate gifts, fund-raising, or educational purposes. Special editions can also be created to specifications. For details, contact the Special Sales Department, Sky Pony Press, 307 West 36th Street, 11th Floor, New York, NY 10018 or info@skyhorsepublishing.com.

Sky Pony® is a registered trademark of Skyhorse Publishing, Inc.®, a Delaware corporation.

Visit our website at www.skyponypress.com.

Authors, books, and more at SkyPonyPressBlog.com.

10 9 8 7 6 5 4 3 2 1

Library of Congress Cataloging-in-Publication Data is available on file.

Cover design by Brian Peterson
Cover image by Getty Images
Interior photography by Jason R. Rich

Print ISBN: 978-1-5107-4971-9
E-Book ISBN: 978-1-5107-4976-4

Printed in the United States of America

TABLE OF CONTENTS

Section 1—Discover the Ever-Changing World
of *Fortnite: Battle Royale* 1
More Ways *Fortnite: Battle Royale* Constantly Changes 5
All Guns Require the Proper Type of Ammunition 7
Your Distance from a Target Matters 9
Most Weapon Types Are Available in Different Tiers 11
Keep Up-to-Date on Weapon Ratings 12
Keep Tabs on Your Soldier's Health and Shield Meters 15
The Six Skills You'll Need to Become a Sharpshooter 16

Section 2—*Fortnite: Battle Royale*
Gaming Basics 23
How to Download and Install *Fortnite: Battle Royale* 25
Customize Your Gaming Experience 26
Consider Upgrading Your Gaming Gear 29
Don't Focus on the Game Settings Used
by Top-Ranked Players 32
Experience *Fortnite: Battle Royale* Using the Fastest
Internet Connection Possible 33
How to Make In-Game Purchases 34
Ways to Customize the Appearance of Your Soldier 35
Visit the Item Shop 42
Purchase a Current Battle Pass 44
An Additional Way to Unlock Cosmetic Items 45
Take Advantage of Twitch Prime Packs 45

Section 3—Jump Right into a
Fortnite: Battle Royale Match and Fight 47
Choose Your Landing Location Wisely 51
Prepare for a Safe Landing 53
Start Building Your Arsenal Right Away 57
Explore and Find What You Need 60

Section 4—How to Accurately Shoot
the Various Types of Weapons 65
Where to Find Weapons on the Island 76
Managing Your Soldier's Inventory 79
How to Rearrange What's in Inventory Slots 81
How to Drop and Share Weapons, Ammo, and Items 81
Discover When and How to Fire Each Weapon 82
How to Accurately Aim and Fire Different
Types of Weapons 84

Section 5—Building for Offensive and
Defensive Purposes 89
The Basics of Building on the Island 91
How to Build a Barrier for Protection 92
Build Ramps and Bridges to Reach Difficult Places 93
Eight Things You Need to Know About Building 97
Learn How to Build a 1x1 Fortress 98
Building Techniques for the End Game 102

Section 6—Popular Health, Shield,
and Loot Items 107
Health and Shield Replenishment Items 109
Useful Loot Items & Tools 110
Weapon-Related Items 113

Section 7—*Fortnite: Battle Royale* Resources 115
Your *Fortnite: Battle Royale* Adventure Continues 120

SECTION 1

DISCOVER THE EVER-CHANGING WORLD OF *FORTNITE: BATTLE ROYALE*

When you step onto the mysterious island where *Fortnite: Battle Royale* takes place, you're always guaranteed to experience plenty of fun, as well as a few surprises.

Epic Games (the game's developer) continuously tweaks Fortnite: Battle Royale by introducing new gaming elements, such as: points of interest (locations) to the island, types of terrain to explore, ways to get around the island, as well as weapons and loot items.

This is how the island map looked during Season 3 of Fortnite: Battle Royale. A lot has changed geographically on the island since then. There have been earthquakes, massive explosions, volcano eruptions, meteor strikes, an ice age, and other terrain-changing disasters.

Shown here is the Season 8 island map. As you can see, there are all-new points of interest, along with vastly different types of terrain and terrain-based challenges. During Season 9 and beyond, expect some additional and rather significant geographic changes to the island.

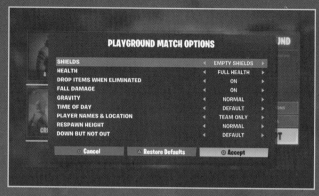

During each Solo (shown above), Duos, or Squads match you experience, for example, you control a single soldier who is visiting the island at the same time as up to 99 other soldiers, each of whom is controlled in real time by a different gamer. Since each gamer's experience level, reaction time, and thought process is different, it's virtually impossible to predict what to expect each time you encounter an enemy on the island.

The Playground mode (shown above) allows you to spend time on the island exploring and experimenting with different weapons and items at your own pace. Creative mode allows you to design your own island from scratch, and then challenge yourself and other gamers in a one-of-a-kind match. There are also temporary game play modes from Epic Games, like Team Rumble, High Explosives, and 50v50 Squads, each of which offers an entirely different way to experience your time on the island.

In addition to the three main *Fortnite: Battle Royale* game play modes—Solo, Duos, and Squads—Epic Games continues to introduce other exciting game play modes that allow you to experience the game in entirely new and challenging ways.

If you're a newb (beginner), playing 50v50 matches typically allows you to stay in matches longer, find and utilize more powerful weapons, and have up to 49 other gamers watching your back in battles.

More Ways Fortnite: Battle Royale *Constantly Changes*

There are also many other things that keep *Fortnite: Battle Royale* interesting and challenging.

The ability to customize the appearance of your soldier is an extremely popular gaming feature, although how your soldier looks has no impact whatsoever on their fighting, exploration, building, or survival capabilities during a match.

From vehicles to airplanes, jetpacks, rifts, hoverboards, balloons, and ziplines, discovering unique ways to use these transportation options can give you a tactical advantage during matches. With one, two, or three balloons attached to your soldier's back, for example, they can defy gravity and make large leaps, and then drift slowly to the ground without injury. The drawback to this transportation method (shown here on an iPad Pro) is that while airborne, your soldier becomes an easier target to see and shoot.

In addition to purchasing or unlocking outfits and cosmetic accessories, including Back Bling (your soldier's backpack), Harvesting Tool (pickaxe) designs, Glider designs, Contrail designs, Emotes, and weapon wraps for your soldier, some of the outfits themselves can be altered using Unlockable Styles. These are typically unlocked by accomplishing specific tasks during game play.

Plus, each time a new way to transport your soldier around the island is introduced, it provides yet another way to protect your soldier, explore more territory faster, and potentially launch creative attacks against your enemies.

Shown here is a soldier riding a hoverboard around the island within the iPad version of Fortnite: Battle Royale. While riding a hoverboard, in addition to traveling much faster than on foot, it's possible to travel over cliffs and go airborne, without the risk of injury resulting from a fall. Many gamers believe this is the most fun way to quickly travel around the island.

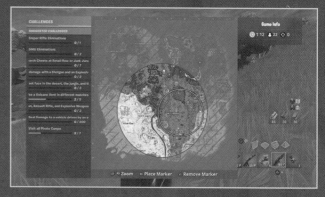

As if fighting against up to 99 other potentially well-armed soldiers isn't difficult enough, while on the island, there's also the deadly storm to contend with. Shortly after each match begins, the storm forms and then slowly expands and moves, while at the same time, making more and more of the island uninhabitable. When viewing the island map, what's displayed in pink (outside of the safe circle) is the area that's no longer safe to be in.

Throughout certain parts of the island, a network of ziplines allow you to get from one location to another. While gliding through the air, you're able to aim and shoot your soldier's active weapon, but you also become a moving target for your enemies.

It's possible to travel from the top to bottom, or from the bottom to the top of a hill or mountain that offers a zipline. Some ziplines offer a horizontal path on which you can travel in either direction.

When exploring the island itself, the edge of the storm looks like a blue wall. Shown here, the soldier is on the safe side of the wall. If he were to cross this blue barrier into the unsafe terrain, his Health meter would immediately begin to diminish. Displayed directly below the mini-map (seen here in the top-right corner of the screen) is a timer that informs you when the storm will be moving and expanding again.

And then there are the heart-pounding firefight and combat elements of Fortnite: Battle Royale. To win a match, your goal is to become the last soldier alive, which means up to 99 adversaries must be eliminated. While during Solo matches you can defeat lots of enemies to boost your player XP and increase your level, only one gamer can actually win each match and achieve #1 Victory Royale.

All Guns Require the Proper Type of Ammunition

At the start of each match, your soldier lands on the island armed only with a Harvesting Tool (pickaxe)—with no other weapons, tools, ammo, or anything that can help him or her survive.

Through exploration, one objective is to find and gather a personal arsenal that'll help you win firefights and battles. As soon as your soldier lands on the island, seek out and grab a weapon and ammo so you can properly protect yourself. The Harvester Tool can be swung at enemies at very close range, but it'll take multiple direct hits to defeat that enemy. Plus, the Harvester Tool is no match for an enemy that's armed with any type of gun.

Don't forget, every type of gun requires compatible ammo. There are different types of ammo to find and stockpile. It's essential that you maintain an ample supply of ammo for the specific weapons your soldier is carrying. Shown above, the soldier is about to pick up a stash of Medium Bullets. This type of ammo is typically used by Assault Rifles.

Rockets are projectile and explosive weapons that get shot from a projectile (explosive) weapon launcher, such as a Rocket Launcher, Quad Launcher, Grenade Launcher, or Guided Missile Launcher. This type of ammo can be shot from a distance, and then typically explodes either immediately on impact or several seconds after impact. Not only is it useful for inflicting major damage on enemies, it can also be used to destroy structures, objects, or fortresses.

Light Bullets are about to be picked up and added to the soldier's inventory. This type of ammo is typically used in smaller, handheld weapons, such as Pistols and some SMGs.

Shells are used in various types of Shotguns. These weapons work well against close- to mid-range targets for a few reasons. When a shell is shot from a Shotgun, the ammo splits apart into many tiny pieces. When those pieces hit one target, each piece of the shell causes damage. However, if two targets are at close range, pieces from a single shell can hit and injure (or even kill) multiple targets at once.

Heavy Bullets are used mainly in Sniper Rifles. This are the highest caliber ammo available on the island. It's useful for inflicting damage on long-range targets. Weapons that use Heavy Bullets tend to have a low fire rate and long reload time, but they also cause the most damage per shot when a direct hit is made.

The drawback to a Shotgun that shoots shells is that if your soldier is too far away from a target when shooting this weapon, the shell fragments spread out a lot. Less of the ammo will hits your intended target, which means each hit causes less damage. Plus, the farther away you are from your target when using a Shotgun, the less accurate your aim becomes.

Your Distance from a Target Matters

Throughout each match, your circumstances and surroundings constantly change, as does the type of terrain you're visiting. As a result, expect your weapon and ammo needs to change during a match.

Sometimes you'll need to focus on close-range fighting, like when you're exploring indoors, or when you're in an area that contains a lot of buildings and structures located close together. At other times, you'll be farther away from your adversaries and need to rely more on mid- to long-range weapons. Various types of Pistols and Shotguns are great close-range weapons.

Assault Rifles (ARs), Grenade Launchers, Pistols, Rocket Launchers, Sniper Rifles, Shotguns, Submachine Guns (SMGs), and Throwable Grenades are among the weapon categories available on the island. Within each category, there are multiple types of weapons. Shown here is an Assault Rifle that's about to be picked up by the soldier (iPad version).

This soldier is using a Heavy Assault Rifle to target the door of a building. As soon as an enemy approaches the door, shooting will begin in hopes of an easy victory.

A Common Suppressed Submachine Gun can do some decent damage relatively quickly, especially when at close- to mid-range from your target. Its magazine holds 30 rounds, and its reload

time is about 2.2 seconds. An Uncommon or Rare Suppressed Submachine Gun also holds 30 rounds, but the reload time is a bit faster and the weapon's DPS goes from 198 (Common) to 207 (Uncommon) to 216 (Rare). Keep in mind, these stats can change in conjunction with game updates.

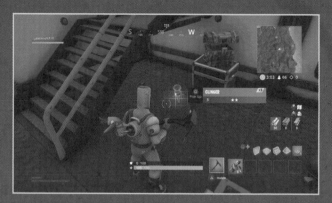

As you'll soon learn, various types of throwable weapons (like Clingers) can be very useful, but only in specific types of fighting situations. For example, when you toss a Grenade at a solid object, such as a wall, it'll bounce off that wall and come back toward your soldier. However, if your target is hiding within an enclosed space, and you toss a Grenade through an open door or window, the resulting explosion could injure or defeat your enemies, plus cause damage to the structure they're hiding in.

In the Pistol category, there are Revolvers, Pistols, Suppressed Pistols, Hand Cannons, Dual Pistols, Six Shooters, and Scoped Revolvers. Each weapon type has its own capabilities that are rated based on their Damage Per Second (DPS), Damage, Fire Rate, Magazine (Mag) Capacity, and reload time. Shown here on an iPad is a Suppressed Pistol that's about to be picked up.

Here's a Suppressed Pistol on an iPad being used as an active weapon by a soldier as she explores within a building and expects to encounter enemies at close range. A Rare Suppressed Pistol's DPS is 181.5, it's Fire Rate is 5.5 bullets per second, it's Mag size is 30, and its reload time is 2.1 seconds. Like all other weapons, this weapon's stats can change in conjunction with game updates.

Most Weapon Types Are Available in Different Tiers

Each weapon type falls into a specific weapon category. Weapons are also ranked based on their tier. *Fortnite: Battle Royale* offers weapons that come in several different, color-coded weapon tiers, which impact their capabilities and ratings. Not all weapon types, however, are available in each of these tiers.

An **Uncommon** version of a weapon has a green hue. It is slightly more powerful than a Common version of that same weapon. This soldier is about to pick up an Uncommon Pistol. These handheld weapons are great for close-range combat, plus their Mag holds 16 rounds of ammo. The reload time is 1.5 seconds.

A **Rare** weapon has a blue hue. It's a bit more powerful than an Uncommon version of that same weapon.

An **Epic** version of the weapon has a purple hue. It can cause even more damage than an identical Common, Uncommon, or Rare tiered weapon. Here, the soldier is about to pick up an Epic Pump Shotgun.

A **Common** version of a weapon has a gray hue and is the weakest. This soldier is about to pick up a Common Suppressed Machine Gun that's lying on the ground within a building.

*The most powerful tier of weapons is **Legendary**. These have a golden (orange) hue. These are powerful weapons that are the hardest to find. This soldier is about to pick up a Legendary Heavy Assault Rifle. If your soldier makes it into the End Game of a match, their arsenal should include as many applicable Legendary weapons as possible.*

After a few more bullet hits, the wall's HP meter hits zero, causing the wall to be destroyed.

Keep Up-to-Date on Weapon Ratings

Every weapon offered within *Fortnite: Battle Royale* is rated based on several criteria. Combined, this determines how much damage a direct hit from that weapon can cause, based on certain situations. For example, a headshot will always cause more damage than a body shot when shooting at enemies.

Each weapon is rated based on its:

Damage Per Second (DPS) Rating—This determines how much damage a weapon can cause per second of continuous firing.

Damage Rating—This is a measure of how much overall damage the weapon can cause per direct hit.

Fire Rate—This determines how many rounds or bullets can be fired per second, either using Continuous or Burst shooting mode, or by quickly pressing the trigger.

Magazine (Mag) Size—Each weapon can hold a pre-determined number of bullets or rounds of ammunition at once before it needs to be reloaded. The Mag Size is the maximum number of bullets/rounds that can be held by the weapon at once.

Likewise, when you shoot at a structure, as opposed to an enemy soldier, the amount of damage each direct hit will cause will be different. When you point a weapon at an object to shoot, that object's HP meter is displayed. The wall that this soldier is shooting at has a 300HP meter when it's maxed out. After several shots, however, the wall's HP meter is down to just 56.

Reload Time—This determines how long it takes to reload a weapon once the magazine is empty. During this time, your soldier is vulnerable to attack and can't shoot back at their enemies. Some of the most powerful weapons in *Fortnite: Battle Royale* offer a small magazine size and slow reload time, but each direct hit causes the most damage to a target. A weapon with a fast reload time might have a smaller Mag Size or use less powerful ammo.

Structure Damage—This is a measure of how much damage a direct hit will cause on a structure, object, or building (as opposed to a soldier).

Some weapons allow you to choose between multiple firing modes. The **Single** fire mode means that one bullet is fired each time the weapon's trigger is pulled. When a weapon uses a **Burst** firing mode, multiple rounds of ammo are fired each time the trigger is pulled. Using **Continuous** fire mode, bullets keep firing continuously as long as you hold down the weapon's trigger or until the weapon runs out of ammo. Keep in mind that not all weapons allow you to switch between all three of these firing modes.

With each new game update that Epic Games introduces, and with each new season of game play, new weapons are typically introduced into the game, while others are removed. In some cases, an existing weapon's ratings get tweaked (making it either stronger or less powerful).

To learn about a specific weapon your soldier is carrying, access the Inventory screen and select the icon for that weapon.

Information about your soldier's active weapon (the one they are carrying and that's ready to use), as well as the other items in their inventory are also displayed as icons on the game screen. The location of this information varies, based on which gaming system you're using. The PS4 version of the game is shown here. The soldier's inventory information is seen in the lower-right corner of the screen.

At any time during a match (but only do it when it's safe), you can access your soldier's Inventory screen. From here, it's possible to rearrange the location of weapons, see what your soldier is carrying, drop items (or share them with others), and learn about each of the items (including your weapons) currently in your arsenal.

Shown here is the main game screen when playing the Windows PC version of Fortnite: Battle Royale. As you can see, basic information about your soldier's current weapons and inventory is also displayed near the bottom-right corner of the screen.

Game	🖥 ⚙ ☀ 🔊 🧑 🔲 🎮 👤

Invert Aircraft Mouse Controls	◄ Off ►
tivity Multiplier For Aircraft Steeri	2
Camera and Display	
Anonymous Mode	◄ Off ►
Hide Other Player Names	◄ On ►
Hidden Matchmaking Delay	0
HUD Scale	0.85
Show Spectator Count	◄ On ►
Peripheral Lighting	◄ On ►
Control Options	
Toggle Sprint	◄ Off ►
Sprint by Default	◄ Off ►
Sprint Cancels Reloading	◄ Off ►
Tap to Search / Interact	◄ Off ►
Toggle Targeting	◄ Off ►

Hide Other Player Names
Hides names of players that are not squad members. Their names will still be tracked for player reporting.

[A] Apply   [R] Reset   [ESC] Back

Whether you're playing the Xbox One, PS4, Nintendo Switch, Windows PC (shown above), or Mac version of Fortnite: Battle Royale, from the game's Settings menu, you're able to somewhat customize what information is displayed on the screen at any given time. Making certain adjustments, as you'll learn from Section 2–Fortnite: Battle Royale Gaming Basics, will help you eliminate non-essential clutter from the screen so you can focus more on the action and what's happening around your soldier on the island.

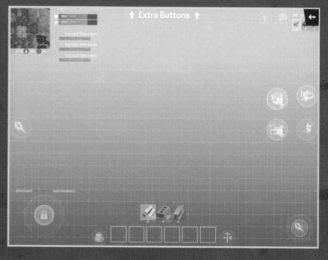

The mobile edition of Fortnite: Battle Royale is shown above on an iPad Pro. Using the game's built-in HUD Layout Tools, you're able to customize the location and display size of key information that's displayed on the HUD (Heads Up Display). To do this, simply access the game's main menu (tap on the icon comprised of three horizontal lines in the top-right corner of the screen) and then select the HUD Layout Tools option.

To stay up-to-date on all of the weapons currently available within *Fortnite: Battle Royale*, and to see the ratings for each weapon, check out any of these independent websites:

- **Fortnite Weapon Stats & Info—** https://fortnitestats.com/weapons
- **Gamepedia Fortnite Wiki—**https:// fortnite.gamepedia.com/Fortnite_Wiki
- **GameSkinny Fortnite Weapons List—**www.gameskinny.com/9mt22/ complete-fortnite-battle-royale- weapons-stats-list
- **Metabomb—**www.metabomb.net/ fortnite-battle-royale/gameplay- guides/fortnite-battle-royale-all- weapons-tier-list-with-stats-14
- **Tracker Network (Fortnite)—**https:// db.fortnitetracker.com/weapons

Keep Tabs on Your Soldier's Health and Shield Meters

Every soldier has Health and Shield meters that contain a certain amount of HP. Likewise, all objects also have an HP meter. Each direct hit with a weapon depletes some of the meter's HP. When a soldier's Health meter hits zero, that soldier is immediately eliminated from the match.

At the start of a match, a soldier's Health meter is maxed out at 100HP and their Shield meter is at zero. This is shown here at the bottom-center of the screen. Each time a soldier gets injured, as a result of an attack or fall, for example, some of their Health HP gets depleted. Again, based on which gaming system you're using, where this information is displayed varies.

Using Health replenishment items, like Bandages, Med Kits, Slurp Juices, Cozy Campfires, or Chug Jugs, it's possible to replenish some or all of your soldier's Health.

To activate and then maintain your soldier's Shield meter, you'll need to use a Shield replenishment item, such as Mushrooms, Small Shield Potions, Shield Potions, or Chug Jugs. Shields will protect your soldier against weapon attacks, but not from injury caused by the storm or falls.

The Six Skills You'll Need to Become a Sharpshooter

To consistently defeat your enemies in firefights and win #1 Victory Royale, you'll need to master the art of survival, be able to build quickly, avoid the deadly storm, and learn how to use the many guns and explosive weapons at your disposal.

However, when it comes to working with weapons during a match, you'll consistently need to use six essential skills:

1. Finding weapons and then adding the best selection of them to your soldier's arsenal. The weapons you collect get stored within your soldier's backpack. It only has slots for up to five weapons and/or loot items (excluding your soldier's Harvesting Tool, which can also be used as a short-range weapon).

2. Choosing the most appropriate weapon based on each combat situation. This means quickly analyzing the challenges and rivals you're currently facing, and selecting a close-range, mid-range, or long-range gun, an explosive weapon, or a projectile explosive weapon that'll help you get the current job done.

3. Collecting and stockpiling the different types of ammunition and making sure you have an ample supply of ammunition for each weapon you want to use.

4. Positioning yourself in the ideal location, with direct line-of-sight to your target(s), so you can inflict damage in the most accurate and efficient way possible. Headshots always cause more damage than a body shot, for example, when targeting enemies.

5. Aiming each type of weapon, so you're able to consistently hit your targets, without wasting ammunition or increasing the risk of your enemies having time to shoot back. When your soldier crouches down while shooting a weapon, their aim will always improve. Having to walk, run, or move while shooting reduces your soldier's accuracy when aiming a weapon.

6. Shooting the active weapon your soldier is holding, and then quickly switching between weapons as needed. You'll also need to take cover each time a weapon needs to be reloaded.

Once you get good at performing each of these tasks, it'll still take a lot of practice to become a highly skilled sharpshooter who is capable of using single shots to defeat enemies. Plus, you'll need to discover how to best use the weapons at your disposal to destroy structures and fortresses in which your enemies may be hiding.

Learning how to effectively and efficiently use the many types of weapons at your disposal when playing *Fortnite: Battle Royale* is the main focus of this unofficial strategy guide. You'll also get a comprehensive overview of the game itself, plus discover tips and strategies for dealing with the many challenges you'll face during each match.

You're also about to discover tips for staying alive longer during matches, for keeping your soldier healthy, and strategies that'll help you explore and loot more efficiently, so you can gather and maintain a powerful arsenal, plus utilize the different types of loot items you'll need to achieve success. This Mounted Turret was sitting out in the open, on a rooftop, and is about to be grabbed by the soldier who found it.

Shown here is a Vending Machine. They're scattered throughout the island and allow you to exchange resources that you collect (Wood, Stone, or Metal) to acquire powerful weapons and other items.

In addition to learning how to best use the weapons available to your soldier, you'll discover how to take advantage of the terrain you're in to obtain the best possible tactical advantage. The island map dramatically changes with each new gaming season. However, the names of specific locations you visit on the map are less important than understanding how to survive when exploring and fighting within the different types of terrain that make up the island.

Some of the terrain types you'll soon encounter include urban (city) areas, suburban neighborhoods, deserts, ice-covered regions, farmland, mountains, valleys, forests, and areas populated with large lakes and windy rivers.

The fighting techniques you'll use at close range, such as when you're inside of any building, structure, or mine shaft, for example, are vastly different than the strategies you should implement when fighting in wide open (outdoor) terrain or mountainous terrain, for example.

Regardless of how you're getting around the island, there are specific strategies for giving your soldier an edge when it comes to winning firefights and staying alive as you're traveling on foot, versus riding in a vehicle, soaring through the air, or while riding ziplines.

Anytime you're out in the open, use surrounding objects, such as trees, rock formations, or bushes (shown above) to provide a hiding place when needed. While solid objects will provide some defensive protection against attacks, a bush will not. A bush can only keep your soldier out of sight. There is a soldier hiding in this bush. If you choose to hide in a bush, keep your weapon drawn and ready to shoot, in case an enemy gets too close.

Meanwhile, if you know an enemy must be hiding somewhere nearby and you can't spot them, start shooting at nearby bushes or throwing explosives into the bushes to lure them out or defeat them. Hiding in a bush is different from using a Bush item (shown here) as camouflage.

When *Fortnite: Battle Royale* first launched, building structures was an essential element in the game. Especially during the End Game (the final few minutes of a match) the gamer who was able to build the tallest, strongest, and most strategically placed fortress was typically the person who won the match. While building is still a gaming element within *Fortnite: Battle Royale*, it's become a far less important one.

Yes, you can and will benefit from quickly being able to build defensive barriers or mini-fortresses to protect yourself during a battle, but building is no longer an absolute must to survive and win matches. However, you should not ignore the building tools offered in the game altogether. Instead, discover when and how to use them when they're absolutely necessary, and make sure you have an ample stockpile of resources on hand to build with. Basic building techniques are also covered later in this unofficial guide.

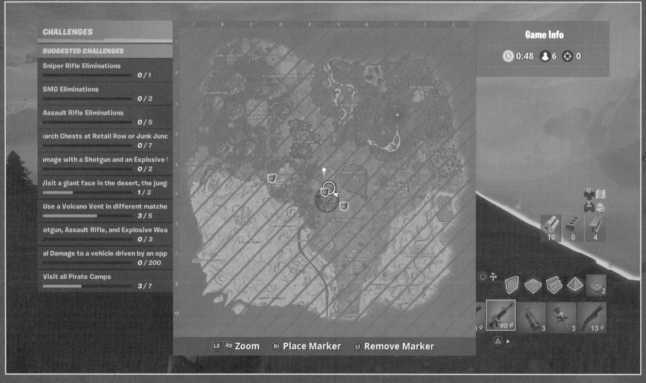

When the inhabitable area of the island becomes very small, and all of the surviving soldiers are forced into extremely close proximity, to defeat the most enemies, take the least amount of risk, boost your player XP, and help ensure you'll consistently make it into the End Game of the matches you participate in, you'll need to understand what the various weapons offered within *Fortnite: Battle Royale* can and should be used for, and more importantly, how to successfully use each type of weapon.

...ractice improving your aiming technique when using different types of weapons (including Sniper Rifles equipped with a powerful scope). Also learn how to choose specific weapons to achieve success in various types of fighting scenarios, regardless of the terrain your soldier is in, or where they are positioned on the map.

Remember, when playing a Solo match, it's your soldier against 99 others. There's only one first place and 98 losers. Ending a match in third (shown here) or even second place still means your soldier has perished. The longer you stay in a match, however, the more enemies you defeat, the more challenges you complete, and the more XP (Experience Points) you'll earn, so as a gamer you'll be able to level up faster.

SECTION 2

FORTNITE: BATTLE ROYALE GAMING BASICS

BATTLE PASS
SEASON 8

GET FORTNITE

100 TIERS, 100 REWARDS.
STILL 950 V-BUCKS!

PLAY BATTLE ROYALE. LEVEL UP. UNLOCK EPIC LOOT.

12:13 PM

Epic Games has made *Fortnite: Battle Royale* free to play. There are, however, a variety of ways to spend real money in order to enhance your gaming experience and customize your soldier.

How to Download and Install Fortnite: Battle Royale

To download and install the Windows PC or Mac version of Fortnite: Battle Royale, launch your favorite web browser and visit www.fortnite.com. Click on the yellow Download button that's displayed in the top-right corner of the browser window or click on the Get Fortnite button displayed on the main webpage.

Click on PC/Mac button, and then follow the on-screen prompts.

To download and install the Xbox One, PS4, or Nintendo Switch version of the game directly to your gaming console, make sure your system is connected to the Internet. Xbox One users should visit the Microsoft Store. To play the game, you'll need to be a paid subscriber to the Microsoft Xbox Live Gold service.

PS4 users should visit the PlayStation Store and Nintendo Switch users should visit the Nintendo eStore. Within the Search field, enter "*Fortnite*" to find the game, and then select and download it.

iOS mobile device users (iPhone and iPad) should visit the App Store from their mobile device, and within the Search field, enter "Fortnite." Click on the Get button to download and install the game.

The Android version of Fortnite: Battle Royale is not available from the Google Play Store. Instead, to download and install it, find it using the Samsung Game Launcher, or from your smartphone or tablet's web browser, visit: www.fortnite.com/android.

Regardless of which gaming system you use, after downloading and installing the game, you'll need to set up a free Epic Games account (https://accounts.epicgames.com). Depending on which gaming system you're using, you may need to link your Epic Games account with a game console–specific account, such as your Xbox Live Gold account.

For online-based help with specific versions of *Fortnite: Battle Royale*, visit: https://epicgames .helpshift.com/a/fortnite. If you need directions on how to link your console-based gaming account with your Epic Games account, visit this webpage: https://epicgames.helpshift.com/a/fortnite/?s= general&f=how-do-i-connect-link-my-console -account-to-my-epic-account.

Customize Your Gaming Experience

There are several ways to customize your *Fortnite: Battle Royale* gaming experience. Because at its core, this is a combat game that involves accurate shooting, you'll want to use the best keyboard/ mouse or controller at your disposal in order to improve reaction time and aiming accuracy.

Some gamers opt to upgrade their standard keyboard/mouse combo to a specialized gaming keyboard and mouse or upgrade their regular controller to one designed for greater precision and faster response time.

If you're a newb, there are some options available from the game's Settings menu that you might want to adjust. To access the Settings menu, from the Lobby screen (shown here on a PC), select the Menu icon (which looks like three horizontal lines). It's displayed in the top-right corner.

Click on the gear-shaped Settings menu option. It can be found in the top-right corner of the screen.

Depending on which gaming platform you're using, a different selection of Settings-related submenu icons is displayed along the top-center of the screen. These include: Video (PC/Mac only), Game, Brightness, Audio, Accessibility, Input, Controller, and Account. The Video submenu is shown here.

To ensure the fastest response time from the game, based on the graphics being generated and displayed, from the Video submenu (The PC version is shown on the previous page.), adjust options like Display Resolution, Frame Rate Limit, and Quality. If you're using a lower-end computer that doesn't have a cutting-edge graphics card, for example, you may need to reduce some of these graphics-related options to optimize game play speed.

Based on your gaming experience and game play style, as well as the hardware you're using, from the Game submenu (shown here on a PC), you may want to tinker with some of the settings below the Input heading in order to increase or decrease the mouse's sensitivity, which has a direct correlation to your aiming capabilities and precision when moving your soldier around, for example.

The same menu is shown here on a PS4. (A similar menu is offered within the Xbox One and Nintendo Switch version of the game.) From the options below the Input heading, you're able to adjust the sensitivity of the controller, which has a direct impact on your control over your soldier, as well as your aiming accuracy when playing Fortnite: Battle Royale.

Scroll down on the Game submenu (shown here on a PC), to adjust options listed below the Control Options heading to customize how certain aspects of the game react to your commands. For example, to make aiming easier, turn on the Aim Assist option. To make building more efficient, turn on the Turbo Building and Auto Material Change feature. To reduce the amount of time it takes to open doors within the game, turn on the Auto Open Doors feature. To automatically pick up weapons and items as you find them, turn on the Auto Pickup Weapons option.

Sound effects play an extremely important role in Fortnite: Battle Royale. For this reason, you definitely want to experience the game while wearing quality headphones. However, if you'll be playing any of the game play modes that require you to interact with a partner or squad mates, you'll benefit greatly by connecting a good quality gaming headset (with a built-in microphone) to your gaming system or computer.

From the Settings menu, select the Audio submenu. Consider turning down the Music Volume option. Some gamers opt to turn off the music altogether. Next, turn up the SoundFX Volume. You want to hear all of the game's sound effects clearly. If you'll be using the game's Voice Chat mode to communicate with your partner or squad mates, also turn up the Voice Chat Volume option.

Gaming headsets have a built-in microphone. This type of optional accessory is available from a wide range of manufacturers. Some of the more popular gaming headsets used by top-ranked Fortnite: Battle Royale gamers come from companies like Logitech G (www.logitechg.com), HyperX (www.hyperxgaming.com/us/headsets), Razer (www.razer.com/gaming-headsets-and-audio), and Turtle Beach Corp. (www.turtlebeach.com). Shown here is a partial lineup of Logitech G headsets, which range in price from $59.99 (US) to $139.99 (US). These are compatible with PCs, Macs, and all popular console-based gaming systems.

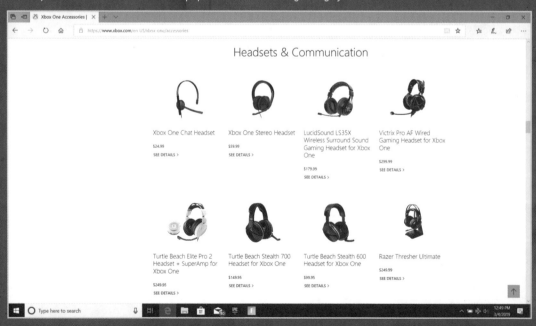

Be sure to check out the online store for your favorite gaming system. Shown here is the selection of optional gaming headsets sold directly from Microsoft's online-based Xbox store (www.xbox.com/en-US/xbox-one/accessories).

When playing Fortnite: Battle Royale *on a PC or Mac, you have the option to use a keyboard/mouse option to control your soldier during each match. Many gamers believe this option offers the best response time and precision. From the Settings menu, select the Input submenu (shown here on a PC). From this menu, you're able to customize all the key bindings associated with each available action and command offered within the game.*

Keep in mind, it's possible for PC/Mac gamers to connect a PS4 or Xbox One gaming controller to their computer system and control the game on their computer using a gaming controller. It's also possible for Xbox One and PS4 gamers to connect an optional keyboard and mouse combination directly to their gaming system.

Consider Upgrading Your Gaming Gear

The reaction time of your keyboard/mouse combo or controller directly impacts your success when playing *Fortnite: Battle Royale*. For this reason, serious gamers often opt to upgrade their equipment to include a specialty gaming keyboard and mouse for their PC or Mac, and/or a more precision-oriented controller for their console-based gaming system.

These are optional purchases that you might want to make after you've played *Fortnite: Battle Royale* for a while, you've tweaked the game controls (in Settings), and you believe your gaming abilities will improve with higher-end equipment.

For some gamers, a keyboard/mouse combo offers the most precise and responsive control options, especially if you're using a specialty gaming keyboard and mouse, such as those offered by Corsair (www.corsair.com), Logitech (www.logitechg.com), or Razer www.razer.com/gaming-keyboards). The Razer Huntsman Elite WR (2018) for the PC ($199.99) is shown here.

Several companies, including Razer (www.razer.com/gaming-keyboards), offer one-handed, reduced-sized gaming keyboards, which feature fewer keys than a traditional keyboard, making it easier to reach only the keys needed to play a specific game, such as Fortnite: Battle Royale.

The Razer Orbweaver Chroma, (shown above), is priced at $129.99 (US). In addition to awesome LED colored lighting effects, it offers 30 programmable keys (which includes 20 programmable mechanical keys). Priced at $34.95, the Fist Wizard One-Handed Gaming Keyboard (https://groovythingstobuy.com/products/fist-wizard-one-handed-gaming-keyboard-1) is a less expensive alternative.

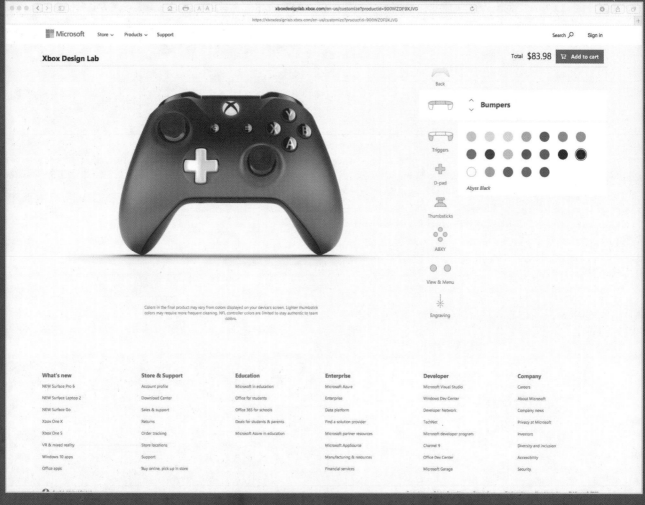

Microsoft offers a service that allows you to custom design a wireless or corded Xbox One controller. These controllers look different cosmetically but offer the same functionality as the controller that comes with the gaming system. The price varies, based on options you choose. Check out https://xboxdesignlab.xbox.com/en-us to learn more about customizing an Xbox One controller's design.

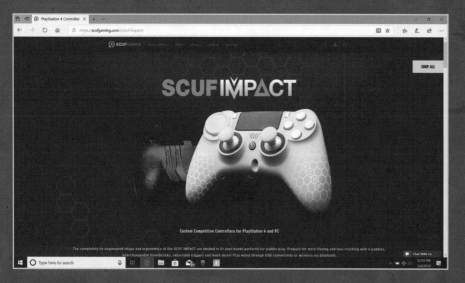

Offering more precision than a standard console controller, several companies, such as SCUF Gaming (www.scufgaming.com), manufacture specialty Xbox One and PS4 controllers designed to cater to the needs of advanced gamers. The SCUF Impact controller for the PS4 ($139.95 US) is shown here. These controllers can also be used with a PC or Mac when playing Fortnite: Battle Royale.

Xbox One or PS4 console-based gamers can use the standard wireless controllers that came bundled with their gaming system or upgrade to more advanced controllers. It's also possible to connect a gaming keyboard and mouse directly to a console-based system. The Turret for Xbox One gaming keyboard and mouse ($249.99 US) from Razer is shown here.

If you'll be experiencing Fortnite: Battle Royale on a Nintendo Switch gaming system, you'll have greater control over your soldier during matches if you upgrade to the Nintendo Switch Pro Controller ($69.99), as opposed to using the Joy-Con controllers that come bundled with the system. More creative gamers have figured out ways to connect a computer keyboard and mouse to a Nintendo Switch (while using the Dock and playing Fortnite: Battle Royale). You'll find directions for how to do this on YouTube.

Regardless of the gaming hardware you're using, memorize the controls for *Fortnite: Battle Royale* and keep practicing using those controls so you develop your muscle memory for the game. When you're able to rely on your muscle memory, you'll be able to react faster without having to think about which key or button to press to accomplish specific tasks.

After accessing the Settings menu, select the Controller menu to customize the controller layout you'll be using to play Fortnite: Battle Royale. The pre-created controller layouts include: Old School, Quick Builder, Combat Pro, and Builder Pro. On most gaming systems, there's also a Custom option which allows you to personalize a controller's button bindings.

If you choose to connect an Xbox One or Play-Station 4 controller to your Windows PC, for example, from the *Fortnite: Battle Royale* Settings menu, select the Controller option. Choose your favorite Controller Configuration, and then select between an Xbox One or PS4 Controller layout from the buttons displayed near the bottom-left corner of the screen.

Don't Focus on the Game Settings Used by Top-Ranked Players

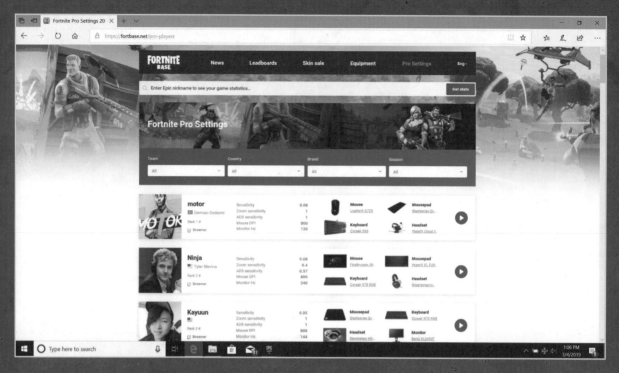

Many of the top-ranked Fortnite: Battle Royale gamers publish details about exactly what game equipment they use, as well as the customizations they've made to the various Settings menu and submenu options. While this information is useful for reference, for several reasons, you should not try to replicate another gamer's exact settings.

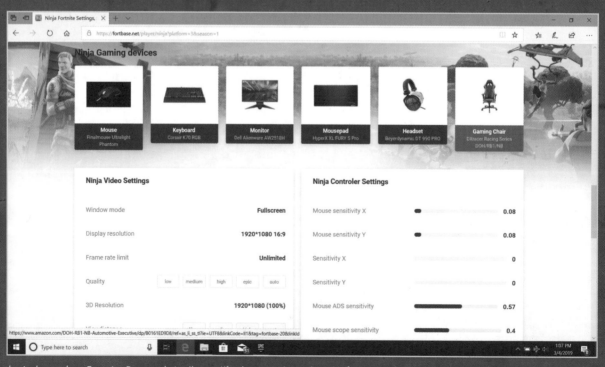

From the independent Fortnite Base website (https://fortbase.net/pro-players), for example, you can look up the player stats, ranking, gaming equipment list, and game-related settings for many of the best Fortnite: Battle Royale players in the world. Shown here is the information from Ninja.

First, unless you have exactly the same gaming equipment and Internet connection speed used by the pro gamer, when you replicate their settings, you'll achieve different results on your own gaming system.

Second, every pro gamer tweaks the game based on their unique gaming style and experience level. If you play using a different style, or your reflexes and game-related muscle memory are not as developed as the pro gamer, copying their game settings will actually be detrimental to your success.

As a newb, you're better off leaving the majority of the *Fortnite: Battle Royale* Settings menu options at their Default settings. Then, once you start getting good at playing, tweak the options you believe will improve your game play. Always make small, incremental adjustments to one setting at a time, and then test out how each change works for you by playing one or two matches. Continue to tweak the settings as you deem necessary.

To discover the gaming equipment and customized settings used by top-ranked and pro *Fortnite: Battle Royale* gamers, check out these websites:

- **Best Fortnite Settings—**https://bestfortnitesettings.com/best-fortnite-pro-settings
- **Fortnite Base—**https://fortbase.net/pro-players
- **Fortnite Pro Settings & Config—**https://fortniteconfig.com
- **GamingScan—**www.gamingscan.com/fortnite-competitive-settings-gear
- **ProNettings.net—**https://prosettings.net/best-fortnite-settings-list

By accessing the free and independent Fortnite Stats & Leaderboard website (https://fortnitestats.com), enter the Epic Games username for any Fortnite: Battle Royale gamer to see their current stats as a player.

Experience Fortnite: Battle Royale *Using the Fastest Internet Connection Possible*

To achieve the most reliable Internet connection speed on a computer or console-based gaming system, connect to the Internet using a physical Ethernet cable, as opposed to using a wireless (Wi-Fi) connection.

All current model Windows PCs and iMacs, as well as the Xbox One and PlayStation 4 have the ability to connect to the Internet via a wireless (Wi-Fi) connection or using a physical Ethernet cable that connects between your computer (or gaming console) and modem (or a router).

Many MacBook and MacBook Air laptop computers, for example, as well as the Nintendo Switch, do not have an Ethernet port built in. In this case, an inexpensive Ethernet adapter can be purchased online or from a popular consumer electronics store. Keep in mind, a standard Ethernet cable (they come in many different lengths) also needs to be purchased separately.

Slow Internet often causes *Fortnite: Battle Royale* to glitch during game play. When this happens, especially during an intense firefight or at the wrong moment, you could find your soldier getting eliminated from a match for no good reason.

When connecting to the Epic Games gaming servers to play Fortnite: Battle Royale, you can choose which region's servers to connect to. This directly impacts your connection speed when playing. From the top of the Game menu within Settings, choose your Matchmaking Region (shown here on a PC). Options include: Auto, North America–East Coast (NA-EAST), North America–West Coast (NA-WEST), Europe, Oceania, Brazil or Asia. In parentheses next to each option is the current connection speed available, measured in milliseconds.

To have the smoothest, glitch-free gaming experience possible, choose the region that offers the fastest connection speed based on your current location. Your best bet is to choose the Auto option and allow the game to select the appropriate and fastest server. However, if you're based in one part of the planet and want to compete against gamers in another region, manually choose which region's servers you want to connect to, knowing that you will likely experience a slower connection to the distant server.

How to Make In-Game Purchases

While you can play Fortnite: Battle Royale as much as you'd like on your favorite gaming systems for free, if you want to participate in Battle Pass Challenges or purchase items that allow you to customize the appearance of your soldier, for example, you'll need to spend real money.

To make in-game purchases, first visit the Store by selecting the Store tab that's displayed at the top of the Lobby screen.

From the Store, acquire V-Bucks. This is Fortnite: Battle Royale's in-game currency. You can purchase bundles of V-Bucks using real money. The larger the bundle of V-Bucks you purchase at once, the more money you'll save. As you can see here, 1,000 V-Bucks costs $9.99 (US). 2,800 V-Bucks costs $24.99. 5,000 V-Bucks costs $39.99, and 13,500 V-Bucks costs $99.99.

In conjunction with each new gaming season, Epic Games offers at least one special V-Bucks Bundle. This includes 600 V-Bucks plus an exclusive outfit that's only available for a limited time. At the start of Season 8, for example, this Cobalt outfit with matching Back Bling was made available as part of The Cobalt Pack for a discounted price of $4.99 (US). This outfit will never be sold in the Item Shop, and after Season 8 ended, it probably won't ever become available again.

As soon as you purchase the Cobalt Pack, or whatever limited time pack is available during the current season, the outfit and related accessories will immediately be added to your Locker.

Ways to Customize the Appearance of Your Soldier

Prior to each match, you have the ability to customize the appearance of your soldier in several ways, using items you've purchased or unlocked that are available from the Locker.

Some available outfits are larger than others, however, *Fortnite: Battle Royale* has balanced the "hit box" associated with each outfit to make it the same. In other words, whether or not an enemy is difficult to target and hit with a weapon

depends almost entirely on the gamer controlling that soldier, regardless of the physical size or appearance of a soldier's outfit.

Wearing a brightly colored outfit or equipping your soldier with bright-colored Back Bling or a flashy-looking Harvesting Tool, however, can make your soldier easier to spot during a match, which could become a disadvantage.

From the Lobby, select the Locker tab that's displayed at the top of the screen. On the left side of the screen is a selection of slots. Each slot represents a different customization option. On the right side of the screen is your soldier's current appearance based on the selected options.

Near the top-left corner of the Locker screen is the Outfit slot. Select this to choose from any of the outfits that you've previously purchased or unlocked.

After selecting the Outfit slot from the Locker screen, this Selecting Outfit screen is displayed. Choose which outfit you want your soldier to wear during the upcoming match. Your selection will remain saved for all future matches, until you return to this menu and select a different outfit.

Directly below the Outfit heading, near the top-center of the screen, are five icons used to sort your Outfit inventory. Options include: All (view all of your available outfits), New (display only your newest outfits), Favorite (display the outfits you've labeled as Favorites), Styles (display outfits that have optional Styles that can be unlocked to alter their appearance), Reactive (view outfits that are classified as Reactive). A Reactive outfit changes based on the way you play or what happens to your soldier during a match.

Choose your desired outfit and click on the Save and Exit button to return to the main Locker screen.

When choosing an outfit, keep in mind that bright colors attract attention and can make your soldier easier to spot on the island, especially when exploring snow or ice-covered terrain. In lush tropical areas, camouflage colors will help your soldier blend in more. While in desert areas, outfits with tan, black, or brown-related colors might work best if your goal is to avoid being noticed.

To the right of the Outfit slot on the Locker screen is the Back Bling slot. Click on this to choose a Back Bling (backpack) design to go with the outfit you've selected. Some outfits come with a matching Back Bling design. You're always free to choose any available Back Bling design to go with any outfit from the Locker. Like everything else available from the Locker, the Back Bling you add is for cosmetic purposes only.

While many Back Bling designs match specific outfits, themes, or sets, there are a few that include an animated pet, such as Bonesy (a dog), Camo (a lizard), and Woodsy (a dog). These animated pets stay in your soldier's backpack and look super cute, but don't impact game play in any way.

A growing number of Back Bling designs are what Epic Games calls Reactive. These change in appearance during a match, based on the number of chests you open, for example.

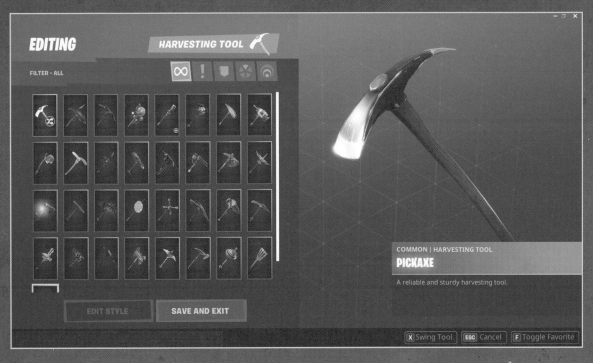

Back at the Locker screen, to the right of the Back Bling slot, is the Harvesting Tool slot. Select it, and then choose from the available Harvesting Tool designs that you've purchased or unlocked, and that are available to your soldier. While the appearance of the different Harvesting Tools varies greatly, they all function exactly the same way during matches.

To the right of the Harvesting Tool slot on the Locker screen is the Glider slot. Select it, and then choose from the available Glider designs that you've purchased or previously unlocked, and that are currently available to your soldier. Once again, the appearances of the Glider designs vary greatly, but they all function exactly the same way.

Your soldier's Glider is used to reduce their rate of descent at the start of the match, to stop their freefall from the Battle Bus, and to ensure a safe landing on the island.

The Glider can also be used at certain times during a match to transport from one location to another. To accomplish this, you'll first need to find and grab a Glider item and add it to your soldier's inventory. Then, when your soldier leaps off a mountain or cliff, for example, select and activate the Glider item to deploy the Glider and keep your soldier from falling to the ground and getting injured or worse. Perfect timing is essential when using this item.

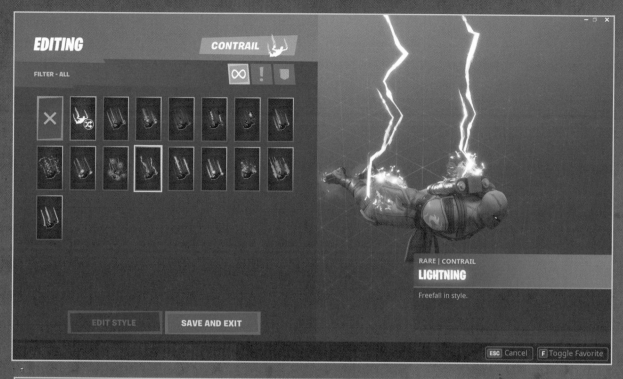

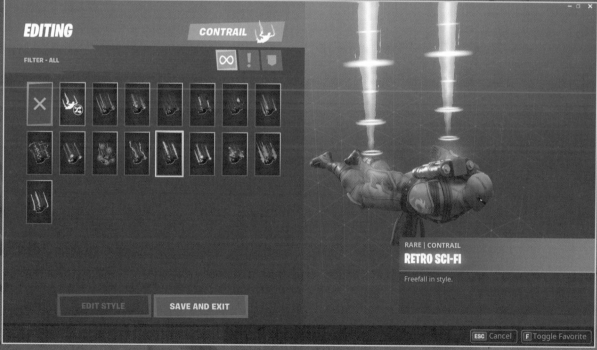

Displayed to the right of the Glider slot on the Locker screen is the Contrail slot. Select this, and then choose a Contrail design that you've previously unlocked. This is an animation that's displayed from your soldier's hands and/or feet during their freefall from the Battle Bus. Again, it's for cosmetic purposes only. Using a Contrail does not speed up your soldier's descent or give you added navigational control during free fall. Contrail designs must be unlocked within the game by accomplishing Challenges or Battle Pass Challenges. They typically cannot be purchased from the Item Shop.

The second row of slots displayed on the Locker screen are used to select six different emotes that your soldier can showcase in the pre-deployment area or anytime during a match.

There are several types of emotes available, including Dance Moves, Emoticons, Spray Paint Tags, and Toys. Place a different emote within each of the six slots.

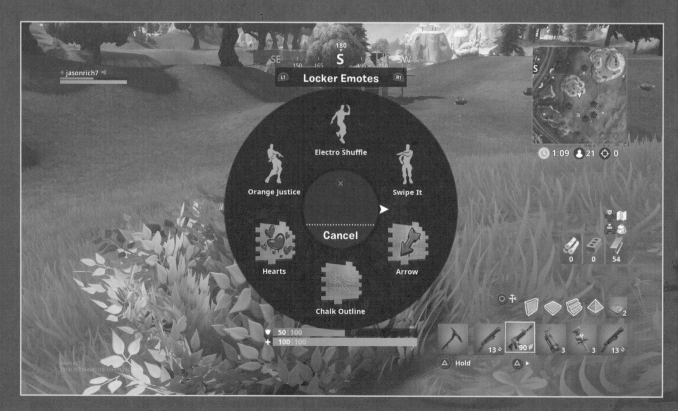

While in the pre-deployment area or during a match, access this Emotes menu to select and showcase an emote. If you're using a keyboard/mouse combo, press the key or mouse button you have assigned to a specific Emote slots to showcase that emote, or access the Emotes menu. There are hundreds of emotes (including many different Dance Moves) to choose from. Some can be purchased from the Item Shop, while others need to be unlocked.

Emoticons are graphic icons that your soldier can toss into the air for everyone in the nearby area to see.

Spray Paint Tags allow you to spray paint any flat object on the island, such as the wall of a building or structure. You're able to mix and match Spray Paint Tags to create original graffiti designs and leave your mark.

Scattered throughout the island are areas for playing with toys. For example, there are basketball courts for playing hoops. You can, however, start playing with a toy almost anywhere on the island. These are for recreational purposes only and have no impact on game play. In fact, they can be detrimental to your soldier's well-being if they're used at an inappropriate time. For example, while playing hoops, an enemy can sneak up and shoot you.

Emotes can be used to communicate with your partner or squad members, to taunt enemies, to showcase your soldier's personality, or just to have fun while exploring the island and participating in matches. As you'll discover, there are hundreds of different emotes to unlock, purchase, and then choose from, but you can only have access to six per match, so choose wisely.

The third row of slots displayed on the Locker Screen allow you to customize the appearance of vehicles and weapons using skins that you've unlocked. First, click on one of the six Wraps slots, then select one of the customizable wrap options that are currently available to you.

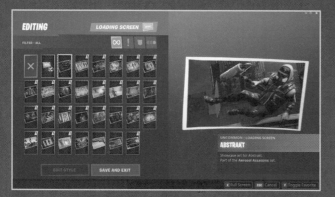

The fourth row of slots on the Locker screen allows you to choose a custom banner, select which background music track you want to hear, and choose your Loading Screen (seen each time you launch Fortnite: Battle Royale). One at a time, click on a slot and then choose from the available options.

Shown here, the Loading Screen slot was chosen, and one of the available graphic options is being selected. Like everything else in the Locker, this has no impact on actual game play.

Visit the Item Shop

Every day within the Item Shop, a different selection of outfits, Back Bling designs, Harvesting Tool designs, Glider designs, and emotes are made available for sale. All of these items are optional and can be purchased using V-Bucks. After visiting the Store to acquire a bundle of V-Bucks, from the Lobby, access the Item Shop to purchase items one at a time.

On the right side of the Item Shop are six additional items, all displayed below the Daily Items heading. These tend to be items that are more common and that get reintroduced into the game periodically. This is also where you'll find Dance Move emotes (each sold separately). Be sure to check the Item Shop each day to see the latest selection of items being offered.

On the left side of the Item Shop, below the Featured Items heading, will be at least two different items per day. These slots tend to showcase the newest, rarest, or most exclusive outfits or items currently available.

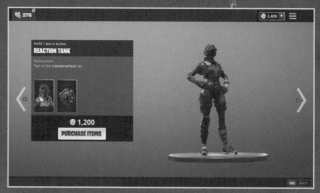

When you see a showcased item you want, highlight and select it. The Purchase screen for that item gets displayed. Choose the Purchase Item(s) button to confirm the purchase. As soon as you do this, the selected item (or items if it's an outfit and Back Bling design bundle, for example) become available immediately within the Locker.

Outfits that are categorized as Legendary are the most exclusive. These are rarely, if ever, reintroduced into the game, and they're only made available for a limited time. These also tend to be the most expensive, although most come with matching Back Bling. While a Rare outfit will typically cost 1,200 V-Bucks (about $12.00 US), a Legendary outfit typically costs 2,000 V-Bucks, which translates to approximately $20.00 (US).

Shown here is the Rare Backbone outfit. It's priced at 1,200 V-Bucks (approximately $12.00 US). This outfit is part of the Biker Brigade set. When an outfit is part of a set, this means that other matching items, such as a Back Bling design, Harvesting Tool design, and/or Glider design have also been released. As you can see here, the outfit's matching Back Bling design is included, but other matching items in the set are each sold separately.

This is an example of an Epic outfit. These tend to be priced at 1,500 V-Bucks (approximately $15.00 US). As you can see, this one is part of the Hardboiled set. It comes with matching Back Bling. Less expensive outfits are considered Uncommon. These are typically priced at 800 V-Buck each (approximately $8.00 US), but usually do not include matching Back Bling. These outfits are also reintroduced into the game every few weeks or months.

Depending on the outfit you choose, you're able to make your soldier look intimidating, whimsical, or menacing, for example. There are also plenty of outfits that are released in conjunction with storylines happening within the current gaming season, or that relate to a holiday or event happening in the real world.

Whichever outfit you choose, remember that it offers no competitive advantage whatsoever during a match, yet by mixing and matching different outfits with accessory items (like Back Bling and a Harvesting Tool), you can make your soldier look truly unique.

Purchase a Current Battle Pass

Every gaming season, Epic Games releases a new Fortnite: Battle Royale *Battle Pass (each sold separately). A Battle Pass allows gamers to participate in Tier-based challenges. A typical Battle Pass includes 100 Tiers. Each time you complete a challenge, it unlocks a prize, such as an outfit, Back Bling design, Harvesting Tool design, Glider design, Contrail design, some type of emote, a Loading Screen graphic, a bundle of 100 V-Bucks, or another item.*

Each Battle Pass includes several outfits that are exclusive. This means they probably won't ever be released elsewhere, such as from the Item Shop. Each gaming season lasts for approximately three months, after which time the Battle Pass expires and a new one is introduced. All of the prizes that you unlock by completing or unlocking Tier challenges are yours to keep forever.

At the time you purchase a new Battle Pass, consider upgrading your purchase to a Battle Bundle. This typically costs 2,800 V-Bucks (approximately $28.00 US).

Upon purchasing a Battle Bundle, you'll automatically unlock the first 25 Battle Pass Tiers and receive those prizes instantly.

In addition to purchasing a Battle Pass, which costs 950 V-Bucks (approximately $9.50 US), if you don't want to complete any of the Tier-based challenges, you can pay a flat fee of 150 V-Bucks (about $1.50 US) to unlock individual Tiers.

To purchase a Battle Pass, see the Tier-related prizes associated with the Battle Pass, or to unlock individual Tiers, from the Lobby, select the Battle Pass option at the top of the screen. Shown here is the Battle Pass screen for Season 8.

An Additional Way to Unlock Cosmetic Items

In addition to the Battle Pass Tier-related challenges, by selecting the Challenges tab from the Lobby, you're able to participate in additional Daily and Weekly challenges, as well as Event challenges and Style challenges. Completing any of these challenges also allows you to win prizes.

Take Advantage of Twitch Prime Packs

Epic Games has teamed up with Twitch.tv and Amazon Prime to offer occasional Twitch Prime Packs for *Fortnite: Battle Royale.* Each of these free promotional packs contains at least one exclusive outfit along with other items. To acquire them when they become available you must be a paid Amazon Prime subscriber, plus have a free Twitch.tv account that's linked with your Epic Games account. To learn more about Twitch Prime Packs, visit: www.twitch.tv/Prime or https://help.twitch.tv/s/article/twitch-prime-guide.

SECTION 3

JUMP RIGHT INTO A *FORTNITE: BATTLE ROYALE* MATCH AND FIGHT

The Solo game play mode of *Fortnite: Battle Royale* is extremely popular. Upon selecting it from the Lobby, your soldier gets placed within the pre-deployment area where they, along with up to 99 other soldiers, wait to depart for the island aboard the Battle Bus (a flying blue bus).

While in the pre-deployment area, feel free to interact with other soldiers, pick up and try out the nearby weapons, or explore the environment. It's also possible to showcase a few emotes or practice using your soldier's dance moves.

It's not possible to harm any enemies, nor can your soldier be harmed while in the pre-deployment area. Anything you collect, in terms of resources, weapons, or ammo will be automatically left behind when your soldier boards the Battle Bus.

One of the more useful ways to spend your time in the pre-deployment area is to check the Map screen. You'll notice that a line (comprised of tiny arrow icons) is displayed across the island. This line depicts the random route the Battle Bus will travel over the island. The direction of the arrows tells you which way the bus will be traveling.

Based on the random route the Battle Bus will take, this is the perfect time to consider a desired landing location or for soldier.

Choose Your Landing Location Wisely

The landing location you choose will determine a few important things that'll impact your experience during that match.

Choosing to land in the heart of a popular location will typically mean that within moments after reaching land your soldier will encounter enemies. Thus, you can expect to engage in firefights almost immediately.

Knowing that you may need to fight right away, as soon as your soldier lands, your first and most important task is to find and grab a weapon (and ammo) so your soldier can defend themselves or attack anyone who poses a threat. Here, the soldier landed on top of the clocktower in Tilted Towers. Upon smashing the roof of the clocktower, you're guaranteed to find at least two chests within the tower, plus additional weapons, ammo, and loot items. You just need to be the first soldier to arrive at this location to grab what's here.

For less experienced gamers, another approach is to choose a landing location that's more remote and less popular. As a result, you'll typically have more time to explore the area and build up a proper arsenal before having to engage in firefights.

Keep in mind, upon landing you won't always see enemies that are in very close proximity. If you're able to find cover, take a moment to listen carefully for the sounds enemies make—like footsteps, weapon fire, sounds generated by building, doors opening or closing, or the sound of nearby vehicles.

As you analyze the island map and consider the route the Battle Bus will take, know that many gamers opt to leap from the bus at the very start of the route (in this case over Botimus Prime's Block), while some wait until the very last possible second to depart from the bus when it reaches the end of its route (in this case over Happy Hamlet).

Since almost every possible route that the bus will take goes either directly over the center of the island (or close to it), points of interest near the center of the map (such as Tilted Towers, Loot Lake, and Dusty Divot) tend to always be popular. As the map changes in conjunction with new game updates, the points of interest near the map's center will always be popular landing spots.

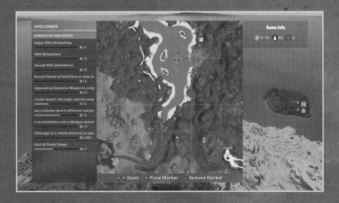

Each gaming season, Epic Games also introduces new points of interest to the map. Lazy Lagoon is shown here. These tend to be extremely popular, especially during the first few weeks of a new season. If you choose to land at one of these locations, it's likely to be populated with a bunch of enemies that you'll encounter quickly–sometimes within seconds after landing.

One of the worst mistakes you can make is landing in the heart of a popular point of interest with no plan whatsoever. If you don't know exactly where to go to discover a chest or weapon stash, you'll likely get shot within seconds of landing.

Near the top of the wooden tower you'll often discover a chest, along with other useful items lying on the ground. What's in the chest will help you quickly build up your soldier's arsenal.

As you study the island map, you'll discover plenty of locations on the outskirts of the island that are remote, but that offer scattered structures where you'll often find chests, as well as weapons, ammo, and loot items lying on the ground. There's a tall wooden tower near Lonely Landing, for example, where you'll often find a chest and plenty of goodies to grab.

The drawback to landing at a very remote section of the island is that your soldier may need to travel a great distance within the first few minutes of the match to stay within the safe area. However, during this travel, your soldier will potentially be well armed and prepared for enemy encounters.

Whenever you need to help your soldier travel a far distance in order to outrun the storm, look for a nearby zipline that points in the right direction, or find a vehicle that'll take you just about anywhere you want or need to go.

Upon choosing one of these locations (which will give you extra time to explore and build your soldier's arsenal), start grabbing what you need, but refer to the map after a few minutes once the storm forms, to determine where the first safe region will be.

Prepare for a Safe Landing

Once you've chosen a landing location, determine the best moment for your soldier to leap from the Battle Bus and begin their freefall.

While still on the Battle Bus, use the directional controls to see the back end of the bus. You'll be able to see when other soldiers make their leap. By waiting for a moment when few soldiers are simultaneously leaving the bus, you're less apt to encounter those enemies immediately upon landing.

During freefall, use your directional controls to help your soldier glide through the air toward the desired landing spot. If you point the soldier straight downward, they will fall faster. Being the first to land at a desired spot, particularly one that's popular, is extremely important. The first soldier to land at a specific location has more time to grab nearby weapons and then start shooting at enemies as they land.

Regardless of when your soldier leaps from the Battle Bus, they should be able to glide in mid-air and cover almost half of the island before landing. You can increase the distance your soldier is able to travel by activating their Glider early, which slows their rate of descent and gives you increased navigational control. However, this is best done only if you're fairly certain you'll be the only soldier landing at the desired landing spot, since it'll take you longer to get there.

To help guide you to your desired landing location when playing a Solo match, or to help your partner or squad mates see a designated rendezvous location, place a Marker on the map. Each gamer has their own colored Marker for easy identification. Here the Marker has been placed on a building in the outskirts of Dusty Divot. Anytime you place a Marker on the map, only you and your partner or squad mates can see it. Markers are not seen by rivals.

Once a Marker is placed on the map, it can be seen by you and your partner or squad mates on the island itself from a distance. This makes it easier to navigate directly to the exact location that's been marked. The blue flare coming from the island is the Marker created by the gamer controlling this soldier.

As your soldier begins approaching land, to ensure a safe landing, their Glider will automatically deploy. Again, this gives you greater navigational control during those final moments of descent.

Be sure to study the land as your soldier is approaching. If you notice other soldiers landing nearby, veer in another direction to put distance between you and the enemy if they'll be landing first and will be able to grab a weapon before your soldier.

Another decision you'll need to make when choosing an exact landing spot is whether you want to land on the ground, on top of an object, or on the roof of a building, house, or structure. Shown here, a soldier has landed on the ground, out in the open, but close to a hut that will hopefully contain at least one weapon and some ammo.

Most houses have an attic, and within the attic, you'll often discover a chest that'll contain useful weapons, ammo, and/or loot. Knowing this, it's faster to land directly on the roof of a house, smash through the roof using your soldier's Harvesting Tool, and then jump down into the attic.

The alternative is to land on the ground outside of a house, enter the house through a door, climb up the stairs, build a ramp that'll allow your soldier to reach the attic (shown on the left), and then use the soldier's Harvesting Tool to smash through the ceiling (shown on the right). This option takes longer. However, as you make your way through the house, you can grab weapons, ammo, and loot items that are lying out in the open, on the floor. Notice that the soldier was already able to grab a weapon that was located on the ground floor of the house.

Always avoid landing in a wide-open space, such as a field. Doing so makes you an easy target for a sniper or any enemy with a mid- to long-range weapon to spot and shoot, since there will be no place to take cover. Remember, if you don't yet have any resources, you can't build either.

On this mountaintop, there was a chest that could be seen before landing, as well as a Hoverboard, so the soldier could easily and quickly make her way off the mountain and continue her exploration.

When choosing a landing spot, if you notice a mountain or hill that has a chest on top, it might make sense to land on the top of that elevation. Look for the golden glow of a chest during the final moments of your soldier's freefall. By landing on a hill or mountain and being able to quickly grab a weapon, this also gives you a potential height advantage over any enemies below, so you can look down and shoot 'em. If there's no weapon to be seen before landing, choose another mountaintop.

Yet another option when choosing a landing spot is to find a small hut or structure that's near, but not directly inside, a popular point of interest. This one is on the outskirts of Tilted Towers. Once you grab a weapon, you can shoot at enemies below, or make your way into this very popular urban area of the island.

Doing this allows you to land, quickly grab a weapon, and then travel into the point of interest once you're armed and ready for battle. The slight delay it'll take you to reach the point of interest might give other soldiers time to pick clean the weapons, ammo, and loot items in the area, but if you're able to defeat those enemies in a firefight, grab the items you want that they leave behind after they've been eliminated from the match.

Just a few steps away from the hut on top of the mountain that overlooks Tilted Towers is this RV with a trailer. During this match, sitting on the trailer is a vehicle that you can hop into and drive. The location of vehicles on the island is not consistent from match to match. You never know where they'll spawn.

Once your soldier is riding in a vehicle, they can head directly into Tilted Towers, or quickly travel to whatever destination you choose.

One of the best ways to choose perfect landing spots is to get to know the terrain and remember what you experienced during past matches or while watching other gamers. Many objects, including chests, respawn in the same location for each match, plus the layout of buildings and structures only changes as a result of game updates made by Epic Games.

Consider where you've been in the past and try to recall exactly what you encountered there. Your past experiences and exploration of the island will help you make more intelligent landing-spot decisions in the future.

Start Building Your Arsenal Right Away

Don't forget, the moment your soldier lands on the island, the only weapon at their disposal is their Harvesting Tool, which is not at all effective against an enemy already holding a gun or explosive.

Immediately upon landing, find shelter if necessary, but make it a priority to grab at least one weapon and some ammo, so you're able to help your soldier defend themselves.

The next objective is to analyze your terrain and determine how you'll use it to your advantage. Consider where you'll be traveling to and exploring in the next few minutes and determine what types of weapons (and ammo) you'll need. For example, if you'll be entering buildings, houses, or pre-existing structures, and you encounter enemies inside, you'll need to engage in close-range combat.

In your mind, try to keep track of the weapons, ammo, and items you collect. By doing this, you'll need to refer to the Inventory screen less often. Anytime you switch to the Inventory screen, this takes your attention away from what's happening around your soldier on the island, which makes them vulnerable to attack. When you need to access the Inventory screen, make sure you first find a safe location to hide.

One of the biggest perks of playing a Duos or Squads match is that you have other soldiers to watch your back and to launch attacks with. You're also able to easily share weapons, ammo, loot items, as well as Health/Shield-replenishment items with your partner or squad mates who are close by. When near an ally, access your soldier's Inventory screen and choose what you want to share. Drop that item in front of another soldier so they can pick it up. Shown here, one squad member just shared a Small Shield Potion with another.

Gathering a well-rounded arsenal early on will help you prepare for all types of fighting situations. Collecting multiple versions of the same weapon is often counterproductive and wastes valuable inventory space.

When it comes to sharing weapons, provide your partner or a squad mate with weapons you know they're more proficient using than you are. For example, if you have a Legendary Suppressed Sniper Rifle, but you know you're not good at shooting enemies from a distance, share that weapon with an ally who will be able to make better use of it than you.

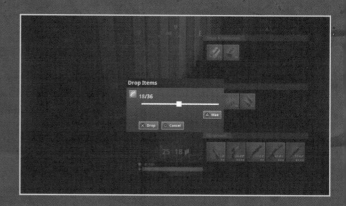

Anytime you're sharing ammo or simultaneously carrying multiples of a particular item, such as Bandages, when you opt to share that item, you'll be able to determine how much of what your soldier is currently carrying you actually want to share. You might want to give away half of a particular type of ammo, or just one set of Bandages, instead of all of an item in your soldier's inventory.

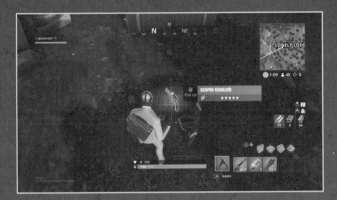

There are many ways to gather weapons (and ammo) on the island. Some will be lying out in the open (on the ground) waiting to be grabbed. Others will be found within chests, Loot Llamas, or Supply Drops. Some powerful weapons can be purchased from Vending Machines.

Especially as you get closer to the End Game, you'll be able to enhance your soldier's arsenal dramatically by picking up the weapons, ammo, and items that eliminated enemies leave behind. After knocking off an enemy, however, make sure the coast is clear before you approach what loot they've left at the spot where they perished.

One of the easiest ways to replenish or stockpile ammo is to find and open Ammo Boxes that are scattered throughout the island. These green boxes do not glow like chests, but when you open them, you'll be able to grab several types of ammo, including some ammo that's not readily available elsewhere. For example, Ammo Boxes are a great source of Rockets that can be used with Grenade Launchers, Rocket Launchers, Quad Launchers, and Guided Missile Launchers.

Explore and Find What You Need

If you'll be traveling between buildings or structures, or need to travel through vast open areas, chances are, you'll notice enemies while they're still a distance away, so you're more likely to engage in mid- to long-range firefights. Here, the soldier is riding on an extremely maneuverable Hoverboard to quickly get through an open area where he's vulnerable. By steering in a zig-zag pattern, it's easier to outmaneuver enemies if they try to target your soldier with their guns.

When you want to enter a building or structure you know has enemies inside, you might be able to lure them out or inflict damage by first sneaking up to a window, peeking through, and shooting the enemies (through the window) while still outside. While your enemies may be guarding the front door of a structure, they often forget to guard the windows or a back door to the structure they're in.

You may also determine that it'll be necessary to breach structures that are already populated by enemies. In this case, you might want to hide a decent distance away from a structure's entrance, and then pick off enemies with a mid- to long-range weapon as they exit. Once enemies are terminated, pick up the weapons, ammo, and loot they collected from inside that structure. This will save you time, since you won't have to search and loot the structure yourself.

Another option for breaching a building or structure is to toss an explosive weapon into an open door or window before entering (shown here), or to shoot a projectile explosive weapon (such as a Grenade Launcher or Rocket Launcher) from a safe distance through the open door or window.

Anytime you're in relatively close proximity to enemies, remember your soldier will generate less movement-related noise if they crouch down and tiptoe around, as opposed to walking or running. Also be mindful that movements your soldier makes will generate noises that others might hear, so if you're planning an ambush or surprise attack, it's important to keep noises to a minimum.

Anytime you're playing a Solo match, a vehicle can help you travel from one location on the island to another much faster than on foot. While you're driving most vehicles, however, you cannot simultaneously shoot your weapon. Thus, you'll need to rely on taking evasive maneuvers to escape enemies trying to attack your vehicle. If you're playing a Duos or Squads match, for example, some types of vehicles hold up to three additional passengers. While one soldier drives, the others can use their weapons and shoot at enemies while in motion.

If you hear an enemy vehicle approaching, always try to shoot at and defeat the driver, or attempt to destroy or incapacitate the vehicle itself. Shooting a moving target is rather difficult, however, especially from a distance. It's typically easier to toss an explosive weapon at a vehicle from close- to mid-range, or to shoot at the vehicle using a projectile explosive weapon, such as a Grenade Launcher or Rocket Launcher.

When it comes to aiming any gun, you'll always achieve better accuracy if you have your soldier crouch down and remain still while aiming. Standing decreases aiming accuracy slightly but moving around while shooting greatly reduces aiming accuracy for virtually all weapons.

When deciding where you'll travel next during your exploration, refer to the map, so you know the location of the storm and can figure out when and where it'll be moving to next. Then, as you travel from region to region, take the time to pick up new weapons that you discover and think will be useful, while dropping weapons and items you no longer want or need.

Many types of vehicles available on the island that can be driven make noise, so enemies are sure to hear your arrival, or hear the vehicle's engine get quieter as you travel farther away. Always be aware of the noise your soldier is generating and listen carefully for audible clues regarding the whereabouts of your enemies.

A Scoped Revolver with its high-magnification scope will be useful during any phase of a match. Without using the scope, this weapon is great for close- to mid-range combat. Using the gun's scope, you can zoom in and target enemies from a distance. This makes the Scoped Revolver one of the most versatile weapons available on the island.

During the End Game, the inhabitable area of the island will be very small, so you'll want to have the most powerful close- and mid-range weapons available, as well as powerful explosive weapons. Sniper Rifles and other long-range weapons won't be that useful during those final minutes of a match when everyone is typically very close together.

It's always a good strategy to close doors behind you anytime you enter a building. You can then position yourself in a tactical location inside and shoot at enemies that come through the door after you, or strategically place Traps to injure or kill enemies that enter later. As you'll discover, the trick to using Traps successfully is to place them where they can't easily be seen by enemies approaching them.

At the start of a match, by default, all doors to houses and buildings are closed. So, anytime you come across a building or structure with an open door, this means that someone has already been there, and they may still be inside. If they've already come and gone, chances are they've already collected anything good worth grabbing, so looting that structure again is probably counterproductive. However, if the enemies are still inside and you're able to defeat them, you'll boost your player XP, plus collect whatever they've already looted while inside.

As you learn how to use each type of weapon, you'll certainly discover your own personal favorites, as well as which ones you're particularly good at working with. Once you know this, make it a priority to gather those weapons, stockpile plenty of ammo for them, and place them within left-most Inventory slots so they're easy to switch between and quickly access.

When organizing your inventory, if one of your favorite weapons is a Shotgun, always place that Shotgun in the same Inventory slot during every match, so you'll always know exactly where it is when you need to switch to it.

Notice that the Assault Rifle is now being positioned in the left-most Inventory slot (seen near the bottom-right corner of the screen) and the Clingers have been placed over to the right.

Anticipating what your weapon, ammo, loot item, and Health/Shield-replenishment needs will be during each phase of a match is as important as making sure you have the right assortment of weapons at your disposal. Then, it's necessary to know how to properly use the weapons and items available to you, so you can make the maximum use of what's currently in your soldier's inventory.

Keep in mind, projectile explosive weapons, such as Rocket Launchers, Grenade Launders, Quad Launchers, or the newer Boom Bow can be used to destroy buildings, structures, or vehicles, but also cause mega damage to enemies caught in the explosion or who get hit head-on by one of these weapons. These weapons use Rockets as ammo, so be sure to stockpile this type of ammo if you plan to use one of these long-range weapons.

SECTION 4

HOW TO ACCURATELY SHOOT THE VARIOUS TYPES OF WEAPONS

You already know that *Fortnite: Battle Royale* offers several distinct weapon categories. These include:

Assault Rifles (ARs)–*These are the most versatile weapons, because they're powerful and useful at close range, mid-range, or even at a distance.*

Cannons–*A Cannon can be pushed around, aimed, and fired. They shoot destructive cannonballs that can defeat enemies or destroy structures. While they're powerful, this weapon's maneuverability is limited due to its large size and weight.*

Cannons—are a weapon introduced in conjunction with Season 8, which featured a Pirates theme. This weapon will likely be vaulted in the future. A soldier cannot carry a Cannon. Due to their size, they can simply be located, pushed around in certain areas, aimed, and then fired. They shoot cannonballs that can blast apart structures or critically injure enemy soldiers.

Crossbows—More often than not, Crossbows get vaulted (not available in *Fortnite: Battle Royale* matches), but they are available when experiencing other game play modes, like Creative. These are mid-to-long-range weapons that make very little noise when shot. They're most useful if you can achieve a headshot when targeting your enemy.

Explosive Projectile Weapon Launchers–*Rocket Launchers, Grenade Launchers, Guided Missile Launchers, and Quad Launchers are examples of over-the-shoulder weapons that shoot Rockets that explode, usually upon impact with their target. These are excellent long-range weapons that can injure or defeat enemies and/or easily and quickly destroy structures. (Not all of these power-packed and destructive weapons are offered within all game play modes of* Fortnite: Battle Royale *at any given time.)*

A Grenade Launcher shoots Grenades (similar to the ones that can be thrown), but with the Grenade Launcher, the Grenades can travel farther before detonating.

*A **Rocket Launcher** is ideal for blasting away buildings, structures, or enemies at almost any range.*

Just aim and shoot, and whatever your target was will explode. Shown here, a bus is being targeted to demonstrate the power of this weapon.

It takes two consecutive shots from a Rocket Launcher, but within moments, the bus is dust! Look above . . . no more bus.

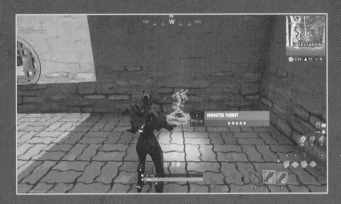

Mounted Turrets—This type of weapon can be found and added to your soldier's inventory until needed. Once activated, this weapon gets placed on the ground (a flat surface is required). Upon hopping onto it, the weapon can be aimed and fired at an enemy target. This weapon offers unlimited ammo but tends to overheat if you shoot continuously for too long. Once this happens, it needs to cool down and be reloaded. This can only be done five times.

The drawback to a Mounted Turret is that once it's placed, any soldier (friend or foe) can use it. Once you set it up and use it to defeat an enemy, it's best to destroy the weapon by shooting at it with another weapon, as opposed to leaving it behind for a potential enemy to use in the future.

Once a Mounted Turret is set up, it cannot be moved.

Pistols—At any given time, several different model Pistols are available on the island (such as Pistols, Hand Cannons, Six Shooters, Suppressed Pistols, Duel Pistols, and Revolvers). These tend to be the weakest type of gun available, and they're best used for close-range fighting (when your soldier is within a building or structure, for example). Some types of Pistols have higher Damage and DPS ratings, a faster Fire Rate, a larger Magazine size, and/or faster Reload time than others.

The most versatile type of Pistol is a Scoped Revolver. Thanks to its scope, it can be used from any distance. Ideally, you want to find and keep a Legendary Scoped Revolver (shown here) in your arsenal.

A Scoped Revolver can be shot "from the hip" at close range with great accuracy, but when you press the Aim button, the weapon's built-in scope permits you to pick off your target from a distance.

The benefit to using a Duel Pistol is that you hold one handgun in each hand and can fire two bullets at once at your enemy.

Shotguns—These too are versatile weapons since they can cause damage from almost any distance. The trick is to find and grab the best ranked and most powerful Shotgun model you can during a match. Shotguns fire Shells, which burst apart when fired, meaning each shot can inflict damage over a greater area, based on the distance a round travels before impact. When the distance is too far, the Shell fragments disburse over a greater area. This reduces the damage each round causes on its target.

The drawback to Shotguns is they typically have a small-size Magazine, capable of holding just one or two Shells at a time before a reload is needed. These weapons also tend to have a slow reload time. For example, a Legendary Double Barrel Shotgun takes 2.7 seconds to reload, but each direct-hit shot can inflict up to 120 Damage. The Pump Shotgun (shown here) works nicely as a close-range weapon when you're exploring the inside of houses, buildings, or structures, for example.

Sniper Rifles–*These are powerful long-range weapons that include a scope. They tend to have a small Magazine size and long reload time, but they're great for achieving headshots from a distance, especially if you catch your enemy off-guard and standing still. The different types of Sniper Rifles are best used during the early- to mid-stages of a match, when enemies can still be far apart. During the End Game, all remaining soldiers are typically very close together, so a Sniper Rifle is less useful.*

Try to find and use a Sniper Rifle with a large Mag Size, so you'll need to reload less frequently during firefights. When using a weapon with a small Mag Size, position your soldier behind a protective barrier when reloading.

Another perk of having a Sniper Rifle (or weapon with a scope) at your disposal is that you can use the scope like binoculars to spy on your enemies from a distance. Remember, anytime you're firing a weapon from a distance, you need to account for "bullet drop." The longer a bullet needs to travel toward its target after being fired, the more it'll fall lower than where it was originally aimed. As the shooter, you often need to aim slightly higher than your intended target when you're very far away.

Submachine Guns (SMGs)–*These weapons are excellent at close- to mid-range, because they have a very fast Fire Rate, can cause a good amount of damage, and their Magazine Size tends to be rather large (20 rounds or more before a reload is required). The farther you are from your target, however, the worse the aiming accuracy will be when using an SMG.*

One benefit to a Legendary Suppressed Sniper Rifle is that it makes very little noise when fired. This makes it harder for your target(s) to pinpoint the shooter's location when they're far away. If your enemy can't figure out where your soldier is, they can't accurately shoot back.

Instead of holding down the trigger and utilizing Automatic Firing mode, SMGs tend to be more accurate if you use Burst mode. In other words, press the trigger for a second or two, release, and then press the trigger again, instead of holding it down.

Fortnite: Battle Royale offers several different types of throwable explosive weapons. These include: Grenades (which explode on impact), Clingers (which attach to a target and explode several seconds after making contact), Stink Bombs (which release a harmful cloud of toxic yellow smoke), and Smoke Grenades (which release a cloud of regular smoke that does not cause damage but decreases visibility in the area). Shown here, a bundle of three Stink Bombs is about to be picked up.

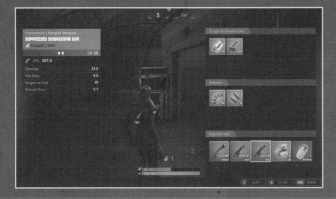

Compared to a regular SMG which has similar stats, a Suppressed Submachine Gun makes less noise. As you can see, it has a Damage rating of 23, a Fire Rate of 9, a Magazine that holds 30 rounds at a time, and a reload time of 2.1 seconds. Other weapons in the SMG category include: Tactical SMGs, Compact SMGs, Drum Guns, and Miniguns.

The soldier's plan here is to toss a Stink Bomb through the window of the house and poison any enemies that may be lurking inside.

Once your soldier's inventory is filled up, you can't pick up another weapon or item until you decide to get rid of an item. Notice the red-colored "Backpack Full" message that's displayed over the banner for the Suppressed Submachine Gun that's lying on the ground. Here, a Common (gray) Tactical Shotgun is being held by the soldier who wants to pick up a Suppressed Submachine Gun that's ranked as Uncommon (green).

This is what the Stink Bomb looks like once it's detonated. The toxic cloud lasts for nine seconds, during which time it'll cause harm to anyone who breathes in the yellow gas. For every half-second of exposure, a soldier's Health meter gets depleted by 5HP. If an enemy were inside, chances are the Stink Bomb would lure him out. To cause additional damage, it's possible to throw multiple Grenades (including Stink Bombs) at the same target in quick succession.

There are also Impulse Grenades, Shock Grenades, Boogie Grenades, Remote Explosives, Dynamite, and Bottle Rockets, for example, that can be tossed at enemies directly, used to lure them out of hiding, inflict damage, cause general disruptions, or to create a distraction. (Again, not all these Grenade types are offered in all game play modes of *Fortnite: Battle Royale* at any given time.)

Two sticks of Dynamite have been thrown near the back door of this house. The soldier who tossed the Dynamite should have run backward to get farther away from the house.

Grenades detonate upon impact and cause an explosion. Dynamite has a five-second fuse that must burn before this weapon explodes. Either can effectively be used to destroy structures, but keep in mind, they bounce off solid objects like walls. It's best to toss one of these explosive weapons through an open door or window, or into an enemy's fortress. Shown here, three sticks of Dynamite are about to be picked up.

After the detonation of the Dynamite, not only did the explosion destroy almost the entire bottom floor of the house (talk about causing some serious destruction), but because the soldier was too close to the explosion, his own Health meter took some damage as well. Notice it's now down to 30HP (from 100HP before the explosion).

The soldier has chosen to toss several sticks of Dynamite at the house in front of him. Notice his own Health meter is currently at 100 percent.

Don't forget, within each weapon or gun category, there are multiple types of weapons, and each weapon type is rated based on its color-coded Rarity (Common, Uncommon, Rare, Epic, or Legendary). A weapon's Rarity helps to determine its overall power and capabilities based on criteria, such as its Damage Per Second (DPS), overall Damage capabilities, Fire Rate, Magazine Size, and reload time.

If you're carrying a specific weapon that you really like and it's rated as Rare, for example, and you're able to find the same weapon but it's ranked Epic or Legendary, always swap it out for the more powerful version of the weapon, unless you have room in your inventory for both weapons. Later, when you need to get rid of a weapon to make room for something else, drop or swap out the weakest weapon you have.

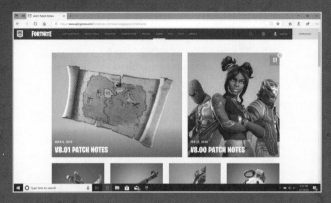

Don't forget, your soldier's Harvesting Tool (pickaxe) can be used as a close-range weapon. Each time you strike an enemy with it, some of their HP gets diminished. To defeat an enemy, however, it'll take multiple direct hits from a Harvesting Tool. Of course, most adversaries won't just stand still and accept the assault, so expect them to jump around and try to run, especially if they're not armed with a gun. Any type of weapon is far more powerful than the Harvesting Tool, so watch out for armed enemies when your soldier is unarmed.

Anytime a new weapon is introduced into Fortnite: Battle Royale, information about it appears on the Epic Games website, within the News section (www.epicgames.com/fortnite/en-US/news).

At any given time, more than 100 different weapon styles and variations are available on the island. With each new game update or gaming season, new weapons are introduced, others are removed altogether, and some have their capabilities tweaked—making them either more powerful or less powerful.

You'll also see announcements about new weapons within the News screen that's featured in the game itself. As news gets released, this screen appears when you launch the game. At any time, however, it can be seen by clicking on the News button that's displayed in the lower-right corner of the Lobby.

From the News screen within the game be sure to click on the Patch Notes button to read the latest details about new weapons, features, and functions added to *Fortnite: Battle Royale*.

When a weapon becomes less powerful in *Fortnite: Battle Royale*, it's referred to as having been "nerfed." Anytime a weapon gets removed from the game, this is referred to as being "vaulted," but that same weapon could be reintroduced into the game anytime in the future.

Where to Find Weapons on the Island

The arsenal your soldier carries must be collected and managed by the gamer controlling that soldier. With limited space in a soldier's inventory, it's important to maintain an arsenal that's useful in all types of fighting situations and terrain types.

Consider a chest's location before running toward it. If the chest is in the center of an open field, and there is no place to take cover as you approach, retreat from, or open the chest, collecting what's inside the chest becomes a dangerous task that involves potentially unnecessary risk. If an enemy spots you from a distance, they'll start shooting.

Weapons (and ammo) can be found lying on the ground, out in the open. These are often found within buildings or structures, but sometimes outside.

Opening chests is another way to build your soldier's arsenal, often without the danger of having to fight off enemies.

If you make it safely to the chest, first build metal walls around your soldier and the chest for protection. Then open the chest. Before adding a door or destroying one of the walls to make your escape, listen carefully for approaching enemies. Don't forget there could still be snipers off in the distance waiting to take you out. Going through this much trouble just to open a chest is not always the best strategy. However, you might consider taking the risk for a Loot Llama or Supply Drop that'll likely offer better loot and more powerful weapons.

Supply Drops that randomly drop from the sky tend to include powerful and rare weapons. However, to grab them, you must be the first person to arrive at and open the Supply Drop.

Many advanced gamers never head directly toward Supply Drops with the intention of opening them. Instead, they find a place to hide near the Supply Drop's landing location, and then use a long-range weapon, such as a Sniper Rifle, to shoot at and attack any enemies that approach the Supply Drop. Be prepared for this and approach a Supply Drop with extreme caution.

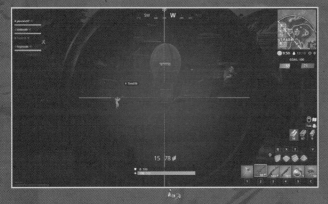

This soldier is using a Thermal Scoped Assault Rifle to target the Supply Drop and wait for an enemy to approach it. What's great about this weapon is that when an enemy can be seen within the scope, they'll appear bright yellow, so they're easy to spot and target. Check out the left side of the soldier's Inventory screen to learn more about this power-packed, long-range weapon.

A Loot Llama looks like a colorful piñata. They get randomly scattered throughout the island but are much rarer than chests. They also tend to contain a larger and more powerful selection of weapons, ammo, and loot items.

Vending Machines are also a great source for acquiring powerful weapons during a match. These too are randomly scattered throughout the island.

Just like with Supply Drops, instead of quickly approaching and opening them, some more experienced gamers tend to keep their distance and then launch a surprise attack on any enemies that approach. Be prepared for this.

If you manage to safely reach a chest, Supply Drop, or Loot Llama, consider quickly building stone or metal walls around yourself to provide an added few seconds of safety against enemies as you open and grab what's inside.

Each Vending Machine offers a different inventory selection. Approach the Vending Machine and watch for items to be displayed. When an item appears that you want, press the Buy button on your keyboard or controller.

Once again, if you're in an area that has enemies lurking around, more experienced gamers will hide near a Vending Machine, wait for someone to make a purchase, and then shoot at and defeat that enemy to acquire what was just purchased and everything else the defeated soldier was carrying.

Especially during the mid to final stages of a match, one of the best ways to quickly and dramatically improve your soldier's arsenal is to fight and defeat enemy soldiers. As soon as a soldier is defeated, not only are they removed from the match instantly, but everything the deceased soldier was carrying falls to the ground and can be grabbed by surviving soldiers. Even if you don't defeat an enemy, you can still grab what a fallen enemy leaves behind after they've lost a firefight against someone else.

The problem is that his inventory is full, so he needed to drop the Assault Rifle he was holding, grab and use the Med Kit (shown here), and then re-take the dropped weapon from the ground.

Managing Your Soldier's Inventory

At any time during a match, an overview of your soldier's inventory is displayed on the screen. Depending on which gaming system you're using, this information is typically found near the bottom-right corner. After this soldier spent some unfortunate time in the storm, his Health meter is dangerously low (at just 5HP out of 100HP). Luckily, he stumbles upon this Med Kit to replenish his health.

In addition to your Soldier's Harvesting Tool, which they always carry and cannot drop at any time, your soldier has six Inventory slots that can hold weapons or certain types of loot items (such as Health and Shield replenishment items).

As you're looking at the inventory icons displayed in the bottom-right corner of the screen, the number associated with each item tells you one of two things. If the icon relates to a weapon, it shows you how much compatible ammo you currently have for that weapon. If the icon is for an item, it shows you how many of that item you have on hand. The weapon or item that's currently selected and active will display a yellow box around its Inventory icon slot.

To see and manage your soldier's entire inventory, it's necessary to access their Inventory screen. This is done by pressing the assigned Inventory button on your keyboard/mouse or controller.

The Inventory screen displays a lot of useful information. On the top-right side of the screen, you'll see a summary of the Resources your soldier is carrying–including wood, stone, and metal. Below this, also on the right side of the screen, is a summary of the ammunition your soldier currently has on hand. Each ammo icon represents one of the five types of ammo (Light Bullets, Medium Bullets, Heavy Bullets, Shells, and Rockets), and shows how many rounds of each ammo type you have available.

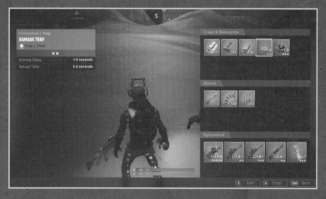

Displayed to the right of your soldier's Resources on the Inventory screen (when applicable) is information about the Traps and other items (such as Cozy Campfires), that are stored in your soldier's Inventory, but that don't take up one of the six main Inventory slots. To access any of these items, while viewing the main game screen, switch to Building mode using the assigned keyboard/mouse key or controller button, and then press the keyboard key, mouse button, or controller button assigned to the additional weapons and tools.

When your soldier is holding multiple Traps or items that are not included within the six main Inventory slots (when playing on a console-based gaming system), you'll need to enter into Building mode, and then keep pressing the appropriate controller button to scroll through the items in order to select the one you want to use. On a computer, each item is bound to a different keyboard key or mouse button.

Displayed in the bottom-right corner of the Inventory screen are the seven main Inventory slots. The left-most slot always holds the Harvesting Tool. However, it's possible to rearrange the items being held in the other six slots to make them easier to access during a match.

As you're looking at the Inventory screen, use the directional controls to highlight and select the weapon, ammo type, or item you want to access or use. The selected item's icon will display a yellow frame around in.

If you have a weapon selected, details about the weapon's category, color-coded rarity, and stats are displayed on the left side of the screen. When you're not sure how to best use a weapon or what type of ammo it requires, for example, this is a quick way to access the information.

Anytime you access your soldier's Inventory screen, this takes your attention away from the main game screen. The match does not pause, so your soldier potentially becomes vulnerable to attack.

Only access the Inventory screen when you're in a safe location (such as small and enclosed room with the door shut). While viewing this screen, even though you can't see what's happening around your soldier, you can still hear sound effects, so pay attention to the sound of approaching enemies or nearby weapons fire. If it sounds like an enemy is approaching or you may soon be under attack, exit from the Inventory screen quickly and be ready to take defensive actions!

How to Rearrange What's in Inventory Slots

Whenever you pick up a new weapon or loot item, it automatically gets placed within an available Inventory slot. Your soldier's Inventory slots initially fill up from left to right.

However, during a match, it's a good strategy to rearrange the items in your inventory so your most powerful and frequently used weapons and items are placed in the left-most slots. To rearrange what's in your Inventory slots, follow these steps:

1. Access your soldier's Inventory screen.
2. Highlight and select one of the items you want to move.
3. On a PC, drag the item from one Inventory slot to another. On a console-based system, select the Move command, and then position the cursor over the slot you want to move the selected item to.

Experienced gamers tend to place their favorite weapon in the left-most Inventory slot, and then their Health/Shield replenishment item(s) in the right-most slots. Throwable weapons (when available) get placed in the middle Inventory slots. This strategy, however, is a matter of personal preference.

In most situations, it makes little or no sense to carry around two of the same weapon, since inventory space is limited and you want to have a well-rounded selection of weapons available.

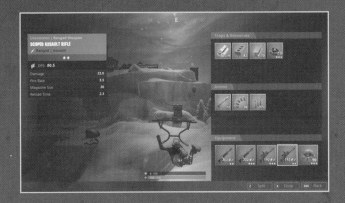

One instance when you might want to carry duplicate weapons is if you have a favorite weapon that has a small Magazine Size and slow reload time. By placing the two identical weapons in Inventory slots directly next to each other, instead of waiting for one weapon to reload when it runs out of ammo, you can quickly switch to the other (identical weapon) and keep firing. You're often able to switch weapons faster than it takes to reload a weapon—especially if you're using a Sniper Rifle that only holds one round of ammo at a time, for example. Shown here, the soldier is carrying two Scoped Assault Rifles and two Assault Rifles, although the rarity of the duplicate weapons is different.

How to Drop and Share Weapons, Ammo, and Items

If your soldier's six Inventory slots are filled up, but you find a new weapon or item you want to grab, it becomes necessary to give something up. First choose which item you want to get rid of and select it. Next, face the item you want to pick up and grab it. The item you're holding (the one you want to trade out) will be dropped, making room for the new item you want to grab.

There will be times when you might just want to drop a weapon or item that you no longer want or there's something that you want to share with a partner or squad mate who is standing close to your soldier. To do this, access the Inventory screen, select the item you want to drop, then press the keyboard key, mouse button, or controller button that's associated with the Drop command.

If you want to share an item from your inventory (in this case Dynamite) and your soldier is currently carrying multiples of that item, select the item you want to share with a nearby ally, and select the Drop command (see in the bottom-right corner of the screen).

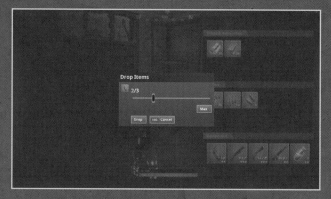

From the Drop Items pop-up window, choose how many of that item you want to drop (share). Press the Drop button to drop that amount of the item. Press the Max button to drop the entire inventory of that item your soldier is carrying.

Instead of wasting valuable time using the Drop Items slider, after selecting an item from the Inventory screen, select the Split command to instantly drop half of the quantity of the item that's selected. So, if you have six Heavy Bullets for example, and you use the Split command, you'll keep three Heavy Bullets in your inventory and drop three for someone else to pick up.

Anytime you opt to Drop or Share a weapon or item, make sure an ally is nearby and picks it up. Otherwise, any soldier (including your enemies) could stumble upon what you've dropped and grab it. Sometimes, in order to pick up a more powerful or useful item, you'll need to drop a less powerful or less useful item and run the risk of an enemy acquiring it.

Discover When and How to Fire Each Weapon

The trick to becoming a skilled soldier in battle is to learn when to use each weapon, based on the fighting situation. If you're at close range with an enemy, choose a weapon that's ideal for the situation.

If you're at a far distance from your enemy, you'll want to use a Sniper Rifle (or weapon with a scope), but make sure you position yourself in a spot that can be protected, but that also offers a clear line-of-sight to your target.

Regardless of where you are, achieving a height advantage when shooting at your enemies is almost always beneficial. You can achieve a height advantage by standing on an object, climbing to the roof of a building or structure, or by building a tall ramp or fortress, for example.

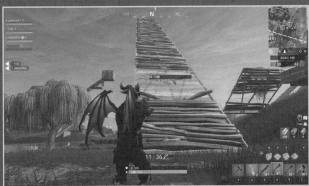

One of the easiest types of forts to build that's functional and that offers adequate protection is a 1x1 Fortress. Check out the directions for building a 1x1 Fortress within Section 5–Building for Offensive and Defensive Purposes, and then practice your building skills. Learning to build quickly is important, especially when enemies are close by and a firefight can begin at any moment.

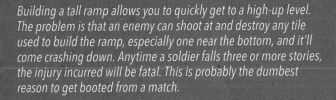

Building a tall ramp allows you to quickly get to a high-up level. The problem is that an enemy can shoot at and destroy any tile used to build the ramp, especially one near the bottom, and it'll come crashing down. Anytime a soldier falls three or more stories, the injury incurred will be fatal. This is probably the dumbest reason to get booted from a match.

Here, the soldier is standing on the roof of the 1x1 Fortress she built and is keeping her eye out for enemy movement within the lodge. For protection, she has the option to crouch behind the pyramid-shaped ceiling tiles that surround the roof of the fortress. Because they're made of metal, they'll offer excellent short-term protection against incoming bullets.

Building a tall fortress takes longer than a ramp, and requires more resources, but it also offers more protection, especially if the fortress is made of stone or metal. Any structure that's made from wood can easily be destroyed by gun fire, an explosive weapon, or even a Harvesting Tool.

Based on the fighting situation you're in, or that you're about to encounter, build up your arsenal accordingly, so you have the right types of weapons and a good supply of ammo. There are many ways to gather ammo during a match. One of the easiest is to open Ammo Boxes that are scattered throughout the island.

How to Accurately Aim and Fire Different Types of Weapons

Depending on the weapon, there are several ways to aim and then fire it.

When any gun is active, point it toward your enemy and pull the trigger to fire it. This strategy works well when you're in close range, when time is more important than aiming accuracy because you're close to the enemy and it'll be difficult to miss your intended target. This is referred to as "shooting from the hip."

By pressing the Aim button before pulling the trigger, you'll have more accurate aim over the weapon you're using, particularly if your soldier is crouching and still or standing still. Notice how small the targeting crosshair is that's displayed on the wall of the structure. You can barely make out the white "+". When you press the Aim button, the viewing perspective changes. You'll see your target from the end of a gun's barrel, and the target will appear closer.

Shown here, the soldier is running toward the building and is ready to fire her weapon. Notice the white aiming crosshairs (seen on the wall of the building) are very large. If she were to fire, the bullet would hit anywhere within this large crosshair area.

Simply by standing still, the targeting crosshairs for the weapon shrink a lot, meaning that your soldier will be able to aim more accurately. To achieve the most precise aim, pressing the Aim button before pulling the trigger works best, but this takes slightly longer. If it were an enemy standing in front of her at close range, the fraction of a second it takes to press the Aim button could give the enemy the time needed to shoot their own weapon first.

Anytime you're using a weapon with a built-in scope, pressing the Aim button activates the scope and changes your view. The farther you are from your target, the more you may need to compensate for bullet drop, so aim slightly higher than your intended target. Learning to accurately account for bullet drop takes lots of practice with each type of long-range weapon.

Whenever you point an active weapon at any target, you'll see its targeting crosshairs. The smaller the crosshairs appear, the more accurate your shot will be. Standing still and crouching will reduce the size of the crosshairs, while walking, running, or jumping will increase the size of the crosshairs and greatly reduce your aiming accuracy.

The aiming process for throwable weapons (various types of Grenades) is different than shooting a gun. Notice the targeting crosshairs look different. When you toss a Grenade, it follows an arc-like trajectory. As you're aiming the Grenade, you'll see an outline for the trajectory for that weapon. In some cases, if you're trying to toss a Grenade through a small open window of a building or fortress, it may be necessary to aim slightly higher than your intended target. Shown here, the soldier is tossing multiple Clingers at a nearby building to destroy it. Once a Clinger reaches its target, it sticks to it, flashes a blue light for a few seconds, and then detonates.

Most types of Grenades bounce off solid walls or objects and will bounce back toward the thrower. If this happens, your soldier could get injured as a result of the explosion. These items are best used when tossed into an enclosed structure—through an open door or window, or when a fortress built by an enemy does not have a roof. (Many gamers forget to add a roof to their fortresses, which makes them vulnerable if you're able to lob a Grenade up and over a wall so it goes through the open roof.)

Notice that when the Grenade Launcher was shot at the house's garage door, it bounced off and the explosion took place in the street, as opposed to causing damage to the house.

As you can see, two Clingers pretty much demolished the small structure. If anyone had been inside, they'd be toast.

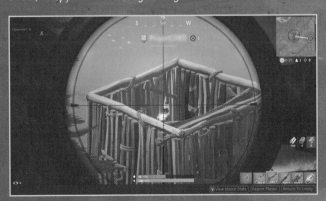

With just two other soldiers left in the match, this one builds a ramp to get higher up, and then aims into an enemy's fortress that does not have a roof.

When shooting a Grenade Launcher, keep in mind that the Grenades can bounce off walls and solid objects, so aim for an open door or window, for example. Rocket Launchers, Guided Missile Launchers, and Quad Launchers can be used to blast apart structures or solid objects, so aim directly for whatever you want to destroy.

Here, the soldier is crouched behind a wooden wall (which offers minimal protection against incoming bullets or explosive weapons but can keep her hidden). She's drinking a Small Shield Potion to boost her Shield meter.

Pay attention to your surroundings and use any wall, building, structure, broken down vehicle (shown here), or solid object at your disposal.

Keep in mind, non-solid objects, like bushes or haystacks, can help you hide, but these offer no protection whatsoever against incoming attacks.

Of course, while your soldier is exploring inside of a house, building, or structure, you'll discover plenty of objects to hide behind. Shown here, the soldier is crouched behind a bed and aiming at the door to the room. She hears an enemy approaching.

Any type of solid wall can provide decent cover during a firefight. Hide behind a wall to reload your weapon or avoid incoming bullets.

You can then peek around that wall to fire your weapon or build a window into the wall. When peeking, always try to look out the right side of a wall or object. This will help keep the majority of your soldier's body protected by the barrier you're hiding behind.

When your soldier peeks out from the left side of a barrier, much more of their body is exposed, because all soldiers carry and hold guns on their right side.

SECTION 5

BUILDING FOR OFFENSIVE AND DEFENSIVE PURPOSES

Knowing how to handle the weapons available on the island will certainly help keep your soldier alive and allow you to boost your firefight victory stats during battles. Beyond exploring and fighting, this section focuses on the building skills you'll also want to master.

The Basics of Building on the Island

There are often times during a match when no reliable pre-built wall or object is available to hide behind, but you need to immediately protect your soldier against an incoming attack. In this situation, building a vertical wall out of stone (shown here) or metal is a quick and easy solution.

Every building tile you create has its own HP meter, which you'll see when you face it. As a building tile is being constructed, it's HP meter increases until it's fully built. This happens with wood tiles the fastest and metal tiles the slowest. This floor tile made of wood, for example, has a maximum 140HP meter when it's full.

Depending on the distance an enemy is when attacking your building tiles, and which weapon they are using, how quickly a tile gets destroyed varies. This happens when a building tile's HP meter hits zero.

Any building tile can be built from wood, stone, or metal. This is shown from left to right in each of these examples. After entering into Building mode, your soldier can choose their building material and then create a vertical wall tile, horizontal floor tile, ramp/stairs tile, or a pyramid-shaped roof tile, one at a time. Based on your available resources, you're able to build by mixing and matching various shaped tiles to create elaborate structures when needed.

Keep in mind, while your soldier is in Building mode, they can't use their weapons. Be sure to practice switching between Combat and Building mode quickly, and then while in Building mode, learn how to build as quickly as possible.

How to Build a Barrier for Protection

To provide your soldier with slightly more protection than a single vertical wall tile, build a vertical wall (using stone or metal), and then build a stone or metal ramp/stairs tile directly behind it.

The easiest way to cross a lake or large body of water is typically to build a bridge and then run over it as fast as possible, since your soldier will be out in the open and vulnerable to a potential attack. Ramps should be made from wood, since this is the fastest material to work with.

When you need safety, crouch down behind the ramp. Your enemy will now need to destroy two layers of barriers (the wall and the ramp) before being able to reach your soldier with their weapon attack.

Build Ramps and Bridges to Reach Difficult Places

While it's certainly possible to participate in a *Fortnite: Battle Royale* match and win Victory Royale, but never need to build a fortress, chances are, you will often need to build ramps or bridges to reach certain areas of the island.

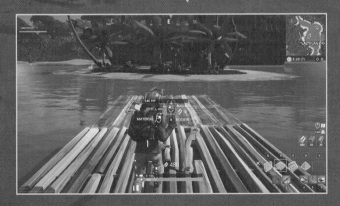

In order to maintain a higher ground when traveling in between houses, structures, or buildings, for example, instead of returning to ground level and walking between buildings, and then climbing back up to the roof of another building, consider building a mid-air bridge between the two structures. Since it's possible your bridge will get shot at by enemies while you're crossing, it's sometimes a better strategy to work with stone or metal for the added protection and strength these building materials offer.

Tall ramps can also be used to help your soldier quickly gain a height advantage over an enemy during a firefight. Wood can be used to build ramps quickly.

Ramp building can be particularly important during the final few moments of a match (the End Game), for example, when only a few soldiers remain alive and the safe area of the island has become extremely small. In this case, the final battle for supremacy might take place vertically within a single structure. The soldier who has the height advantage typically has the overall tactical advantage in these situations.

The problem with tall ramps made of wood is that an enemy can quickly shoot them down and destroy them (with you on them) from almost any distance. Simply by shooting at and destroying one tile, the entire ramp will come crashing down, along with whoever is standing on it.

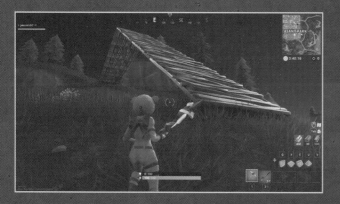

In addition to building ramps that face a hill or mountain to help you reach the top, it often makes more sense to build a ramp along the side of a mountain, like the one shown on the right.

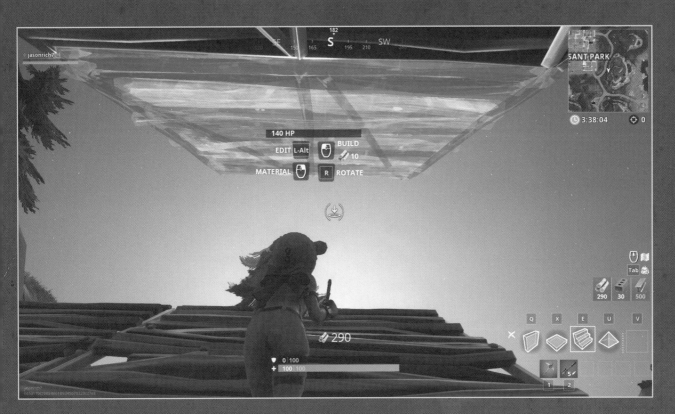

An Over/Under Ramp allows you to simultaneously build a ramp and have a roof over that ramp to protect your soldier from potential threats from above. This takes twice the resources, but it's useful when climbing up a mountain where enemies could be lurking above you. Instead of pointing the cursor toward the ground as you're walking or running and building a regular ramp, place the cursor in front of your soldier (pointing slightly upward) to build an Over/Under Ramp.

There are many items and vehicles on the island that can help you travel up (or down) a hill or mountain quickly. One thing you never want to do is leap off a mountain and fall to the bottom. This will result in serious injury or worse. It is possible, however, to stay along the edge of a steep mountain and slide down it. This will not result in injury.

Many vehicles and items, such as ATKs, Quad-crasher, Hover Boards, Balloons (shown), Launch Pads, Rift-To-Go items, Shopping Carts, Gliders, and Grappling Hooks can also help your soldier climb up or down a tall hill or mountain quickly and safely. All vehicles and items used to transport your soldier require some practice to steer or use effectively.

Keep in mind, not all these vehicle types and items are available within *Fortnite: Battle Royale* at all times. Some get periodically vaulted and then reintroduced into the game later.

Using two balloons at once will help your soldier defy gravity when he leaps upward. (Use the directional controls while airborne to steer.) Using three balloons at once allows your soldier to float up high into the air. You can then pop (release) one balloon at a time to lower your soldier back down to land when needed.

An ATK (All-Terrain Kart) is a souped-up golf cart. It can hold multiple passengers, move at a decent pace, and has a HP meter that maxes out at 400HP. Once it sustains too much damage, it gets destroyed.

Once you acquire and store a Glider item in your soldier's inventory, upon leaping from a very tall object (such as a building's roof or a cliff), during the fall downward, deploy your soldier's Glider to ensure a safe landing. When using the Glider item, choose the item from your inventory before making the leap. Perfect timing is then needed to deploy it while in mid-air, so you don't let your soldier splat on the ground. Gliders offer a great way to quickly reach the bottom of a building or mountain, and at the same time, have some navigational control while your soldier is airborne.

Quadcrashers are fast-moving, all-terrain vehicles that are more maneuverable, faster, and able to cross more rugged terrain. These have a Boost feature (shown here) that allows for short bursts of extra-fast speed.

Eight Things You Need to Know About Building

1. To build or edit anything, your soldier must switch from Combat mode to Building mode. While in Building mode, he/she cannot use a weapon.
2. In most situations, you're able to build indoors (within homes, buildings, or structures), or just about anywhere outdoors.
3. You're able to build directly on top of pre-built buildings or structures.
4. Anything that another soldier builds on the island, your soldier can destroy, edit, or expand upon. Explosive weapons are one way to destroy a structure quickly.
5. Many gamers forget to build a roof on their fortresses. If you know an enemy is hiding in a fortress without a roof, build a ramp to get higher up than the fortress and then drop some throwable

Hoverboards (also referred to as Driftboards) allow a single rider to soar in the air (just above ground level). They're fast, whether going up or down hills, or across flat terrain, and are extremely maneuverable. You can also go airborne while riding one yet have a safe landing with no Health damage. In addition to using your directional controls to steer, a Hoverboard can "jump," which is useful to do tricks, plus it offers a slick Boost feature. Use a Hoverboard to "slide" down a mountain or hill, ride off the top of a mountain or hill and go airborne (shown here), or ride up a hill and defy gravity.

explosive weapons directly into the enemy fortress, or shoot downward using any weapon. A projectile explosive weapon will cause the most damage the fastest in this situation.

6. Resources can be collected by harvesting them (using your soldier's Harvesting Tool), by finding and grabbing resource bundle icons that are scattered throughout the island, or by defeating an enemy and grabbing the resources they were carrying at the time of their demise.

7. Creativity is as important as speed when it comes to building. First quickly determine what the purpose for building is, and then build in the most efficient way possible based on your immediate goals.

8. During the early and mid-stages of a match, sometimes it's better to keep moving and to make a quick escape from an enemy instead of sticking around and using resources to build a structure for protection.

Learn How to Build a 1x1 Fortress

A fortress can be used for added protection from an incoming attack, provide a safe place for your soldier to launch an attack from (using mid- to long-range weapons), or to provide a safe place where your soldier can replenish their Health and/or Shield meters when appropriate items are at their disposal.

Once a fortress is built, activating a Cozy Campfire inside the fortress is one way to replenish your soldier's Health meter. Using a Med Kit, Bandages, or consuming a Chug Jug, for example, will also do the trick. Each of these items take time to use and require your soldier to stand still and be vulnerable to attack. This is why using these items within the safety of a fortress is advisable.

With practice, you can quickly build a 1x1 fortress. A sample of this type of fortress (made of metal) is shown here. Building any protective barrier made of wood is absolutely pointless. It's quick but offers too little protection. Building from stone takes a bit longer but offers more protection. Ideally, you want to build a fortress from metal. This offers the strongest level of protection.

To create a 1x1 fortress, follow these steps. Learning to do this quickly is important, so keep practicing your building techniques. The first step to building anything in *Fortnite: Battle Royale* is to acquire and stockpile resources (wood, stone, and metal), so you have an ample supply to build with when they're needed.

Collecting resources is the primary use of your soldier's Harvesting Tool. Use it to smash objects on the island to collect wood, stone (brick), and metal. As you explore the island, you'll also discover resource bundles. Pick them up to collect a bunch of wood, stone, or metal at once.

Harvesting (smashing) anything on the island made of wood allows you to gather the wood resource. Harvesting anything made of stone or brick allows you to gather the stone resource. Harvesting anything made of metal, such as vehicles or appliances in a kitchen, allow you to collect the metal resource. Resources are used for building, as well as for currency for Vending Machines that are scattered throughout the island.

Step 2–Build four vertical wall tiles around the floor tile, creating a box. If you want, build a door on the bottom level. This is an option that takes a few extra seconds to create. (While in Building mode, you need to switch to Edit mode.)

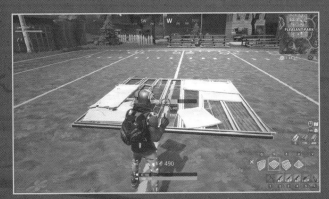

Step 1–Find a flat surface or build one floor tile on the ground.

Step 3–Within the box you just created, build one ramp tile. As the ramp tile is being constructed, jump onto it and move upward. The first level of your 1x1 fortress is now completed.

Step 4—*To add another level, build four additional wall tiles on top of the other ones.*

Step 5—*Add another ramp tile within the structure. Repeat steps 3 and 4 as often as necessary to build the 1x1 fortress as tall as you want or need it.*

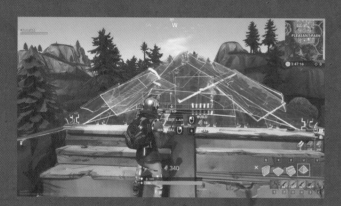

Step 6—*At the top of your fortress, add ceiling tiles around the outer edges that you can peek out from to shoot at enemies.*

Step 7—*On the top level, consider building a floor tile, so you have space to move around. This flat space is also ideal for placing a Cozy Campfire, Launch Pad, or Bouncer Pad, for example.*

As time permits, you can add a ramp stemming off from the roof of your fort so you can reach a higher level quickly, or add walls with windows so you're able to see and shoot out. In addition to speed, successful building requires creativity.

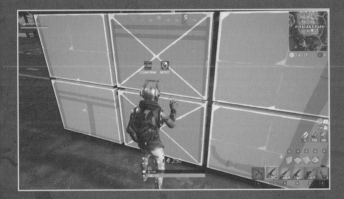

Shown here is a door being built (from the outside) on the bottom level of a 1x1 fortress. If you build the first level from the outside and then build a door to get in, an enemy could later use that same door to follow you inside and attack from within (if he's able to get close enough without being defeated during his approach). One way to prevent this is to place Damage Traps on the inside of the fortress.

Any building tile can later be repaired (using resources) or edited to add a door, window, or opening, for example. Anytime you add something to the tile, however, it lowers that tile's HP level. For example, a solid metal (vertical) wall has a 500HP, but a vertical wall with a door built into it has a maximum level of 480HP.

The drawback to building a window into a wall or fortress is that just as you can see and shoot out, an enemy can see and shoot in. If you need to reload your weapon, for example, crouch down and move away from the window. Shown here is the soldier within a 1x1 fortress looking out through a window on the first level.

Shown here, the same soldier is outside of the 1x1 fortress looking at the wall containing a window. As you can see from the wall tile's HP meter, the tile containing the window has a maximum HP level of 480.

During the mid-stage of a match, don't waste time or resources building elaborate fortresses. Usually something basic, like a 1x1 Fortress, works well. In this case, the soldier shown here is trying to destroy the mid-section of the distant fortress and force her enemy to show himself.

If you don't have the time or skills necessary to quickly build a fortress, seek out and grab a Port-A-Fort or Port-A-Fortress item and keep in stored in your soldier's inventory until it's needed. When you need to build a quick and sturdy fortress, toss this item where you want the fort created, and it'll build itself instantly (and require zero resources to build).

A Port-A-Fort or Port-A-Fortress can be extremely useful during the End Game, for example, if there's no place else that's safe for your soldier to hide or take cover.

Building Techniques for the End Game

As *Fortnite: Battle Royale* has evolved, Epic Games has put less emphasis on the need to build tall, strong, and elaborate structures and fortresses in order to stay alive. There are, however, plenty of gamers who still fully utilize the building tools available to them, and who have mastered the art of building quickly and efficiently during matches, either for offensive or defensive purposes, to provide a safe place to replenish their soldier's Health and Shield meters, or to gain a height advantage over enemies.

You're about to see just a few samples of how various gamers tapped their building skills during the End Game phase of various matches. Even if you don't plan to focus your End Game strategy on building, it's still important to fine-tune your building skills, just in case the final adversaries you face at the end of a match are master builders.

Just four soldiers remain in this match. The soldier doing the shooting is at ground level, but she's making it rain bullets on the distant fortress being built by her adversary. The goal is to weaken the fortress, make it collapse, and force the soldier within it to also fight at ground level to make it a more even match by eliminating the enemy's height advantage.

The soldier in the tall fortress made one lethal mistake. The foundation of the fortress is made of wood and very narrow. Instead of focusing on shooting the enemy within the fortress, the soldier can shoot from below, target the weak spot, and bring the entire fortress crashing down. This will cause the last remaining enemy to plummet to the ground and perish.

Seven soldiers remain in this match. One is building a simple, but tall wooden fortress. The soldier using the scoped weapon is waiting for his enemy to peek their head above the wall, so he can take a headshot.

From the safety and comfort of her own fort, this soldier sees one of her enemies taking to the sky via their Glider in order to relocate to another location. With just three enemies left to eliminate, she tries to shoot the adversary while he's in mid-air. Especially during the End Game, you always need to know where your enemies are, and try to keep them from reaching a higher elevation than you.

The soldier seen here entered the End Game with all Legendary weapons (a really smart move). With just one enemy remaining in the match, she's hiding behind a stone ramp that she built. She is also using a Rocket Launcher to cause as much devastation as possible on the enemy's fortress. The soldier with the Rocket Launcher does not have a height advantage here, so bringing down the enemy's fort is a good strategy.

During this End Game, with just two soldiers left in the match, both were striving to achieve a height advantage and building tall ramps and high-up platforms. Unfortunately for the soldier in the distance, she wound up losing the match by crashing hard on the ground when the ramp was destroyed right out from under her feet.

In the heat of a firefight, don't worry about building a well-designed fortress. Instead, focus on building a structure that'll give you a height advantage, but simultaneously protect your sides or attacks from overhead, based on the location of your remaining adversaries. When possible and to conserve resources, build over or edit part of a structure that another soldier has already built. During the End Game, building quickly, and then switching back to Combat mode is essential.

Sometimes in the final moments of an intense match, when you lose track of your enemy's location, the best strategy is to sit tight, be as quiet as possible, and wait for your adversary to reveal their location. Use the time to replenish your soldier's Health and Shields.

Here's another situation where the storm is closing in, and one of the two remaining soldiers has a height advantage over the other. The soldier at the disadvantage is held up within a structure and is forced to build and then repair protective walls until he can make an escape. Without exiting the building and going directly into the storm, the soldier has limited escape options.

Shown here, multiple soldiers have built on top of existing buildings in order to stay protected and prepare for the End Game. Notice the reinforced ramps made from stone, as well as the metal ramps used to link buildings together.

SECTION 6

POPULAR HEALTH, SHIELD, AND LOOT ITEMS

There's always a selection of Health and Shield replenishment items, along with other loot items and tools that can be found, stored in a soldier's inventory, and then used when they're needed. The various items available at any given time in the game changes, but a good selection of these items is always available. Each needs to be used at the appropriate time in order to help your soldier stay alive longer during a match.

This section offers details about many of the most popular items available on the island. Sometimes these can be found lying on the ground, out in the open. They're also sometimes available in chests, as well as sometimes within Loot Llamas or Supply Drops.

As you'll discover, some items get stored within one of your soldier's six main Inventory slots, while others can also be stored within your soldier's inventory, but in a slot found on the Inventory screen to the right of your soldier's Resources. To use them, you must first switch from Combat mode to Building mode, and then select and activate the selected item.

Health and Shield Replenishment Items

LOOT ITEM	HOW LONG IT TAKES TO USE OR CONSUME	POWERUP BENEFIT	STORAGE LOCATION	MAXIMUM NUMBER YOU CAN CARRY
Apples	Almost Instantly	Increases your soldier's Health meter by 5 points per Apple that's consumed.	Apples must be consumed when and where they're found (which is usually under trees). They cannot be carried and used later.	None
Bandages	4 seconds	Increases your soldier's Health meter by 15 points.	Requires one backpack Inventory slot	15
Chug Jug	15 seconds	Replenishes your soldier's Health *and* Shield meter to 100.	Requires one backpack Inventory slot.	1
Cozy Campfire	25 seconds	Boosts each soldier's Health HP by 2 points for every second they are standing near the flames for up to 25 seconds. If fully utilized, it boosts a soldier's Health meter by 50 points.	Stored with a soldier's resources, so it's accessed from Building mode, not Combat mode.	Unknown

(Continued on next page)

LOOT ITEM	HOW LONG IT TAKES TO USE OR CONSUME	POWERUP BENEFIT	STORAGE LOCATION	MAXIMUM NUMBER YOU CAN CARRY
Med Kits	10 seconds	Replenishes your soldier's Health meter back to 100.	Requires one backpack Inventory slot.	3
Mushrooms	Almost instantly	Increases your soldier's Shield meter by 5 points (up to 100).	Mushrooms must be consumed when and where they're found. They cannot be carried and used later.	None
Shield Potion	5 seconds	Replenishes your soldier's Shield meter by 50 points (up to 100 maximum).	Requires one backpack Inventory slot.	2
Slurp Juice	Approximately 2 seconds to consume and 37.5 seconds to achieve its full benefit	A soldier's Health *and* Shield meter increases by one point (up to 75 points) for every half-second this drink is being consumed.	Requires one backpack Inventory slot.	1
Small Shield Potion	2 seconds	Replenishes your soldier's Shield meter by 25 points.	Requires one backpack Inventory slot.	10

Useful Loot Items & Tools

LOOT ITEM	HOW IT'S USED	BENEFITS & LIMITATIONS	DURATION OF USE
Balloons	After collecting this item and adding it to inventory, upon selecting it, one, two, or three balloons can be attached to your soldier's back at once.	Using one balloon at a time allows your soldier to jump higher or leap farther. Using two balloons at a time, a soldier can jump even higher and stay airborne longer to cover more territory. Using three balloons, your soldier can defy gravity and float high into the air. As you pop each balloon, one at a time, they will descend safely back toward land.	Balloons stay inflated and attached to your soldier once activated, until they are popped.

LOOT ITEM	HOW IT'S USED	BENEFITS & LIMITATIONS	DURATION OF USE
Bouncer Pad	In addition to being used as a weapon (when used creatively to put your enemy into an endless bouncing loop), a Bouncer Pad can be used to catapult your own soldier up into the air. They will land with zero damage.	A Bouncer Pad does not allow your soldier to reach the same altitude as similar items, like a Launch Pad, but unlike a Launch Pad, it can be placed on a ramp tile, as well as any other flat surface.	Once placed, a Bouncer Pad can be used repeatedly, but it can't be relocated.
Bush Loot Item	Wear this item as camouflage and your soldier will look like a bush when they are standing still. Use this to hide from enemies when outside.	While a Bush will hide you, it offers zero protection. If you get spotted, an enemy will attack you, and the Bush will immediately disappear.	Until it's destroyed, the Bush will provide camouflage. If you crouch down and remain still, you typically won't get spotted. If you walk around while wearing the Bush, you'll immediately attract attention.
Campfire	Scattered throughout the island (mostly around camp sites) you'll discover unlit Campfires. These Campfires cannot be picked up and moved. They must be used at their existing location.	Walk up to a Campfire and light it. For every second your soldier stands near the flame, their Health meter will be slightly replenished.	25 seconds
Cozy Campfire	This is an item that can be found, picked up, and stored in inventory until needed. It can then be placed on any flat surface, such as within a fortress, in a building, or behind a protective barricade.	Set up the Cozy Campfire on a flat surface and light it. For every second a soldier stands near the flame, their Health gets replenished by 2HP.	25 seconds. Multiple soldiers can stand near the same Cozy Campfire and all benefit from its Health replenishment powers.
Glider	After being placed in your soldier's inventory and selected, they can leap off a tall building, hill, or mountain, for example, deploy the Glider, and travel safely back to land.	Perfect timing is essential. You must select the Glider item before jumping, and then must activate it while airborne.	Each time you pick up a Glider item, it includes 10 uses.

(Continued on next page)

LOOT ITEM	HOW IT'S USED	BENEFITS & LIMITATIONS	DURATION OF USE
Grappler	Shoot this item at a nearby target and as soon as it makes contact, your soldier will be catapulted forward, toward the target area.	It's a quick way to reach higher up (or lower down) areas without sustaining injury. Use it to rush enemies or move to another location fast with no setup. You can use this item repeatedly to swing from target to target, like Spider-Man®.	Each time you add a Grappler to your arsenal, it offers 15 shots.
Launch Pads	Place a Launch Pad on a flat surface and then jump on it. Your soldier will be catapulted into the air. Use the directional controls to navigate as they fall (and then glide) back to land.	The same Launch Pad can be used many times by any soldiers that jump on it. Use it to quickly reach the top of a building, to escape a fortress that's being attacked, or to help your soldier escape the storm.	Once you determine where and when it gets placed, a Launch Pad remains there until it's manually destroyed (by shooting at it or blowing it up).
Port-A-Forts	After collecting a Port-A-Fort, when you need to quickly build a metal fortress, toss it at the desired building location, and the fort will be created instantly—without requiring any resources.	During the first few seconds as its being built, a Port-A-Fort is somewhat vulnerable to attack. An enemy soldier can enter with you or follow you into the fortress later. You definitely want to seal the entranceway.	A Port-A-Fort will offer protection until it's destroyed by enemy gunfire or an explosive weapon. Like any other type of structure, it too can be destroyed. Because it's made from metal, it can first withstand a lot of damage, however.
Rift-to-Go	Use this item to quickly get catapulted into the air and be able to navigate to a desired (nearby) landing spot.	This item works like a Launch Pad or Bouncer Pad but requires no setup. It also catapults your soldier higher into the air.	Each Rift-to-Go item can only be used once. Use it to make a fast emergency escape or to relocate yourself fast.

Weapon-Related Items

LOOT ITEM	DAMAGE	MAXIMUM NUMBER YOU CAN CARRY	STORAGE LOCATION
Boogie Bombs	Once detonated (by tossing it at an enemy), this bomb causes a soldier to dance uncontrollably for 5 seconds. During this time, they are defenseless against other weapon or explosive attacks.	10	Requires one backpack Inventory slot.
Bouncer Pads	If positioned correctly, these can be used to send an enemy into a bouncing loop, during which time, they will be defenseless against other types of attack. To use it as a weapon, you need to be creative.	Unknown	Stored with a soldier's resources, so it's accessed from Building mode, not Combat mode.
Bottle Rockets	This is a throwable fireworks weapon that works at mid-range. Once detonated, 45 rockets explode over a 9-second period. How much damage is caused depends on how close an enemy is to the explosion and how many rockets they are hit by. This weapon can also damage a structure that it's detonated in.	Pick up two Bottle Rockets at a time and store up to six within your soldier's inventory. Toss multiple Bottle Rockets at the same target to increase the destructive power. This item makes a lot of noise when detonated, so it attracts attention.	Requires one backpack Inventory slot.
Clingers	Up to 100HP damage can be caused if a soldier or object is caught in the explosion. Use this to defeat enemies or blow up objects or structures.	10	Requires one backpack Inventory slot.
Damage Traps	A Damage Trap can be placed on a wall, floor, or ceiling—within a structure built by a soldier or a pre-existing building, for example. If an enemy gets caught by a Damage Trap, they'll perish. It's best to place them where they can't be seen by enemies. Be creative when placing them.	No limit	Stored with a soldier's resources, so it's accessed from Building mode, not Combat mode.

(Continued on next page)

LOOT ITEM	DAMAGE	MAXIMUM NUMBER YOU CAN CARRY	STORAGE LOCATION
Dynamite	A throwable weapon that detonates 5 seconds after hitting its target and causes an explosion. An explosion can cause at least 70HP damage to a soldier and up to 800HP damage to a structure.	10	Requires one backpack Inventory slot.
Grenades	Up to 105HP damage can be caused if a soldier or object is caught in the explosion. Use this to defeat enemies or blow up objects or structures. Unlike Dynamite, for example, Grenades detonate immediately upon impact.	10	Requires one backpack Inventory slot.
Impulse Grenades	When thrown at enemies, this special grenade will catapult an enemy soldier away from the explosion's point of impact. This item does not damage structures or objects.	10	Requires one backpack Inventory slot.
Mounted Turret	This weapon gets mounted and stays in one location after it gets activated. It must be placed on a flat surface. While you can continuously fire a Mounted Turret, it lasts longer if you shoot in bursts.	Unknown	Stored with a soldier's resources, so it's accessed from Building mode, not Combat mode.
Remote Explosives	Damage to enemy soldiers varies, based on how close a target is to the explosion. If placed on a structure or object, it will blow it up. Use multiple Remote Explosives together to create a bigger bang.	10	Requires one backpack Inventory slot.
Shockwave Grenades	When tossed, this type of grenade will send whoever is in its path flying backward. This is more powerful than an Impulse Grenade but causes no actual damage when a soldier lands from their fall.	6	Requires one backpack Inventory slot.
Stink Bombs	Once tossed, a Stink Bomb generates a toxic cloud of yellow smoke that lasts for 9 seconds. For every half-second an enemy is caught in the smoke, they receive 5HP damage. This weapon works best when deployed in a confined area.	4	Requires one backpack Inventory slot.

SECTION 7

FORTNITE: BATTLE ROYALE RESOURCES

On YouTube (www.youtube.com), Twitch.TV (www.twitch.tv/directory/game/Fortnite), or Facebook Watch (www.facebook.com/watch), in the Search field, enter the search phrase "*Fortnite: Battle Royale*" to discover many game-related channels, live streams, and prerecorded videos that'll help you become a better player.

Also, be sure to check out the following online resources related to *Fortnite: Battle Royale*:

WEBSITE OR YOUTUBE CHANNEL NAME	DESCRIPTION	URL
Best Fortnite Settings	Discover the custom game settings used by some of the world's top-rated *Fortnite: Battle Royale* players.	www.bestfortnitesettings.com
Corsair	Consider upgrading your keyboard and mouse to one that's designed specifically for gaming. Corsair is one of several companies that manufacture keyboards, mice, and headsets specifically for gamers.	www.corsair.com
Epic Game's Official Social Media Accounts for *Fortnite: Battle Royale*	Visit the official Facebook, Twitter, and Instagram Accounts for *Fortnite: Battle Royale*.	Facebook: www.facebook.com/fortnitegame Twitter: https://twitter.com/fortnitegame Instagram: www.instagram.com/fortnite
Fandom's *Fortnite* Wiki	Discover the latest news and strategies related to *Fortnite: Battle Royale*.	http://fortnite.wikia.com/wiki/Fortnite_Wiki
FantasticalGamer	A popular YouTuber who publishes *Fortnite* tutorial videos.	www.youtube.com/user/FantasticalGamer
FBR Insider	The *Fortnite: Battle Royale Insider* website offers game-related news, tips, and strategy videos.	www.fortniteinsider.com
Fortnite Config	An independent website that lists the custom game settings for dozens of top-rated *Fortnite: Battle Royale* players.	https://fortniteconfig.com
Fortnite Gamepedia Wiki	Read up-to-date descriptions of every weapon, loot item, and ammo type available within *Fortnite: Battle Royale*. This Wiki also maintains a comprehensive database of soldier outfits and related items released by Epic Games.	https://fortnite.gamepedia.com/Fortnite_Wiki

(Continued on next page)

WEBSITE OR YOUTUBE CHANNEL NAME	DESCRIPTION	URL
Fortnite Intel	An independent source of news related to *Fortnite: Battle Royale*.	www.fortniteintel.com
Fortnite Scout	Check your personal player stats, and analyze your performance using a bunch of colorful graphs and charts. Also check out the stats of other *Fortnite: Battle Royale* players.	www.fortnitescout.com
Fortnite Skins	This independent website maintains a detailed database of all *Fortnite: Battle Royale* outfits and accessory items released by Epic Games.	https://fortniteskins.net
Fortnite Stats & Leaderboard	This is an independent website that allows you to view your own *Fortnite*-related stats or discover the stats from the best players in the world.	https://fortnitestats.com
Fortnite: Battle Royale for Android Mobile Devices	Download *Fortnite: Battle Royale* for your compatible Android-based mobile device.	www.epicgames.com/fortnite/en-US/mobile/android/get-started
Fortnite: Battle Royale Mobile (iOS App Store)	Download *Fortnite: Battle Royale* for your Apple iPhone or iPad	https://itunes.apple.com/us/app/fortnite/id1261357853
Game Informer Magazine's *Fortnite* Coverage	Discover articles, reviews, and news about *Fortnite: Battle Royale* published by *Game Informer* magazine.	www.gameinformer.com/fortnite
GameSkinny Online Guides	A collection of topic-specific strategy guides related to *Fortnite*.	www.gameskinny.com/tag/fortnite-guides
GameSpot's *Fortnite* Coverage	Check out the news, reviews, and game coverage related to *Fortnite: Battle Royale* that's been published by GameSpot.	www.gamespot.com/fortnite
IGN Entertainment's *Fortnite* Coverage	Check out all IGN's past and current coverage of *Fortnite*.	www.ign.com/wikis/fortnite
Jason R. Rich's Websites and Social Media	Learn about additional, unofficial game strategy guides by Jason R. Rich that cover *Fortnite: Battle Royale*, *PUBG*, and *Apex Legends* (each sold separately).	www.JasonRich.com www.GameTipBooks.com Twitter: @JasonRich7 Instagram: @JasonRich7
Microsoft's Xbox One *Fortnite* Website	Learn about and acquire *Fortnite: Battle Royale* if you're an Xbox One gamer.	www.microsoft.com/en-US/store/p/Fortnite-Battle-Royalee/BT5P2X999VH2

WEBSITE OR YOUTUBE CHANNEL NAME	DESCRIPTION	URL
MonsterDface YouTube and Twitch.tv Channels	Watch video tutorials and live game streams from an expert *Fortnite* player.	www.youtube.com/user/ MonsterdfaceLive www.Twitch.tv/MonsterDface
Ninja	On YouTube and Twitch.tv, check out the live and recorded game streams from Ninja, one of the most highly skilled *Fortnite: Battle Royale* players in the world. His YouTube channel has more than 22 million subscribers.	YouTube: www.youtube.com/user/ NinjasHyper Twitch: https://twitch.tv/Ninja
Official Epic Games YouTube Channel for *Fortnite: Battle Royale*	The official *Fortnite: Battle Royale* YouTube channel.	www.youtube.com/user/epicfortnite
Pro Game Guides	This independent website maintains a detailed database of all *Fortnite: Battle Royale* outfits and accessory items released by Epic Games.	https://progameguides.com/fortnite/ fortnite-features/fortnite-battle-royale- outfits-skins-cosmetics-list
ProSettings.com	An independent website that lists the custom game settings for top-ranked *Fortnite: Battle Royale* players. This website also recommends optional gaming accessories, such as keyboards, mice, graphics cards, controllers, gaming headsets, and monitors.	www.prosettings.com/game/fortnite www.prosettings.com/ best-fortnite-settings
SCUF Gaming	This company makes high-end, extremely precise, customizable wireless controllers for the console-based gaming systems, including the SCUF Impact controller for the PS4. If you're looking to enhance your reaction times when playing *Fortnite: Battle Royale*, consider upgrading your wireless controller.	www.scufgaming.com
Turtle Beach Corp.	This is one of many companies that make great quality, wired or wireless (Bluetooth) gaming headsets that work with all gaming platforms.	www.turtlebeach.com

Your Fortnite: Battle Royale *Adventure Continues . . .*

If there's one thing you should have learned from this unofficial strategy guide about *Fortnite: Battle Royale*, it's that there's so much more to this gaming experience than just trying to achieve #1 Victory Royale while playing Solo mode. Even without your soldier becoming the last one alive at the end of a match, as a gamer, there are still many ways to enjoy everything this game offers.

Beyond just playing a Solo, Duos, or Squads match when playing Fortnite: Battle Royale, *as a gamer, you can focus on trying to complete the ever-changing selection of Battle Pass Challenges, Daily Challenges, and Weekly Challenges that are promoted on the left side of the Lobby screen, or when you select the Challenges or Events tab that's displayed at the top of the Lobby screen.*

If you need help accomplishing any Daily or Weekly challenges, be sure to take advantage of the game's Party Assist feature. Simply click on a listed Challenge and then click on the Party Assist button.

There's also an ever-changing selection of limited-time game play modes created by Epic Games that are available from the Game Play mode menu. Any of the 50v50 or Team Rumble matches, for example, offer an entirely different gaming experience than a Solo, Duos, or Squads match.

From the Lobby, you can also accept invitations from others, or send out your own invites prior to each match.

When playing a Duos or Squads match, use the No Fill option to handpick your partner or squad mates from your online friends. Choose the Fill option to allow the game to randomly select the other gamers you'll team up with.

Meanwhile, **Playground** mode allows you to explore the island and experiment with all the different weapons, loot items, and vehicles at your own pace—without having to deal with the deadly storm.

Since becoming a skilled gamer when it comes to playing *Fortnite: Battle Royale* involves practice—an awful lot of practice—Playground mode is just one way to fine-tune your skills and practice your strategies once you discover where your weaknesses lie after playing Solo, Duos, or Squads matches.

After choosing Duos or Squads mode and the No Fill option, to invite online friends to participate as your partner or squad mates, invite them from the Lobby by clicking on one of the three "+" icons near the center of the screen.

MY ISLAND

| GAME | GAME SETTINGS | ISLAND TOOLS | DESCRIPTION | PERMISSIONS |

SCORE PRESET	◄	FREE PLAY	►
TEAMS	◄	FREE FOR ALL	►
TIME LIMIT	◄	5 MINUTES	►
ELIMINATIONS TO WIN	◄	OFF	►
COLLECT ITEMS TO WIN	◄	OFF	►
SPAWNS	◄	INFINITE	►
LAST STANDING	◄	OFF	►
SPAWN LOCATION	◄	SPAWN PADS	►
POST-GAME SPAWN LOCATION	◄	ISLAND START	►

When the game completes your island will be restored to its pre-game state

Restore Defaults   **START GAME**

ESC Close

MY ISLAND

| GAME | GAME SETTINGS | ISLAND TOOLS | DESCRIPTION | PERMISSIONS |

TIME OF DAY	◄	DEFAULT	►
STARTING HEALTH	◄	FULL HEALTH	►
STARTING SHIELDS	◄	EMPTY SHIELDS	►
INFINITE AMMO	◄	OFF	►
INFINITE RESOURCES	◄	ON	►
PICK AXE BUILDING DAMAGE	◄	DEFAULT	►
DROP ITEMS WHEN ELIMINATED	◄	ON	►
FALL DAMAGE	◄	OFF	►
GRAVITY	◄	NORMAL	►

Restore Defaults   **APPLY**

ESC Close

The **Creative** mode allows you to design your own mysterious island from scratch, and then set the rules of engagement for a match that you alone, you and your online friends, or you and a selection of random gamers can experience.

The **Save the World** gaming experience allows you to follow a detailed storyline as a unique combat adventure unfolds on the island.

As if offering so many different game play modes weren't enough, what keeps *Fortnite: Battle Royale* continuously challenging, fresh, and fun are the new game updates released every week by Epic Games, and the major updates made to the game at the start of each new gaming season.

If you're a newb, don't expect to achieve success right away. Your soldier is going to perish often! Keep practicing and stay focused. Learn from your mistakes, take time to study the island itself, and watch what experienced gamers are doing to help ensure their own survival.

One of the best ways to do this is to stay in Spectator mode after being eliminated from a match, or to watch the live streams of top-ranked players on YouTube, Twitch.tv, or Facebook Watch. There are also several other full-color, unofficial guides in this *Fortnite: Battle Royale Master Combat* series by Jason R. Rich that'll help you master specific aspects of the game, so be sure to check them out as well. Visit **www.GameTipBooks.com** for details!

Have fun and good luck!

ZAGAT®

Seattle
Restaurants
2008

LOCAL EDITOR
Alicia Comstock Arter
STAFF EDITOR
Allison Lynn

Published and distributed by
Zagat Survey, LLC
4 Columbus Circle
New York, NY 10019
T: 212.977.6000
E: seattle@zagat.com
www.zagat.com

ACKNOWLEDGMENTS

We thank Gail Miller, Julia
Morris, Lei Ann Shiramizu and
Steven Shukow, as well as the
following members of our staff:
Kelly Stewart (assistant editor),
Sean Beachell, Maryanne
Bertollo, Amy Cao, Sandy Cheng,
Reni Chin, Larry Cohn, Alison
Flick, Jeff Freier, Roy Jacob,
Natalie Lebert, Mike Liao, Dave
Makulec, Chris Miragliotta,
Andre Pilette, Kimberly Rosado,
Becky Ruthenburg, Robert Seixas,
Sharon Yates and Kyle Zolner.

About This Survey

Here are the results of our **2008 Seattle Restaurants Survey**, covering 759 of the best eateries in the city of Seattle and its outlying areas. Like all of our guides, this one is based on the collective opinions of thousands of local consumers who have been there before you.

WHO PARTICIPATED: Input from 3,165 frequent diners forms the basis for the ratings and reviews in this guide (their comments are shown in quotation marks within the reviews). Of these surveyors, 45% are women, 55% men; the breakdown by age is 8% in their 20s; 26%, 30s; 24%, 40s; 23%, 50s; and 19%, 60s or above. Collectively they bring roughly 500,000 annual meals worth of experience to this Survey. We sincerely thank each of these participants – this book is really "theirs."

HELPFUL LISTS: Whether you're looking for a celebratory meal, a hot scene or a bargain bite, our lists can help you find exactly the right place. See Most Popular (page 7), Key Newcomers (page 7), Top Ratings (pages 9–14) and Best Buys (page 15). We've also provided 41 handy indexes.

OUR EDITORS: Special thanks go to our local editor, Alicia Comstock Arter, who covers the Seattle-area dining scene as a contributing editor for *Northwest Palate* magazine and serves as the national grassroots chair for the International Association of Culinary Professionals.

ABOUT ZAGAT: This marks our 29th year reporting on the shared experiences of consumers like you. What started in 1979 as a hobby involving 200 of our friends has come a long way. Today we have well over 300,000 surveyors and now cover dining, entertaining, golf, hotels, movies, music, nightlife, resorts, shopping, spas, theater and tourist attractions worldwide.

SHARE YOUR OPINION: We invite you to join any of our upcoming surveys – just register at **zagat.com,** where you can rate and review establishments year-round. Each participant will receive a free copy of the resulting guide when published.

AVAILABILITY: Zagat guides are available in all major bookstores, by subscription at **zagat.com** and for use on Web-enabled mobile devices via **Zagat To Go** or **zagat.mobi.** The latter two products should allow you to contact any restaurant by phone with one click.

FEEDBACK: There is always room for improvement, thus we invite your comments and suggestions about any aspect of our performance. Is there something more you would like us to include in our guides? We really need your input! Just contact us at **seattle@zagat.com.**

New York, NY
December 5, 2007

Nina and Tim Zagat

Contents

About This Survey	4	Views	168
What's New	5	Visitors on Expense Acct.	169
Most Popular	7	Waterside	169
Key Newcomers	7	Winning Wine Lists	170
Ratings & Symbols	8	Worth a Trip	171
Top Ratings:		**Wine Chart**	172
Food	9		
Decor	13		
Service	14		
Best Buys	15		

RESTAURANT
DIRECTORY

Names, Locations, Contact
Info, Ratings & Reviews   17

INDEXES

Cuisines   126
Locations   137
Special Features:
Breakfast   147
Brunch   147
Buffet   148
Business Dining   148
Catering   148
Celebrity Chefs   150
Child-Friendly   150
Dancing   151
Delivery/Takeout   151
Dessert   154
Dining Alone   154
Dramatic Interiors   154
Entertainment   155
Fireplaces   156
Game in Season   156
Historic Places   157
Hotel Dining   158
Late Dining   158
Meet for a Drink   159
Natural/Organic   160
Noteworthy Newcomers   161
Offbeat   161
Outdoor Dining   161
Parking   163
People-Watching   164
Power Scenes   165
Private Rooms   165
Quiet Conversation   165
Raw Bars   166
Romantic Places   166
Senior Appeal   167
Singles Scenes   167
Theme Restaurants   168
Trendy   168

Most Popular

Each surveyor has been asked to name his or her five favorite places. This list reflects their choices.

①	Wild Ginger	㉑	Cafe Campagne
②	Dahlia Lounge	㉒	Harvest Vine
③	Metropolitan Grill	㉓	Nishino
④	Canlis	㉔	Volterra
⑤	Restaurant Zoë	㉕	Lark
⑥	Flying Fish	㉖	Mistral
⑦	El Gaucho	㉗	Brooklyn Sea/Steak
⑧	Rover's	㉘	Lola
⑨	Daniel's Broiler	㉙	Cascadia
⑩	Seastar	㉚	McCormick & Schmick's
⑪	Etta's Seafood	㉛	Crush
⑫	Cafe Juanita	㉜	Cheesecake Factory
⑬	Herbfarm, The	㉝	Salty's*
⑭	Anthony's HomePort	㉞	Le Pichet
⑮	JaK's Grill	㉟	Palisade*
⑯	Ray's Boathouse	㊱	Elliott's Oyster Hse.
⑰	Palace Kitchen	㊲	Union
⑱	Oceanaire	㊳	Brasa
⑲	Campagne	㊴	Georgian, The
⑳	Purple Cafe	㊵	Il Terrazzo Carmine*

It's obvious that many of the above restaurants are among the Seattle area's most expensive, but if popularity were calibrated to price, we suspect that a number of other restaurants would join their ranks. Given the fact that both our surveyors and readers love to discover dining bargains, we have added a list of 80 Best Buys on page 15. These are restaurants that give real quality at extremely reasonable prices.

KEY NEWCOMERS

Our editors' take on the most notable new arrivals of the past year. For a full list, see the Noteworthy Newcomers index on page 161.

Austin Cantina	Opal
Bakery Nouveau	Porcella Urban Market
Beàto Food & Wine	Portage
Betty	Qube
Café Presse	Serious Pie
Coupage	Steelhead Diner
Entre Nous	TASTE
Made in Kitchen	Tavolàta
O/8 Seafood	Tilth

* Indicates a tie with restaurant above

Ratings & Symbols

Zagat Top Spot	Name	Symbols	Cuisine	Zagat Ratings			
				FOOD	DECOR	SERVICE	COST

Area, Address & Contact

Ⓩ **Tim & Nina's** ◖ *Pacific NW* | ▽ 23 | 9 | 13 | $150

Pike Place Market | 999 Pike Pl. (1st Ave.) | 206-555-6000 | www.zagat.com

Review, surveyor comments in quotes

Surveyors of "hearty soul and iron gut" "keep the anoraks on" to dodge the drips and drafts at this "leaky-roofed" fisherman's shack known for its "combustible" confusion of Southern Italian and Northwest cuisines (think hamachi antipasti) based on Captain T's catch of the day; prices are "pay-what-you-weigh" – even though you have to serve yourself.

Ratings

Food, Decor and **Service** are rated on the Zagat 0 to 30 scale.

0	–	9	poor to fair
10	–	15	fair to good
16	–	19	good to very good
20	–	25	very good to excellent
26	–	30	extraordinary to perfection
	▽		low response	less reliable

Cost reflects our surveyors' average estimate of the price of a dinner with one drink and tip and is a benchmark only. Lunch is usually 25% less.

For **newcomers** or survey **write-ins** listed without ratings, the price range is indicated as follows:

I	$25 and below
M	$26 to $40
E	$41 to $65
VE	$66 or more

Symbols

Ⓩ	Zagat Top Spot (highest ratings, popularity and importance)
◖	serves after 11 PM
Ⓢ	closed on Sunday
Ⓜ	closed on Monday
⌿	no credit cards accepted

Top Food Ratings

All ratings are to the left of names, which are listed in order of descending scores and exclude places with low votes, unless indicated by a ▽.

29 | Herbfarm, The

28 | Bakery Nouveau
Mistral
Rover's
Cafe Juanita
Sitka & Spruce
Armandino's Salumi

27 | Paseo
Kisaku Sushi
Inn at Langley
Nishino
Szechuan Chef*
Canlis
Cafe Besalu
Phoenecia/Alki
Maneki
Restaurant Zoë
Belle Pastry
Lark
Le Gourmand

Monsoon
Shiro's Sushi
Il Terrazzo Carmine

26 | Eva
Carmelita
La Carta de Oaxaca
Crush
Campagne
Chiso
Lynn's Bistro
Maltby Cafe
Elemental@Gasworks
Georgian, The
Saito's Japanese
Harvest Vine
Chez Shea
Thai Tom
Tropea
Seastar
JaK's Grill

BY CUISINE

AMERICAN (NEW)

28 | Mistral
27 | Restaurant Zoë
Lark
26 | Eva
Crush

AMERICAN (TRAD.)

26 | Maltby Cafe
Glo's
23 | Dish, The
Hi Spot Cafe
22 | Hilltop Ale House

BBQ/SOUL/SOUTHERN

25 | Pecos Pit BBQ
24 | Ezell's
23 | Kingfish
22 | Jones BBQ
Dixie's BBQ

CHINESE

27 | Szechuan Chef
24 | Kau Kau BBQ
23 | Jade Garden
22 | Shanghai Garden
21 | House of Hong

DELIS/SANDWICHES

28 | Armandino's Salumi
25 | Other Coast Cafe
24 | Three Girls Bakery
23 | Buffalo Deli
Baguette Box

DESSERTS

28 | Bakery Nouveau
27 | Cafe Besalu
Belle Pastry
25 | Macrina
24 | Gelatiamo

ECLECTIC

28 | Sitka & Spruce
26 | Elemental@Gasworks
24 | Yarrow Bay Grill
23 | Circa
22 | Black Bottle

FRENCH

28 | Mistral
Rover's
27 | Le Gourmand
26 | Campagne
Lynn's Bistro

GREEK

- 24 Lola
- Vios Cafe
- 23 Panos Kleftiko
- Santorini Greek
- 22 Yanni's

ITALIAN

- 28 Cafe Juanita
- Armandino's Salumi
- 27 Il Terrazzo Carmine
- 26 Tropea
- 25 La Rustica

JAPANESE

- 27 Kisaku Sushi
- Nishino
- Shiro's Sushi
- Maneki
- 26 Chiso

MEDITERRANEAN

- 27 Phoenecia/Alki
- 26 Carmelita
- 25 La Medusa
- Brasa
- Primo Grill

MEXICAN

- 26 La Carta de Oaxaca
- 24 Ooba's Mexican Grill
- Señor Moose Café
- 23 Peso's Kitchen
- 22 Agua Verde

PACIFIC NORTHWEST

- 29 Herbfarm, The
- 27 Inn at Langley
- Canlis
- 26 Georgian, The
- Chez Shea

PAC. RIM/PAN-ASIAN

- 25 Wild Ginger
- 23 Coupage
- Lee's Asian
- 22 Shallots
- 20 Madoka

PIZZA

- 25 Serious Pie
- 23 Via Tribunali
- Tutta Bella
- 22 Pagliacci Pizza
- La Vita É Bella

SEAFOOD

- 26 Seastar
- 25 Flying Fish
- Shuckers
- 24 Waterfront Seafood
- Ray's Boathouse

STEAKHOUSES

- 26 JaK's Grill
- Metropolitan Grill
- 25 El Gaucho
- Daniel's Broiler
- 24 Morton's

THAI

- 26 Thai Tom
- 23 Thai Siam
- 22 Bai Pai Fine Thai
- Thai Ginger
- Typhoon!

VIETNAMESE

- 27 Monsoon
- 25 Green Leaf
- 24 Tamarind Tree
- 22 Pho Thân Bros.
- 20 Pho Cyclo Café

BY SPECIAL FEATURE

BREAKFAST

- 26 Georgian, The
- Glo's
- 25 Macrina
- 24 6·7
- 23 Dish, The

BRUNCH

- 28 Sitka & Spruce
- 27 Monsoon
- 26 Lynn's Bistro
- 25 Cafe Campagne
- Volterra

HOTEL DINING

- 27 Inn at Langley
- 26 Georgian, The
  (Fairmont Olympic)
- 25 Shuckers
  (Fairmont Olympic)
- 24 Barking Frog
  (Willows Lodge)
- Lola
  (Hotel Andra)

10

LATE DINING

26 Elemental@Gasworks
25 El Gaucho
   Flying Fish
   Volterra
   La Isla

MEET FOR A DRINK

26 Campagne
   Metropolitan Grill
25 El Gaucho
   Brasa
   Volterra

NEWCOMERS (RATED)

28 Bakery Nouveau
26 Portage
25 Serious Pie
   Tilth
24 Porcella Urban Market

OFFBEAT

25 Mashiko
22 Dixie's BBQ
   Pink Door
   Agua Verde
21 Madame K's Pizza

PEOPLE-WATCHING

27 Restaurant Zoë
26 Crush
   Seastar
25 Flying Fish
   Volterra

POWER SCENES

28 Rover's
27 Canlis
26 Crush
   Georgian, The
   Seastar

RAW BARS

26 Seastar
25 Izumi
   Shuckers
24 Waterfront Seafood
23 Elliott's Oyster Hse.

SINGLES SCENES

27 Restaurant Zoë
26 Metropolitan Grill
25 Wild Ginger
   Daniel's Broiler
24 Lola

TRENDY

28 Bakery Nouveau
   Sitka & Spruce
   Armandino's Salumi
27 Cafe Besalu
   Restaurant Zoë

WINNING WINE LISTS

29 Herbfarm, The
28 Mistral
   Rover's
   Cafe Juanita
27 Canlis

WORTH A TRIP

29 Herbfarm, The
   Woodinville
27 Inn at Langley
   Langley
26 Christina's∇
   Eastsound
25 Four Swallows
   Bainbridge Island
24 Salish Lodge
   Snoqualmie

BY LOCATION

BALLARD/SHILSHOLE

27 Cafe Besalu
   Le Gourmand
26 La Carta de Oaxaca
25 Volterra
   Other Coast Cafe

BELLEVUE

27 Szechuan Chef
   Belle Pastry
26 Seastar
   Tosoni's
25 Daniel's Broiler

BELLTOWN

28 Mistral
27 Restaurant Zoë
   Shiro's Sushi
26 Saito's Japanese
25 El Gaucho

CAPITOL HILL

27 Lark
   Monsoon
26 Glo's
24 Osteria La Spiga
   Ezell's

DOWNTOWN

26 Georgian, The
   Metropolitan Grill
   Union
25 Wild Ginger
   Dahlia Lounge

EASTLAKE/
LAKE UNION

28 Sitka & Spruce
27 Canlis
26 Elemental@Gasworks
25 Daniel's Broiler
24 Serafina

FREMONT/
WALLINGFORD

27 Paseo
26 Chiso
25 Kabul Afghan
   Tilth
   Asteroid Ristorante

GREEN LAKE/
GREENWOOD/
PHINNEY RIDGE

27 Kisaku Sushi
26 Eva
   Carmelita
25 Nell's
24 Stumbling Goat Bistro

KIRKLAND

28 Cafe Juanita
26 Lynn's Bistro
25 Izumi
24 Yarrow Bay Grill
   Mixtura

MADISON PARK/
MADISON VALLEY

28 Rover's
27 Nishino
26 Crush
   Harvest Vine
23 Essential Baking Co.

PIKE PLACE MARKET

26 Campagne
   Chez Shea
25 Cafe Campagne
24 Le Pichet
   Beecher's Cheese

PIONEER SQUARE/
SODO

28 Armandino's Salumi
27 Il Terrazzo Carmine
25 Pecos Pit BBQ
22 Jones BBQ
   Zaina Food

QUEEN ANNE/
SEATTLE CENTER

26 Portage
25 Macrina
   Boat Street Cafe
24 Shiki
   Ototo Sushi

WEST SEATTLE

28 Bakery Nouveau
27 Phoenecia/Alki
26 JaK's Grill
25 La Rustica
   Mashiko

Top Decor Ratings

28	Georgian, The
27	Canlis
	Indochine Asian
26	SkyCity at Needle
	Palisade
	Salish Lodge
	6 · 7
	Herbfarm, The
	Bai Pai Fine Thai
25	Waterfront Seafood
	Cascadia
	Boka Kitchen & Bar
	Barolo Ristorante
	Il Terrazzo Carmine*
24	Geneva
	Osteria La Spiga
	Brasa
	Umi Sake House
	Rover's
	Marrakesh Moroccan

Seastar
Ray's Boathouse
Hunt Club
Calcutta Grill
Yarrow Bay Grill
El Gaucho
Dahlia Lounge
Campagne

23	Daniel's Broiler
	icon Grill*
	Carnegie's
	Mission*
	Third Floor Fish*
	O'Asian
	Inn at Langley
	Wild Ginger
	Il Bistro
	Capitol Club
	Ponti Seafood Grill
	Purple Cafe

OUTDOORS

Anthony's HomePort
Barking Frog
Belltown Bistro
Copacabana Cafe
Maggie Bluff's

Marjorie
Pink Door
Purple Cafe/Kirkland
Ray's Cafe
Yarrow Bay Grill

ROMANCE

Cafe Campagne
Cafe Juanita
Chez Shea
Lark
La Rustica

Le Gourmand
Mistral
Pink Door
Place Pigalle
Rover's

ROOMS

Andaluca
Barking Frog
Brouwers
Café Presse
Maximilien

Oceanaire
Qube
Trader Vic's
Union
Yama at the Galleria

VIEWS

Canlis
Chandler's Crabhouse
Daniel's Broiler/Lake Union
Ivar's Salmon House
Palisade

Ray's Boathouse
Salty's
6 · 7
SkyCity at Needle
Waterfont Seafood

Top Service Ratings

28 Herbfarm, The

27 Canlis
Rover's

26 Georgian, The
Cafe Juanita
Mistral
Phoenecia/Alki
Le Gourmand
El Gaucho
Il Terrazzo Carmine

25 Lark
Salish Lodge
Metropolitan Grill
Campagne
Chez Shea
Bis on Main
Geneva
Restaurant Zoë
La Fontana Siciliana
Tropea

24 Seastar
St. Clouds
6 · 7
Rist. Italianissimo*
Daniel's Broiler
Asteroid Ristorante
Barking Frog
Tosoni's
Nishino
Waterfront Seafood
Shuckers
Eva
Cascadia
Morton's
La Medusa
Lynn's Bistro*
Flo

23 Dahlia Lounge
Dish, The
Market St. Grill

Best Buys

In order of Bang for the Buck rating.

1. Uptown Espresso
2. Cafe Besalu
3. Crumpet Shop
4. Bakery Nouveau
5. Gelatiamo
6. Dick's Drive-In
7. Belle Pastry
8. Pho Thân Bros.
9. Pecos Pit BBQ
10. Piroshky Piroshky
11. Other Coast Cafe
12. Noah's Bagels
13. Le Panier
14. Bakeman's
15. Matt's Gourmet Hot Dogs
16. Three Girls Bakery
17. Beecher's Cheese
18. Ooba's Mexican Grill
19. Buffalo Deli
20. Dish, The
21. Kidd Valley
22. Red Mill Burgers
23. Bagel Oasis
24. Malena's Taco Shop
25. Thai Tom
26. Pho Cyclo Café
27. Shultzy's
28. Essential Baking Co.
29. Gordito's Healthy Mex.
30. Paseo
31. Ezell's
32. Baguette Box
33. Original Pancake
34. Macrina
35. Glo's
36. Dilettante Chocolates
37. Louisa's Cafe
38. Armandino's Salumi
39. Alki Bakery Café
40. Sunfish

OTHER GOOD VALUES

Assimba Ethiopian
Austin Cantina
Burrito Loco
Cafe Campagne
Café Darclee
Cellar Bistro
Crash Landing Pizza
Crepe de France
Diggity Dog's
El Gallito
Entre Nous
FareStart
FareStart/2100
Fuji Sushi
Fu Man Dumpling
Jack's Fish Spot
Judy Fu's
Kaosami
Kau Kau
Kusina Filipina
La Cocina del Puerca
Lemon Grass
Made in Kitchen
Mae Phim Thai
Mee Sum Pastries
Mike's Noodle House
Noodle Ranch
Pan Africa
Philadelphia Fevre
Phnom Penh
Pho Bac
Remedy Teas
Rhodie's Smokin' BBQ
Tacos Guaymas
Than Vi
Turkish Delight
Udupi Palace
Vegetarian Bistro
Volunteer Park Café
World Class Chili

RESTAURANT
DIRECTORY

| | FOOD | DECOR | SERVICE | COST |

Abbondanza Pizzeria 🛇 Ⓜ *Pizza* ▽ 18 | 9 | 15 | $22

West Seattle | 6503 California Ave. SW (Fauntleroy Way) | 206-935-8989

"Pizza is the way to go" at this "fun", no-frills "Italian joint" where "it's great to take the kids"; the West Seattle parlor gets "crowded" and service "can be uneven" and "unfriendly", so pickier diners opt for takeout and "and eat it somewhere else."

Acorn Eatery & Bar *Italian* ▽ 17 | 14 | 15 | $25

Crown Hill | 9041 Holman Rd. NW (Mary Ave.) | 206-297-0700 | www.acorneatery.com

In nearly cuisine-free Crown Hill, locals "hang" at this "pleasant" "neighborhood" Italian for "good" pastas, *secondis* and a thin-crust pizza that's the cafe's "best-kept secret"; some snipe that the ambiance is "dull" and not worth a trip, though families with kids appreciate the extras – crayons, puzzles and a kids' menu.

Agua Verde Cafe & Paddle Club *Mexican* 22 | 16 | 15 | $16

University District | 1303 NE Boat St. (Brooklyn Ave.) | 206-545-8570 | www.aguaverde.com

UW students and hungry boaters brave "ridiculous" lines for "great local interpretations" of Baja-style Mexican, including "homemade salsas" and margaritas "like icy nectar", at this "extremely popular" and affordable University District taco "shack" on Portage Bay; kayak rentals below deck and "beautiful views" on top make up for the "humble", "uninspiring" interior and a staff that's "kind of harried, since there's always a rush on."

Al Boccalino 🛇 *Italian* 22 | 18 | 20 | $35

Pioneer Square | 1 Yesler Way (Alaskan Way) | 206-622-7688

At this star in Luigi DeNunzio's Italian mini-empire, "top-notch" fare is made with fresh, local ingredients; the "romantic" old brick dining room "in the heart of Pioneer Square" is "unpretentious", as if straight out of "a small town in Italy", though business types, tourists and sports fans on their way to the nearby stadiums can make for a "noisy" evening.

Alborz *Persian* ▽ 23 | 18 | 22 | $26

Redmond | 8461 164th Ave. NE (85th St.) | 425-883-1080 | www.alborzrestaurant.net

One of the "best Persian restaurants" in the area, this "beautifully decorated" Redmonder proffers "mouthwatering skewers" and other "distinctive" dishes made with "quality" ingredients like halal chicken and lamb; though the prices are "slightly high", service is "helpful" and the room features "quiet" nooks that are perfect for a "small business lunch."

Alibi Room *Pacific NW* 19 | 21 | 17 | $29

Pike Place Market | Pike Place Mkt. | 85 Pike St. (1st Ave.) | 206-623-3180 | www.seattlealibi.com

Diners who can find this "cinematic hole-in-the-wall" "down a very old alley" in Pike Place Market will "discover" a "cool and hip" nook that's "great" for a "date" or a "secret rendezvous"; local art and stacks of film scripts round out the decor, and while they serve "good daily specials" and a "reasonably priced" Pacific NW menu to the local indie film crowd, some say it's "more of a place for drinks than dinner."

Alki Bakery Café *Bakery*   21 | 13 | 17 | $14
Georgetown | 5700 First Ave. S. (Orcas St.) | 206-762-5700 🗷
West Seattle | 2738 Alki Ave. SW (61st Ave.) | 206-935-1352
www.alkibakery.com
Sugar and carb lovers swoon over the "homemade pastries" and "bakery bread" sandwiches at this American twinset that's also praised for its "good coffee", soups and salads; service "can be spotty", but the West Seattle site compensates with a "lovely view" of Elliott Bay and the Olympic Mountains, while the Georgetown outpost shines as a "lunch getaway" in an industrial area.

Alki Homestead *American*   20 | 22 | 22 | $30
West Seattle | 2717 61st Ave. SW (Alki Ave.) | 206-935-5678
Set across from the Alki Beach party scene, this "historic" 1902 "log house" (formerly The Fir Lodge) in West Seattle draws nostalgists with its "old-fashioned", "grandmotherly" charm – "think doilies, lace" and a stone fireplace; the kitchen turns out "good", "homestyle" American standards like fried chicken and meatloaf, complemented by "stiff drinks" and a bill that "won't break the bank."

All-Purpose Pizza & Ale *Pizza*   16 | 14 | 15 | $17
Capitol Hill | 2901 S. Jackson St. (29th Ave.) | 206-324-8646 |
www.allpurposepizza.com
This "family-friendly" pizzeria specializing in "sourdough-crust" pies is a "convenient" addition to an "under-restaurant-served" slice of Capitol Hill, plus there's a "kids' kitchen" where munchkins can "play with dough" and give "moms and dads a break"; another appeal for locals: "they deliver!"

Andaluca *Mediterranean*   24 | 23 | 23 | $43
Downtown | Mayflower Park Hotel | 407 Olive Way (4th Ave.) |
206-382-6999 | www.andaluca.com
"Extremely talented" chef Wayne Johnson's "innovative" Mediterranean cuisine is the draw at this "totally cool" Downtowner, where a "welcoming", "attentive" staff delivers tapas, steak and more; tucked into the "elegant" Mayflower Hotel, it's "quiet" and "intimate", with "comfy booths to hide in" – "perfect for discussing romance over Rioja."

Andre's Eurasian Bistro 🗷 *French/Vietnamese*   19 | 15 | 17 | $28
Bellevue | 14125 NE 20th St. (140th Ave.) | 425-747-6551 |
www.andresbistro.com
"Vietnam meets France" in the "fresh", "sophisticated" fare on offer at this "friendly", "reasonably priced" Bellevue bistro; despite the "simple" atmosphere and strip-mall setting, it's "popular with the Microsoft crowd" and "particularly dependable" for lunch.

	FOOD	DECOR	SERVICE	COST

☑ Anthony's HomePort   *Pacific NW/Seafood*   20 | 21 | 20 | $35

Shilshole | 6135 Seaview Ave. NW (near Shilshole Marina) |
206-783-0780

Kirkland | Moss Bay Marina | 135 Lake St. S. (Kirkland Ave.) |
425-822-0225

Des Moines | Des Moines Marina | 421 S. 227th St. (Marine View Dr.) |
206-824-1947

Edmonds | Edmonds Marina | 456 Admiral Way (Dayton St.) |
425-771-4400

Everett | Everett Marina Vlg. | 1726 W. Marine View Dr. (18th St.) |
425-252-3333

Tacoma | 5910 N. Waterfront Dr. (bet. Pearl St. & Vashon Ferry Dock) |
253-752-9700

Gig Harbor | 8827 N. Harborview Dr. (Stinson Dr.) |
253-853-6353

Bellingham | Squalicum Harbor Marina | 25 Bellwether Way (Roeder Ave.) |
360-647-5588

Olympia | Marina | 704 Columbia St. NW (Market St.) |
360-357-9700
www.anthonysrestaurants.com

"To-die-for" waterfront views are the trademark of this "friendly"
31-year-old chain whose "Northwest" woodsy decor and "solid" if
"not spectacular" NW seafood reel in "locals" and "out-of-towners"
alike; sure, they can be "noisy" and a few critics carp about "inconsistent" quality, but the "happy-hour bar menu" and lower-priced
"sunset dinners" are an "awesome" deal.

Anthony's Pier 66   *Pacific NW/Seafood*   21 | 21 | 20 | $39

Seattle Waterfront | Pier 66 | 2201 Alaskan Way (Wall St.) |
206-448-6688 | www.anthonysrestaurants.com

A "cut above" the others in the Anthony's food chain, this "higher-end"
Waterfronter also trades in "surprisingly good" NW fish and "killer
views" of Elliott Bay and "the ferries"; an "attentive" staff, "good wine
list" and "fabulous deck" make it work for more than just "tourists."

Aoki Japanese   19 | 17 | 18 | $24
Grill & Sushi Bar   *Japanese*

Capitol Hill | 621 Broadway E. (Roy St.) | 206-324-3633

Just the ticket for film aficionados catching a flick at the Harvard Exit
Theater, this no-frills Capitol Hill Japanese serves "standard" sushi
and sukiyaki at "reasonable prices"; service can be "slow when
busy", but on the upside, it's chef-run with "no sign of pretension."

☑ Armandino's   28 | 11 | 20 | $16
Salumi ☒ Ⓜ   *Italian/Sandwiches*

Pioneer Square | 309 Third Ave. S. (bet. Jackson & Main Sts.) |
206-621-8772 | www.salumicuredmeats.com

"Unforgettable" "handmade" Italian sandwiches and salamis draw
crowds and kudos to this Pioneer Square "hawg heaven" where
Armandino Batali (Mario's dad) cranks out "amazing" "homemade"
cured meats in the back; the "shoebox"-size cafe is "cramped", the
mood "fun" and the lines "out the door" as both regular folk and "every food luminary in the world" make the pilgrimage.

	FOOD	DECOR	SERVICE	COST

Assaggio Ristorante ⑤ *Italian* | 23 | 20 | 22 | $39

Downtown | 2010 Fourth Ave. (Virginia St.) | 206-441-1399 |
www.assaggioseattle.com

"Even strangers get a bear hug" from "irrepressible" owner Mauro
Golmarvi at his "bustling" Downtown trattoria that fans call "one of
the best places for pasta" and Italian wines; factor in "attentive" service, a "classy, casual" frescoed interior and a patio that "faces west,
for maximum sun", and few mind if the "tables are too close together."

Assimba Ethiopian Cuisine ⑤ *Ethiopian* ▽ 22 | 10 | 18 | $14

Capitol Hill | 2722 E. Cherry St. (MLK Jr. Way) | 206-322-1019

The few who have "discovered" this Capitol Hill sleeper say it serves
"solid", "comforting" Ethiopian fare in "generous" portions (the
sampler platter is a "best bet") alongside "tangy" injera; the decor
may be "basic" (travel posters, a portrait of Haile Selassie), but so
are the prices, with "friendly" service as a bonus.

Asteroid Ristorante | 25 | 21 | 24 | $36
e Bar Italiani ⑤ *Italian*

Fremont | 3601 Fremont Ave. N. (36th St.) | 206-547-9000 |
www.asteroidcafe.com

"Stellar" food showcasing "fresh ingredients" in "simple
preparations" – i.e. "what traditional Italian cuisine is all about" –
sends fans of this Fremont *cucina* over the moon; the modish room
is more "spacious" than the "funkier" original Wallingford digs, but
the staff remains "engaging" and prices aren't too steep, prompting
regulars to wish they "could keep this a secret."

Athenian Inn *American/Seafood* | 16 | 14 | 16 | $18

Pike Place Market | Pike Place Mkt. | 1517 Pike Pl. (Pine St.) | 206-624-7166

Tourists and locals alike flock to this "quintessential" "greasy
spoon" (made famous in *Sleepless in Seattle*) that "hasn't changed
since the early 20th century", drawing Pike Place Market shoppers
and "waterfront characters" with its American breakfasts, "fish every which way" and "multitude of beer choices"; the decor may be
"lacking", but there are "unbeatable" views of Elliott Bay from the
"many window tables"; no dinner.

Atlas Foods *American/Eclectic* | 16 | 16 | 17 | $25

University Village | University Vill. | 2820 NE University Vill.
(bet. 26th & 28th Aves.) | 206-522-6025 | www.chowfoods.com

"A decent option" if "you must be in the mall", this "noisy", "family-
friendly" American-Eclectic offers an "extensive" menu that
changes regional theme quarterly and "caters to University Village
shoppers" in search of "well-prepared food at a fair price"; some say
"brunch is the best" bet, ergo it "can be stroller hell on Sundays."

NEW Austin Cantina Ⓜ *Tex-Mex* | - | - | - | I

Ballard | 5809 24th Ave. NW (bet. 58th & 59th Sts.) | 206-789-1277 |
www.austincantina.org

Get your enchilada on at this near-tony yet affordable Tex-Mex
newcomer in Ballard where formally trained chef-owner Jefe Birkner

minds the beer-braised pot roast, hot empanadas and banana fritters; soft buttery yellow walls, aged wood tables and Lone Star music set a laid-back Austin-esque vibe.

Ayutthaya *Thai*   ▽ 22 | 12 | 20 | $15
Capitol Hill | 727 E. Pike St. (Howard St.) | 206-324-8833
This Capitol Hill Thai is considered a "great neighborhood" place thanks to its "quick, cheap", "consistently good" offerings; maybe it's "a trifle cramped" and the "decor could use some work", but fans don't seem to mind.

Azteca *Mexican*   14 | 15 | 16 | $18
Eastlake | 1823 Eastlake Ave. E. (bet. Blaine St. & Yale Pl.) | 206-324-4941
Northgate | Northgate Mall | 401 NE Northgate Way (5th Ave.) | 206-362-0066
Bellevue | 150 112th Ave. NE (bet. Main & 2nd Sts.) | 425-453-9087
Kirkland | 11431 NE 124th St. (116th Ave.) | 425-820-7997
Kent | 25633 102nd Pl. SE (bet. 104 & Smith Sts.) | 253-852-0210
Federal Way | 31740 23rd Ave. S. (320th St.) | 253-839-6693
Tacoma | 4801 Tacoma Mall Blvd. (SW 48th St.) | 253-472-0246
Mill Creek | 15704 Mill Creek Blvd. (Bothell-Everett Hwy.) | 425-385-2209
Tukwila | 17555 Southcenter Pkwy. (south of Minkler Blvd.) | 206-575-0990
www.aztecamex.com
"Basic" but "reliable" typifies reaction to this chain of "Ameri-Mexican" hangouts where the "huge portions" are frequently topped with "gooey cheese" and the "margaritas on the rocks rock"; the atmosphere is "colorful", service "cheerful" and "the price is right", yet detractors still yawn "average."

Azul Restaurant ● *Pan-Latin*   ▽ 23 | 22 | 22 | $25
Mill Creek | 15118 Main St. (bet. 151st & 153rd Sts.) | 425-357-5600 | www.azullounge.com
For a "special dinner" in Mill Creek, this "upscale" Pan-Latin hot spot satisfies with a "spicy" menu that offers "something for almost everyone"; its "cool" blue room is especially energetic during the "happening happy hour", when the vibe can get "a bit loud for conversation."

Bad Albert's Tap & Grill *Pub Food*   16 | 10 | 18 | $17
Ballard | 5100 Ballard Ave. NW (Dock Pl.) | 206-782-9623 | www.badalberts.com
On "hip" Ballard Avenue, this "gritty neighborhood pub" stands firm with cheap bar food, burgers, an "amazing weekend breakfast" and "none of the irritating waiting-to-be-seated-and-seen crowd"; live music on Thursday nights and Sunday afternoons helps distract from the "'80s decor", including "neon beer lights"; N.B. 21-and-over only.

Bagel Oasis *Deli*   21 | 7 | 11 | $9
Ravenna | 2112 NE 65th St. (bet. Ravenna & 21st Aves.) | 206-526-0525
"The aroma alone is enough to make you swoon" at this Ravenna "oasis of authenticity" that purveys the "best bagels in Seattle"; at lunchtime they make "a good sandwich", although snippier sorts say "life's too short" to put up with the "disorganized" service that causes "unacceptable" waits.

	FOOD	DECOR	SERVICE	COST

Baguette Box *Sandwiches*

23 | 11 | 15 | $12

Capitol Hill | 1203 Pine St. (Minor Ave.) | 206-332-0220
NEW **Fremont** | 626 N. 34th St. (bet. Evanston & Fremont Aves.) |
206-632-1511
www.baguettebox.com

"Messy but worth the extra napkins" is the verdict on the "mouth-watering sandwiches" found at this duo from Monsoon's Eric Bahn; the "famous" "drunken chicken" on a baguette (natch) and the "must-try" truffle french fries win the loudest raves from diners at both its quaint Capitol Hill outpost and the spare Fremonter, though surveyors sigh that service "can be maddeningly slow."

Bahn Thai *Thai*

20 | 17 | 19 | $24

Queen Anne | 409 Roy St. (5th Ave. N.) | 206-283-0444 |
www.bahnthaimenu.com

A "good" pre-theater option on Queen Anne (a block from the Seattle Center), the staff at this "long-established", "welcoming" Thai moves diners "in and out pretty quickly"; the "wide variety" of "great flavors" keeps the crowds coming, so reservations are suggested.

☒ Bai Pai Fine Thai *Thai*

22 | 26 | 20 | $22

Roosevelt | 2316 NE 65th St. (23rd Ave.) | 206-527-4800 |
www.baipairestaurant.com

"Calming", "elegant" decor elevates this "slightly pricey" Roosevelt Thai "a welcome step up" from the rest of the pack; the cuisine is "creative", though a few detractors wish "they'd spend more attention on the food than the decor."

Bakeman's ☒✒ *Deli*

22 | 6 | 14 | $9

Downtown | 122 Cherry St. (2nd Ave.) | 206-622-3375

Downtowners flock to this "downright-cheap" luncheonette for deli classics like "excellent" soups and "very fresh" turkey sandwiches – "add a little cranberry sauce and a slice of pie, and you're halfway to heaven"; intentionally "hostile" service is "part of the game", causing some to call this the West Coast's answer to the soup nazi.

☒ NEW Bakery Nouveau *Bakery/French*

28 | 15 | 20 | $10

West Seattle | 4737 California Ave. SW (Alaska St.) | 206-923-0534 |
www.bakerynouveau.com

It's "Paris in West Seattle" at this "working bakery" serving "scrumptious" French pastries that are "well worth the calories"; chef-owner William Leaman is a "rock star" who "beat the French at their own game" (he led the U.S.'s winning team at the 2005 World Cup of Baking), and rush times can be "chaotic", so some forgo the few indoor tables and head out to the sidewalk seats.

NEW Bambino's
East Coast Pizzeria *Pizza*

▽ 19 | 15 | 19 | $17

Belltown | 401 Cedar St. (4th Ave.) | 206-269-2222 |
www.getbambinos.com

"Satisfy your NY-style pizza cravings" at this Belltowner where eco-friendly East Coast exiles bake "wonderfully thin-crust" pies in their

| | FOOD | DECOR | SERVICE | COST |

"centerpiece [wood-fired] brick oven"; dieters dote on "salads that are a meal in themselves", and though the in-house service is "minimalist", "they deliver"; N.B. no liquor license.

Bamboo Garden Szechuan Restaurant Chinese
- | - | - | I

Bellevue | 202 106th Pl. NE (2nd St.) | 425-688-7991
In a Bellevue strip mall infamous for its adult toy store, this modern, affordable Szechuan dishes up spicy fare (hot pots, whole fish and even offal) to satisfy heat-seekers, and offers milder selections (hand shaven noodles, tofu) for everyone else; the interior is colorful, and as for outside, just look for the red awning and you'll know you're in the right place.

Bamboo Garden Vegetarian Cuisine Chinese
18 | 11 | 18 | $17

Queen Anne | 364 Roy St. (bet. 3rd & 4th Aves.) | 206-282-6616 | www.bamboogarden.net
This kosher vegetarian Queen Anner near the Opera House gets props from vegheads looking for a light Chinese meal before a heavy night of Wagner; "surprisingly good fake meat" beefs up dishes like the popular "curry 'chicken' hot pot", and "friendly owners" cause hungry locals to "come back time and again" – hence, it can get "crowded."

Bambuza Bistro ⊠ Vietnamese
19 | 18 | 16 | $23

Downtown | 820 Pike St. (bet. 8th & 9th Aves.) | 206-219-5555 | www.bambuza.com
"Interesting", "fresh" Vietnamese fare in "elegant presentations" draw pre-show diners to this "cool" spot "right across the street" from the Convention Center and the Paramount Theater; "slow service" and "hit-or-miss" dishes deter some, though most concede that the food is "better than you'd expect in such a hotel-filled area."

B&O Espresso ◑ Coffeehouse
20 | 18 | 16 | $19

Capitol Hill | 204 Belmont Ave. E. (Olive Way) | 206-322-5028
Just off a "too-hip-for-me" Capitol Hill street corner, this "epitome of the eclectic-hippie coffeehouse" has caffeine-hounds "drooling" over "awesome desserts" and savory bites; an "expedient" staff keeps things moving in the "funky", antiques-filled space, which can get "pretty crowded and loud"; P.S. "coffee can be ordered with a kicker from the bar."

Barking Dog Alehouse Pub Food
17 | 17 | 14 | $19

Ballard | 705 NW 70th St. (7th Ave.) | 206-782-2974
On a Ballard residential street, this "hard-to-find" "neighborhood joint" pours a "booya beer selection" (19 on tap) alongside "upscale" American "pub food" that's "familiar and tasty" with a "twist"; the "light-filled", "eco-friendly space" is also "kid-friendly" – which means it can be "really loud" – and stern surveyors find the "incredibly slow" service "lacking."

	FOOD	DECOR	SERVICE	COST

Barking Frog *Pacific NW* | 24 | 23 | 24 | $48

Woodinville | Willows Lodge | 14580 NE 145th St.
(Woodinville-Redmond Rd.) | 425-424-2999 |
www.willowslodge.com

A "great alternative" to neighbor The Herbfarm, this more casual
but still "pricey" Willows Lodger holds its own with "imaginative"
Pacific NW "favorites" (many of which are "organic" or "line caught,
thank you") and a "fabulous selection" of "superb" local wines;
"attentive" waiters and a "comfortable" atmosphere make it "worth
the drive" to Woodinville – no wonder it's become "the lunch
place" of choice for digerati and venture capitalists eager to "see
and be seen."

NEW **Barolo Ristorante** *Italian* | 22 | 25 | 22 | $47

Downtown | 1940 Westlake Ave. (6th Ave.) | 206-770-9000 |
www.baroloseattle.com

The "young and beautiful, and those who used to be" hang out at
this Downtown Italiano where the "sparkly" "modern/baroque" decor is "very South Beach" and the vibe is "fun"; its "inventive"
Northern-inspired cuisine takes *cucina* cognoscenti "back to
Piemonte", and thanks to the "amazing happy hour" and "good
people-watching", few complain about the "smallish" portions and
"snooty but decent" service.

Bayou on First *Cajun* | - | - | - | I

Pike Place Market | Pike Place Mkt. | 1523 First Ave. (bet. Pike & Pine Sts.) |
206-624-2598

This "small dive" in the Pike Place Market is a "godsend for locals
who work nearby" (and tourists too, given its locale), providing "a
little Cajun spice" in the form of "surprisingly good" jambalaya and
catfish; the service is so "entertaining and friendly" that you can tell
that the staffers "appreciate your business."

Beach Cafe at the Point *Eclectic/Seafood* | 18 | 21 | 17 | $29

Kirkland | 1270 Carillon Pt. (Lake Washington Blvd.) | 425-889-0303 |
www.ybbeachcafe.com

You can't beat the "spectacular setting on Lake Washington" ex-
claim enthusiasts who also come for the "good" Eclectic seafood
("the halibut rocks") at this downstairs "sister" of Yarrow Bay Grill;
the "relaxed" atmosphere is a boon to locals, though some sigh over
the "slow" service and only "adequate" fare that's a disappointment
"given the prices."

NEW **Beàto Food & Wine** Ⓜ *Italian* | 23 | 21 | 23 | $40

West Seattle | 3247 California Ave. SW (bet. Hanford & Hinds Sts.) |
206-923-1333 | www.beatoseattle.com

Its name is Italian for 'blessed', which is exactly how this pricey
West Seattle yearling "makes one feel" aver voters who've tasted
the "simple yet creative" "seasonally inspired" fare served in
"small" portions; an "expert" staff helps navigate the "spectacular"
wine list – just know that the "beautiful" room is pint-sized, so be
sure to make reservations.

Beecher's Handmade Cheese *Cheese* | 24 | 15 | 19 | $13 |

Pike Place Market | Pike Place Mkt. | 1600 Pike Pl. (Pine St.) |
206-956-1964 | www.beecherscheese.com

"Snag a seat" on a milk-can stool at this Pike Place Market "must"
for *fromage* fans and "watch the cheese being made" while you
munch on "perfect grilled cheese sandwiches" and mac 'n' cheese
that's "a thing of beauty"; Downtown locals add to the "tourist
throng", so expect "crowds" – and tabs that can be "pricey for lunch"
but still "worth the splurge."

Belle Epicurean *Bakery/French* | ▽ 26 | 22 | 23 | $24 |

Downtown | Fairmont Olympic Hotel | 1206 Fourth Ave. (bet. Seneca &
University Sts.) | 206-262-9404 | www.belleepicurean.com

An "elegant" "respite" for tired Downtown shoppers, this "hidden
gem" of a bakery in the Fairmont Olympic Hotel brims with "excellent" French pastries, "*jambon-fromage* sandwiches" and "melt-in-
your-mouth" buns; owner Carolyn Bianchi Ferguson holds a Grande
Diplome from Le Cordon Bleu Paris, and it shows in her food – but
not in the prices, which remain "reasonable."

◪ Belle Pastry *Bakery/Dessert* | 27 | 18 | 18 | $11 |

Bellevue | 10246 Main St. (bet. 102nd & 103rd Aves.) | 425-289-0015 |
www.bellepastry.com

This "slice of Paris in Downtown Bellevue" is "wildly popular" with
local *bon vivants* thanks to its "gorgeous" pastries, "wickedly scrumptious" desserts, "simple lunch" items and coffee like "the café latte
that first stole your heart"; it's authentically French right down to
the often "excruciatingly slow" service and slightly "pricey" tabs.

Bell Street Diner *Seafood* | 18 | 20 | 17 | $26 |

Seattle Waterfront | Pier 66 | 2201 Alaskan Way (Bell St.) | 206-448-6688 |
www.anthonysrestaurants.com

A "casual counterpart" to Anthony's Pier 66 (which is right upstairs), this Seattle Waterfront seafooder offers "good" cheaper fare –
fans hail the fish tacos – and the same "beautiful views" of Elliott Bay;
though service can be hit-or-miss, the site "really shines in summer"
when you can "eat outside" and watch ferries and cruise ships float by.

Belltown Bistro ● *American* | 18 | 18 | 19 | $27 |

Belltown | 2322 First Ave. (bet. Battery & Bell Sts.) | 206-728-2000 |
www.bluwaterbistro.com

"Very good", frequently "innovative" American fare is the draw at this
"warm" Belltowner (begat by the BluWater folks) that's prime as a
"date place" and "late-night haunt" (serving until 1 AM nightly); reasonable prices and "funny, quick" bartenders are a bonus, and the
"sidewalk dining" is "heaven" on "gorgeous summer evenings."

Belltown Pizza *Pizza* | 20 | 14 | 16 | $17 |

Belltown | 2422 First Ave. (bet. Battery & Wall Sts.) | 206-441-2653 |
www.belltownpizza.net

The "really tasty", "thin-crust" pies at this "always crowded" pizza
joint in the heart of Belltown have just enough "heft" that they "don't

stray into the territories of soggy or hard as a cracker"; the digs are "lively" (forget "intimate conversations"), and be sure to "get there early", as the "spacious booths" "fill up fast with regulars."

Benihana *Japanese* 18 | 17 | 20 | $34

Downtown | 1200 Fifth Ave. (Seneca St.) | 206-682-4686 | www.benihana.com

Diners get "not only a meal" but also "a show" at this 38-year-old Downtown outpost of the famous Japanese teppanyaki chain, where juggled knives and flying steak make it a "favorite" for "kids", "groups of friends and business associates"; the sushi's "good too" say fans who claim the food's still got its edge – and even those who deem the cuisine "average" and decor "dated" concede that a night here is "entertaining", no matter how you slice it.

NEW Bennett's 22 | 21 | 20 | $32
Pure Food Bistro *American*

Mercer Island | 7650 SE 27th St. (bet. 76th & 77th Aves.) | 206-232-2759 | www.bennettsbistro.com

"Vibrant" and green-leaning, this sibling of Beecher's Handmade Cheese is hailed as "just what Mercer Island needed", serving "inventive" New American dishes made with "fresh", "natural" ingredients; even Islanders who argue that the atmosphere's a "little austere" and "noisy" admit that once the proprietors "relax about their uber-organic-ness" (as in "no diet drinks because they use all those chemicals"), "it will be great."

NEW Betty *American* 22 | 21 | 20 | $35

Queen Anne | 1507 Queen Anne Ave. N. (Galer St.) | 206-352-3773

This new sister of the always-packed Crow (just down the hill) is already "hopping" thanks to a "succinct" menu of "hip", "tasty" New American dishes that "hit every time"; the "cool" quasi-"industrial" Queen Anne space can be "fairly loud" and the "friendly" service doesn't always have its "timing" down, but "reasonable prices" and "excellent cocktails" numb the pain.

Bick's Broadview Grill *American* 21 | 17 | 18 | $26

Greenwood | 10555 Greenwood Ave. N. (107th St.) | 206-367-8481

"Lively and loud" (expect "deafening decibels" at prime time), this Greenwood "neighborhood joint" is known for its "spicy", "quirky" takes on American "comfort food", made with "local ingredients"; the "wonderful" tap beers and wines are poured by "knowledgeable" servers who warm up the "casual" atmosphere.

Bing's Bodacious Burgers *American* 16 | 12 | 17 | $19
(fka Bing's Bar & Grill)

Madison Park | 4200 E. Madison St. (42nd Ave.) | 206-323-8623

Well-heeled locals chill at this Madison Park American "standby" where "generously portioned" "burgers and salads" are doled out at "reasonable" prices; a toe-tapper jukebox and "fast", "family-friendly" service add to the allure.

	FOOD	DECOR	SERVICE	COST

Bis on Main *American* | 24 | 22 | 25 | $43 |

Bellevue | 10213 Main St. (102nd Ave. NE) | 425-455-2033 |
www.bisonmain.com

Bellevue "boomers" feel "right at home" at "suave" Joe Vilardi's
"Eastside treasure" on Main Street, where the "delicious" New
American cuisine is paired with "well-chosen" wines and "smooth"
service; the "classy" (recently expanded and remodeled) dining
room is "bustling", as is the "comfy" bar – a "destination unto itself."

Blackbird Bistro *American* | 19 | 21 | 19 | $29 |

West Seattle | 2329 California Ave. SW (College St.) | 206-937-2875 |
www.blackbirdbistro.com

West Seattleites who flock to this neighborhood "up-and-comer"
crow about its "solid" American comfort food with "a smidgen of
creativity"; smart "yet unstuffy", it's "good" for a "neighborhood
night out", even if the "hit-or-miss" service can be for the birds;
N.B. breakfast and lunch are served on weekends.

Black Bottle ❶ *Eclectic* | 22 | 21 | 19 | $28 |

Belltown | 2600 First Ave. (Vine St.) | 206-441-1500 |
www.blackbottleseattle.com

This "cool" Belltown spot draws "hipsters" with "inventive" Eclectic
small plates that are a "good value"; "nice" for a "first date" (and
conveniently "way too noisy" for "small talk"), with "midpriced wines"
and cocktails, it's also "the place to make your regular watering hole."

Black Pearl *Chinese* | 15 | 10 | 15 | $18 |

Wedgwood | 7347 35th Ave. NE (75th St.) | 206-526-5115
Shoreline | 14602 15th Ave. NE (146th St.) | 206-365-8989

These no-frills Chinese "depots" have been longtime Wedgwood
and Shoreline "neighborhood favorites" thanks to their homemade
noodles, "unusual combinations" and "fast and easy" delivery; admirers still laud the "lover's eggplant" and "bargain" prices, but the
Food score has taken a dive, causing one former fan to note "something has changed and it wasn't for the better."

Blue C Sushi *Japanese* | 15 | 17 | 15 | $22 |

Fremont | 3411 Fremont Ave. N. (34th St.) | 206-633-3411
University Village | University Vill. | 4601 26th Ave. NE (Montlake Blvd.) |
206-525-4601
www.bluecsushi.com

Experience "modern-day hunting and gathering" at this twinset
where "conveyor belts" deliver sushi to plate-snagging diners; the
selection is "pretty conservative" and quality "average" say
Japanophiles used to the real deal, but "decent" prices make it "fun"
for both raw-fish "newbies" and finatics angling for a "quick, casual"
bite in "simple" University Village and Fremont settings.

Blue Onion Bistro Ⓜ *American* | 17 | 15 | 15 | $27 |

University District | 5801 Roosevelt Way NE (58th St.) | 206-729-0579 |
www.theblueonionbistro.com

Think kitsch and a plate of sautéed hot dog mac 'n' cheese, and you
get the gist of this American eatery serving tweaked "comfort food"

in a "retired" University District gas station; nostalgists and neighbors mingle in the "true funk", knickknack filled space, though frus-
trated raters mark it down for slow service that causes "long waits"
even when it isn't crowded.

BluWater ● American   16 | 18 | 16 | $30

Lake Union | 1001 Fairview Ave. N. (Ward St.) | 206-447-0769
Green Lake | 7900 E. Green Lake Dr. N. (Ashworth Ave.) | 206-524-3985
Leschi | 102 Lakeside Ave. (Lake Washington Pl.) | 206-328-2233
NEW Kirkland | 2220 Carillon Pt. (Lake Washington Blvd.) |
425-822-4000
www.bluwaterbistro.com

At these "always busy" waterside watering holes, the "gorgeous"
views are backed up by "filling", "modestly" priced American fare
that may be "a bit bland", but at least there are "options for everyone"; a "yuppie vibe" pervades at the Lake Union branch, where
"scantily clad urbanites" gather on the deck in sunny weather.

Boat Street Cafe Ⓜ French   25 | 21 | 23 | $37

Queen Anne | 3131 Western Ave. (Denny Way) | 206-632-4602 |
www.boatstreetcafe.com

This "wildly intimate" bistro in lower-lower Queen Anne proffers "exquisite" French "comfort food" prepared with "local and seasonal"
ingredients – and "remarkable care", to boot; add in "warm" service
and "industrial-chic" surroundings (complete with "whitewashed
walls" and "soft lighting") and you've got a "friendly, delicious spot."

NEW Boka Kitchen & Bar Pacific NW   22 | 25 | 22 | $45

Downtown | 1010 First Ave. (Madison St.) | 206-357-9000 |
www.bokaseattle.com

It's all *Sex and the City* at this Downtown boîte where the "lighted
walls change color" every 90 seconds and a "diverse crowd" sips
herb-infused martinis; the Pacific NW menu features "well-executed"
"twists" on the basics, and while tabs can be "expensive" (except at
the "downright-cheap" happy hour), service is "warm as a reunion
with an old friend"; N.B. the Food score does not reflect a chef change.

Bonefish Grill Seafood   19 | 19 | 21 | $31

Lake Union | 711 Westlake Ave. N. (Valley St.) | 206-405-2663
Bothell | 22616 Bothell Everett Hwy. (228th St. SE) | 425-485-0305
www.bonefishgrill.com

With lines cast in both Lake Union and Bothell, this seafood duo nets
lunch and dinner diners with "inventive" specials and an "attentive
staff" that doesn't blanch when large parties appear; "surprisingly
nice", "comfortable" surroundings and "good-value" prices cause
skeptics to say these spots are "better than expected" given that
they're links in a "national chain."

NEW Bottle Rocket Café Ⓩ American   – | – | – | I

Wallingford | 1605 N. 45th St. (bet. Densmore & Woodlawn Aves.) |
206-545-4555 | www.bottlerocketcafe.com

This "cute" Wallingford American fills the tiny crater left after the
Asteroid Café flew to Fremont, and serves low-key traditional break-

fast, lunch and dinner – including "tasty" soups and sandwiches – to locals; N.B. there's free delivery all day.

Brad's Swingside Cafe 🗷 *Italian* 24 | 17 | 21 | $32

Fremont | 4212 Fremont Ave. N. (bet. 42nd St. & Motor Pl.) | 206-633-4057
Chef Brad Inserra swings "complex, creative" riffs on Italian "standards" at this "quirky", unpretentious" Fremonter where everything is cooked "with love"; expect old knotty pine and sports memorabilia on the walls along with a "mellow, slow-paced feel" that makes diners want to "take their time" over the "large portions"; N.B. the wine list is almost bigger than the restaurant.

☑ Brasa *Mediterranean* 25 | 24 | 22 | $45

Belltown | 2107 Third Ave. (bet. Blanchard & Lenora Sts.) | 206-728-4220 | www.brasa.com
Iron Chef contender Tamara Murphy keeps customers happy with her "bold", "smooth" and "complex" Mediterranean fare at this "spendy but trendy", comfortable Belltowner; the wine list boasts "interesting" Spanish and Portuguese treasures, and reviewers rave about the "value"-packed "happy hour."

Brasserie Margaux *French/Pacific NW* 19 | 17 | 19 | $38

Downtown | Warwick Seattle Hotel | 401 Lenora St. (4th Ave.) | 206-777-1990 | www.margauxseattle.com
The Warwick Seattle Hotel's "informal" eatery offers *un petit respite* from the Downtown bustle with "good value" French-NW fare and "pleasant" service; despite "uninspired" decor, it's "inviting" enough for "small family get-togethers" and "after-work" drinks.

Bricco della Regina Anna 🌗 *Italian* 22 | 22 | 21 | $28

Queen Anne | 1525 Queen Anne Ave. N. (bet. Galer & Garfield Sts.) | 206-285-4900 | www.briccoseattle.com
"Inventive" Italian food and a whopper of a boutique beverage list earn bravos from Queen Anne cognoscenti who declare this "small", "dark", "sublime" spot as "congenial" as a "real" European wine bar; "knowledgeable" servers ("when you have their attention") deliver "terrific", affordable panini, cured meats and artisan cheese.

Broadway Grill, The 🌗 *American* 16 | 14 | 14 | $21

Capitol Hill | 314 Broadway E. (bet. Harrison & Thomas Sts.) | 206-328-7000
The "place to be for Sunday brunch", this newly remodeled American is also a "fun" Capitol Hill spot for meeting your "fabulous" friends after clubbing (it's open until 3 AM); the "perky and flirty" service "can get a bit tiresome" and some consider the food "unspectacular" – yet the people-watching, complete with "drag stars", is anything but.

☑ Brooklyn Seafood, Steak & Oyster House *Seafood* 23 | 20 | 22 | $43

Downtown | Brooklyn Bldg. | 1212 Second Ave. (University St.) | 206-224-7000 | www.thebrooklyn.com
Oyster lovers vie for seats on the "comfy" "swiveling captain's chairs" at this "crowded" Downtowner in the stately 1890 Brooklyn

	FOOD	DECOR	SERVICE	COST

Building where the mollusks, seafood and steaks are "impressive"; its "classic" "clubby" decor wins raves from the pre-concert crowd (Benaroya Hall is nearby), and even equivocators say the only "downside" is the price.

Brouwer's Belgian
| 20 | 23 | 19 | $23 |

Fremont | 400 N. 35th St. (Phinney Ave.) | 206-267-2437 | www.brouwerscafe.com

This "lively" Flemish Fremont pub stirs up the fun with "excellent", affordable Belgian frites, "top-notch" mussels and over 64 "phenomenal" tap beers served in the appropriate "steins"; "cave"-like warehouse environs remind some of a "Belgian castle circa 1200 A.D.", but the "hipster" hordes who descend at night are decidedly modern; N.B. 21-and-over only.

Buca di Beppo Italian
| 14 | 18 | 17 | $25 |

Queen Anne | 701 Ninth Ave. N. (Broad St.) | 206-244-2288
Lynnwood | 4301 Alderwood Mall Blvd. (44th Ave.) | 425-744-7272
www.bucadibeppo.com

"Big" boisterous "groups" eat up the "loopy atmosphere" at the Queen Anne and Lynnwood branches of this "quirky" national chain serving "family-style" portions of "decent" Southern Italian fare; "bring a big car for the leftovers", pack "earplugs" and be advised the bill can "sneak up on you" warn regulars who note that "if it doesn't leave you thrilled, at least you will be full."

Buckley's On Queen Anne ◑ American
| 19 | 16 | 20 | $21 |

Seattle Center | 232 W. First Ave. (bet. John & Thomas Sts.) | 206-691-0232 | www.buckleysseattle.com

Sports fans cheer this old-skool American "sports" bar near Seattle Center for its burgers and "sweet potato fries" that "surpass" pub grub "expectations"; with a "decent" selection of draft beers and the game "always on", you'll "feel like you're in college again" minus the term papers.

Buenos Aires Grill Argentinean
| 23 | 19 | 21 | $39 |

Downtown | 220 Virginia St. (2nd Ave.) | 206-441-7076

Slip into a world of "wonderful" meats and "tango" beats at this "noisy" Argentinean Downtowner where the mixed grill "parrillada", "chimichurri" sauce and weekend dancers leave voters "drooling for more"; although the usually "excellent" service can be "occasionally inattentive", prices are reasonable and, all in all, it's always an "interesting experience."

Buffalo Deli ⑤ Deli
| 23 | 8 | 15 | $11 |

Belltown | 2123 First Ave. (bet. Blanchard & Lenora Sts.) | 206-728-8759

"Sandwiches" rule at this bare-bones "quickie" "Buffalo-style deli" (the owner hails from Buffalo, NY) with "plenty" of choices and "top-of-the-line" Boar's Head meats; how better to spend a lunch hour than sitting on a stool in the window and eating a roast beef "on a weck"?

	FOOD	DECOR	SERVICE	COST

Burrito Loco *Mexican* ▽ 22 | 15 | 16 | $16

Crown Hill | 9211 Holman Rd. NW (13th Ave.) | 206-783-0719
This "unconventional" Crown Hill eatery serves "excellent",
"healthy" Mexican that "hasn't been completely Americanized"
("no chain glop here"); its colorful interior doesn't score as high as
the food, but fans of the cheap chicken mole and "outstanding"
beans aren't arguing.

Bush Garden *Japanese* ▽ 19 | 15 | 19 | $30

International District | 614 Maynard Ave. S. (bet. Lane & Weller Sts.) |
206-682-6830 | www.bushgarden.net
Fifty-five years old and counting, this "moderately" priced ID stalwart reminds locals of their "little kid" days with its "classic"
"American-style Japanese" decor and cuisine – think tatami rooms,
karaoke, sukiyaki and sushi; naysayers note the "spotty" service and
natter "it's not the great destination it used to be."

Cactus *Southwestern* 22 | 20 | 19 | $27

Madison Park | 4220 E. Madison St. (43rd Ave.) | 206-324-4140
NEW **West Seattle** | 2820 Alki Ave. SW (62nd Ave.) | 206-933-6000
Kirkland | 121 Park Ln. (bet. Central Way & Lake St.) | 425-893-9799
www.cactusrestaurants.com
"Tasty" and "original" Southwestern tapas are the ticket at this trip-
let of cantinas that specialize in "hybrid" dishes with "just-south-of-
traditional" accompaniments; "wild" razzmatazz decor and
"delicious" margaritas that "make you forget you're not in Mexico"
add to the "festive" feel that draws "long lines" of "spouse-hunters"
on weekend nights.

Cafe Bengodi *Italian* ▽ 19 | 15 | 20 | $24

Pioneer Square | 700 First Ave. (Cherry St.) | 206-381-0705
This "fun" Italian on a cozy corner of Pioneer Square is a "secret you
don't want to share" say reviewers who've discovered Luigi
DeNunzio's casual counterpoint to his more formal Luigi's Grotto; the
"good", "cheap" housemade pastas and pizzas draw business folks
at lunchtime, and as night falls, barhoppers seeking sustenance.

Z Cafe Besalu **M** *Bakery* 27 | 17 | 19 | $9

Ballard | 5909 24th Ave. NW (bet. 59th & 60th Sts.) | 206-789-1463
"Walking through the door" of this Ballard bakery/cafe "is like falling
in love" rave rapturous fans of its "exquisite, buttery" European
pastries and "excellent" coffee, all served by an "enthusiastic" staff;
you'll want "to linger and enjoy reading the newspaper", though
"serpentine" lines can mean that seating is competitive but worth
it – since while some flinch at the "spendy" prices, most insist it's
"cheaper than a flight to Paris, and just as genuine."

Z Cafe Campagne *French* 25 | 21 | 21 | $36

Pike Place Market | Pike Place Mkt. | 1600 Post Alley (bet. 1st & Pine Sts.) |
206-728-2233 | www.campagnerestaurant.com
Tucked away on the Pike Place Market's vine-covered Post Alley, this
"lovely" and less-pricey sister to Campagne (upstairs) is a "Paris

throwback", serving "marvelous" country French bistro dishes like "sublime" brunchtime *"oeuffs en meurette"* and *cassoulet* that's "to die for" at night; service is "warm, friendly" and authentically "slow", so "reserve a window seat" and be prepared to linger over a "great glass of wine."

Café Darclée *French*

-	-	-	I

Belltown | Fisher Plaza | 100 Fourth Ave. N. (Denny Way) | 206-404-2233 | www.cafedarclee.com

"My favorite crêperie" say business and broadcast types who duck into this petite, affordable Belltown European in the Fisher Plaza/ KOMO TV building for french pancakes, "soup specials" and luxe hot chocolate; the relaxed, condo-cool atmosphere has a light, industrial-chic feel.

Cafe Flora *Vegetarian*

22	21	20	$29

Madison Park | 2901 E. Madison St. (29th St.) | 206-325-9100 | www.cafeflora.com

Even the "most rapacious carnivores" "won't miss the meat" when eating at this upscale Madison Park "vegetarian hot spot" where the food "bursts with flavor"; the digs are "tranquil" (especially in the "arboretumlike" "fountain room"), the servers "personable" and "attentive", and the prices "reasonable"; P.S. the "weekend brunch is a must."

☑ Cafe Juanita *Italian*

28	22	26	$57

Kirkland | 9702 NE 120th Pl. (97th St.) | 425-823-1505 | www.cafejuanita.com

Chef Holly Smith's Northern Italian cuisine is "consistently" "stunning" thanks to her "creative" touch with "impeccably" fresh local ingredients say the legions of satisfied suppers who've "battled traffic" to get to this "foodie" destination housed in a Kirkland rambler redo; its "deep" wine list features "lots" of *Italiano* "hard-to-finds", and "informed" servers add to the abundant "sense of competence and bonhomie" – so while it's "not cheap", it is "worth every penny."

Cafe Lago *Italian*

23	18	20	$34

Montlake | 2305 24th Ave. E. (Lynn St.) | 206-329-8005 | www.cafelago.com

"Delizioso" croon the multitudinous fans of this "informal", "candlelit" Montlake Italian serving "very good" homemade pasta, "luscious" lasagna and "wood-fired" "thin-crust" pizzas; bills that some consider "a tad pricey for what you get" are offset by "friendly", "quick" service.

Cafe Nola *American*

21	18	19	$35

Bainbridge Island | 101 Winslow Way E. (Madison Ave.) | 206-842-3822 | www.cafenola.com

Fresh-off-the-ferry day-trippers join Winslow locals in lauding the "Northwest-inspired" New American fare at this "very cute", "informal" bistro, "one of the better places to eat" on Bainbridge Island; some argue that the service can be "island (too) casual", but undeterred acolytes fill up the "weekend brunch", turning the "warm" yellow room "lively" (and "noisy").

	FOOD	DECOR	SERVICE	COST

Café Ori ⇗ *Chinese* — 21 | 8 | 13 | $15

Bellevue | 14339 NE 20th St. (bet. 140th & 148th Aves.) | 425-747-8822
"Well-prepared" "Hong-Kong-style" Cantonese is the draw at this Bellevue strip-maller catering to expats and savvy digerati who gather for "huge" plates of noodles, "pork chop" soup, "French toast and spaghetti" (that's the Hong Kong influence); the decor and service are "bare-bones", but few complain since it's such a "great value"; N.B. cash only.

NEW Café Presse ◑ *French* — - | - | - | M

Capitol Hill | 1117 12th Ave. (E. Spring St.) | 206-709-7674 | www.cafepresseseattle.com
This sibling of the popular Le Pichet sits on Capitol Hill's now-trendy 12th Avenue and serves polished Gallic cafe standards (French pastries, steak frites, croque monsieurs) in chic, former-garage digs; a surfeit of international magazines and newspapers invite eaters to linger (from 7 AM–2 AM daily), as does the European futbol on the bar TV.

Café Septieme *American* — 16 | 16 | 15 | $20

Capitol Hill | 214 Broadway E. (bet. John & Thomas Sts.) | 206-860-8858
Trendinistas "chat, read, drink and fall in love" over "burgers" and "desserts" at this Capitol Hill American "mainstay of Broadway culture"; an "attentive", "accommodating" staff presides over the "moody" room (note the "original artwork" on the walls), making this an ideal "local cafe."

Café Soleil ▥ *American/Ethiopian* — ▽ 20 | 16 | 23 | $22

Madrona | 1400 34th Ave. (Union St.) | 206-325-1126
On an "exceedingly quiet" Madrona corner, this often "overlooked" spot has two identities: on weekend mornings it serves American breakfasts, and at night it draws in the local intelligencia with "fresh", "surprisingly good" Ethiopian fare; responders rate it "reasonably priced" and rave about its "cheerful" service and "lovely" owner "who treats every diner like family"; N.B call first, as hours and days vary.

Cafe Veloce *Italian* — ▽ 21 | 19 | 20 | $21

Kirkland | 12514 120th Ave. NE (Totem Lake Blvd., opp. Totem Lake Mall) | 425-814-2972 | www.cafeveloce.com
Near Evergreen Hospital, this motorcycle-themed Kirkland cafe gets checkered flags for its "large selection" of Italian pizzas and pastas and "delicious" chicken scampi, served amid "vintage" bikes and memorabilia; easy riders get a discount on the already-affordable nosh.

Café Yarmarka *Russian* — - | - | - | I

Pike Place Market | Pike Place Mkt. | 1530 Post Alley (bet. Pike Pl. & Pine St.) | 206-521-9054
Just off Post Alley, this unassuming Russian eatery gets "overshadowed" by "the other piroshky place" in the Pike Place Market, but this one's "much less crowded"; expect "friendly" service from

husband-and-wife owners who serve, in addition to the "tasty" namesake vittles, stuffed cabbage and other bargains to "eat at the counter" or "take out."

Caffé Minnie's ◐ *American* | 12 | 10 | 11 | $15 |

Queen Anne | 101 Denny Way (1st Ave.) | 206-448-6263 | www.minniescafe.com

This 24-hour Queen Anne "dive" is "slacker heaven" for punkers and after-hours barhoppers looking for a "quick" American "bite in the middle of the night" or when "nursing a hangover" the next morning; objectors knock the lack of atmosphere and say it "keeps trying but hasn't gotten there yet", though it's been open for 14 years.

Calabria Ristorante Italiano *Italian* | 17 | 15 | 16 | $28 |

Kirkland | 132 Lake St. S. (Central Way) | 425-822-7350 | www.calabriakirkland.com

Kirklanders come to this "cozy", "candlelit" Southern Italian for "good", "solid" classics, though some sigh that the fare has become "inconsistent" since "they lost their longtime chef"; others warn that the "friendly" service can be "spotty", but still it remains a "local favorite."

Calcutta Grill *American* | 20 | 24 | 20 | $40 |

Newcastle | Golf Club at Newcastle | 15500 Six Penny Ln. (New Castle Coal Creek Rd.) | 425-793-4646 | www.newcastlegolf.com

Named for "the golf betting game, not the city", this wood-beamed dining room at Bellevue's tony Golf Club at Newcastle offers a "spectacular view" of the city's skyline and Lake Washington, especially from "out on the deck"; the "food's good as well" say duffers who munch on New American victuals served by a "friendly but not always polished staff"; P.S. post-dinner, head upstairs to the clubby Wooly Toad pub "for a drink" and a game of billiards.

☑ Campagne *French* | 26 | 24 | 25 | $55 |

Pike Place Market | Pike Place Mkt. | 86 Pine St. (1st Ave.) | 206-728-2800 | www.campagnerestaurant.com

At this "elegant" yet "unpretentious" "oasis" in the Pike Place Market, chef Daisley Gordon doles out "heavenly" country French cuisine accompanied by a "sophisticated but quirky wine list" by sommelier Jake Kosseff; the "*magnifique*" interior (white tablecloths, a snazzy bar) has a "great view" of the market, though regulars recommend dining alfresco on the patio; the service combines "American warmth" with "European attention" to detail, and as for the pricey tab, "ooh-la-la."

☑ Canlis 🅂 *Pacific NW* | 27 | 27 | 27 | $71 |

Lake Union | 2576 Aurora Ave. N. (Halladay St., south of Aurora Bridge) | 206-283-3313 | www.canlis.com

"Spoil yourself" royally at this old-schooler that's been the city's "gold-standard" "special-event restaurant" for more than 50 years; the "world-class" Pacific NW food and wine are matched by "million-dollar" Lake Union views from a "chic", and some say "formal", mid-century modern room, and by the "gracious" "how-did-they-know" service that borders on magic; so leave your worries at home, but don't forget to "bring your platinum card."

Capitol Club *Mediterranean* | 19 | 23 | 21 | $31 |

Capitol Hill | 414 E. Pine St. (bet. Bellevue & Summit Aves.) | 206-325-2149 | www.thecapitolclub.net

A "great place for a party" say swanky sorts who enjoy the "exotic" Moroccan decor, "belly dancers" and "city" views at this Capitol Hill hot spot; the Mediterranean menu is "better than average", though most agree "it seems to be more about the drinks."

☑ Carmelita Ⓜ *Mediterranean* | 26 | 22 | 23 | $33 |

Greenwood | 7314 Greenwood Ave. N. (bet. 73rd & 74th Sts.) | 206-706-7703 | www.carmelita.net

Vegetarians unite at this pricey meat-free Med mecca known for its "amazing feats of vegetable" (they "make rutabaga sexy"); the "up-scale" wood and cream-toned Greenwood setting is "refined" yet "casual" with "none of that crunchy-hippie-granola vibe", and the "garden seating during summer" is "especially memorable."

Carnegie's Ⓢ Ⓜ *French* | 21 | 23 | 20 | $38 |

Ballard | 2026 NW Market St. (Russell Ave.) | 206-789-6643 | www.carnegiesrestaurant.com

There's "charm to spare" at this bistro in the "beautiful" 1907 Ballard Carnegie Library building where the chef "circulates" among guests as they check out his "casual" French fare; some say this "elegant" respite from the nearby bars is too staid ("no loud voices in the library") and needs to "please, lighten up."

☑ Cascadia Ⓢ *American* | 25 | 25 | 24 | $55 |

Belltown | 2328 First Ave. (bet. Battery & Bell Sts.) | 206-448-8884 | www.cascadiarestaurant.com

Chef Kerry Sear's "awe-inspiring", "beautifully presented" New American cuisine is matched by an "elegant" atmosphere and "first-rate" service at this Belltown foodie favorite; if the standard plates seem pricey, opt for the "surprisingly reasonable" tasting menus or munch on "gourmet sliders" at the bar during the "not-to-be-missed" happy hour.

Caspian Grill Persian Cuisine Ⓜ *Persian* | – | – | – | M |

University District | 5517 University Way NE (bet. 55th & 56th Sts.) | 206-524-3434 | www.caspiangrill.com

"Consistent, fresh" flavors are the hallmark of this midpriced Persian in the University District, which hits the spot when a craving strikes; sensitive palates may find some dishes "spicier than expected", but most say it's "definitely worth a try – or several"; N.B. there's live music and belly dancers on Friday and Saturday nights.

Catfish Corner Ⓢ *Soul Food* | ▽ 21 | 9 | 15 | $17 |

Capitol Hill | 2726 E. Cherry St. (MLK Jr. Way) | 206-323-4330 | www.mo-catfish.com

A "neighborhood fixture", this "bustling" Capitol Hill soul food haven keeps it real with "tasty", "down-home" fried catfish, buffalo

| | FOOD | DECOR | SERVICE | COST |

fish and hushpuppies that make you downright "grateful for taste buds"; the digs are frills-free, and takeout is a popular option.

Cellar Bistro, The Ⓜ Italian
| - | - | - | M |

Capitol Hill | 2355 10th Ave. E. (bet. Lynn & Miller Sts.) | 206-709-8744 | www.cellarbistro.com

"You swear you're going to run into Frank Sinatra" at this Capitol Hill Northern Italian that's like a "time warp to the '50s", right down to its hanging "plastic grapes" decor; some say the pasta is a "little greasy", but the staff is "excellent" and the prices "very reasonable."

Chaco Canyon Café Vegan
| - | - | - | I |

University District | 4757 12th Ave. NE (50th St.) | 206-522-6966 | www.chacocanyoncafe.com

Veggiemeisters hie to this University District raw-food mecca for "good-value", "good-vegan" permutations, including "Thai grinders" and low-temp lasagna; the "spacious" new digs boast "high ceilings", "congenial" service and, hey, "free Internet" (a draw for UW students).

Chandler's Crabhouse Seafood
| 22 | 21 | 22 | $43 |

Lake Union | 901 Fairview Ave. N. (Valley St.) | 206-223-2722 | www.schwartzbros.com

Pescatorians clamor for the "well-executed" fish and "amazing" crab concoctions, including the fan-favorite "whiskey crab soup", at this Lake Unioner with "fabulous" water views and "friendly" service; critics carp that while the whole experience is "good", it's "expensive" and a "little tired" too.

Chanterelle Specialty Foods Eclectic
| ▽ 19 | 17 | 16 | $25 |

Edmonds | 316 Main St. (bet. 3rd & 4th Sts.) | 425-774-0650

This Eclectic Edmonds eatery "charms" locals with "something for every taste" at breakfast, lunch and especially dinner, when a four-course prix fixe is offered; a few suggest the kitchen can be "unpredictable" and that a "smile" at the door would go a long way.

Ⓩ Cheesecake Factory ◑ American
| 17 | 17 | 17 | $25 |

Downtown | 700 Pike St. (7th Ave.) | 206-652-5400
Bellevue | 401 Bellevue Sq. (NE 4th St.) | 425-450-6000
www.thecheesecakefactory.com

Even skeptics call the melting-pot fare "surprisingly good" at these "noisy" Belltown and Downtown chain links known for "gargantuan" portions, an American menu "the size of a dictionary" and mountains of "glorious" cheesecake; despite "efficient" service, be prepared to endure "long waits" with a "pager" before being granted a seat.

Chez Shea Ⓜ French/Pacific NW
| 26 | 23 | 25 | $54 |

Pike Place Market | Pike Place Mkt. | 94 Pike St. (1st Ave.) | 206-467-9990 | www.chezshea.com

"Absolute perfection" gush lovers of this "intimate" Pacific NW–French in the Pike Place Market where "wonderful views" and an "excellent use" of seasonal bounty "guarantee romance in every booth and bite"; "talented" service ensures that each meal is a "special occasion", so just swoon along and "don't worry about the wallet."

China Gate ◑ *Chinese*   20 | 12 | 16 | $19

International District | 516 Seventh Ave. S. (King St.) | 206-624-1730

"Authentic" "dim sum" served by "solid, polite" waiters is offered daily (and into the wee hours on the weekend) at this large, "real-deal" Chinese in the ID; the two golden dragons hovering over the front door can be a little "off-putting", but "live seafood tanks" and "terribly fun" karaoke bring cheer to the interior.

Chinoise Café *Pan-Asian*   19 | 15 | 17 | $24

Wallingford | 1618 N. 45th St. (bet. Densmore & Woodlawn Aves.) | 206-633-1160
Madison Valley | 2801 E. Madison St. (28th Ave.) | 206-323-0171
Queen Anne | 12 Boston St. (Queen Anne Ave.) | 206-284-6671
www.chinoisecafe.com

This inexpensive, "consistent" trio proffering "good" Pan-Asian "for any taste" hits the spot "when you want sushi, but your date wants Thai"; a "customer-friendly" staff keeps the crowds moving through the art-filled dining rooms, though the take-out service "takes a while."

Chinook's at Salmon Bay *Seafood*   21 | 19 | 20 | $28

Magnolia | Fishermen's Terminal | 1900 W. Nickerson St. (18th Ave.) | 206-283-4665 | www.anthonys.com

Right on the Fishermen's Terminal dock (home of the North Pacific fishing fleet), this "noisy", "friendly" Magnolia eatery is a "favorite" with families thanks to its "simple, but very, very fresh" seafood and "to-die-for" focaccialike cannery bread at "bargain" prices; expect "lotsa local color" in the "casual", "nautical" digs where it's always "come as you are"; P.S. early-risers tout the "real Seattle breakfasts" on weekends.

☑ Chiso Restaurant *Japanese*   26 | 22 | 23 | $33

Fremont | 3520 Fremont Ave. N. (36th St.) | 206-632-3430 | www.chisoseattle.com

The "marvelous" sushi is "inventive, but not over-the-top crazy" at this "hip" Fremonter whose "hot dishes rank high too", and include plenty of "hometown" flavors "not often found on this side of the Pacific"; the service is as "upbeat" as the scene at the bar, where local condo dwellers and software serfs roll in for the fun.

Christina's *Pacific NW*   ▽ 26 | 20 | 22 | $50

Eastsound | Porter Bldg. | 310 Main St. (Horseshoe Hwy.) | 360-376-4904 | www.christinas.net

Christina Orchid's refuge of "outrageously fresh" and "flavorful" Pacific NW cuisine provides "yet another reason" to "take the ferry to Orcas Island"; the staff is "on its toes", whether catering to indoor diners or to the regulars who "bring a sweater" and dine on the back deck overlooking East Sound.

Ciao Bella *Italian*   21 | 17 | 20 | $28

University Village | 3626 NE 45th St. (bet. 35th & 40th Aves.) | 206-524-6989

This "charming" Italian in a "new location" near University Village welcomes *amici* with "huge portions" of "good, solid" staples served in a "very cozy" setting that's "terrific for a date"; "reasonable" prices and "seasoned" waiters enhance the "authentic", "homestyle" aura.

Circa Neighborhood Grill & Ale House *Eclectic*

23 | 18 | 20 | $22

West Seattle | 2605 California Ave. SW (Admiral Way) | 206-923-1102
In West Seattle, this "sincerely good" Eclectic pub serves "hearty" hamburgers, brisk brews, "yam tacos" and a "legendary" steak salad for just the right price; a "relaxed", "capable" and "sometimes irreverent (in a good way)" staff makes the frequent waits tolerable; P.S. the "creative" weekend brunch is "excellent."

CJ's Eatery *Diner*

21 | 10 | 21 | $15

Belltown | 2619 First Ave. (bet. Cedar & Vine Sts.) | 206-728-1648
"Ample servings" of "quick" diner-style breakfasts and lunches (but no dinner) keep this "relaxed", reasonably priced Belltown storefront hopping seven days a week; the "no-frills" space is serviced by "hardworking", "friendly" servers who will customize your breakfast "any way you want."

Coastal Kitchen *American/Eclectic*

20 | 17 | 19 | $25

Capitol Hill | 429 15th Ave. E. (bet. Harrison & Republican Sts.) | 206-322-1145 | www.chowfoods.com
This "lively" Eclectic-American perks up the "sedate" side of Capitol Hill with a wide "variety" of wild finfish – on both its basic menu and an additional "theme" slate highlighting a new global "coastal" region every season; the vittles may be "sometimes grand, sometimes bland", but service is always "way friendly" and even the "I-hate-brunch" crowd lines up to feast on weekend mornings.

Coho Cafe *Pacific NW/Seafood*

18 | 18 | 17 | $25

Issaquah | 6130 E. Lake Sammamish Pkwy. SE (62nd St.) | 425-391-4040
Redmond | 8976 161st Ave. NE (Redmond Woodinville Rd.) | 425-885-2646
www.cohocafe.com
These "casual" and "quite noisy" Redmond-Issaquah seafooders score with "flavorful" Pacific NW cookery like "halibut and chips" and "killer" burgers that satisfy the whole family; "bright" contemporary digs and patio seating add to what some call the "fun" but others claim is "nothing to write home about."

Coldwater Bar & Grill *Pacific NW/Seafood*

20 | 18 | 19 | $38

Downtown | Westin Hotel | 1900 Fifth Ave. (Stewart St.) | 206-256-7697 | www.westinseattle.com
Off the Downtown "beaten track", this "underrated" enclave in the Westin Hotel dishes out "decent if unremarkable" Pacific NW seafood and an "excellent" raw-bar selection; with "upscale" decor and "impressive" service, it "does a fine job of keeping the people satisfied."

Coliman 🅱 *Mexican*

- | - | - | I

Georgetown | 6932 Carleton Ave. S. (E. Marginal Way) | 206-767-3187
Head south to Georgetown for "terrific" prawn flautas and freshly made guacamole at this "affordable and good" cantina owned by a

family from the Pacific Coast state of Colima, Mexico; the large, unassuming space has a dash of south-of-the-border decor, *authentico*
music and a rustic little bar in the back.

Columbia City Ale House *Pub Food*   18 | 16 | 18 | $20
Columbia City | 4914 Rainier Ave. S. (bet. Ferdinand & Hudson Sts.) |
206-723-5123 | www.seattlealehouses.com
In Columbia City, this "friendly local tavern" tempts suds-hounds with
burgers, "spicy" gumbos and other pub grub plus a "broad" selection
of microbrews; the staff is "clever and efficient", but on the downside, "high ceilings and TVs = lots of noise"; N.B. 21-and-over only.

Copacabana Cafe *S American*   20 | 15 | 20 | $23
Pike Place Market | Pike Place Mkt. | 1520½ Pike Pl. (Pine St.) |
206-622-6359
The "generous", "well-seasoned" Bolivian bites are nearly outshone
by a "heavenly" "bird's-eye" view from the terrace at this "casual"
South American cafe overlooking Pike Place Market and Elliott Bay;
affordable prices and an accommodating staff make you almost
forget that there's "no decor."

Costas Greek Restaurant *Greek*   17 | 10 | 17 | $20
University District | 4559 University Way NE (46th St.) | 206-633-2751
Academics with a hankering for "simple", "fast" Aegean eats appreciate the "friendly ambiance" of this "unpretentious" University
District longtimer; gyros, "skordalia" (garlic dip) and other Greek
specialties get an *opa*, as do the weekend "belly dancers", though
some raters reckon it "could use a face-lift and a spark of liveliness."

Costas Opa *Greek*   19 | 15 | 18 | $22
Fremont | 3400 Fremont Ave. N. (34th St.) | 206-633-4141
In a "can't-be-beat" funky Fremont location, this retro *taverna* welcomes with "old-style" Greek dishes, including "terrific" apps and rich
meat preps that leave surveyors "satisfied, but not overloaded"; the
"casual" setting is overseen by owners who are "always there" and a
staff that "functions like a family, albeit a highly dysfunctional one."

NEW Coupage *French/Pan-Asian*   23 | 18 | 22 | $50
Madrona | 1404 34th Ave. (Union St.) | 206-322-1974 |
www.coupageseattle.com
Asian cuisine (that leans toward Korea) meets French flair in the
"delightfully surprising" menu at Tom Hurley's Madrona bistro where
the "foie gras burger" lives up to the "buzz"; the modish, small room
has a vibe that's neither "stuffy" nor "noisy", bolstered by "polished",
"attentive" service; N.B. the Food score may not reflect a chef change.

Coyote Creek Pizza *Pizza*   20 | 14 | 17 | $16
Kirkland | 228 Central Way (2nd St.) | 425-822-2226
Redmond | 23525 Novelty Hill Rd. NE (bet. Trilogy Pkwy. & 234th Pl.) |
425-868-8700
www.coyotecreekpizza.com
Pie-eyed *paesani* head to this colorful Redmond-Kirkland twosome
for "very good" stuffed pizzas, calzones and panini with "creative

flavors" from all over the globe – "for a thrill", try the apple-walnut variation; a "relaxed" atmosphere and "very slow" service round out the picture.

Crash Landing Pizza *Pizza* ▽ 18 | 6 | 16 | $10

Ballard | 702 NW 65th St. (7th Ave.) | 206-706-1480
A genuine "pizza dive" with "cheap", "fast" Philadelphia-style pies, this mostly take-out joint brings a bite of the East Coast to Ballard; while well-fed surveyors "love that crust", grudging graders think its "not worth traveling to" and advise that unless you're in the neighborhood, fuhgeddaboudit.

Crave *American* 20 | 14 | 17 | $26

Capitol Hill | Capitol Hill Arts Ctr. | 1621 12th Ave. (Pine St.) | 206-388-0526 | www.cravefood.com
"Decadent yet homey" New American comfort food comes out of the "tiniest" kitchen at this Capitol Hill Arts Center canteen where the French toast is a hit at breakfast and brunch; elbow-to-elbow seating is de rigueur with the "eye-candy" types who cram inside to take advantage of "good" prices, and seem undeterred by the perennially "haphazard" and "aloof" service.

Crémant *French* 24 | 20 | 22 | $44

Madrona | 1423 34th Ave. (Union St.) | 206-322-4600 | www.cremantseattle.com
Madrona *confreres* say *mais oui* to this "true French bistro" where "simple but full-flavored" traditional fare is served in "American-sized" portions, set off by a "brilliant sparkling wine (*cremant*) list"; wood accents and chichi wallpaper evoke the "Left Bank" – and as for the "noisy" "din" (thanks to cement floors and walls), most voters insist that "the food" and "service make up for it."

Crepe de France 🄢🄜 *French* ▽ 23 | 13 | 19 | $12

Pike Place Market | Pike Place Mkt. | 93 Pike St. (1st Ave.) | 206-624-2196
It's "not quite France", but surveyors still swoon over this "fun and fresh" crêperie in the Pike Place Market serving "wonderful" Gallic-y roll-ups in "sweet" and "savory" varieties; "red walls" and hip photographs make the cafeteria-style service (and paper-and-plastic place settings) more palatable.

Crocodile Cafe *Eclectic* 14 | 10 | 13 | $17

Belltown | 2200 Second Ave. (Blanchard St.) | 206-448-2114 | www.thecrocodile.com
Best known as a nighttime "mecca" for rock "music aficionados", this Belltowner serves cheap, Eclectic "good home cooking" for weekday lunch and dinner (and Sunday brunch); the fashionably "unhelpful" staff may be one reason a cadre of critics insists it's better to come here "for a drink and a show" only.

Crow Restaurant & Bar *American* 23 | 20 | 20 | $36

Queen Anne | 823 Fifth Ave. N. (bet. Aloha & Valley Sts.) | 206-283-8800
The "relatively cheap" New American "standard bearers" (including a "must"-try prosciutto-wrapped roast chicken) are "always good"

	FOOD	DECOR	SERVICE	COST

at this "trendy" Queen Anner with "industrial" wood-and-metal decor; the vibe is "simple, fun and loud", though some say a "laid-back" staff means "astronomical waits" for food; P.S. chef-watchers coo over the "cool" seating at the "kitchen bar."

Crumpet Shop, The *Bakery*

24	11	20	$9

Pike Place Market | Pike Place Mkt. | 1503 First Ave. (Pike St.) | 206-682-1598

"Terrific" "made-to-order" crumpets, scones and loads of toppings make this "homey" Pike Place Market "nook" the toast of the town and a "great place to plan your day"; "wonderful" sandwiches on homemade bread are on offer for lunch, and "lovely" service adds to the allure; N.B. no dinner.

🇿 Crush 🅈🅼 *American*

26	23	23	$54

Madison Valley | 2319 E. Madison St. (23rd Ave.) | 206-302-7874 | www.crushonmadison.com

A "tiny" century-old Madison Valley house coddles this "sleek", "modern" New American that "lives up to the hype" courtesy of celeb chef Jason Wilson's "daring" cookery that will "please any foodie", plus a "surprisingly rounded" wine list; the kitchen's "delicious thrills" make up for "expensive" tariffs, "uncomfortable chairs", service that can be "inconsistent" and a crush for the "hard-to-get" reservations.

Cucina De-Ra *Italian*

▽ 21	21	19	$43

Belltown | 2801 Western Ave. (Clay St.) | 206-728-9600 | www.cucinadera.com

This Belltown ristorante with Elliott Bay vistas serves "tasty" Northern Italian with "clean flavors" in a "very nice" modern dining room near the Seattle Art Museum Sculpture Park; pickier sorts say that service is "quirky" and "given the prices" they "expect more" from the food.

Cutters Bayhouse *Pacific NW/Seafood*

19	20	20	$38

Pike Place Market | 2001 Western Ave. (Virginia St.) | 206-448-4884 | www.cuttersbayhouse.com

Situated near the Pike Place Market, this "old reliable" fish house lands "classic" Pacific NW seafood "for all palates" at a "good price point"; set against a backdrop of "primo" "panoramic" views of Elliott Bay and Mt. Rainier, it's no surprise that there are "busloads of tourists", but "you'll never be treated as an outsider" by the "friendly, unassuming" staff; P.S. at the popular happy hour, the bar scene "hops."

Cyclops *Eclectic*

17	17	14	$21

Belltown | 2421 First Ave. (Wall St.) | 206-441-1677 | www.cyclopsseattle.com

"Ask for the Elvis booth" at this "funky" Belltown icon (and "young crowd" hangout) that boasts "good" burgers, Eclectic pub dishes, a nice "selection of beers on tap" and what some call "best hangover breakfast in town"; service is a "little slow", but that goes with the "comfortingly casual" territory.

	FOOD	DECOR	SERVICE	COST
	-	-	-	I

Dahlak Eritrean *Eritrean*

South Seattle | 2007 S. State St. (20th Ave.) | 206-860-0400

At this warm, unassuming eatery, suppers use injera bread to scoop up spicy, slow-cooked Eritrean stews; the daunting exterior (it's in a windowless former strip club off Rainier Avenue S.) opens to a simple blue-and-white room fragrant with incense and cheap eats.

	FOOD	DECOR	SERVICE	COST
	25	24	23	$48

☒ Dahlia Lounge *Pacific NW*

Downtown | 2001 Fourth Ave. (Virginia St.) | 206-682-4142 | www.tomdouglas.com

Tom Douglas' pricey flagship may be "not as exciting as it once was", but it remains an über-popular "perennial favorite" proffering "delightful" Pacific NW cuisine that riffs on Asian flavors, capped off by the "world's best coconut cream pie" (available to go at Douglas' bakery next door); there's "lots of space" between tables in the "whimsical", "gorgeous" Downtown room, so settle in for a "comfortable sit-down meal" served by a "thoughtful" staff.

	FOOD	DECOR	SERVICE	COST
	25	23	24	$58

☒ Daniel's Broiler *Steak*

Lake Union | 809 Fairview Pl. N. (Valley St.) | 206-621-8262
Leschi | Leschi Marina | 200 Lake Washington Blvd. (Alder St.) | 206-329-4191
Bellevue | Bellevue Pl. | 10500 NE Eighth St. (Bellevue Way) | 425-462-4662
www.schwartzbros.com

Replete with "stylish" steakhouse ambiance, "phenomenal" views and "accommodating" service, this beefy trio sates with "big, juicy" prime cuts and fresh seafood; "expense-account" prices mean it's a "great place" for "business" dinners or "more formal nights out" – though un-millionaires can get a bargain at happy hour by "making a dinner" out of the "well-priced" apps.

	FOOD	DECOR	SERVICE	COST
	21	21	21	$44

Dash Point Lobster Shop *Seafood*

Tacoma | 6912 Soundview Dr. NE (Markham Ave.) | 253-927-1513

Lobster Shop, The *Seafood*

Tacoma | 4015 Ruston Way (McCarver St.) | 253-759-2165
www.lobstershop.com

Seafood that's "don't-let-it-escape" fresh, plus "magnificent" views of Puget Sound, qualify this dynamic seafood duo in Tacoma and Dash Point as "worth the drive"; "close but pleasant quarters" and "wonderful" service make for a "quiet, relaxing" meal.

	FOOD	DECOR	SERVICE	COST
	15	17	15	$34

DC's Steakhouse *Steak*

Sammamish | 22850 NE Eighth St. (228th Ave.) | 425-898-1231

Sammamish carnivores say this "close-to-home" steakhouse from the Metropolitan Grill's owners is "good", if a "little generic"; though service can be "inconsistent", its "huge portions" are reasonably priced.

	FOOD	DECOR	SERVICE	COST
	17	11	15	$17

Delfino's Chicago Style Pizza *Pizza*

University Village | University Vill. | 2631 NE University Vill. (25th Ave.) | 206-522-3466

Windy City pie-*sani* say this University Village hideaway is "close to the real deal", "satisfying nostalgic pangs for Chicago deep-dish" amid decor reminiscent of a "sterile cafeteria"; the pizzas "take forever to cook" and the "servers are slow", so those looking for a "quick fix" phone their orders in ahead.

Deluxe Bar & Grill ◑ *Burgers* 16 | 14 | 18 | $19

Capitol Hill | 625 Broadway E. (Roy St.) | 206-324-9697

Capitol Hill's "landmark" neighborhood pub has been serving burgers and comfort food "to please the beast inside" for 45 years; a "rotation" of "interesting" beers on tap makes it a "quintessential" place to "hang after work" or "late in the evening", with "friendly", "quick" service, even when busy.

De Nunzio's 🖼 *Italian* ▽ 16 | 14 | 14 | $26

Pioneer Square | 102 Cherry St. (First Ave.) | 206-343-9517 | www.luigislittleitaly.com

Inside an over-the-top, tchotchke-filled underground Pioneer Square space (it used to be Luigi's Grotto), the effervescent Luigi De Nunzio sets out his take on Italian fare; though graced with a notable wine list, vexed voters say the food is disappointing and geared toward "people who don't know any better."

Desert Fire *Southwestern* 16 | 19 | 16 | $24

Redmond | Redmond Town Ctr. | 7211 166th Ave. NE (Bear Creek Pkwy.) | 425-895-1500 | www.desertfiremex.com

A "fine" "standby", this Redmond Southwesterner is set in a rustic room with a center stage "fire pit", and patio seating in warm weather; the "decent" dishes can lean toward "more style than substance" say surveyors who call it "mediocre Mex", though most agree that the Sunday brunch is a "great value."

Dick's Drive-In ◑⊄ *Burgers* 19 | 8 | 17 | $7

Capitol Hill | 115 Broadway E. (bet. Denny Way & John St.) | 206-323-1300
Crown Hill | 9208 Holman Rd. NW (15th Ave.) | 206-783-5233
Wallingford | 111 NE 45th St. (bet. 1st & 2nd Aves.) | 206-632-5125
Lake City | 12325 30th Ave. NE (Lake City Way) | 206-363-7777
Queen Anne | 500 Queen Anne Ave. N. (Republican St.) | 206-285-5155
www.ddir.com

"Deluxe" burgers, "bargain-basement" prices and "lightning-fast" service ("order, pay and move") have kept this "everlasting institution" of a fast-food chain popular for more than 50 years; hand-cut "real potato" fries and "scrumptious" shakes round out the "guilty-but-wonderful" menu that draws "lines" right up to 2 AM closing time, when you'll find a "bunch of characters" (from post-prom kids to famous techies, depending on the location) cramming in a final "grease" fix.

Die BierStube *German* - | - | - | I

Roosevelt | 6106 Roosevelt Way NE (bet. 61st & 62nd Sts.) | 206-527-7019 | www.diebierstube.com

Every day is Oktoberfest at Roosevelt's raucous German pub where barrels of "really good" on-tap and bottled Bavarian *bier* "you won't find anywhere else" are the draw; the "hot, soft pretzels", "brats" and other beer garden fare don't win many raves, but still college students (who can handle the decibels) come to party.

Diggity Dog's Hot Dogs & Sausages *Hot Dogs*
▽ 19 | 8 | 17 | $8

Wallingford | 5421 Meridian Ave. N. (bet. 54th & 55th Sts.) | 206-633-1966

This "neighborhood joint" in Wallingford goes to the dogs with "good, cheap" frankfurters and a "toppings bar" that makes it "worth the trip"; its low-key storefront quarters are perfect for a pig-out, so "have more than one or two" declare delineators doggedly, and don't forget to "bring your Tums."

Dilettante Chocolates *Dessert*
23 | 15 | 15 | $14

Capitol Hill | 416 Broadway E. (bet. Harrison & Republican Sts.) | 206-329-6463 ◑

Downtown | Westlake Ctr. | 400 Pine St. (4th Ave.) | 206-903-8595

www.dilettante.com

"Skip the main courses" and get right to the "amazing desserts" at these "divine" coffee and sweets "destinations" that are "elegant ways to round out" an evening; the "pricey" handmade chocolates are "rich, rich, rich", the decor is "intimate" (though the Downtowner is new, some say the older Capitol Hill outpost is "in need of an update") and if the service "struggles to keep up", the "treats" "make up for it."

Dinette ⌧ Ⓜ *European*
24 | 19 | 23 | $35

Capitol Hill | 1514 E. Olive Way (bet. Denny Way & Howell St.) | 206-328-2282 | www.dinetteseattle.com

On Capitol Hill, this "tiny" "gem" "shines" with "lovely" rustic European fare, including an entire "toast" menu of "fresh and savory" ingredients buoyed by bread; you'll feel like you entered your "best friend's kitchen" in the "homey, yet arty" environs, complete with "attentive" servers who add to the "overall wonderful feel."

Dish, The Ⓜ⌖ *American*
23 | 14 | 23 | $14

Fremont | 4358 Leary Way NW (8th Ave.) | 206-782-9985

There's always a crowd at this "bustling" Fremont breakfast joint that pours "excellent" coffee in "unmatched" mugs while you wait for your chance at "huge" all-American egg dishes like the "slacker *especial*", and sides of "great" bacon and scones; the line moves fast thanks to "friendly" servers happy to rush diners who've "lingered long enough, thank you very much"; N.B. no dinner.

NEW Dish D'Lish Ⓜ *American*
18 | 13 | 16 | $15

Ballard | 5136 Ballard Ave. NW (bet. Ione Pl. & 20th Ave.) | 206-789-8121 | www.kathycasey.com

Chef Kathy Casey brings "creative", "high-class" New American takeout to Ballard with this "casual", cafeteria-style "wonderful addition" to the neighborhood; penny-pinchers posit it's "pricey" for newfangled "comfort food", but others are content to pay for such "consistent quality."

	FOOD	DECOR	SERVICE	COST

NEW Divine **M** *Greek* — — — M

Maple Leaf | 7919 Roosevelt Way NE (bet. 79th & 80th Sts.) |
206-526-7919 | www.divineseattle.com

This "gem" of a *taverna* serves "innovative", "simply delectable"
modern Greek specialties in a vintage Maple Leaf house with a serious "neighborhood feel"; the value is so "good" and service so
friendly that admirers aver it's "like having your best friend open
a trendy restaurant."

NEW DiVino *Italian* ∇ 22 21 23 $31

Ballard | 5310 Ballard Ave. NW (Vernon Pl.) | 206-297-0143 |
www.divinoseattle.com

"Everyone seems to be having fun" in this Italian wine bar that brings
"Euro-hipness" to Ballard with more than 300 labels (and a "narrow
by-the-glass list"), "fun" cocktails and "surprisingly good" Northern
Italian small plates; while some view the "space-aged", "Milan run-
way" decor as "trying too hard", most find the vibe "friendly"
and prices "reasonable."

Dixie's BBQ **S≠** *BBQ* 22 8 12 $13

Bellevue | 11522 Northup Way (116th Ave. NE) | 425-828-2460
Bellevue 'cue-seekers "satisfy a basic craving" at this lunch-only
former auto shop where the focus is on "tasty" BBQ pork and beef
with "all the fixin's", washed down with classic "good ol' Southern
sweetened tea"; there's a show each time staffers cajole patrons to
"meet the man" – a dollop of "volcanic" hot sauce dropped on their
food ("bring your hankies").

Dragonfish Asian Cafe **◑** *Pan-Asian* 20 18 17 $28

Downtown | Paramount Hotel | 722 Pine St. (8th Ave.) | 206-467-7777 |
www.dragonfishcafe.com

Inside the Paramount, this trendy Downtown Pan-Asian draws par-
tiers and theatergoers with "pleasing twists" on "dependable" fusion fare, especially at the post–10 PM happy hour when prices are
seriously discounted; its "lively", Eastern-influenced atmosphere is
"fun" for "hanging out with friends", as long as they don't mind the
often "indifferent" service.

Duke's Chowder House *Seafood* 18 16 17 $27

Lake Union | 901 Fairview Ave. N. (south shore of Lake Union) |
206-382-9963 **◑**
Green Lake | 7850 E. Green Lake Dr. N. (bet. Ashworth & Densmore Aves.) |
206-522-4908
West Seattle | 2516 Alki Ave. SW (58th St.) | 206-937-6100
Kent | 240 W. Kent Station St. (bet. 1st Ave. & 2nd Pl.) | 253-850-6333
NEW Tacoma | 3327 Ruston Way (bet. N. Alder & N. 40th Sts.) |
253-752-5444 **◑**
www.dukeschowderhouse.com

"Stick to the basics" – i.e. "yummy" chowders that are always "fresh
and hot" – at this "solid" chain of "casual" seafood "classics" that
are still going strong; few fuss over the "slightly overpriced" tabs
after factoring in its "aah"-inspiring views.

	FOOD	DECOR	SERVICE	COST

Dulces Latin Bistro 🅢 Ⓜ *Eclectic* `21` `22` `23` `$39`

Madrona | 1430 34th Ave. (bet. Pike & Union Sts.) | 206-322-5453 |
www.dulceslatinbistro.com

Latin lovers say it's a "mystery" why this "quiet and classy" Madrona
Eclectic "isn't full every night", given its "consistently good" Eclectic
Spanish-Mexican-French-Italian bistro cuisine, a wine list "unri-
valed among peers" and "phenomenal" staff; only a few suggest that
it's "a bit overpriced."

Earth & Ocean *American* `22` `22` `21` `$48`

Downtown | W Hotel | 1112 Fourth Ave. (Seneca St.) | 206-264-6060 |
www.earthocean.net

"Hip" describes the food, vibe and crowd at this New American in
Downtown's, yes, "hip" W Hotel; admirers applaud chef Adam
Stevenson's "imaginative" cuisine – "especially the 'ocean' options" –
but some complain that the "sophisticated" if "stark" space ("feels
like a hotel lobby . . . oh wait, it is") "can be a little loud" when the
"sizzling bar" heats up, and most find tabs "pricey."

Eats Market Café Ⓜ *American* `20` `15` `16` `$21`

West Seattle | Westwood Vill. | 2600 SW Barton St. (26th Ave.) |
206-933-1200 | www.eatsmarket.com

"Hidden in a corner" of Westwood Village Mall, this West Seattle
American dishes out "comfort food" including deli staples like
Reuben sandwiches and matzo ball soup; the "diner setting" and
surrounding big box stores belie the number of dishes that are
homemade, so while service "can take forever" and some find tabs
"slightly high", the food keeps believers "coming back."

Eggs Cetera's `15` `11` `15` `$17`
Blue Star Cafe & Pub *American*

Wallingford | 4512 Stone Way N. (bet. 45th & 46th Sts.) | 206-548-0345
This publike "neighborhood" American slings coffee and omelets in
the morning and beer and Black Angus burgers at night, making it a hit
with Wallingford's "I'm-too-lazy-to-cook" crowd; the "unorganized"
service is as "relaxed" as the atmosphere, but at least the tabs are
"relatively cheap", especially at the popular weekend brunch.

El Camino Ⓜ *Mexican* `21` `20` `19` `$27`

Fremont | 607 N. 35th St. (Evanston Ave.) | 206-632-7303 |
www.elcaminorestaurant.com

The combo of "sophisticated" "regional" Mexican food ("the freshest fish tacos this side of the Yucatán") and "fabulous margaritas"
keeps this "festive" Fremonter filled with chile-hounds and imbibers; whether hoping for a table inside or on the heated year-round
"back deck", compadres know to come "early to beat the rush."

El Chupacabra *Mexican* `▽ 14` `14` `14` `$16`

Greenwood | 6711 Greenwood Ave. N. (bet. 67th & 68th Sts.) |
206-706-4889

"One step above your favorite dive", this "cheap" Greenwood
Mexican serves "spicy salsa" and "powerful" margaritas in an old

bungalow whose Day of the Dead decor hits some "gritty" kitsch notes; when the "noise level" annoys, amigos opt for the "great deck" where you can "watch the world go by"; as for service, critics say "prepare to be ignored."

		FOOD	DECOR	SERVICE	COST

☑ Elemental@Gasworks ● ☒ Ⓜ Eclectic | 26 | 18 | 23 | $45 |

Lake Union | 3309 Wallingford Ave. N. (Northlake Way) | 206-547-2317 | www.elementalatgasworks.com

More like an "avant-garde dinner party" than a restaurant, this "tiny" Lake Union Eclectic pairs chef Laurie Riedeman's "sublime", "well-priced" fare with "abundant" wine, but "no wine list" – instead, co-owner/"sommelier-waiter-host" Phred Westfall chooses the vinos and "flawless" cocktails (and only sometimes reveals what's in the pour); "it's not for everyone", but those willing to "relinquish control" call it a "dazzling" "gem" and only regret that "no reservations" mean it's often "impossible to get in."

El Gallito *Mexican*   ▽ 18 | 9 | 13 | $17 |

Capitol Hill | 1700 20th Ave. (Madison St.) | 206-329-8088

Look for the old pink building with the rooster (el gallito himself) sign to find this "undiscovered" Capitol Hill Mexican "joint"; while some crow about its "authentic" flavors ("home of the best chiles rellenos north of the border"), others squawk that the food is "pretty standard" and the interior is "lacking."

☑ El Gaucho ● *Steak* | 25 | 24 | 26 | $65 |

Belltown | 2505 First Ave. (Wall St.) | 206-728-1337
Tacoma | 2119 Pacific Ave. (S. 21st St.) | 253-272-1510
www.elgaucho.com

"It doesn't get better" than these "dark", "swanky" "supper clubs" with "impeccably cooked" steaks that "melt in your mouth" and "old-school" "flambé kebabs and desserts"; the waiters are "beyond extraordinary", whether serving "business" tycoons in Tacoma, or the "NBA stars" and local hotties who fill up the mink-upholstered booths in Belltown – just know that the "fun" is so "expensive" some recommend "taking out a loan" before you come.

El Greco Ⓜ *Mediterranean* | 23 | 17 | 21 | $24 |

Capitol Hill | 219 Broadway E. (John St.) | 206-328-4604 | www.elgrecorestaurant.com

"Tucked away" on Capitol Hill's trendy Broadway, this "best-kept secret" entices with "simple, interesting" midpriced Med meals and a "to-die-for" weekend brunch; an "attentive" staff keeps thing moving in the "tiny", "romantic" space that gets "packed" at peak times.

Elliott Bay Brewery & Pub ● *Pub Food* | 20 | 15 | 19 | $20 |

West Seattle | 4720 California Ave. SW (Alaska St.) | 206-932-8695 | www.elliottbaybrewing.com

A West Seattle standby, this "friendly" microbrewery is "always hopping" with "wall-to-wall" beer hounds who lap up the "excellent" fresh ales and stouts along with organic burgers and "good quality" American grub; expect a "typically" "noisy and dark" "neighborhood pub" setting.

	FOOD	DECOR	SERVICE	COST

Z Elliott's Oyster House *Seafood*   23 | 18 | 21 | $38

Seattle Waterfront | 1201 Alaskan Way (Seneca St.) | 206-623-4340 |
www.elliottsoysterhouse.com

"Snapping fresh" oysters "are the stars" at this "just plain fun" seafood "institution" on the Seattle Waterfront where the finfish is "reliable" (though some say "overpriced") too; inside, diners perch on
ringside seats at the bar where a "national prize-winner" shucks bi-
valves, while outside eaters sit on the patio, "disregard the mobs" of
"tourists" and enjoy "outstanding" views of Elliott Bay and the ferries.

El Puerco Lloron *Mexican*   21 | 12 | 13 | $13

Pike Place Market | 1501 Western Ave. (Pike Pl. Hillclimb) | 206-624-0541 |
www.elpuercolloron.com

"You'll swear you're south of the border" as you "watch the cook
make tortillas" at this popular "authentic" "hole-in-the-wall" on the
Hillclimb at the Pike Place Market; the no-frills "kitschy" setting is
pure "taqueria meets school cafeteria" but fans don't care since it's
"cheap" and one of the "best" Mexican spots around.

El Ranchon Family   ∇ 15 | 12 | 21 | $16
Mexican Restaurant Ⓢ *Mexican*

Magnolia | 3416 W. McGraw St. (34th Ave.) | 206-281-9233

This affordable Magnolia neighborhood joint serves "basic"
"Americanized" Mexican in a cheery cantina setting; some say the
service outshines the food, especially given that the waiters "love"
children, making this a good spot for "kids of any age."

Emmett Watson's Oyster Bar *Seafood*   22 | 13 | 15 | $20

Pike Place Market | Pike Place Mkt. | 1916 Pike Pl. (bet. Stewart &
Virginia Sts.) | 206-448-7721

"Hard to find, but worth it", this "dive" in the Pike Place Market
shells out "vast varieties" of "fresh and fabulous" seafood; "popular" with tourists as well as local "chowderheads", the waiters really
"know their oysters", and the "old-time" "grungy-casual" decor is
part of the lure.

Endolyne Joe's *American*   19 | 19 | 18 | $26

West Seattle | 9261 45th Ave. SW (Wildwood Pl.) | 206-937-5637 |
www.chowfoods.com

"You never get bored" at this "fun", "noisy" brick eatery on the old
West Seattle trolley line (named for one of the now-defunct route's
conductors) with its lineup of "solid" American regional breakfasts,
burgers and an "eclectic rotating menu" (e.g. Little Italy, The
Islands); the cutesy decor revolves with the revolving theme, and
the service, while sometimes "slow", is "friendly"; P.S. frequent diners get "tokens" for future discounts.

NEW Entre Nous Ⓢ *French*   - | - | - | M

Downtown | 216 Stewart St. (bet. 2nd & 3rd Aves.) | 206-905-1633 |
www.entrenousseattle.com

Provence specialties like ratatouille and Gallic fondue are the raison
d'être of this French hideaway on Downtown's Stewart Street; the

vivid black, white and red setting gets a turbo boost at night when old movies are screened on the ceiling.

Essential Baking Company *Bakery*

| 23 | 14 | 14 | $13 |

Wallingford | 1604 N. 34th St. (Woodlawn Ave.) | 206-545-0444
Madison Park | 2719 E. Madison St. (27th Ave.) | 206-328-0078
www.essentialbaking.com

Chatty neighbors cram into this "lively" Wallingford and Madison Park duo of bakeries to nosh on the "most exquisite carbs" including "incredible" pastries, "wonderful" bread and "fabulous sandwiches"; quibblers find the staff at the counter somewhat crummy and even downright "surly", yet undeterred acolytes keep coming, and even "break down in tears if the chocolate croissants are sold out."

Ⓩ Etta's Seafood *Pacific NW/Seafood*

| 24 | 19 | 22 | $39 |

Pike Place Market | 2020 Western Ave. (bet. Lenora & Virginia Sts.) | 206-443-6000 | www.tomdouglas.com

Owner Tom Douglas is an *Iron Chef* winner, so it's no wonder "tourists flock" to his flashy fish spot by the Pike Place Market for "terrific", if "pricey", Pacific NW seafood – including crab cakes that even locals laud as "disks of crustacean heaven"; the room swims with "elegance", stylish "Seattle funk" and "enthusiastic" service.

Ⓩ Eva *American*

| 26 | 21 | 24 | $37 |

Green Lake | 2227 N. 56th St. (Kirkwood Pl.) | 206-633-3538

At this "top-notch" "little neighborhood" bistro, chef Amy McCray wins raves for her "classy", "innovative" New American fare with a focus on "organic" and "homemade" ingredients; the "cozy", "romantic" atmosphere and "impressively reasonable" prices have many whispering that it's the "best-kept secret" in Green Lake.

Ezell's Famous Chicken *American*

| 24 | 5 | 13 | $11 |

Capitol Hill | 501 23rd Ave. (Jefferson St.) | 206-324-4141
South Seattle | 11805 Renton Ave. S. (72nd Ave.) | 206-772-1925
Lynnwood | 7531 196th St. SW (bet. 74th & 76th Aves.) | 425-673-4193
www.ezellschicken.com

Fans of "as-good-as-it-gets" Southern-style fried chicken flock to these "legendary" no-frills American "take-out joints" (Oprah's a fan) where the regular and "spicy" birds are "worth a heart attack" – and a bargain, to boot; surveyors squawk that "the service isn't friendly" and "decor doesn't really apply", but hey, "it doesn't matter."

NEW Facing East Ⓜ *Chinese*

| - | - | - | I |

Bellevue | Belgate Plaza | 1075 Bellevue Way NE (bet. 10th & 12th Sts.) | 425-688-2986

Expats and lovers of Taiwanese cuisine line up at this "much needed" "inexpensive" newcomer hidden in Bellevue's Belgate Plaza where hurried servers ferry "interesting" eats and teas to the tables; even though the "benches are uncomfortable" and "don't invite one to linger", it's packed, so come early.

	FOOD	DECOR	SERVICE	COST

Fado Irish Pub *Irish* | 14 | 17 | 14 | $22 |

Pioneer Square | 801 First Ave. (Columbia St.) | 206-264-2700 |
www.fadoirishpub.com

Pioneer Square meets Dublin at this pub serving "classic" Irish victuals for the football/rugby crowd; settle into the "cozy" "nooks" and
order boxty (potato pancakes) and a pint of Black and Tan, or hit the
bar where a "great beer selection" outweighs the "surly" service.

FareStart 🅕 *Pacific NW* | 22 | 18 | 22 | $23 |

Downtown | 700 Virginia St. (7th Ave.) | 206-267-7601 | www.farestart.org

Diners "do good while eating well" at this Downtowner where prom-
inent local chefs train the homeless for restaurant jobs – and turn
out "creative, delicious" Pacific NW fare in the process; open for
lunch on Monday–Friday, dinner is served on Thursdays only and
"sells out" quickly, so reserve ahead since, say regulars, these nighttime meals are some of "Seattle's best dining deals."

FareStart Café @ 2100 🅕 *Deli* | – | – | – | I |

South Seattle | 2100 Bldg. | 2100 24th Ave. S. (Walker St.) | 206-407-2195 |
www.farestart.org

In South Seattle, this cafe (where disadvantaged and homeless "students" get on-the-job culinary experience) serves perhaps the "best
lunch in town" at a "great price" with the proceeds going to a "terrific cause"; expect "right-on" pastries, soups and sandwiches, and
if the service is "slow", "that's the point, it's a training spot."

Feierabend *German* | 18 | 19 | 19 | $21 |

Lake Union | 422 N. Yale Ave. (bet. Harrison & Republican Sts.) |
206-340-2528 | www.feierabendseattle.com

"Get your schnitzel on" at this inexpensive Lake Union German pub
where "basic" *"Deutches"* grub plays second fiddle to the "great
biers" served in "their appropriate glassware"; it draws an "older
crowd" than sibling Die BierStube, and hopsters hail it as a perfect
lunch (beware of getting "soused") or "after-work" "hangout."

Firenze Ristorante Italiano *Italian* | 22 | 16 | 19 | $32 |

Bellevue | Crossroads Mall | 15600 NE Eighth St. (156th Ave.) |
425-957-1077 | www.firenzerestaurant.com

Locals name this "classy" Bellevue white-tableclother one of "the
best Eastside Italians" for its "fabulous" dishes "matched" with a
"wonderful wine selection"; the ambiance is old-world, right down
to the stucco walls and "charming" waiters with "accents", though
some find the prices too new-world "for a strip-mall" spot.

Fish Club *Mediterranean* | 22 | 20 | 20 | $46 |

Seattle Waterfront | Seattle Marriott Waterfront | 2100 Alaskan Way
(bet. Virginia & Wall Sts.) | 206-256-1040 | www.fishclubseattle.com

This "isn't your standard hotel restaurant" coo converts to Todd
English's "expensive" Med mecca in the Seattle Marriott Waterfront
with a "highbrow" menu of "creative", "well-prepared" seafood; the
open, airy dining room and "lovely" patio offer "great views" of Elliott
Bay, a welcome distraction from the "inconsistent" service.

	FOOD	DECOR	SERVICE	COST

5 Point Café ● 🛇 Ⓜ *American* | 19 | 12 | 16 | $15

Belltown | 415 Cedar St. (4th Ave.) | 206-448-9993

With "breakfast, booze and rock 'n' roll" fans ask "how can you go wrong?" at this "cheap", "24-hour" Belltown American "dive" whose slogan – 'alcoholics serving alcoholics since 1929' – is part of the "fun"; "greasy spoon" lovers keep it "packed for brunch" and "late-night", especially when the urge for "a 4 AM gut bomb" hits.

5 Spot ● *American* | 20 | 17 | 19 | $22

Queen Anne | 1502 Queen Anne Ave. N. (Galer St.) | 206-285-7768 | www.chowfoods.com

"My spot" crow enthusiasts about this "old-school" Queen Anne American serving "comfort food supreme" as well as a "rotating" "geographically themed" menu (e.g. Memphis, Brooklyn, Bourbon Street); the staff is sometimes "friendly", sometimes "indifferent", but all agree that "breakfast is the bomb" with lines "out the door", so "get there early" to beat the "stroller patrol."

Flo 🛇 *Japanese* | 25 | 22 | 24 | $37

Bellevue | 1150 106th Ave. NE (12th St.) | 425-453-4005 | www.florestaurant.com

"Modern", "beautiful sushi" and Asian-inspired cooked food draw Bellevue-ites to this "diamond in the rough" where "plenty of sake" flows and the "omakase (chef's choice) is phenomenal"; the "small portions" don't come cheap, but epicures happily pay to dine in the "calm", "stylish" digs.

🛿 Flying Fish ● *Asian/Seafood* | 25 | 21 | 22 | $44

Belltown | 2234 First Ave. (Bell St.) | 206-728-8595 | www.flyingfishseattle.com

This "posh" Asian seafood "institution" soars thanks to chef-owner Chris Keff's "fabulous" fish "creations" served by a "well-informed" staff; "lively" crowds of beautiful people fill up the "bright, airy" room where, in summer, the garage-door facade flips open to turn the space alfresco; P.S. while the main dining room can be "very noisy", the "mezzanine is more conducive to conversation."

Fort St. George *Japanese* | - | - | - | I

International District | 601 S. King St. (6th Ave.) | 206-382-0662

Modish and cheap, this IDer appeals to young scenesters craving "Japanese bachelor food", including a "fun" roster of spaghettis topped with "steak, curry" or garlic mayonnaise; those who can find it – up a flight of stairs and easy to miss from street level – say a meal here is like "eating in east Asia" even though Safeco Field is only a few blocks away.

Four Seas *Chinese* | ▽ 17 | 11 | 16 | $19

International District | 714 S. King St. (8th Ave.) | 206-682-4900 | www.fourseasrestaurant.com

Dishing out "decent" Cantonese dim sum, this destination has been an ID "standby" for years, with a dining room large enough for big parties (there's free parking too) and a "very friendly" staff; detractors deride the "tired" 1960s decor, but nonetheless, the bar scene continues to "rage."

Four Swallows 🅂🅼 *Italian/Pacific NW* 25 | 21 | 23 | $42
Bainbridge Island | 481 Madison Ave. N. (Madrona Way) | 206-842-3397 | www.fourswallows.com
Some call this Pacific NW–Italian "the best dining" on Bainbridge Island with "consistently well-prepared" food that "emphasizes seasonal ingredients over fancy fusion recipes"; in a "lovely" 19th-century farmhouse, it's full of vintage wood and high-backed booths that encourage "romance", even if the service can be "spotty."

14 Carrot Cafe *American* 18 | 10 | 16 | $17
Eastlake | 2305 Eastlake Ave. E. (Lynn St.) | 206-324-1442
Its "friendly" hippie vibe and what some locals call the "best breakfast around" draw crowds to this "kitschy", low-cost Eastlake American, which serves lunch too (but no dinner); insiders tout the "chalkboard" "daily specials" and say come early "on weekends" or prepare to wait "on the sidewalk and watch the neighborhood go by."

Fox Sports Grill *American* 12 | 17 | 14 | $23
Downtown | 1522 Sixth Ave. (bet. Pike & Pine Sts.) | 206-340-1369 | www.foxsportsgrill.com
"Beer, burgers, ballgames and babes" abound at this Downtown "happening" American sportsbar where there's "not a bad seat in the house, assuming you can find one"; while it gets "packed" on game days, most say the merely "good" food can't compete with the "flat-panel wide-screen TVs."

Frankie's Pizza & Pasta *Italian* 20 | 15 | 20 | $20
Redmond | 16630 Redmond Way (166th Ave.) | 425-883-8407 | www.frankiesredmond.com
Families cram into this "casual", "noisy" Redmond Italian for affordable, "good pizza and pastas" that change "seasonally"; locals' only grouse is that "more seating would help", since on weekends you have to "stand in line forever" to get in.

**Fremont Classic
Pizzeria & Trattoria** *Italian* ▽ 19 | 16 | 19 | $21
Fremont | 4307 Fremont Ave. N. (43rd St.) | 206-548-9411 | www.fremontpizza.com
A "solid choice" for Fremonters seeking "simple" Italian fare and "good" pizza, this "unpretentious, intimate" neighborhood spot is no-frills; it's also "seldom crowded", making it a fine choice for a spontaneous meal.

**Friday Harbor
House Restaurant** *Pacific NW/Seafood* - | - | - | E
Friday Harbor | Friday Harbor House Inn | 130 West St. (1st St.) | 360-378-8455 | www.fridayharborhouse.com
This high-end seafooder at the boutique-y Friday Harbor House Inn proffers Pacific NW cuisine (including "excellent breakfasts") prepared with fresh local produce and fish, giving diners a true taste of

the island; the appealing space looks out on the harbor, though a minority warns that it's trying "too hard."

From Russia With Love 🛇 *Russian* | - | - | - | I |

Bellevue | 1424 156th Ave. NE (15th St.) | 425-401-2093 | www.frwldeli.com

Lunch at this cornucopia of "true Eastern European foods" in Bellevue's Crossroads Mall is a tasty trip, featuring imported smoked whitefish, borscht and cabbage rolls; just know that while the staff is fluent in happy gesturing, there's "little English spoken here."

Frontier Room, The ●🛇Ⓜ *BBQ* | 19 | 16 | 18 | $25 |

Belltown | 2203 First Ave. (Blanchard St.) | 206-956-7427 | www.frontierroom.com

"Pretty good" barbecue right in the "heart" of trendy Belltown draws a stampede of buckaroos to this "fun" Wild West-y "joint" housed in a former geezer "dive"; wet blankets claim the food is only "so-so", but most admit it's at least "decent" for "happy hour and weekend drinks."

Fuji Sushi *Japanese* | ▽ 25 | 19 | 22 | $21 |

International District | 520 S. Main St. (bet. 5th & 6th Aves.) | 206-624-1201

"Sit at the sushi bar" or in the sleek dining room for "wonderful, fresh seafood" at this the IDer that may be "one of the best" "reasonably priced" Japanese eateries in town; "lunch bento boxes" are a "value" and extras like tatami rooms and "free parking" (a rarity in the neighborhood) make responders croon "I love this place."

Fu Man Dumpling House 🛇Ⓜ *Chinese* | ▽ 19 | 6 | 17 | $16 |

Greenwood | 14314 Greenwood Ave. N. (bet. 143rd & 144th Sts.) | 206-363-0526

Greenwooders jonesing for a "dumpling fix" search out the bright yellow sign marking this strip-mall Chinese near Shoreline Community College; "authentic" potstickers and "simple" noodle dishes allow folks to stay local rather than "fight traffic" to get to the International District, but be aware that it's small and gets "jammed" on weekends.

F.X. McRory's *Seafood/Steak* | 17 | 19 | 16 | $30 |

Pioneer Square | 419 Occidental Ave. S. (King St.) | 206-623-4800 | www.fxmcrorys.com

Seahawks and Mariners fans pile into this surf 'n' turf "crowd-pleaser" "before the game" for prime rib, "great oysters" and "scotch and bourbon" from the packed and "noisy" bar; the dark-wood and marble decor also works for "business lunches", though a few former fans think "it's seen better days."

Galanga Thai Cuisine 🛇 *Thai* | ▽ 24 | 14 | 19 | $21 |

Tacoma | 1129 Broadway (bet S. 11th & S. 13th Sts.) | 253-272-3393 | www.galangathai.com

In Tacoma's bustling financial district, this colorful cafe pleases with "great", "fast" Bangkok bites, including perennial favorites like pad Thai, at a fair price; the simple setting has an upscale Southeast Asian "diner" feel.

	FOOD	DECOR	SERVICE	COST

Galerias *Mexican* `22` `23` `20` `$25`

Capitol Hill | 611 Broadway E. (Mercer St.) | 206-322-5757 |
www.galeriasgourmet.net

"Highfalutin Mexican food" that's "flavorful" and "innovative" makes
this "pricey", "upscale" cantina a Capitol Hill "favorite"; handmade
wooden furniture fills the dining room, which is presided over by a
staff that will "entertain you while you eat"; P.S. the "tequila selection" on its own "deserves a visit."

Garage ◐ *American* `13` `19` `15` `$18`

Capitol Hill | 1130 Broadway E. (Madison St.) | 206-322-2296 |
www.garagebilliards.com

This he-man "hangout" in a retro former Capitol Hill garage serves
"good" American bar food and beer to patrons as they play pool,
making it a "great setting for meeting with friends"; those who are
less bowled over snipe that the "overpriced" grub is only "decent."

🆕 Gaudi *Spanish* `-` `-` `-` `M`

Ravenna | 3410 NE 55th St. (bet. 34th & 35th Aves.) | 206-527-3400

The kitchen at this "authentic" Ravenna Spaniard "really knows
what it's doing" thanks to an expat chef who whips up "fantastic"
"tapas and paella"; uneven service doesn't detract from the
Southern *España* decor, which "swaddles you in coziness", making
this a "refuge" on "Seattle's gray days."

Gelatiamo 🅢 *Dessert* `24` `14` `18` `$9`

Downtown | 1400 Third Ave. (Union St.) | 206-467-9563 |
www.gelatiamo.com

"Gelati buonissimi" cheer aficionados of the "superb" gelato at this
Downtown parlor that also offers "very good" Italian pastries, sandwiches and coffee; the space has "just a few tables", so it's "not the
most inviting", ergo most munchers take the "pricey"-but-"worth-
it" sweets "to go."

Geneva 🅢 Ⓜ *Continental* `25` `24` `25` `$48`

First Hill | 1106 Eighth Ave. (Spring St.) | 206-624-2222 |
www.genevarestaurant.com

Avid devotees call this "elegant" First Hill Continental the "best
restaurant you've never heard of", citing its "excellent", "very
traditional" cuisine; a classic chandelier hangs over the "romantic",
old-world domed room, and "gracious" service and a convenient location (near the Convention Center and Paramount Theater) round
out the picture.

Ⓩ Georgian, The *French/Pacific NW* `26` `28` `26` `$65`

Downtown | Fairmont Olympic Hotel | 411 University St. (bet. 4th &
5th Aves.) | 206-621-7889 | www.fairmont.com

This "regal" dining room in the Downtown Fairmont Olympic Hotel
has been a "special-occasion" destination for more than 80 years,
boasting "high-high ceilings", "crystal chandeliers", 11 shades of
yellow paint on the walls and a No. 1 Decor ranking in this Survey;
its "impeccable" staff doles out "superb" French–Pacific NW break-

fasts, lunches, dinners and a "not-to-be-missed" tea service; just be sure to bring your gold card – "or grandma, when she's in town and buying"– since it's "expensive, but worth every penny."

Geraldine's Counter ☒ American   20 | 18 | 18 | $18

Columbia City | 4872 Rainier Ave. S. (Ferdinand St.) | 206-723-2080 | www.geraldinescounter.com

"Upscale" "comfort food" sates the hungry who line up at this "bright, cheery" American in Columbia City for "homestyle" breakfasts (lunch and dinner are served too); the sibling of El Greco, it's popular with families, especially since the "dinerlike" digs and "friendly staff" "ooze congeniality."

Gilbert's Main Street Bagel Deli *Deli*   22 | 13 | 16 | $17

Bellevue | 10024 Main St. (bet. 100th & 102nd Aves.) | 425-455-5650

"Wonderful" soups, salads, sandwiches and bagels are the ticket at this meet-and-greet with portions so big "you'll have to bring home half"; Bellevue-ites wait on line to nosh in the "cramped" interior or "sit out" on the Main Street patio, and though gripers groan over the fares ("I'd rather have more moderate prices and smaller portions"), "that doesn't keep people away."

Glo's *American*   26 | 14 | 16 | $15

Capitol Hill | 1621 E. Olive Way (bet. Belmont & Summit Aves.) | 206-324-2577

"Crowded, cheap, greasy" breakfasts – the way they're "intended" to be – abound at this "tiny" American "institution" on Capitol Hill where "it's obvious from the taste" that "everything is made with fresh ingredients"; despite "service that gives new meaning to slow" and "kind of pricey" tabs, crowds line up on weekends, so "expect to wait on the curb for a while"; N.B. no dinner.

Goldbergs' Famous Delicatessen *Deli*   17 | 13 | 12 | $19

Bellevue | 3924 Factoria Blvd. SE (40th Ct.) | 425-641-6622 | www.goldbergsdeli.com

This Bellevue Jewish deli proffers "East Coast–style" sandwiches and specialties, including what may be the "best Reuben in town"; though it's "family-friendly" and they "try hard", a few kvetch about the "absurd waits" and others groan "oy vey", "this is anything but authentic."

Gordito's Healthy   22 | 10 | 17 | $12
Mexican Food *Mexican*

Greenwood | 213 N. 85th St. (Greenwood Ave.) | 206-706-9352

Amigos gorge on "burritos as big as your head" and "bursting with flavor" at this "cheap, quick and tasty" Greenwood Mexican "hole-in-the-wall"; the "fun" vibe makes it a 'happy place to dine", but as for service and decor "there's not much to say."

Gordon Biersch *American*   14 | 15 | 15 | $24

Downtown | Pacific Pl. | 600 Pine St. (6th St.) | 206-405-4205 | www.gordonbiersch.com

Downtown power shoppers and movie-goers grab "above-average" American "pub food" at this "busy" chain brew house in Pacific

	FOOD	DECOR	SERVICE	COST

Place mall with a menu so "large" most find "something to please their palate"; though service can lag, the "comfortable" space draws crowds "after work", when it morphs into a "meat market" scene.

Grazie Ristorante Italiano *Italian*

| 20 | 17 | 20 | $28 |

Bellevue | Factoria Square Mall | 3820 124th Ave. SE (bet. I-90 & I-405) | 425-644-1200
Bothell | 23207 Bothell-Everett Hwy. (232nd St. SE) | 425-402-9600
Tukwila | 16943 Southcenter Pkwy. (Strander Blvd.) | 206-575-1606
www.grazieristorante.com

An Italian "mainstay", this trio with a "cozy mom-and-pop feel" pleases with "fresh" fare and a "wine list that's strong as well"; the "quaint, faux Tuscan" decor and "friendly but slow" staff don't charm a minority that finds the whole experience "mediocre."

Greenlake Bar & Grill *American*

| 16 | 14 | 16 | $22 |

Green Lake | 7200 E. Green Lake Dr. N. (72nd St.) | 206-729-6179 | www.greenlakebarandgrill.com

This "cheap and cheerful" American across from Green Lake sets out "solid" "bar-and-grill" offerings boosted by "good drinks" and a "great" twice-a-day happy hour; sun worshipers hie to the "outdoor seating" and "watch the motivated people jog around the lake", though the less enthused yawn "don't expect to be dazzled."

Green Leaf *Vietnamese*

| 25 | 13 | 23 | $18 |

International District | 418 Eighth Ave S. (Jackson St.) | 206-340-1388

"Wowza" say fans of this Vietnamese "foodie" nook in the ID with "consistently wonderful" dishes featuring a "mélange of novel and familiar flavors" – at a "low price" to boot; the "amiable" staff "truly cares" and keeps things running smoothly, even when the tiny, bamboo-heavy space is "crowded", i.e. any "Friday or Saturday night."

Hale's Ales Brewery & Pub *Pub Food*

| 17 | 16 | 17 | $20 |

Fremont | 4301 Leary Way NW (bet. 7th & 8th Aves.) | 206-782-0737 | www.halesales.com

Fremonters "meet friends" for "hearty portions" of "solid" eco-friendly "pub grub" at this affordable and "down-to-earth" brew-house with "always great" English-style ales; the atmo is "typical brewery" punctuated by local artwork and the "smell of brewing beer", though in warm weather, ale aficionados know to "snag spots" on the patio.

Ⓩ Harvest Vine, The *Spanish*

| 26 | 21 | 22 | $44 |

Madison Valley | 2701 E. Madison St. (27th Ave.) | 206-320-9771 | www.harvestvine.com

For "great foodie entertainment", perch at this Basque bastion's "convivial" "copper-topped" bar and "watch the chefs" prepare "in-tricate", "extremely flavorful" tapas that are "so good" "you can't stop ordering"; the all-Spanish wine list is "extensive", and the staff "paces itself with military precision"; the "only negative", say most, is that the "very small" Madison Valley venue is "too hard to get into."

| | FOOD | DECOR | SERVICE | COST |

Hattie's Hat *Diner* | 16 | 13 | 15 | $16 |

Ballard | 5231 Ballard Ave. NW (Vernon Pl.) | 206-784-0175
This century-old Ballard "landmark" is a go-to spot for "hangover breakfasts" and "late-night dinners" of "decent" American "comfort food"; the prices are mild, the "dive" decor is part of the "fun" and though the staff can be "abrupt", fans still "hope it never changes"; P.S. "check out the fish tank" in the "newly jazzed-up" back room.

Z Herbfarm, The M *Pacific NW* | 29 | 26 | 28 | $163 |

Woodinville | 14590 NE 145th St. (Woodinville-Redmond Rd.) | 425-485-5300 | www.theherbfarm.com
A "once-in-a-lifetime dining experience", the "sublime" cuisine at this "over-the-top" "oasis" – ranked No. 1 for Food and Service – features "vibrant herbs" in a nine-course Pacific NW prix fixe menu (plus paired wines) that changes nightly, delivered by an "impeccable" staff; a "quick tour" of the garden is de rigueur before settling into the "lush" dining room in Woodinville's wine belt, and the bill, while "huge", covers four or five hours of "exquisite" eating; N.B. a new chef took the reins post-Survey.

Hi Life *American* | 18 | 20 | 18 | $22 |

Ballard | 5425 Russell Ave. NW (Market St.) | 206-784-7272 | www.chowfoods.com
Part of the Chowfoods mini-empire, this New American has "cool" digs (in a converted firehouse) and a menu that "rotates" every few months to cover the world's wine regions (to wit, France, Italy); though it strikes some as "not the best" of the food chain, its "friendly service" and "lively, casual" vibe easily pleases Ballard's "kiddie-clientele."

NEW Hills' Food & Wine M *Pacific NW* | ∇ 23 | 18 | 20 | $30 |

Shoreline | 1843 NW Richmond Beach Rd. (bet. 15th & 20th Aves.) | 206-542-6353
Lauded as a "real find" with "fresh fish", steaks and what may be "the best seafood chowder ever", this Pacific NW bistro "raises" the stakes in the under-restaurant-served Shoreline; the "understated" setting includes a "wine bar" tucked in the corner and outdoor seating – a welcome refuge on weekends, when it "can get crowded."

Hilltop Ale House *American* | 22 | 16 | 19 | $19 |

Queen Anne | 2129 Queen Anne Ave. N. (Boston St.) | 206-285-3877 | www.seattlealehouses.com
Regulars "kick back and relax" at this Queen Anne American where "swell sandwiches", "fantastic" homemade soups and "solid" fish tacos pair nicely with the "fabo" local "craft brews"; the "loud but energizing" scene evokes "English pub houses", making it an "excellent", inexpensive "neighborhood hangout"; N.B. 21-and-over only.

Hi Spot Cafe *American* | 23 | 18 | 18 | $16 |

Madrona | 1410 34th Ave. (Union St.) | 206-325-7905 | www.hispotcafe.com
In a "homey" Madrona Victorian that looks like "grandma's house" (full of "cute little alcoves"), this "funky" "coffee shop" hits the spot

with "excellent" American breakfasts and brunches – the scones are "to die for" – served by a "personable" staff; "get there early" advise enthusiasts who note that the lines are "long" "on Saturdays and Sundays"; N.B. no dinner.

Ho Ho Seafood Restaurant ◑ *Chinese/Seafood*

FOOD	DECOR	SERVICE	COST
21	10	17	$21

International District | 653 S. Weller St. (bet. Maynard & 7th Aves.) | 206-382-9671

The standard menu at this ID Chinese seafooder goes on for pages, but adventurous eaters know to fish from the "chef's specials" instead, for "well-prepared", "nicely spiced" fare that "tastes authentic"; a recent remodel spiffed up the formerly "spartan" room – a popular perch for nightclubbers, since it stays open until 1 AM.

Honey Bear Bakery & Cafe *American*

FOOD	DECOR	SERVICE	COST
▽ 21	14	16	$16

Lake Forest Park | Third Place Books | 17171 Bothell Way NE (Ballinger Way) | 206-366-3330 | www.thirdplacebooks.com

Nestled in Third Place Books, this "comfy", inexpensive Lake Forest Park cafe has a "homey" bent, beckoning to browsers with "sweet and savory" American goodies made from "fresh ingredients"; "sandwiches big enough to split" are a hit, and the "cakes are better than my mom used to make" effuse enthusiasts.

Honey Court ◑ *Chinese*

FOOD	DECOR	SERVICE	COST
▽ 23	8	14	$15

International District | 516 Maynard Ave. S. (bet. King & Weller Sts.) | 206-292-8828

Sinophiles salute the "fabulous" dim sum made from ingredients "at their peak of freshness" on offer at this ID "longtimer" where Chinese classics share cart space with a "few things" that might "scare" timid palates; "very reasonable" tabs and late-night hours add to the allure.

Hosoonyi Restaurant *Korean*

FOOD	DECOR	SERVICE	COST
▽ 24	9	12	$18

Lynnwood | 23830 Hwy. 99 (bet. 238th & 240th Sts.) | 425-775-8196

"Down-home" fare like "sizzling hot plates" and "great" seafood pancakes make this Lynnwood favorite a contender for "best Korean" around; families and groups gravitate to the "tatami room", though the rest of the decor scores low and even some who "love the food, hate the service", which can "have attitude."

NEW Hot Dish *American*

FOOD	DECOR	SERVICE	COST
-	-	-	I

Ravenna | 2255 NE 65th St. (bet. Ravenna & 23rd Aves.) | 206-524-5555 | www.hotdishseattle.com

At this sophomore "neighborhood" American, Ravenna locals warm up with "comfort foods" like "chicken and mashed potatoes" served by a "friendly" staff; despite having "real art on its walls", some insist the space "could use some sprucing up."

House of Hong ◑ *Chinese*

FOOD	DECOR	SERVICE	COST
21	13	17	$20

International District | 409 Eighth Ave. S. (Jackson St.) | 206-622-7997 | www.houseofhong.com

This ID "classic" is on a roll with "fab" Cantonese flavors and "can't-be-beat" dim sum; even service that sometimes sports a "what's taking you so long?" attitude and atmosphere "reminiscent of an operating room" don't deter regulars who are drawn in by the surplus of space and cheap tabs.

	FOOD	DECOR	SERVICE	COST

Hunan Garden *Chinese*
▽ 18 | 12 | 15 | $18

Bellevue | 11814 NE Eighth St. (116th Ave.) | 425-451-3595
"Good to very good" Chinese served in "big portions" is the hallmark of this Bellevue standby on busy NE Eighth Street, a strip-mall oasis for drive-time diners seeking a "good value"; live seafood tanks are the decor highlight, and for the hurried, there's takeout.

Hunt Club *Pacific NW*
22 | 24 | 23 | $50

First Hill | Sorrento Hotel | 900 Madison St. (Terry St.) | 206-343-6156 | www.hotelsorrento.com
"Dark" and mahogany-paneled, this First Hill "sleeper" (in the 1900 Sorrento Hotel) has a "classy", "gentleman's club" feel, making it a "haven on rainy nights" when sippers drink by the "lobby fireplace"; breakfasts are "elegant", and Pacific NW dinners, featuring a "good selection of game and fish", are "pricey but worth it."

Ibiza ●🅑Ⓜ *Spanish*
▽ 19 | 21 | 17 | $35

Pioneer Square | 528 Second Ave. (bet. James St. & Yesler Way) | 206-381-9090 | www.ibizadinnerclub.com
Watch the glitterati watch each other at this popular, and some say "pretentious", Pioneer Square Spanish *restaurante* in a chic, "modern" room fronted by "classy", "tall windows"; the cocktail scene is lively, the martinis "wonderful" and the small plates "great for sharing", though some suggest hoarding the larger selections "all for yourself."

icon Grill *American*
20 | 23 | 20 | $35

Downtown | 1933 Fifth Ave. (Virginia St.) | 206-441-6330 | www.icongrill.net
Diners "feel like they fell down the rabbit hole" at this "whimsical" Downtown "date place" packed with "Seattle art glass" and "kitsch"; the kitchen turns out "large portions" of American "comfort food" that surveyors say is "slightly expensive" (you're "paying for the decor"); P.S. don't miss the "amusing reader board" out front and the "giggle"-worthy TVs in the ladies' room.

Il Bistro ● *Italian*
23 | 23 | 23 | $41

Pike Place Market | Pike Place Mkt. | 93A Pike St. (1st Ave.) | 206-682-3049 | www.ilbistro.net
A "favorite" for 35 years, this dreamy grotto "under the Pike Place Market" continues to tempt with "attentive" service and "terrific" Italian fare incorporating "fresh local" ingredients from the bounty upstairs; with a "low-lit" dining room, it's "*très* romantic", and since the "mellow" bar is open late, it's also prime for "swanky drinks."

Il Fornaio *Italian*
20 | 19 | 20 | $34

Downtown | Pacific Pl. | 600 Pine St. (6th Ave.) | 206-264-0994 | www.ilfornaio.com
This "light-filled" "rustic" Italian (the northern link in a California chain) in Downtown's Pacific Place is a convenient "oasis" for sho-

paholics whose "feet hurt", offering "high-quality", "eclectic" staples in three different venues: a "calming" sit-down ristorante, a "casual" bakery/cafe for a "quick espresso and a pastry", and downstairs, a "great value" risotteria; alas, due to its "popularity", there's "not enough staff."

I Love Sushi *Japanese*

<table>
<tr><td>23</td><td>15</td><td>19</td><td>$30</td></tr>
</table>

Lake Union | 1001 Fairview Ave. N. (Mercer St.) | 206-625-9604
Bellevue | 11818 NE Eighth St. (118th Ave.) | 425-454-5706
Bellevue | 23 Lake Bellevue Dr. (118th Ave.) | 425-455-9090
www.ilovesushi.com

"Always reliable" Japanese fare reels 'em in at this trio showcasing "super-fresh" raw and cooked fish; "omakase" at the bar and a "wow" of a view at the Lake Union location make it even better, though quibblers say service "can be surprisingly slow"; as for the decor, "what the atmosphere lacks", the "sushi delivers."

☑ Il Terrazzo Carmine ⑤ *Italian*

<table>
<tr><td>27</td><td>25</td><td>26</td><td>$47</td></tr>
</table>

Pioneer Square | 411 First Ave. S. (bet. Jackson & King Sts.) | 206-467-7797 | www.ilterrazzocarmine.com

"Veal is spoken fluently" at Carmine Smeraldo's "gold standard" Italian, a "classic and classy" Pioneer Square "institution" that's always packed with "politicians" and "power-lunchers" seeking "superb" traditional cuisine; "tucked away" in an office building's courtyard, its "lovely" Tuscan dining room calms the spirit, as does the "flawless" service; all in all, expect to have a "lush, sexy and unsurpassed" experience.

NEW Inchin's
Bamboo Garden *Chinese/Indian*

<table>
<tr><td>-</td><td>-</td><td>-</td><td>I</td></tr>
</table>

Redmond | 16564 Cleveland St. (bet. 164th & 166th Aves.) | 425-284-0670 | www.bamboo-gardens.com

Modern yellow walls and Asian art mark this affordable Redmond strip-mall purveyor of Chinese-Indian cuisine, a combo that's "common back in India"; expats working the software gig nearby come "craving" the "Chicken 65 and Chicken Manchurian" from "their school days."

India Bistro *Indian*

<table>
<tr><td>23</td><td>14</td><td>19</td><td>$19</td></tr>
</table>

Ballard | 2301 NW Market St. (Ballard Ave.) | 206-783-5080 | www.seattleindiabistro.com

"Excellent quality" Northern Indian food thrives at this "crowded" Ballard blue storefront proffering "piping hot naan" and "fresher, lighter takes" on the standards; a "quick and pleasant" staff enlivens the "recently remodeled" ("though poorly lit") interior, and the "buffet lunch – what a value!"

☑ Indochine
Asian Dining Lounge ⑤ *Asian Fusion*

<table>
<tr><td>23</td><td>27</td><td>18</td><td>$32</td></tr>
</table>

Tacoma | 1924 Pacific Ave. (bet. 19th & 21st Sts.) | 253-272-8200 | www.indochinedowntown.com

"Gorgeous" decor – a tableside "pond", blown-glass artwork and window tables with a view of the passing Pacific Avenue parade –

makes this Asian fusion palace a Tacoma winner; the "creative", "intensely flavorful" food is "artistically presented", and though service can be "sketchy", most call the whole experience "stylish to the hilt."

Z Inn at Langley M *Pacific NW* | 27 | 23 | 22 | $90 |

Langley | Inn at Langley | 400 First St. (Anthes Ave.) | 360-221-3033 | www.innatlangley.com

Not just a meal, an "experience" awaits Seattleites who ferry to this Whidbey Island inn for Matt Costello's "exquisite" and expensive six-course prix fixe that focuses on "fresh, honest" Pacific NW market finds; in the "intimate" kitchen/dining room, gourmands get a gander of the chatty chef at work, and may end up so sated that they'll want to "stay the night"; N.B. only open Thursdays–Sundays in the summer, and Fridays–Sundays the rest of the year.

Ivar's Acres of Clams *Seafood* | 20 | 15 | 17 | $24 |

Seattle Waterfront | Pier 54 | 1001 Alaskan Way (Madison St.) | 206-624-6852 | www.ivars.net

"Clams, clams and more clams" plus "fantastic" views are the draw at this "über-casual" Waterfront Pacific Northwesterner specializing in "oh-so-yummy" seafood; opened in 1938 as an aquarium, it's still a "Seattle tradition" with "lots of character and characters" to entertain tourists and natives seeking a "nice dinner after a ferry ride"; P.S. penny-pinchers opt for "fish 'n' chips on the fly" from the cheaper outdoor Fish Bar.

Ivar's Mukilteo Landing *Seafood* | 21 | 22 | 22 | $29 |

Mukilteo | Mukilteo Ferry Dock | 710 Front St. (Mukilteo Spdwy.) | 425-742-6180 | www.ivars.net

This "fun", "inexpensive" fin-farer is a go-to spot for its "famous clam chowder and fish 'n' chips" say locals who laud the "traditional seafood" menu as a whole; to boot, its location on the Mukilteo ferry dock means there are "wonderful" Puget Sound views.

Ivar's Salmon House *Pacific NW/Seafood* | 19 | 21 | 19 | $30 |

Lake Union | 401 NE Northlake Way (north shore of Lake Union) | 206-632-0767 | www.ivars.net

Inside a cedar "Indian longhouse" replica "right on" Lake Union, this Seattle "landmark" has been serving "affordable" Pacific NW "fish a'grillin' on the alder fire" for 38 years; "Native American artifacts" warm the room, and the lakeside patio delivers "the sights, sounds and smells" of the city; P.S. the "walk-up window" in front is a "favorite" for a quick bite.

Izumi M *Japanese* | 25 | 15 | 19 | $32 |

Kirkland | Totem Lake West Ctr. | 12539 116th Ave. NE (124th St.) | 425-821-1959

Kirkland sushi sharks "swear that the fish was caught today" at this unassuming, "wonderfully authentic" Japanese joint in the Totem Lake West mall; though its "decor could use some updating", the welcoming staff "always" has "a smile", especially the "courteous, erudite" chef.

	FOOD	DECOR	SERVICE	COST

Jack's Fish Spot *Seafood* 20 | 10 | 17 | $13

Pike Place Market | Pike Place Mkt. | 1514 Pike Pl. (Post Alley) |
206-467-0514 | www.jacksfishspot.com

"There nothing like" this Pike Place Market "fishmonger" for a "basic",
"bargain" lunch of "fish 'n' chips" and "fresh" seafood plucked right
off the ice in front of you; owner Jack Mathers is a local celeb, so the
seats at the small counter fill up fast, leaving "standing room only."

Jade Garden ❶ *Chinese* 23 | 9 | 14 | $17

International District | 424 Seventh Ave. S. (King St.) | 206-622-8181
A contender for "best dim sum" in a dim sum–obsessed town, this
tiny IDer offers "incredibly fresh" plates and steamer baskets from
the carts, as well as "family-style" Chinese fare from the kitchen; the
service is "swift" and prices "screamingly affordable", so few care
about the nothing-special decor.

☒ JaK's Grill *Steak* 26 | 17 | 23 | $38

Laurelhurst | 3701 NE 45th St. (37th Ave.) | 206-985-8545
West Seattle | 4548 California Ave. SW (bet. Alaska & Oregon Sts.) |
206-937-7809
Issaquah | 14 Front St. N. (Sunset Way) | 425-837-8834
www.jaksgrill.com

This "outstanding" neighborhood trio – proffering "superb" corn-fed
Nebraska beef in "dark", "noisy" settings – "competes with the big
steakhouses at half the price"; its "friendly" staff "really knows the
food and wine", just be aware that the "no-reservations policy"
means "long" waits for a table.

Jalisco Mexican Restaurant *Tex-Mex* 17 | 12 | 19 | $17

Capitol Hill | 1467 E. Republican St. (15th Ave.) | 206-325-9005
Georgetown | 8517 14th Ave. S. (Cloverdale St.) | 206-767-1943
Green Lake | 1205 NE 65th St. (12th Ave.) | 206-524-1707
Lake City | 12336 31st Ave. NE (Lake City Way) | 206-364-3978
Queen Anne | 122 First Ave. N. (bet. Denny Way & John St.) |
206-283-4242 ☒
Queen Anne | 129 First Ave. N. (bet. Denny Way & John St.) |
206-282-1175 ❶
Kirkland | 115 Park Ln. (Lake St.) | 425-822-3355
Bothell | 1715 228th St. SE (bet. 15th & 19th Aves.) |
425-481-3931

For 30 years this local chain has been dishing out "hearty" Tex-Mex
tastes "done right" to crowds who call it "the Mexican *Cheers*"
(where "everybody knows your name"); factor in "inexpensive"
prices and "fast" service, and few mind that the decor is as "cheesy"
as the quesadillas.

Joeys ❶ *Eclectic* 19 | 22 | 20 | $34

Lake Union | 901 Fairview Ave. N. (Aloha St.) | 206-749-5639
NEW **Bellevue** | 800 Bellevue Way NE (8th St.) | 425-637-1177
www.joeysmedgrill.com

Twentysomethings seeking the "singles and date scene" flock to
these "snappily" decorated Lake Union–Bellevue sites (part of a
Canadian chain) where a "surprisingly good" Eclectic menu is

served until 2 AM; they "seem to have hired every hottie in the region", which may be why some surmise it's "known more for the staff than the food."

	FOOD	DECOR	SERVICE	COST

Jones, The *American*
20 | 16 | 18 | $25

Maple Leaf | 8824 Roosevelt Way NE (bet. 88th & 89th Sts.) | 206-527-5480 | www.thejonesbistro.com

Maple Leaf locals jonesing for "cranked up" New American hit this "fine neighborhood hangout" for "carefully prepared" upscale meals "without the high-end cost"; there's been "so much buzz it should sound like a beehive" inside the somewhat "lacking" digs, but mostly you'll hear sighs over the "sloooow" service and lip-smacks once the food arrives.

Jones Barbeque *BBQ*
22 | 9 | 15 | $15

Columbia City | 3810 S. Ferdinand St. (Rainier Ave.) | 206-722-4414 Ⓜ
SODO | 2454 Occidental Ave. (Lander St.) | 206-625-1339 Ⓩ
Bellevue | Crossroads | 15600 NE Eighth St. (156th Ave.) | 425-746-3955
www.jonesbarbeque.net

The "meaty, memorable" ribs and "standout" brisket "never disappoint" at these three bastions of BBQ, just be sure to have a "fire hose" handy "if you order the spicy sauce"; "funky" digs and a "friendly" staff complete the "down-home" experience; N.B. no liquor.

Judy Fu's Snappy Dragon *Chinese*
19 | 11 | 17 | $21

Maple Leaf | 8917 Roosevelt Way NE (89th St.) | 206-528-5575 | www.snappydragon.com

It's "handmade noodle" "heaven" at this "legendary" Chinese in Maple Leaf serving "solid", though "not authentic", fare to customers who come from "all parts of Seattle"; the simple, "cozy" room gets packed, making "carryout" an attractive option, and due to the homemade dough, it's "a bit pricier" than your average dumpling joint.

Julia's *American*
16 | 15 | 14 | $19

Capitol Hill | 300 Broadway E. (Thomas St.) | 206-860-1818
Wallingford | 4401 Wallingford Ave. N. (44th St.) | 206-633-1175
NEW Queen Anne | 1825 Queen Anne Ave. N. (bet. Blaine & Howe Sts.) | 206-282-0680
Issaquah | 375 Gilman Blvd. NW (7th Ave.) | 425-557-1919
www.eatatjulias.com

"Creative takes" on breakfast draw weekend crowds to this "kid-friendly" American foursome that also serves "down-home" lunches and dinners; "slow service" and prices that seem high "for the quality" have more than a handful deeming the experience merely "ordinary."

Kabob House Ⓜ *Pakistani*
▽ 23 | 5 | 11 | $18

Greenwood | 8202 Greenwood Ave. N. (82nd St.) | 206-782-3611

"Authentic" Pakistani plates are "made to order" at this Greenwood "hole-in-the-wall" that even Indian expats call "one of the best" around; there may be little decor to speak of, but at least there's a clay tandoori oven, which puts out "great homemade naan."

	FOOD	DECOR	SERVICE	COST

Kabul Afghan Cuisine *Afghan*

| 25 | 18 | 23 | $25 |

Wallingford | 2301 N. 45th St. (Corliss Ave.) | 206-545-9000 |
www.kabulrestaurant.com

"Amazing "Afghan cuisine is the hallmark of this Wallingford longtimer known for its "excellent" "vegetarian and meat" dishes and "gentle" spicing that "makes taste buds sing"; old maps and "haunting" photos of Afghanistan decorate the walls, and the "very friendly" vibe is enhanced by sitar music on Tuesdays and Thursdays.

Kallaloo ⊠ *Caribbean/Creole*

| - | - | - | I |

Columbia City | 3820 S. Ferdinand St. (Rainier Ave.) | 206-760-7766 |
www.kallalooseattle.com

At this Caribbean-Creole joint in Columbia City, "good" food (including callaloo greens and jerk pork chop) is complemented by "reasonably priced" island libations like coconut water and rum punch; accordion windows and ceiling fans add to the breezy, laid-back plantation feel.

Kaosamai *Thai*

| - | - | - | I |

Fremont | 404 N. 36th St. (Phinney Ave.) | 206-925-9979 |
www.kaosamai.com

The bright paint on the outside is as colorful as the "fresh and flavorful" food inside this "excellent", cheap Fremont Thai that "rises above the rest"; its "large deck" is a pleasure on "summer evenings", and delivery is offered, as well.

Karam's
Lebanese Cuisine ⊠ Ⓜ *Lebanese*

| ▽ 19 | 14 | 16 | $22 |

Capitol Hill | 340 15th Ave. E. (bet. Harrison & John Sts.) | 206-324-2370 |
www.garlicsauce.com

On Capitol Hill this "family-run" lair has been dishing out "flavorful" Lebanese fare for over 20 years, much of it infused with an "addictive" signature garlic sauce; though the restaurant is "a bit hidden" on 15th Avenue East's bustling Restaurant Row, boosters say "it should be known", despite its "kind of drab" interior.

Kasbah Ⓜ *Moroccan*

| - | - | - | M |

Ballard | 1471 NW 85th St. (bet. 15th & Mary Aves.) | 206-788-0777 |
www.kasbahmoroccanrestaurant.com

This "elegant" Ballard oasis lures with billowy tents and ottoman seats that harken "straight back to the casbah", an experience made even more "magical" on weekends when belly dancers perform; the "delicious" Moroccan cuisine is a bargain (especially the $25 five-course feast), and service is "friendly."

Kauai Family Restaurant ⊠ Ⓜ *Hawaiian*

| ▽ 21 | 9 | 15 | $13 |

Georgetown | 6324 Sixth Ave. S. (Michigan St.) | 206-762-3469 |
www.kauaifamilyrestaurant.com

It's "like eating at the best plate-lunch place" on the "islands" say surveyors who've supped at this "friendly" Georgetown purveyor of "soulful" Hawaiian chow, including "loco moco" and the "requisite spam" at prices that "can't be beat"; the decor is "nothing fancy" and clockwatchers say service is "a bit slow", but hey, aren't we on beach time?

Kau Kau Barbeque Market *Chinese*

24	6	15	$17

International District | 656 S. King St. (Maynard Ave.) | 206-682-4006
It's all "about the meat" hanging in the window at this low-key ID Chinese spot where the barbecue duck and pork are "fresh" and "delicious"; though there are tables in back, most order "takeout" at the window inside the front door and can't resist "digging into it on the drive home."

Kells Irish Restaurant & Pub *Irish*

17	20	19	$23

Pike Place Market | Pike Place Mkt. | 1916 Post Alley (bet. Stewart & Virginia Sts.) | 206-728-1916 | www.kellsirish.com
This "clubby and pubby" hideaway down a "quaint alley" in the Pike Place Market is "what an Irish bar in America should be", chock-full of "solid", inexpensive Emerald Isle fare (think shepherd's pie and sausage rolls) and "a great pint" of Guinness; the old-world atmosphere attracts "boisterous gatherings", and the nightly Eireophile music is "fantastic."

Kidd Valley *Burgers*

18	8	14	$10

Green Lake | 4910 Green Lake Way N. (Stone Way) | 206-547-0121
Northgate | Northgate Mall | 418 NE Northgate Way (bet. 3rd & 5th Aves.) | 206-306-9516
North Seattle | 14303 Aurora Ave. N. (143rd St.) | 206-364-8493
Queen Anne | 531 Queen Anne Ave. N. (bet. Mercer & Republican Sts.) | 206-284-0184
Ravenna | 5502 25th Ave. NE (55th St.) | 206-522-0890
Bellevue | 15259 NE Bellevue-Redmond Rd. (152nd Ave.) | 425-643-4165
Kirkland | 5901 Lake Washington Blvd. NE (59th St.) | 425-827-5858
Kenmore | 6434 Bothell Way NE (65th Ave.) | 425-485-5514
Lynnwood | Alderwood Mall | 3000 184th St. SW (bet. Alderwood Mall Pkwy. & 36th Ave.) | 425-771-4905
Renton | 1201 Lake Washington Blvd. (Park Dr.) | 425-277-3324
www.kiddvalley.com
"Better than most fast food", the "oh-so-satisfying" "made-to-order" burgers at these chain joints are among the "best in town", especially when paired with "awesome" fries, milkshakes and seasonal specials like Walla Walla onion rings; there's "not much" decor and the service varies, but the price is always right.

Kikuya ⑤ *Japanese*

▽ 22	14	19	$24

Redmond | 8105 161st Ave. NE (bet. 83rd St. & Redmond Way) | 425-881-8771 | www.kikuyausa.com
A Redmond "standard", this Japanese strip-maller serves a "wonderful selection" of "consistently good" sushi, "lunch bento boxes" and family-style dinners; some say the food has "declined" since the ownership changed a few years ago, and opinions are split on the service ("overly chummy" vs. "fantastic").

	FOOD	DECOR	SERVICE	COST

Kimchi Bistro *Korean*
| | - | - | - | I |

Capitol Hill | 219 Broadway E. (Alder St.) | 206-323-4472

"Hidden in a mini-mall" in Capitol Hill's Broadway district, this Korean satisfies with "cheap 'n' yummy" bibimbop and squid hot pots rife with "nicely balanced" flavors; it wins props for being one of the few Seoul food spots within the city limits, even if the decor doesn't garner raves.

Kingfish *Soul Food*
| | 23 | 21 | 20 | $28 |

Capitol Hill | 602 19th Ave. E. (Mercer St.) | 206-320-8757 | www.thekingfishcafe.com

"Put some south in your mouth" at this "top-notch" Capitol Hill purveyor of "haute" and "heavy" soul food that includes "awesome fried chicken" and enormous slices of classic red velvet cake; "always charming" service and "old family photographs" hanging on the walls make for a "welcoming" experience, just expect to "spend a while in the bar waiting" for a table, since reservations are not accepted.

☑ Kisaku Sushi *Japanese*
| | 27 | 20 | 23 | $31 |

Green Lake | 2101 N. 55th St. (Meridian Ave.) | 206-545-9050 | www.kisaku.com

"You cannot go wrong" when you "let the chef" choose your food at this Green Lake Japanese that sates with a "startling array" of "exceedingly fresh", "creative sushi"; serene decor and "reasonable prices" make this a "favorite", affordable haunt for locals who'd rather keep it their "secret."

Krittika Noodles & Thai Cuisine *Noodle Shop*
| | ▽ 22 | 15 | 17 | $17 |

Green Lake | 6411 Latona Ave. NE (64th St.) | 206-985-1182

For "tasty and fast" Thai tastes, Green Lakers turn to this small family-run "neighborhood" noodle nook that's a local "fall-back" spot; the quarters are "low-key" and "minimalist", just like the "reasonable" prices.

Kusina Filipina *Filipino*
| | - | - | - | I |

Beacon Hill | 3201 Beacon Ave. S. (Hanford St.) | 206-322-9433

Hard-to-find Filipino home cooking at a cheap price attracts expats and neighbors to this cheerful, unassuming Beacon Hill venue; a congenial staff and bright orange decor enliven the "cafeteria-style" setup.

☑ La Carta de Oaxaca ☒ *Mexican*
| | 26 | 18 | 18 | $20 |

Ballard | 5431 Ballard Ave. NW (22nd Ave.) | 206-782-8722 | www.lacartadeoaxaca.com

"As authentic as the Mexican hat dance", this "hopping" Ballard storefront wins raves for its "fantastic" Oaxacan mole and other "truly interesting" south-of-the-border fare; the spare, "artistic" surroundings are a "nice departure from the usual" fiesta decor – add in a "homemade salsa" bar and "mean margaritas", and you've got "rather long" lines.

	FOOD	DECOR	SERVICE	COST

La Casa del Mojito *Pan-Latin*
▽ 21 | 15 | 21 | $21

Lake City | 7545 Lake City Way NE (11th Ave.) | 206-525-3162
NEW **University District** | 5253 University Way NE (bet. 52nd & 55th Sts.) | 206-524-4615 **M**
www.lacasadelmojito.com

Fueled by the growing south-of-the-border food craze, this "friendly" Lake City Pan-Latin purveyor proffers *"muy* yummy" and *"muy caliente"* cookery that spans the map "from Cuba to Venezuela"; "sublime" namesake libations help soothe diners' achy ears when the brightly painted but "so small" quarters get "rather loud"; N.B. a University District location opened after surveying was complete.

La Cocina del Puerco *Mexican*
20 | 14 | 13 | $13

Bellevue | 10246 Main St. (bet. 102nd & 103rd Aves.) | 425-455-1151

Hotheads warn that "wussies" won't be able to weather the heat at this festive Bellevue cantina where the Mexican "diner food" is spicy and the cervezas cost a "reasonable" number of pesos; "tin tables" and a "fun" atmosphere make regulars feel "like they're on the beach" "even in winter", though some say the service can do with some warming up.

La Fontana Siciliana *Italian*
24 | 22 | 25 | $38

Belltown | 120 Blanchard St. (bet. 1st & 2nd Aves.) | 206-441-1045 | www.lafontanasiciliana.com

An "old-school jewel", this "quaint" Belltowner offers "basic" Sicilian fare that's "everything good Italian food should be"; the authenticity trickles down to its waiters, who have "real accents", and the atmosphere, which evokes "rustic charm" inside and "romance" in the courtyard (complete with a fountain); N.B. there's live piano music on weekends.

La Isla ● *Puerto Rican*
25 | 17 | 17 | $20

Ballard | 2320 NW Market St. (bet. 22nd & 24th Aves.) | 206-789-0516 | www.laislaseattle.com

"Fabulous" and "spicy", the Puerto Rican plates rate high at this "wonderful, small" restaurant where the "unique" bites are passed out by a "personable" staff; located just half a block away from the happening Ballard bar scene, it gets "packed" with passels of flirting cocktailers who take advantage of the 10 PM-midnight happy hour.

La Medusa ⊠ **M** *Italian/Mediterranean*
25 | 19 | 24 | $35

Columbia City | 4857 Rainier Ave. S. (Edmunds St.) | 206-723-2192 | www.lamedusarestaurant.com

The food is "full of life" at this "casual" Columbia City Italian-Mediterranean serving "succulent" Sicilian fare (just like a "grandmother would make") that's full of "fresh flavors" from the nearby farmer's market; regulars bask in the "unassuming", "airy" room and let the "friendly but not obtrusive" staff guide the way to a "great experience."

	FOOD	DECOR	SERVICE	COST

Lampreia 🅂 Ⓜ *Pacific NW* 　25 | 21 | 22 | $69

Belltown | 2400 First Ave. (Battery St.) | 206-443-3301 |
www.lampreiarestaurant.com

This "amazing" "foodie" favorite wins praise for "gruff" chef Scott
Carsberg's "inventive" Pacific NW-New American cuisine that's "on
a par with the best"; "efficient" waiters work the "subdued"
Belltown room where prices are "spendy, spendy, spendy" say fans
who urge others to "just bring extra credit" or "skim the grocery
budget – but go!"; the less impressed say it's slipping as "high con-
cept combinations often trump the flavors."

☒ Lark Ⓜ *American* 　27 | 23 | 25 | $49

Capitol Hill | 926 12th Ave. (bet. E. Marion & Spring Sts.) |
206-323-5275 | www.larkseattle.com

Sybarites swoon over chef John Sundstrom's "bonanza" of New
American small plates prepared with "stellar" "organic" ingredients –
and a healthy dose of "love"; some say the "simple" "farmhouse"
setting on Capitol Hill can be "uncomfortable" and quibble over tabs
that are "too pricey by the ounce", but all agree on the "engaging",
"gracious" service; N.B. no reserving means there's often a line,
which patrons wait out at the owners' bar next door.

La Rustica Ⓜ *Italian* 　25 | 22 | 22 | $33

West Seattle | 4100 Beach Dr. SW (Carroll St.) | 206-932-3020

"You feel like you're eating at the owner's house" in this "delightful"
midpriced ristorante where the "excellent" Southern Italian fare
melts in your mouth"; an experienced staff keeps things flowing in
the "intimate" (read: "packed together like sardines") West Seattle
dining room, which is balanced, in summer, by "outdoor seating"
with views "onto Puget Sound."

La Vita É Bella *Italian* 　22 | 17 | 21 | $29

Belltown | 2411 Second Ave. (bet. Battery & Wall Sts.) | 206-441-5322 |
www.lavitaebella.us

"Real" midpriced Italian is the come-hither at this "intimate, family-
owned" joint just a block from the Belltown cocktail circuit; a staff
that's "efficient when busy, friendly when time allows" reigns over the
divided room (one side is a pizzeria, the other serves pasta and carne).

Lee's Asian Restaurant *Pan-Asian* 　23 | 6 | 16 | $17

West Seattle | 4510 California Ave. SW (Oregon St.) | 206-932-8209

A West Seattle "icon", this spot offers an "incredibly flavorful" "mix
of various Asian cuisines" that's so "reasonably priced" neighbors
call it "a poor man's Wild Ginger"; with only basic "shopfront" decor,
regulars opt for takeout so often that it's on their "speed dial."

Le Fournil, Ltd. 　21 | 9 | 14 | $12
French Bakery Ⓜ *Bakery/French*

Eastlake | 3230 Eastlake Ave. E. (bet. Fuhrman & Harvard Aves.) |
206-328-6523 | www.le-fournil.com

"Good food, quick service" sums up this Eastlake French bakery and
cafe with baked goods for breakfast and "great baguette sandwiches"

at lunchtime; the simple setting is as "relaxed" as the prices, which carbophiles insist are "lower than other" *patisseries* "in town."

☒ Le Gourmand ☒ Ⓜ *French*   27 | 22 | 26 | $64

Ballard | 425 NW Market St. (6th Ave.) | 206-784-3463

At Bruce and Sara Naftaly's "lovely" French bistro, "fresh herbs grown in the backyard garden" meet traditional Gallic preps that are "extraordinary" even as "you feel your arteries clog"; the "slightly funky, yet charming" Ballard dining room features hand-painted murals and down-filled silk pillows, and the service is "impeccable without being stuffy", making for a "just plain superb" experience.

Lemon Grass *Vietnamese*   ▽ 20 | 15 | 18 | $17

International District | 1207 S. Jackson St. (12th Ave.) | 206-568-8788

This affordable, "hole-in-the-wall" IDer is a "pretty good option" for Vietnamese thanks to a vibe that's slightly more upscale than other Little Saigon sites; expect a simple setting with, appropriately, walls the color of lemongrass.

Le Panier *Bakery/French*   23 | 14 | 16 | $11

Pike Place Market | Pike Place Mkt. | 1902 Pike Pl. (Stewart St.) | 206-441-3669 | www.lepanier.com

"The smell is heavenly" inside this Pike Place Market bakery/cafe serving "strong coffee" (among the "best in Seattle, *sans doute*") and "excellent" French bread, baguettes, sandwiches and pastries; though there are a few "stools to sit on", most locals get "takeaway" and "walk across the market" to eat outside while enjoying the views.

☒ Le Pichet *French*   24 | 19 | 20 | $33

Pike Place Market | Pike Place Mkt. | 1933 First Ave. (Virginia St.) | 206-256-1499 | www.lepichetseattle.com

Boisterous and "delightful", this "itty-bitty" French *demimonde* in the Pike Place Market boasts "wonderful" standards (roast chicken for two is a favorite!) at "reasonable prices"; stylish waifs cram "elbow to elbow" into the "plain-Jane" room and lap up "great wines" by the "*pichet* (pitcher) and *demi-pichet*", barely caring that, *à la* Paris, the staff can "have an attitude."

NEW Local Vine, The ● *Eclectic*   - | - | - | M

Belltown | 2520 Second Ave. (Wall St.) | 206-441-6000 | www.thelocalvine.com

Traditional Seattle coffeehouse comfort (plush chairs and free WiFi) meets high-end Belltown wine bar fare at this temple to the grape that boasts an Eclectic menu; dishes like truffled popcorn, spiced pork tenderloin and gnocchi are paired with a by-the-glass lineup that includes at least one cult wine priced at several hundred dollars per pour – so it's no surprise that the crowd skews slightly older than at the bars nearby.

Lockspot Cafe *American/Seafood*   18 | 10 | 16 | $16

Ballard | 3005 NW 54th St. (32nd Ave.) | 206-789-4865

A Ballard "treasure" since 1920, this American seafood "dive" by the Hiram Chittenden Locks draws "old-timers", "hipsters who've strayed from their usual stomping grounds" and "a few tourists" for "fried fish and cold beer" that all agree is "worth the stop"; locals recommend eating the cheap grub "at the bar", and warn "don't expect gourmet food."

⨯ Lola ◐ Greek   24 | 20 | 23 | $39

Downtown | Hotel Andra | 2000B Fourth Ave. (Virginia St.) | 206-441-1430 | www.tomdouglas.com

Inspired by Tom Douglas' wife's Hellenic heritage, this "chic Greek" (in Downtown's Hotel Andra) forks out "top-notch" eats with a "modern" twist like "octopus for breakfast" and "goat cheese pie"; the "cool" caramel and chocolate walls emit a "relaxed" vibe even when it's "loud and bustling", and the "happening" bar pours "very good ouzos" and Aegean cocktails that "take the edge off your day", if not off the slightly pricey tabs.

Louie's Cuisine of China ◐ Chinese   15 | 14 | 15 | $20

Ballard | 5100 15th Ave. NW (51st St.) | 206-782-8855 | www.louiescuisine.com

Ballardites "grew up with" this inexpensive 31-year-old "icon" specializing in "American-style" Chinese fare that's "good", "if not exciting" and appeals to the "blue-haired" set; a "flashback to the '70s" ("wicker and all"), it's still "always busy" and the bar is a "lounge lizard's heaven."

Louisa's Cafe & Bakery American   21 | 10 | 12 | $12

Eastlake | 2379 Eastlake Ave. E. (Louisa St.) | 206-325-0081 | www.louisascafe.com

Find your hippie self at this "funky" Eastlake "joint" where low-key locals "meet friends" and chitchat while devouring the "wonderful baked goods" and "very special" sandwiches on "homemade bread"; the coffee is "self-serve" and food "ordered at the counter" – just watch out for the "grumpy, no nonsense" staff that surveyors say "could use an attitude adjustment."

Lowell's American   17 | 16 | 15 | $20

Pike Place Market | Pike Place Mkt. | 1519 Pike Pl. (bet. Pike & Pine Sts.) | 206-622-2036 | www.eatatlowells.com

"Tremendous" views of Elliott Bay and "good" American "roadhouse diner fare" sum up the experience at this "crowded" bi-level Pike Place Market "cafeteria", which attracts tired marketers and "tourist throngs"; the waitresses still call patrons 'honey', and at the end of the day it's "nothing fancy", but still a "great value."

Luau Polynesian Lounge Polynesian   15 | 20 | 18 | $21

Green Lake | 2253 N. 56th St. (Kirkwood Ave.) | 206-633-5828 | www.luaupolynesianlounge.com

"Tiki decor" and "flaming pupu platters" lure Honolulu lulus to this "fun", "corny" Green Lake Polynesian beach hut that's "great for groups", albeit a "bit overpriced"; the "killer" Hawaiian cocktails delivered by cuties and dudes (happy hour starts at noon, "love that!") cause some to comment that it may be a "better bar than restaurant."

	FOOD	DECOR	SERVICE	COST

Luigi's Pizza & Pasta *Italian* ▽ 16 | 9 | 19 | $21

Magnolia | 3213 W. McGraw St. (32nd Ave.) | 206-286-9000

Magnolians get their "Italian fix" at this "good", family-owned pizza parlor that's been right on the main drag for the past 14 years; its casual cafe digs matches the reasonable prices.

Luisa's Mexican Grill *Mexican* ▽ 16 | 13 | 19 | $16

Greenwood | 9776 Holman Rd. NW (6th Ave.) | 206-784-4132 | www.luisasmexicangrill.com

"Fresh" "home-spun tortillas" are being made "as you walk in" to this inexpensive Greenwood hacienda known for its "large portions" of "fine Mexican fare"; "swift", "nice" service, a children's menu and family-friendly environs round out the experience.

Luna Park Cafe *American* 15 | 18 | 13 | $15

West Seattle | 2918 SW Avalon Way (Spokane St.) | 206-935-7250

"Burgers, shakes, fries . . . oh my" effuse West Seattleites about this "kicky" '50s-style American "diner" that "makes you feel like a kid again" (it's named for a 1910 amusement park) with "big and satisfying breakfasts" and a "retro" room; though critics carp about the "sometimes slow service" and "standard fare", it still gets "really crowded" on weekends.

Z Lynn's Bistro M *Asian Fusion/French* 26 | 20 | 24 | $40

Kirkland | 214 Central Way (Main St.) | 425-889-2808 | www.lynnsbistro.com

"Wonderful" say aficionados of chef Lynn Tran's "special" Kirkland French-Asian niche where "not-to-be-missed" crêpes and a "lovely" smoked salmon plate are "well worth" the "slightly expensive" prices; "pleasant" service and digs so "quaint" "you'd think you were in Paris" prompt raters to name this "not your typical trendy find."

Machiavelli ⑤ *Italian* 21 | 14 | 20 | $23

Capitol Hill | 1215 Pine St. (Minor Ave.) | 206-621-7941 | www.machiavellis.com

A "diverse" Capitol Hill crowd calls this "rambunctious" ristorante its "mainstay" for "simple but good" "working-class" Italian, including "crave"-worthy pastas and bread that's "to die for", all at a price that's "right"; flickering candles and "tons of windows" keep the space bright, and the service is "as warm as the gnocchi."

Macrina Bakery & Cafe *Bakery/Dessert* 25 | 15 | 16 | $15

Belltown | 2408 First Ave. (Battery St.) | 206-448-4032
Queen Anne | 615 W. McGraw St. (6th Ave.) | 206-283-5900
www.macrinabakery.com

"Delightful" breakfast, brunch and lunch stops, these "wonderful working bakeries" in Belltown and Queen Anne have built a reputation on their "divine" artisan breads, "superb" pastries and fancy "cakes to die for"; the "rustic" eating areas are "very small", so solution-focused surveyors say "get there early" if you want to dine in, and steel yourself for inexplicably "slow" and "sometimes surly" service, even if you're ordering to go.

	FOOD	DECOR	SERVICE	COST

Madame K's Pizza Bistro *Pizza*
21 | 22 | 21 | $20

Ballard | 5327 Ballard Ave. NW (Vernon Pl.) | 206-783-9710
The owners of this "old-time" "former brothel" in Ballard kept the "bordello" theme when they turned it into this "very affordable" "adults-only pizza place", purveying "greasy", "deep-dish" pies with a side of "attitude" – and "chocolate chip" "orgasms" for dessert; the staff of "beguiling wenches" is "fun", "sassy" and scantily clad.

NEW Made in Kitchen 🅜 *Pan-Asian*
∇ 21 | 24 | 21 | $20

International District | 725 S. Lane St. (bet. 7th & 8th Aves.) | 206-625-0909 | www.mikbistro.com
A "great addition" to the "ID dining scene", this "sleek and hip" Pan-Asian venue gets bonus points for its "private tatami room" and extra "area for groups"; at lunchtime the "delightful noodle bowls" draw workers from the Amazon offices nearby, while at night it's a "nice first date" spot.

Madison Park Cafe 🅜 *French*
22 | 19 | 22 | $32

Madison Park | 1807 42nd Ave. E. (Madison St.) | 206-324-2626 | www.madisonparkcafe.ypguides.net
Up a side street in posh Madison Park, this "hidden" neighborhood "bistro" soars with "old-school/new-school French" fare at "reasonable prices"; "fresh flavors", "lovely baked goods" and a "friendly owner" make it a "homey" "brunch destination" on weekends, especially for sun-seekers who "love the outdoor patio."

Madoka 🅜 *Pacific Rim*
20 | 20 | 19 | $42

Bainbridge Island | 241 Winslow Way W. (Madison Ave.) | 206-842-2448 | www.madokaonbainbridge.com
"We weren't expecting to find this jewel on Bainbridge" say surprised visitors about this "sophisticated" Pacific Rim restaurant that's just a "ferry ride from Seattle"; the "beautiful" "Asian-influenced" setting soothes sorts who say the service can be "inexperienced" and fare a bit "overpriced."

Mae Phim Thai Restaurant *Thai*
21 | 5 | 16 | $12

Downtown | 94 Columbia St. (bet. 1st & Western Aves.) | 206-624-2979 | www.maephim.com
"Stand in line" at this tiny Thai spot for "yummy" basics that may be the "best deal Downtown for lunch", and dinner too; the setting is just "so-so" and the service *modus operandi* is "eat it and beat it", so many order takeout (and know to "call ahead" to "avoid having to wait").

Mae's Phinney Ridge Cafe *American*
18 | 16 | 16 | $14

Phinney Ridge | 6412 Phinney Ave. N. (65th St.) | 206-782-1222 | www.maescafe.com
Phinney Ridgers have a "cow", man, over the "gigantic" portions of American "diner" eats ("omelets sized for lumberjacks") served at this breakfast and lunch (but no dinner) "favorite"; the "fun-for-kids", "über-kitschy" bovine decor, including an "udder booth", is nothing less than "moo-valous", just "be prepared to wait for a table" during the weekend stampede.

	FOOD	DECOR	SERVICE	COST

Maggie Bluff's *Burgers* — 18 | 17 | 19 | $23

Magnolia | Elliott Bay Marina | 2601 W. Marina Pl. (Garfield St.) |
206-283-8322 | www.r-u-i.com

Elliott Bay Marina is the "awesome" backdrop for this "casual"
Magnolia pub where families and the "boating crowd" scarf down
"sloppy burgers" while checking out the "superb view" from the
deck; even skeptics who say the "moderately priced" vittles are
"nothing to write home about" admit the "location is stunning";
P.S. there's "dog parking outside" for "your little Sparky."

Malay Satay Hut *Malaysian* — 24 | 11 | 15 | $20

International District | Orient Plaza | 212 12th Ave. S. (bet. Boren Ave. &
Jackson St.) | 206-324-4091
Redmond | 15230 NE 24th St. (bet. 152nd & 154th Sts.) | 425-564-0888
www.malaysatayhut.com

"Interesting combinations" of "delicious" flavors bring lunchtime
throngs to this Malaysian ID-Redmond duet that caters to both expats and suits with "good, cheap, fast" food; though the service
"lags" and the decor doesn't win raves, most gush "if you have never
tried" this "exotic" cuisine, "don't wait."

Malena's Taco Shop *Mexican* — 20 | 5 | 15 | $10

Ballard | 2010 NW 56th St. (20th Ave.) | 206-789-8207
Queen Anne | 620 W. McGraw St. (bet. 6th & 7th Aves.) |
206-284-0304 ⊟

"True to their name", tacos are the thing at these Queen Anne and
Ballard "holes-in-the-wall" known for their "plentiful and cheap"
south-of-the-border plates and "friendly service"; as for the
"sparse" atmosphere, "who cares?" say diners "satisfied" with their
"quick Mexican fix."

Z Maltby Cafe *American* — 26 | 17 | 22 | $18

Maltby | 8809 Maltby Rd. (87th Ave. NE) | 425-483-3123 |
www.maltbycafe.com

"Biscuits as big as my car" abound at this "down-home", historic
Maltby ex-schoolhouse where "breakfast rules" and the cinnamon
rolls "rock this world"; on weekends it gets "busy", but the "friendly" (if
"uneven") servers move the orders "fast" through the "kitschy"
quarters where the eats are priced "very reasonably"; N.B. no dinner.

Mama's Mexican Kitchen *Mexican* — 17 | 16 | 18 | $18

Belltown | 2234 Second Ave. (Bell St.) | 206-728-6262 | www.mamas.com
This "crazy, fun" Belltown Mexican gets "crammed" with folks looking
for "quick", "solid" staples at a "great price"; "tattooed" waitresses
provide "sassy" service amid the "mismatched chairs" and "funky"
decor – and even those who call the grub "only alright" admit that
the "Elvis Room" and Lava Lounge are pure Latino lagniappe.

Mamma Melina *Italian* — 21 | 16 | 21 | $29

University District | 4759 Roosevelt Way NE (bet. 47th & 50th Sts.) |
206-632-2271
The Varchetta family's "cozy" University District Italian is a "neighborhood fave" for its "unpretentious" cooking, "cordial" service and

a setting that's "romantic" – except on the weekend, when "live opera" turns the "small" space "jolly" and "noisy"; cineastes drop in on their way to the Seven Gables Theater, which is right upstairs.

☑ Maneki Ⓜ *Japanese* | 27 | 17 | 21 | $26 |

International District | 304 Sixth Ave. S. (bet. Jackson & Main Sts.) | 206-622-2631

The "oldest" Japanese restaurant in Seattle, this "authentic" hideaway tucked into an ID hillside offers "homestyle" "comfort food" alongside what fans consider the "best deal" for "top-quality sushi" in the city, plus a large sake selection; the vintage decor is sweet, but the secret's out, so "you need a reservation, even on Tuesday night."

Maple Leaf Grill *Eclectic* | 18 | 13 | 18 | $24 |

Maple Leaf | 8929 Roosevelt Way NE (90th St.) | 206-523-8449 | www.mapleleafgrill.com

"As mellow as it gets", this "comfortable" Eclectic eatery in an old Maple Leaf house offers "tasty" "everyday fare" like "great burgers" and homemade desserts; with 10 microbrews on tap, locals find it a "great place to meet a friend" or to hang with the "good natured crowd" at the "little bar", where most don't mind the often "slow" service.

Marco's Supperclub *Eclectic* | 21 | 17 | 19 | $35 |

Belltown | 2510 First Ave. (bet. Vine & Wall Sts.) | 206-441-7801 | www.marcossupperclub.com

When hipsters want "whimsical", they "rely" on this midpriced Eclectic "grotto" that offers "innovative takes" on the "standards" – "the fried sage leaves are a must" – in an "inviting" Belltown setting that leans toward "bohemian" "camp" (i.e. "mismatched" place settings); Marco himself "greets you at the door", and there's an "alfresco" back deck that's an "oasis."

Marina Park Grill *Seafood* | ▽ 22 | 22 | 19 | $31 |

Kirkland | 89 Kirkland Ave. (Lake St. S.) | 425-889-9000 | www.marinaparkgrill.com

"Good food", a fine Sunday brunch and an "unbeatable" marina "location" make this Kirkland seafooder a "popular spot" for neighbors looking to "relax and people-watch"; some find the eats "overpriced" and call the service "disinterested", but "who cares when you have a drink in one hand and the [Lake Washington] scenery to look at?"

Marjorie Ⓢ Ⓜ *Eclectic* | 22 | 20 | 22 | $38 |

Belltown | 2331 Second Ave. (Battery St.) | 206-441-9842 | www.trenchtownrocks.com

Both locals and "world travelers" find the "delicious" and sometimes "courageous" Eclectic cuisine (think China meets Indian meets New American) at Donna Moodie's midpriced Belltowner to be "fun, funky and different"; the "vibrant atmosphere" (some call it "deafening") inside is matched by a "lovely courtyard", making this "a friendly" "date" place.

	FOOD	DECOR	SERVICE	COST

Market Street Grill *American*

25 | 20 | 23 | $35

Ballard | 1744 NW Market St. (17th St.) | 206-789-6766 |
www.marketstreetgrill.net

Ballard tastemakers tout this "outstanding" New American for its
"inventive", but "non-fussy" posh noshes served by a "gracious"
staff; while some find the colorful setting a little too "early '90s",
most declare it cozy enough to be the place "where you go when you
get home and discover you forgot it was your anniversary."

Marrakesh Moroccan Restaurant *Moroccan*

21 | 24 | 21 | $30

Belltown | 2334 Second Ave. (bet. Battery & Bell Sts.) | 206-956-0500 |
www.marrakeshseattle.com

"Go with people you like" to this "fun" Belltown Moroccan, since you
"share dishes" and eat "with your fingers"; the "convincingly authentic" fare comes in "big portions" (especially the five-course
meals), and is set on "low tables" amid the "usual dine-in-a-tent decor"; N.B. belly dancers perform Wednesday–Sunday nights.

Mashiko *Japanese*

25 | 16 | 19 | $29

West Seattle | 4725 California Ave. SW (bet. Alaska & Edmunds Sts.) |
206-935-4339 | www.sushiwhore.com

A "trendy crowd" scarfs down "inventive" and "ultrafresh" sushi at
this "sassy" West Seattle Japanese with a "simple" setting; to get
around what some call "rude", "slow" service, sit at the bar and let
owner Hajime Sato "take care of you" with an omakase menu – and
if the tarrifs are "a bit higher than they need to be", few complain
given the "excellent quality."

Matt's Gourmet Hot Dogs *Hot Dogs*

18 | 8 | 14 | $8

Pioneer Square | 6615 E. Marginal Way S. (4th Ave.) | 206-768-0418 ⊠
Seattle Waterfront | Pier 52 | 801 Alaskan Way (Marion St.) |
206-264-0446
University District | 1301 45th Ave. NE (Brooklyn Ave.) | 206-545-4490
Kirkland | 12561 116th Ave. NE (124 St.) | 425-814-3760
Renton | 101 SW 41st St. (E. Valley Rd.) | 425-656-5917
www.mattshotdogs.com

Raters relish these "doggity good" frankfurters shops with "to-die-
for" Chicago dogs that "pop when you bite 'em", plus "the best" NY
"Coney Island–style" franks; servers fluent in "big city rudeness"
complete the "inexpensive" and "so casual" experience.

Matt's in the Market ⊠ *Pacific NW/Seafood*

– | – | – | E

Pike Place Market | Pike Place Mkt. | 94 Pike St. (1st Ave.) |
206-467-7909 | www.mattsinthemarket.com

Newly expanded and spiffed up, this pricey Pacific NW seafooder in
the Pike Place Market is routinely packed with a near-cult following
of locals lured by the smoked catfish salad and tasty lamb burger; insiders know to get a reservation, preferably for a table by the arched
windows that overlook the shopping, or at the counter to keep an
eye on the cooks in the gleaming new kitchen.

	FOOD	DECOR	SERVICE	COST

Matts' Rotisserie & Oyster Lounge *American*

	20	19	19	$28

Redmond | Redmond Town Ctr. | 16651 NE 74th St. (166th Ave.) | 425-376-0909 | www.mattsrotisserie.com

"The name don't lie" say boosters who get "anything cooked on the rotisserie" at this Redmond American where "quite good" "seafood, steaks and burgers" are served by a somewhat "confused" staff; with the bar as its "centerpiece", the space gets "loud" when the "after-work crowd" arrives.

Maximilien *French*

	21	23	20	$38

Pike Place Market | Pike Place Mkt. | 81A Pike St. (1st Ave.) | 206-682-7270 | www.maximilienrestaurant.com

"Sit by the window" and enjoy "magnificent" views of Elliott Bay at this "romantic" Pike Place Market hideaway with an "old-world" feel; "well-prepared" "bistrolike" French dishes and service that's authentically "professional, quick and efficient" make it feel like a trip to "Montmartre"; P.S. the bar upstairs has equally "fabulous" views.

May ● *Thai*

	▽ 20	24	19	$26

Wallingford | 1612 N. 45th St. (Woodlawn Ave.) | 206-675-0037 | www.mayrestaurant.com

"Beautiful", "traditional" decor, "inside and out", sets this "lovely" Wallingford Thai apart from the pack, as does its "fresh" and "not standard" cuisine (the sauces and curries are homemade); a "knowledgeable" staff explains any food "you may not be used to", and there's a "raging" late-night happy hour until 1 AM closing.

Mayuri *Indian*

	▽ 25	13	16	$20

Bellevue | 15400 NE 20th St. (154th Ave.) | 425-641-4442 | www.mayuriseattle.com

"Fabulous biryanis and lamb dishes" are just the tip of the "excellent cuisine" offered at this popular Bellevue Indian in a "mundane" strip mall "near Microsoft"; a "full range of authentic spices" and "fresh ingredients" flavor the "bargain" fare, which draws digerati and "East Indian families" for "leisurely dinners" and "quick work lunches."

⊠ McCormick & Schmick's *Seafood*

	21	19	21	$40

Downtown | 1103 First Ave. (Spring St.) | 206-623-5500
Bellevue | 700 Bellevue Way NE (8th St.) | 425-454-2606
www.mccormickandschmicks.com

These Downtown and Bellevue "fish houses" (links in a national chain) swim with "traditional" seafood that's "always good"; "clubby", "brass and dark-wood" digs draw "powerful" locals, and at happy hour frugalists join the scene for "cheap eats."

McCormick & Schmick's Harborside *Seafood*

	21	21	21	$37

Lake Union | 1200 Westlake Ave. N. (southwest end of Lake Union) | 206-270-9052 | www.mccormickandschmicks.com

Check out the "gorgeous" views of "seaplanes landing" on Lake Union from this dockside chain link offering a "large variety of fresh fish and seafood" at "modest prices"; a "great happy hour" and "dependable service" up the ante, though detractors declare the "quality has become inconsistent."

McCormick's Fish House & Bar *Seafood* | 21 | 19 | 22 | $40 |

Downtown | 722 Fourth Ave. (bet. Cherry & Columbia Sts.) | 206-682-3900 | www.mccormickandschmicks.com

It's all about the "fresh sheets" at this Downtown "grande dame" that's a comfortable cousin to the rest of its namesake seafood chain; "classic" "dark-wood" ambiance and a "professional staff" make it a "go-to" spot for "business luncheons" or with out-of-town guests, and tipplers toast the "old-school bar" that pours plenty of "no nonsense" drinks.

Mediterranean Kitchen *Lebanese/Mediterranean* | 22 | 12 | 19 | $22 |

Bellevue | 103 Bellevue Way NE (1st St.) | 425-462-9422 | www.mediterraneankitchens.net

"You'll never have a problem with vampires" after eating at this charming Bellevue Mediterranean-Lebanese lair where the "fresh" garlic-laden cuisine is good enough to coax diners back "a million times", even if there's "not much atmosphere"; the "serving sizes" are "ridiculously" "large", so plan on taking some home for "your next meal."

Mee Sum Pastries *Chinese/Dessert* | ▽ 21 | 4 | 13 | $8 |

Pike Place Market | Pike Place Mkt. | 1526 Pike Pl. (bet. Pike & Pine Sts.) | 206-682-6780

Locals say every trip to the Pike Place Market should include a "hot", golden "BBQ pork hom bow" from this "streetside walk-up counter" specializing in Chinese pastries; the "heavenly beauties" are flavorful and "light", mixing savory and sweet – and better yet are "easy on your wallet."

Melrose Grill *Steak* | ▽ 27 | 22 | 23 | $38 |

Renton | 819 Houser Way S. (Well St.) | 425-254-0759

This Renton hallmark is a "standout" thanks to its "limited" menu of "excellent steaks" that come "inclusive" with "all the sides"; situated in the saloon of an "old hotel", there's "lots of personality" (years ago a boxing ring stood near the bar), which extends to the "friendly" service and "right" prices.

Melting Pot, The *Fondue* | 19 | 19 | 19 | $43 |

Seattle Center | 14 Mercer St. (Queen Anne Ave.) | 206-378-1208
Bellevue | 302 108th Ave. NE (2nd Pl.) | 425-646-2744
Tacoma | 2121 Pacific Ave. (S. 21st St.) | 253-535-3939
www.meltingpot.com

These chainsters are "dipping heaven" thanks to their arrays of fondue for cooking "at your table"; dip-somaniacs call them "awesome" for a "romantic evening" or "with a group", but unsatisfied surveyors say to bring a "full wallet" because it's "cook-your-own-food" at "it-should-be-cooked-for-you prices."

	FOOD	DECOR	SERVICE	COST

☑ Metropolitan Grill *Steak*

| | 26 | 22 | 25 | $62 |

Downtown | 820 Second Ave. (Marion St.) | 206-624-3287 |
www.themetropolitangrill.com

This "old-fashioned" Downtown "power scene" is a "perennial favorite" thanks to its "absolutely outstanding" aged steaks (which could "make a cardiologist weep") and "colossal" lobsters; the "manly" 1940s-style dining room has a "classic" feel and the service is "near perfect", so most don't fret the "pricey" tabs – just "loosen your wallet" or "bring the corporate card", since it's "worth every penny and then some."

Mexico Cantina Y Veracruz *Mexican*

| 20 | 16 | 19 | $22 |

Downtown | Pacific Pl. | 600 Pine St. (6th Ave.) | 206-405-3400 |
www.eatatmexico.com

"Fresh" "Veracruz-style" vittles lure "mall walkers" and movie mavens to Downtown's posh Pacific Place galleria for this Mexican's "beautifully presented" meals; fiesta digs, a happy vibe and "large margaritas" make it "worth dodging" the shopping crowds to get a seat inside.

Mike's Noodle House ⊘ *Noodle Shop*

| ▽ 25 | 6 | 15 | $10 |

International District | 418 Maynard Ave. S. (Jackson St.) | 206-389-7099

Expats and oodles of foodies "fight for a table" at this ID noodle shop where the congee soups, sui kau dumplings and numerous Asian pastas are "cheap, filling and good"; the no-frills atmosphere doesn't disturb fans who cram in for the "comfort food at its best."

Mioposto *Italian*

| – | – | – | I |

Mt. Baker | 3601 S. McClellan St. (34th Ave.) | 206-760-3400 |
www.chowfoods.com

"Very good" pizzas, stromboli and simple fare come out of the oven at this Mount Baker Italian where a dressed-down crowd lounges around the vintage brick-and-wood room; it's part of the Chow Foods mini-empire, and espresso and pastries are served in the mornings, when locals hold "business meetings over coffee."

Mission *Pan-Latin*

| 20 | 23 | 18 | $24 |

West Seattle | 2325 California Ave. SW (College St.) | 206-937-8220 |
www.missionbar.com

With an "intimate", "dark" room, the scene is set for tacos, enchiladas and "steak nachos" at this West Seattle Pan-Latin canteen catering to cravers of "very spicy" chow; the "cool" vibe is bolstered by a stone wall set with candles, icy blue-and-yellow decor and low prices.

☑ Mistral 🅂 🅼 *American/French*

| 28 | 21 | 26 | $107 |

Belltown | 113 Blanchard St. (bet. 1st & 2nd Aves.) | 206-770-7799 |
www.mistralseattle.com

A "must-stop for any serious gourmet", chef-owner William Belickis' "magical" New American–New French "haute cuisine" haven "could be tops in any city in the country, if not the world"; "decadent" tasting menus provide a "symphony of tastes" set against a "sparse but romantic" Belltown room and service that's "impeccable" – as for the final check, well, "baby, is it a stunner!"

	FOOD	DECOR	SERVICE	COST

Mixtura *Peruvian*
24 | 21 | 19 | $38

Kirkland | 148 Lake St. S. (bet. Kirkland Way & 2nd Ave.) | 425-803-3310 |
www.mixtura.biz

"Lovely nuevo Andean food" is the name of the game at this "intriguing", avant-garde Kirkland enclave where "gastronomic twists" are turned on Peruvian fare; prices are "not inexpensive", and the simple dining room is so "hip" (despite its "great view of the parking lot") that some are "surprised it's not in Belltown", especially on Wednesday–Saturday nights when there's live entertainment.

Moghul Palace *Indian*
22 | 13 | 18 | $21

Bellevue | 10303 NE 10th St. (Bellevue Way) | 425-451-1909 |
www.moghulpalace.net

Eastsiders go to this "reliable", "very friendly" Downtown Bellevue venue for "super" Indian Moghul specialties that emphasize spice over heat; its decor is "not the best", but the lunch buffet is a "delectable bargain", plus the waiters "know the food" and "describe it well."

Mona's Bistro & Lounge *Mediterranean*
▽ **23 | 20 | 21 | $32**

Green Lake | 6421 Latona Ave. NE (65th St.) | 206-526-1188 |
www.monasseattle.com

This "little" Green Lake "hideaway" sates with a "small" Med menu of "interesting tapas, salads, seafood and meats", plus a "very good" wine list and "live music" several nights a week; "lingering" after dinner in the "dramatic red and purple" environs is "highly recommended", since the "scenester" "fun" breaks out "late-night."

Mondello Ristorante *Italian*
23 | 22 | 23 | $32

Magnolia | 2435 33rd Ave. W. (McGraw St.) | 206-352-8700 |
www.mondelloristorante.com

"Mama's in the kitchen" keeping the recipes "honest" at this Magnolia "family-run" Sicilian spot that's "as good as a trip to Italy"; those who deem the food only "good", "not terrific", find solace in the "reasonably priced" Italian wine list and "extremely friendly" servers who "make you feel like *famiglia*."

☑ Monsoon *Vietnamese*
27 | 19 | 21 | $35

Capitol Hill | 615 19th Ave. E. (bet. Mercer & Roy Sts.) | 206-325-2111 |
www.monsoonseattle.com

"Oohs and aahs" erupt from satisfied suppers at Eric and Sophie Banh's "upscale" Capitol Hill Vietnamese venue where the "delightful", "complex flavors" "never disappoint"; a "superb" European and American wine list (including some cult pours) wins raves from raters who are split over the "small", "minimalist" room ("beautiful" vs. "feels like the company cafeteria") and sometimes "inattentive" service, though all advise "don't hesitate to eat here."

Mor Mor Bistro *Mediterranean*
▽ **18 | 15 | 19 | $36**

Poulsbo | 18820 Front St. NE (Lincoln Rd.) | 360-697-3449 |
www.mormorbistro.com

There's "something for everyone" at this eco-conscious Poulsbo pub where the "very good" Med meals "range" from "meatloaf and mac 'n' cheese" to "lobster-filled ravioli"; monthly "wine-tasting dinners" lure locals and day-trippers to the simple space "warmed with whimsical family photos", though the penurious peck that it's "getting pricey."

Morton's, The Steakhouse *Steak* | 24 | 21 | 24 | $64 |

Downtown | 1511 Sixth Ave. (bet. Pike & Pine Sts.) | 206-223-0550 | www.mortons.com

"You can't go wrong" with the "huge portions" of "awesome" steaks and seafood at this "top-drawer" Downtown link in the Chicago chain; it feels "very big city" with "Rat Pack decor", "formal waiters" and "expense-account" prices, which fans insist are "worth it."

Moxie *American* | 21 | 19 | 21 | $36 |

Queen Anne | 530 First Ave. N. (bet. Mercer & Republican Sts.) | 206-283-6614 | www.moxieseattle.com

This "pre-theater, pre-game" Queen Anne storefront tempts taste buds with "unusual" New American eats ("the lamb burger is wonderful") that tend toward the bold side; "snazzy" "red walls", candlelight and an old-world/new-world wine list add to the allure, but "if you want quiet", wait and go "after the curtains rise" at nearby Seattle Center.

Musashi's 🅢 Ⓜ 🚭 *Japanese* | ▽ 21 | 6 | 17 | $16 |

Wallingford | 1400 N. 45th St. (Interlake Ave.) | 206-633-0212

"Expect to wait" at this always "crowded" Wallingford Japanese where the "huge", "delicious" sushi dinners come at prices so "low" you can "pig out for cheap"; service is "friendly", but given the "cramped", "no-frills" space, some say it's "better for takeout."

MuyMacho *Mexican* | - | - | - | I |

South Park | 8515 14th Ave. S. (bet. Cloverdale & Sullivan Sts.) | 206-763-3484

Taco and torta freaks seek out this inexpensive, easygoing (despite its Mexican revolutionary art gallery) Mexican cafe in South Park for a "great variety" of "taco fillings" that are "authentically prepared"; if the border town decor doesn't rate high, at least it puts more emphasis on the flavors on the plate.

Nell's *American* | 25 | 19 | 23 | $49 |

Green Lake | 6804 E. Green Lake Way N. (bet. 2nd & 4th Aves.) | 206-524-4044 | www.nellsrestaurant.com

Chef Phil Milhaski's cooking at this "well-kept" Green Lake "secret" "transports" with "elegant" New American flavors and "zero pretension" at an "expensive" price; detractors deem the "quiet", "romantic" room in need of "an upgrade" and dismiss the service as "extremely slow", but neighborhood fans insist it's still the "best food around."

Neville's at the British Pantry Ltd. *British* | 20 | 15 | 14 | $19 |

Redmond | 8125 161st Ave. NE (bet. 83rd St. & Redmond Way) | 425-883-7511 | www.thebritishpantryltd.com

A "real touch of England" in jolly old Redmond, this purveyor of all things Union Jack serves "authentic" (just ask the "expats at the table next to you") fish 'n' chips and "bangers 'n' mash"; expect to be treated with "fine British indifference", and be sure to call for the hours, which vary by day of the week; P.S. head to the attached market for "teas, treats" and "fresh pastries."

New Orleans Creole Cajun/Creole   14 | 15 | 14 | $21

Pioneer Square | 114 First Ave. S. (bet. Washington St. & Yesler Way) | 206-622-2563 | www.neworleanscreolerestaurant.com

This Pioneer Square Cajun-Creole joint sets out "large portions" of "cheesy, greasy" fare that's a "decent facsimile" of Big Easy cuisine, at "bargain" prices; the old brick room houses a party-hearty vibe as hepcats dig the live jazz and "great blues bands" that start up after dinner.

New York Pizza Place, A Pizza   ▽ 25 | 13 | 18 | $15

Roosevelt | 8310 Fifth Ave. NE (83rd St.) | 206-524-1355 | www.anewyorkpizzaplace.com

Favored by East Coast expats for serving what may be the "best New York–style pizza" around, this Roosevelt parlor excels with "chewy" crusts, "rich sauce" and "reasonable prices"; whether "by the slice" or whole round, the fare is "consistent" and the service "on time", but as with many NYC pie shops, "you don't go here for the decor."

94 Stewart M American   21 | 16 | 20 | $42

Pike Place Market | Pike Place Mkt. | 94 Stewart St. (1st Ave.) | 206-441-5505 | www.94stewart.com

Satisfied surveyors wish "Seattle had more bistros like this one", a "cozy" New American that's "tucked" into a "cavelike" nook in the Pike Place Market; the "attentive" staff "makes you feel like part of the family", and a "simple but well-executed" menu featuring "fresh, local" ingredients is complemented by an "extensive" (if "pricey") wine list.

⊠ Nishino Japanese   27 | 21 | 24 | $50

Madison Park | 3130 E. Madison St. (Lake Washington Blvd.) | 206-322-5800 | www.nishinorestaurant.com

For a "nirvanic" experience, sushistas and Seattle movers-and-shakers "let the chefs go crazy" in concocting "fabulous" "omakase" dinners at this "refined, if expensive" Madison Park Japanese; if it seems like "Nobu for half the price", that's because owner Tatsu Nishino is a Nobu Matsuhisa protégé, so it's little surprise that this "spectacular" spot is "the real deal."

Noah's Bagels Bakery   17 | 10 | 12 | $8

Capitol Hill | 220 E. Broadway (E. John St.) | 206-720-2925
Queen Anne | 2133 Queen Anne Ave. N. (bet. Boston & Crockett Sts.) | 206-282-6744
Mercer Island | 7808 28th St. SE (78th St.) | 206-232-8539
www.noahs.com

The "chewy and fresh" bagels at these "not quite New York" triplets are "always reliable" and "delicious" in a "West Coast" way; though service can be "slow" and the subway-tile decor doesn't rate high, they get packed, so go "early on weekends", before the goods "run out."

	FOOD	DECOR	SERVICE	COST

Noble Court *Chinese*
`21` `13` `16` `$21`

Bellevue | 1644 140th Ave. NE (Bellevue-Redmond Rd.) | 425-641-6011
"Dim sum" and then some brings Bellevueites to this parlor where "ancient China comes alive" with traditional "cart" service at lunch and larger plates at dinner; the staff is "eager to offer assistance" to the "patrons of every ethnic origin" who "pack" the place, some of whom warn it's "on the pricier side" and hasn't been updated in a "long time."

Noodle Ranch 🗷 *Noodle Shop*
`17` `10` `15` `$16`

Belltown | 2228 Second Ave. (bet. Bell & Blanchard Sts.) | 206-728-0463
White-collar types "slurp away work worries" with "oodles and oodles of noodles" at this "trendy" Asian "jewel" in Belltown where the vittles are "cheap, fast" and "good"; its "crowded", "noisy" quarters are lit by wok-and-chopstick lamps, and a handy location makes this an "easy stop before [hitting] the bars" at night.

Noosh Café *Deli*
`-` `-` `-` `I`

Queen Anne | 1629 Queen Anne Ave. N. (bet. Blaine & Garfield Sts.) | 206-285-1125
This affordable, diminutive Queen Anne Avenue stop offers "great soup and salad selections", handmade sandwiches and "excellent" French pastries; noosh means "enjoy" in Farsi and owner Ali Jafari "takes pride in his work", so though the room's egg-yolk-yellow walls evoke a "school cafeteria", it's still "worth the trip."

Northlake Tavern & Pizza House *Pizza*

`21` `9` `16` `$20`

University District | 660 Northlake Way NE (Pasadena Pl.) | 206-633-5317 | www.northlaketavern.com
UWers and Husky alums have been packing this University District "legend" "since the beginning of time" to wolf down "heavy" Seattle pizzas that are "the size of Mt. Rainier"; its "servers and bartenders are all great", and as for the "not fancy" decor, doh!, "it's a tavern", so "grab the baseball team" and hie here for a "pie and a pitcher."

NEW O'Asian *Chinese*
`20` `23` `18` `$28`

Downtown | 800 Fifth Ave. (Columbia St.) | 206-264-1789 | www.oasian.net
In the former Ruth's Chris digs, this Downtown Chinese is "the size of a stadium" – albeit a "sleek", "sophisticated" one, smack in the financial district; the "artfully done" lunch (of dim sum and larger regional specialties) breaks through the workday blahs, though some say it's "ok, but not great" and at dinner it's often nearly empty.

Z Oceanaire Seafood Room *Seafood*
`23` `23` `23` `$53`

Downtown | 1700 Seventh Ave. (Olive Way) | 206-267-2277 | www.theoceanaire.com
"Intriguing", "quality" seafood from all over the map is the bait at this Downtown outpost of a Midwest chain with the "clubby" air of an "old-time" ocean liner's "dining salon"; daily "fresh sheets" flesh out the menu and portions are "out-of-hand" "huge", causing most surveyors to fall hook, line and sinker – even if the "cost might set you out to sea."

	FOOD	DECOR	SERVICE	COST

NEW O/8 Seafood Grill *Pacific NW* | 21 | 21 | 20 | $43 |

Bellevue | Hyatt Regency | 900 Bellevue Way (bet. 8th & 10th Sts.) |
425-637-0808 | www.08seafoodgrill.com

This "hip" newcomer in the Hyatt Bellevue holds its own with "generous portions" of "right-on" seafood in "creative" Pacific NW presentations, alongside "fantastic" (if "pricey") wines by the bottle, glass or flight; when there's live music (Wednesday–Sunday nights) it can be too noisy for "any sort of conversation", but most contend that, in time, "it should become a local favorite."

'Ohana ● *Hawaiian* | 21 | 17 | 17 | $25 |

Belltown | 2207 First Ave. (Blanchard St.) | 206-956-9329 |
www.ohanabelltown.com

A "great start for a night on the town", this wacky "tiki" Belltowner boasts an "*ono*" ("delicious") Hawaiian menu of midpriced sushi, "kahlua pork" and "sake bombs"; bamboo booths and "huge lava lamps" add up to an atmosphere that's both "full of life" and "laid-back"- not a contradiction but, you know, "just like Maui."

NEW Oliver's Twist 🅂 *Pacific NW* | ▽ 25 | 24 | 21 | $31 |

Phinney Ridge | 6822 Greenwood Ave. N. (70th St.) | 206-706-6673 |
www.oliverstwistseattle.com

The "tiny kitchen" at this "swanky" Phinney Ridge Pacific NW newcomer turns out "mouthwatering", "little bites" that are "fun to try" (don't miss the "addictive truffle butter popcorn"); "slow" service in the "elegant", low-lit space ("more lounge than restaurant") doesn't hamper the bon vivants who turbo their evening experience with "exotic and interesting" cocktails from the bar.

Olives Cafe & Wine Bar 🅂 *Mediterranean* | 23 | 18 | 20 | $30 |

Edmonds | 107 Fifth Ave. N. (Main St.) | 425-771-5757 |
www.olivesgourmet.com

"Hip and happening", this Edmonds Mediterranean bistro pleases with "well-priced" "small plates beautifully done" and an "excellent wine list" featuring 60 pours by the glass; the "intimate" room is "great for a business lunch" or a "dinner date" and, all in all, it thankfully "belies the 'deadmonds' moniker."

Olympia Pizza & Spaghetti House *Pizza* | 18 | 8 | 18 | $16 |

Capitol Hill | 516 15th Ave. E. (bet. Mercer & Republican Sts.) |
206-329-4500 | www.olympiapizza3.com
Wallingford | 4501 Interlake Ave. N. (45th St.) | 206-633-3655
Queen Anne | 1500 Queen Anne Ave. N. (Galer St.) |
206-285-5550 | www.olympiapizzaonqueenanne.com

For "good, thick, Greek-style" pizza with a "crunchy yet chewy crust" and "no skimping" on the "toppings", "this is the place"; what's more, tabs are "inexpensive", service is "prompt and polite" and there's outside seating at the Capitol Hill and Queen Anne branches.

Ooba's Mexican Grill *Mexican* | 24 | 14 | 18 | $13 |

Bellevue | 55 108th Ave. NE (20th St.) | 425-646-4500
Redmond | 15802 NE 83rd St. (158th Ave.) | 425-702-1694

(continued)

Ooba's Mexican Grill

Woodinville | 17302 140th Ave. NE (175th St. NE) | 425-481-5252 🖼

"Quick" Mexican-American fare (like "awesome" seafood burritos) is served with "freshly fried nacho chips" and a "great salsa bar" at this "creative" Eastside trio; with cheap tabs, simple "Southwestern" decor and a "friendly" staff, it's no wonder they're "crazy busy at lunch."

NEW Opal 🅼 *Pacific NW*

▽ 25 | 25 | 25 | $44

Queen Anne | 2 Boston St. (Queen Anne Ave.) | 206-282-0142 | www.opalseattle.com

"The food and drinks are like art" gush admirers of chef Andy Leonard's "innovative", "seasonal" Pacific NW cookery at this "excellent addition" to Queen Anne; "attentive service" adds to the "warm, classy" interior, even if the tabs strike one surveyor as "pricier than my comfort zone."

Original Pancake House, The *Diner*

21 | 12 | 20 | $13

Ballard | 8037 15th Ave. NW (bet. 80th & 83rd Sts.) | 206-781-3344
Kirkland | Parkplace Ctr. | 130 Park Pl. (Central Way) | 425-827-7575
www.originalpancakehouse.com

"Walk in, waddle out" of these affordable American "breakfast pig-out places" in Kirkland and Ballard offering "Swedish pancakes and Dutch babies" that will "knock your socks off"; "diner"-y decor makes "you feel like you're on a road trip in the Midwest" – the "only real drawback" is the no-reserving rule, as it means "crazy waits" on weekends.

Osteria La Spiga *Italian*

24 | 24 | 18 | $34

Capitol Hill | 1429 12th Ave. (bet. Pike & Union Sts.) | 206-323-8881 | www.laspiga.com

Relocated to an "industrial chic" Capitol Hill space that once housed an automotive shop, this "vast, airy" Italian "favorite" continues to please with "rustic" Emilia-Romana "comfort cuisine" that will "change how you view fresh pasta", plus a "great wine selection" for washing it down; one thing that doesn't thrive in its new home is the service, which is "so slow it's silly."

Other Coast Cafe *Sandwiches*

25 | 10 | 16 | $11

Ballard | 5315 Ballard Ave. NW (bet. 22nd Ave. & Vernon Pl.) | 206-789-0936 🤝
NEW Downtown | 2 Union Sq. | 601 Union St. (6th Ave.) | 206-624-3383
www.othercoastcafe.com

West Coasters get a taste of "East Coast hoagies" at these Ballard-Downtown delis where "serious", "two-handed" sandwiches" are "loaded" with "healthy" dollops of "all the fixings"; "extremely slow" service and a "no-frills" atmosphere don't bother regulars who advise: "order only a half if you value your arteries."

Ototo Sushi *Japanese*

24 | 18 | 18 | $31

Queen Anne | 7 Boston St. (Queen Anne Ave.) | 206-691-3838 | www.ototosushi.com

Sushi and other Japanese offerings that are "fresh" and "beautifully done" are the attraction at this "casual" cafe on the top of Queen

Anne Hill (the name is Japanese for 'fish'); "hipster-trendy" meets "family-friendly" in its "sparse" decor that evokes "the set of *Star Trek*, the original", and a few critics complain that "service can be slow", so be "prepared to wait."

Outback Steakhouse *Steak*

15 | 12 | 17 | $27

Lake Union | 701 Westlake Ave. N. (Broad St.) | 206-262-0326
North Seattle | 13231 N. Aurora Ave. (N. 130th St.) | 206-367-7780
Bellevue | 15100 38th St. SE (150th Ave.) | 425-746-4647
Kirkland | 12120 85th St. NE (122nd Ave. NE) | 425-803-6880
Bothell | 22606 Bothell Everett Hwy. (228th St. SE) | 425-486-7340
Everett | 10121 Evergreen Way (100th St. SW) | 425-513-2181
Federal Way | 2210 S. 320th St. (S. 23rd Ave.) | 253-839-1340
Tacoma | 3111 S. 38th St. (S. Cedar St.) | 253-473-3669
Tukwila | 16510 Southcenter Pkwy. (Strander Blvd.) | 206-575-9705
www.outback.com

Carnivores crowd into these Aussie outposts for affordable steaks (some say you'll "need to pay three times as much to get better"), ribs, chicken and salmon that are "surprisingly good for a chain"; "friendly service" and "acceptable" decor make them appealing for families.

Oyster Bar on Chuckanut Drive, The *Seafood*

▽ 24 | 20 | 23 | $36

Bow | 2578 Chuckanut Dr. (Oyster Creek Ln.) | 360-766-6185 | www.theoysterbaronchuckanutdrive.com

Perched in the small town of Bow, "this is the place" for "fine dining" and "special-occasion" eats when day-tripping in the Skagit Valley; the "serene" room offers "spectacular" views of "sparkling" Samish Bay and the San Juan Islands, where many of the "great, fresh" oysters served here were found.

Pabla Indian Cuisine *Indian*

▽ 20 | 13 | 17 | $20

Downtown | 1516 Second Ave. (bet. Pike & Pine Sts.) | 206-623-2868 | www.pablaindiancuisine.com

"Really good, cheap" Indian food – including "hot and fresh" naan, a lunch buffet and "lots of vegetarian options" – is the draw at this "great value" Downtowner; the decor is simple and the service "quick and cordial."

Pacific Grill ⊠ *Seafood/Steak*

– | – | – | E

Tacoma | Waddell Bldg. | 1502 Pacific Ave. (S. 15th St.) | 253-627-3535 | www.pacificgrilltacoma.com

This polished Pacific Avenue go-to from chef-owner Gordon Naccarato offers pricey steaks, chops and fish specials that lure local foodies, business types and profs from the nearby UW-Tacoma; set in the historic Waddell building, the interior is lively and glam.

Paddy Coynes Irish Pub ● *Pub Food*

18 | 21 | 17 | $23

Downtown | 1190 Thomas St. (Minor Ave.) | 206-405-1548 | www.paddycoynes.net

"Charming and heart-warming", this Downtown Irish pub "well represents" its home country with "delicious fish 'n' chips" and "good brews"; the dark atmosphere and "nice" fireplace and deck make it a prime hang for local condo dwellers, staff from *The Seattle Times* and the occasional "friendly" "rugby team"; N.B. 21-and-over only.

Pagliacci Pizza *Pizza*   22 | 11 | 17 | $14

Capitol Hill | 426 Broadway E. (Harrison St.) | 206-324-0730
Queen Anne | 550 Queen Anne Ave. N. (Mercer St.) |
206-285-1232
University District | 4529 University Way NE (bet. 45th & 47th Sts.) |
206-632-0421
Bellevue | Bellevue Sq. | 563 Bellevue Sq. (Bellevue Way NE) |
425-453-1717
www.pagliacci.com

This mega-popular mini-chain serves some of "the best pizza in town" say satisfied surveyors who salivate over the "thin-crust" "Seattle-style" standards and "seasonal" specials made with eco-chic artisanal ingredients (hence the slightly spendy tabs); design quibblers circumvent the "not-much-to-look-at" decor by turning to the "well-oiled" delivery service, and Bellevue Square neighbors can pick up "takeout" in the parking garage "without having to leave their cars."

Pair ⧉Ⓜ *American*   25 | 22 | 23 | $32

Ravenna | 5501 30th Ave. NE (55th St.) | 206-526-7655 |
www.pairseattle.com

"Awesome" New American tasting plates are paired with "affordable" wines at Ravenna's "sweet" "gem" of a bistro where the focus is on "perfectly fresh" ingredients from local farms; the "country-style" setting and "knowledgeable" staff appease most, though a few nitpick that "those small plates are really small" and with "no reservations" (except for large parties), you have to "roll the dice and hope you get in quick."

Ⓩ Palace Kitchen ☽ *American*   24 | 21 | 23 | $40

Downtown | 2030 Fifth Ave. (Virginia St.) | 206-448-2001 |
www.tomdouglas.com

The Downtown royals who swamp Tom Douglas' "casually" "swanky" New American declare the "sexy", "satisfying" food fit for "the Queen herself"; "arty" gilded mirrors, "low lighting" and the fact that its "always packed" (and "boisterously" "loud") make it a "hip scene" with "top-notch" service that pleases the club kids who've claimed this as their "late-night spot" – "where rock 'n' roll" comes to roost.

Ⓩ Palisade *Seafood*   23 | 26 | 23 | $52

Magnolia | Elliott Bay Marina | 2601 W. Marina Pl. (Garfield St.) |
206-285-1000 | www.palisaderestaurant.com

"Stunning" city and "water views" in the middle of a "gorgeous" Magnolia marina ("arrive by boat if you can") have surveyors crooning that this "off-the-beaten-path" seafood citadel is "the best place to impress a client" or "out-of-town guest"; in the "modern" "supper club"-y digs, a "professional" staff delivers "pricey" Polynesian-inspired fare, though less ardent responders rank the food a long "second" to the setting.

| | FOOD | DECOR | SERVICE | COST |

Palomino   *Italian*

21 | 21 | 21 | $36

Downtown | City Centre Bldg. | 1420 Fifth Ave. (bet. Pike & Union Sts.) |
206-623-1300 | www.palomino.com

A "stylish" hangout for Downtown's "shopping" and "theater"
crowds, this "nontraditional" Italian in the "upscale" City Centre
mall gets it right with "reliably good" chop chop salads and "wood-
fired" pizzas; the "airy" space is full of "beautiful" locally blown
glass (the mall itself has Chihulys on view), though the "happy-
hour" crowd tends to stick around the bar, which "rocks."

Pan-Africa Cafe   *African*

▽ 21 | 13 | 19 | $17

Pike Place Market | Pike Place Mkt. | 1521 First Ave. (bet. Pike & Pine Sts.) |
206-652-2461 | www.panafricamarket.com

Serving "wonderfully spiced" African stews and a wide array of
"tempting vegetarian choices", this "very casual" "little find" in the
Pike Place Market easily pleases "bargain"-hunters and the "downtown crowd in-the-know"; if service is "a bit slow", that's only because everything is "prepared from scratch."

Panos Kleftiko   ⏴   *Greek*

23 | 14 | 20 | $25

Queen Anne | 815 Fifth Ave. N. (Valley St.) | 206-301-0393

"Off the beaten path" at the bottom of Queen Anne Hill (just blocks
from the Seattle Center), Panos Marinos' "Greek taverna" gets
"opas!" for its "spectacularly authentic" Hellenic dishes (especially
the appetizers, which "you can make a whole meal of"); the
"quaint", "close" quarters, named for a freedom fighter's hideout,
are "perfect for a date" and take well-traveled surveyors
"back" to "Greece."

Paragon Restaurant & Bar   *Pacific NW*

19 | 18 | 19 | $28

Queen Anne | 2125 Queen Anne Ave. N. (bet. Boston & Crockett Sts.) |
206-283-4548 | www.paragonseattle.com

This Queen Anne "stalwart" features "good" Pacific NW food with
"lots of local ingredients" that "flies under the radar", overshadowed by the joint's "live music" on most nights and a "jumping bar"
scene on weekends; it's especially "inviting" in winter, when the
"large fireplace is in action"; N.B. a chef change is not reflected in
the Food score.

⏴ Paseo   ⏴ ⏴ ⏴   *Caribbean*

27 | 7 | 13 | $12

Fremont | 4225 Fremont Ave. N. (bet. 42nd & 43rd Sts.) |
206-545-7440

The "aroma will draw you in" to this "funky" Fremont "shack" proffering "generous" portions of "killer" Cuban sandwiches and
Caribbean on the "cheap"; a "cramped" interior includes only a few
seats (at the counter, where service is "friendly"), so it's best if you
"don't plan on eating in" and opt for takeout; N.B. cash only, no liquor.

Pasta & Co.   *Italian*

22 | 13 | 18 | $17

Queen Anne | 2109 Queen Anne Ave. N. (Crockett St.) | 206-283-1182
University District | University Vill. | 4622 26th Ave. NE (Blakeley St.) |
206-523-8594

(continued)

Pasta & Co

Bellevue | 10218 NE Eighth St. (Bellevue Way) | 425-453-8760
Redmond | 7624 170th Ave. NE (Redmond Way) | 425-881-1992
www.pastaco.com

For "fresh" pasta, sauces and entrees that taste like they were "made at home", busy bees turn to this "slightly pricey" mini-chain of "gourmet" Italian "delis"; though "primarily takeout", the small stores have a few tables and chairs, which are "great" when "grabbing a light lunch."

Pasta Bella *Italian*

19 | 16 | 19 | $24

Ballard | 5913 15th Ave. NW (bet. 59th & 60th Sts.) | 206-789-4933
Queen Anne | 1530 Queen Anne Ave. N. (Garfield St.) | 206-284-9827
www.pastabellaseattle.com

This Ballard–Queen Anne duo offers "simple Italian fare", including "good" "staples" ("saltimbocca, lasagna, various pastas") and more "creative" specialties at an affordable cost; the "country home" atmosphere lends a "neighborhood" feel that's "great" for a "first date", so locals forgive the "always slow" service.

Pecos Pit BBQ ⊠⊅ *BBQ*

25 | 8 | 17 | $10

SODO | 2260 First Ave. S. (bet. Holgate & Lander Sts.) | 206-623-0629
"Cheap, meaty, messy and spicy" describes the BBQ at this "funky", cash-only SODO shack that many argue is "the best in the city", known for its "volcanic hot sauce" that will "rip your shorts off" (even "pepper-lovers" tend to opt for the milder "medium"); there's no inside dining, so be ready to eat at a "picnic table" in the parking lot year-round; N.B. closed on weekends.

Pegasus Pizza *Pizza*

20 | 9 | 14 | $18

West Seattle | 2758 Alki Ave. SW (bet. 61st & 62nd Aves.) | 206-932-4849
"Fluffy yet crispy" crusts and lots of toppings (especially on the "Tom's Special") meet "huge salads" at this West Seattle standby; sure, the decor is "lacking, big time", but "they do a great job" of "moving you through" with a "perky smile" – and its location at Alki Beach means every visit is "like a vacation."

NEW Perché No
Pasta & Vino ●Ⓜ *Italian*

22 | 20 | 23 | $29

Green Lake | 1319 N. 49th St. (Green Lake Way) | 206-547-0222 |
www.perchenopastaandvino.com

Chef David Kong "makes you feel like family" at this Italian "gem" that "charms" with "freshly made pasta", "homemade proscuitto" and "great-value" wine flights; a longtime Queen Anne staple, its new Green Lake space is "huge" (and "often loud") with a "fun and friendly" staff.

Persimmon Ⓜ *American*

▽ 22 | 15 | 19 | $26

Fremont | 4256 Fremont Ave. N. (bet. 43rd St. & Motor Pl.) |
206-632-0760 | www.persimmoncafe.com

An "often overlooked prize", this "sweet" spot up the hill from the center of Fremont "makes everyday into gourmet" with moderately priced New American food that's "delicious" and "fresh"; there's a "warm" feel to the persimmon-colored space, but a few fuss that the "kitchen isn't built for speed", ergo "don't visit if you're in a hurry."

Peso's Kitchen & Lounge ● Mexican   23 | 19 | 17 | $25
Queen Anne | 605 Queen Anne Ave. N. (bet. Mercer & Roy Sts.) | 206-283-9353 | www.pesoskitchen.com
"Crowded and noisy", this "scene" at the bottom of Queen Anne Hill excels with "interesting, yet still traditional" Mexican fare and a daily breakfast that may be the "best-kept secret in town"; its cantina-esque interior buzzes with a "super-trendy crowd" and perhaps the "hottest" staff "in the land", so who cares if the service is "spotty"?

P.F. Chang's China Bistro Chinese   19 | 19 | 18 | $28
Downtown | 400 Pine St. (4th Ave.) | 206-393-0070
Bellevue | Bellevue Sq. | 525 Bellevue Way (NE 8th St.) | 425-637-3582
www.pfchangs.com
This "popular place" is a "chain done right", doling out "dependable" "Americanized" Chinese plates (the "lettuce chicken wraps" are "fantastic") to the "somewhat-sophisticated masses"; its nod-to-China dining rooms are "very busy" and a "go-to" for "groups", with service that splits pollsters ("good" vs. "hard to find"); a few cut it no slack, calling it "faux" Asian "mall food" and yawning that the experience is "tired."

Philadelphia Fevre Deli   ∇ 23 | 6 | 15 | $10
Madison Valley | 2332 E. Madison St. (John St.) | 206-323-1000 | www.phillysteakshop.com
For "superb", "real" Philly cheese steaks, confreres from the City of Brotherly Love "have the fevre" for this tiny, no-frills Madison Valley deli/cafe proffering the low-cost sandwiches "wit" the toppings; "they even have scrapple!", crinkle fries that "rule" and "Tasty Kakes."

Phnom Penh Cambodian   - | - | - | I
International District | 660 S. King St. (Maynard Ave.) | 206-748-9825
"Consistently wonderful", this affordable ID storefront is a "favor-ite" for Cambodian cooking, including "great bowls of pho" and "just the best" "battambang noodles"; its grass-hut decor evokes a Southeast Asian cafe, and the service is "fast!"

Pho Bac Vietnamese   ∇ 21 | 4 | 13 | $9
International District | 1214 S. Jackson St. (12th Ave.) | 206-323-4387
The "perfect antidote to rainy-Seattle-day blahs", this ID pho shop is a local "standby" for its "steaming bowls" of mac daddy North Vietnamese noodle soups served with "fresh lime" and "basil"; its "good value" makes up for the "austere" linoleum-heavy decor.

Pho Cyclo Café Vietnamese   20 | 14 | 16 | $12
Capitol Hill | 406 Broadway E. (Terrace St.) | 206-329-9256
SODO | 2414 First Ave. S. (Stacy St.) | 206-382-9256 Ⓢ
www.phocyclocafe.com
These "convenient" SODO and Capitol Hill Vietnamese siblings sate with "cheap", "good-quality" pho soups (that seem "healthier than

others'") and "nice" *banh mi* sandwiches; decorated with cyclo bicycle carts, they get "very busy" at lunch when the "highly efficient" service kicks into gear to keep the crowds moving.

☑ Phoenecia at Alki Ⓜ *Mediterranean* 27 | 16 | 26 | $32

West Seattle | 2716 Alki Ave. SW (bet. 60th & 61st Aves.) | 206-935-6550
"Relax, ignore the menu" and let owner Hussein Khazaal "make something very special just for you" at this "hidden" Med "treasure" that turns out "awesome" seafood, "spicy" chicken and "charred flatbreads"; though it can "get expensive", the trade-off is a "great location" on West Seattle's Alki Beach with "wonderful" Elliott Bay views.

Pho Thân Brothers ⊗ *Vietnamese* 22 | 7 | 15 | $8

Ballard | 2021 NW Market St. (20th Ave.) | 206-782-5715
Capitol Hill | 516 Broadway E. (Republican St.) | 206-568-7218
Green Lake | 7714 Aurora Ave. N. (77th St.) | 206-527-5973
University District | 4207 University Way NE (bet. 42nd & 43rd Sts.) | 206-633-1735
West Seattle | 4822 California Ave. SW (Edmunds St.) | 206-937-6264
Bellevue | 1299 156th Ave. NE (13th St. NE) | 425-818-4905
Redmond | 7844 Leary Way NE (Cleveland St.) | 425-881-3299
Edmonds | 22618 Hwy. 99 (76th Ave. W.) | 425-744-0212
Everett | 500 SE Everett Mall Way (bet. 3rd & 7th Aves.) | 425-353-8906
Tacoma | 10435 Pacific Ave. S. (bet. 104th & 106th Sts.) | 253-548-8886
www.thanbrothers.com
Additional locations throughout the Seattle area
It's an every day noodle "pho"-nomenon at this popular Vietnamese soup chain where "steaming, fragrant" bowls with "all the fixin's" arrive "lightning fast" ("as soon as your butt hits the chair") and with a "complimentary cream puff" on the side; "ridiculously low prices" and a "veggie" option offset the decor, which is "not much to look at"; N.B. cash only.

Piecora's NY Pizza *Pizza* 21 | 13 | 14 | $15

Capitol Hill | 1401 E. Madison St. (14th Ave.) | 206-322-9411 | www.piecoras.com
"Classic" pizza that may be "as close to NY 'za as you'll get" comes out of the oven at this "nothing-fancy" parlor that's "appreciated" by Capitol Hill pie-*sani*; service can be as "super-cheesy" as the slices and comes with "attitude", so grab a "cold brew" and focus on the food.

Pig Iron Bar-B-Q ☒ *BBQ* ▽ 22 | 9 | 16 | $17

South Seattle | 5602 First Ave. S. (Findlay St.) | 206-768-1009 | www.pigironbbq.net
"Bring your tattoos" and dig into the "excellent barbecue", homemade sauces and "sides almost as good" as the meat at this South Seattle "joint"; a "motorcycle culture" vibe makes it a "colorful" lunch and dinner option at "a fair price."

Pike Pub & Brewery *Pub Food* 16 | 16 | 17 | $21

Pike Place Market | 1415 First Ave. (Union St.) | 206-622-6044 | www.pikebrewing.com
"Better-than-pub" grub meets "made-in-house" brews at this "always fun" Pike Place Market "break" space for hungry shoppers; it's

| | FOOD | DECOR | SERVICE | COST |

one of the area's "few" "sit-down" venues that "isn't a major invest-ment", though imbibers implore to "skip" the "uninspired dining" and "have another beer" instead.

Pink Door, The *Italian*   22 | 22 | 21 | $35

Pike Place Market | Pike Place Mkt. | 1919 Post Alley (bet. Stewart & Virginia Sts.) | 206-443-3241 | www.thepinkdoor.net

"Consistently good", "imaginative" Italian food plus cabaret acts – like "swinging" acrobats who hang from the ceiling – wait behind a pink Post Alley door at this "quirky" Pike Place Market "find" with a "personable staff"; add in an "eccentric" bar scene and "outdoor" "roof garden" with long views of Elliott Bay, and you get a "favorite" where, naturally, it's "hard to get a table" on weekends.

Piroshky Piroshky *Russian*   23 | 6 | 17 | $9

Pike Place Market | Pike Place Mkt. | 1908 Pike Pl. (bet. Stewart & Virginia Sts.) | 206-441-6068 | www.piroshkybakery.com

This takeout-only "hole-in-the-wall" in the Pike Place Market pur-veys "huge" Russian pastries ("like Bubbie used to make") that are the "best handheld lunch" say Moscow mavens; "watch" the food being prepped and breathe in the "ridiculously amazing scents" while you wait in the "long line."

Place Pigalle
Restaurant & Bar ⑤ *Pacific NW*   23 | 22 | 23 | $44

Pike Place Market | Pike Place Mkt. | 81 Pike St. (Pike Pl.) | 206-624-1756 | www.placepigalle-seattle.com

"Watch the ferries" from this "quiet", "refined" corner of the Pike Place Market where the "creative" Pacific NW food ("the mussels are divine") is even "better than the view"; there' a "great small bar", the staff is "attentive" and as for its hard-to-find, "almost labyrin-thine location", its an "added bonus", making this "hidden treasure" even more "romantic."

NEW Poco Wine Room ◐ *Eclectic*   - | - | - | I

Capitol Hill | 1408 E. Pine St. (14th Ave.) | 206-322-9463 | www.pocowineroom.com

A "limited" but lauded selection of Eclectic sandwiches, cheeses and meats from local artisans are "well-paired" with a "great" list of 40 "unusual and interesting" Pacific NW pours at this "welcoming" Capitol Hill wine bar; a "friendly neighborhood staff" works the warm, modern room, which has a cool second floor loft.

Pogacha *Croatian/Pacific NW*   18 | 13 | 17 | $24

Bellevue | Bellevue Plaza | 119 106th Ave. (Main St.) | 425-455-5670
Issaquah | 120 NW Gilman Blvd. (Front St.) | 425-392-5550
www.pogacha.com

"Fresh from the oven" Croatian "pogacha breads" are the draw at this good-value Pacific NW duo where the "interesting blend of fla-vors" makes for a "delicious" meal; the locations differ in atmo-sphere and menu – the Issaquah branch is the place to head for happy hour, while the Bellevue outpost is more "casual."

| | FOOD | DECOR | SERVICE | COST |

Pomegranate Bistro *American*

FOOD 25 | DECOR 17 | SERVICE 21 | COST $28

Redmond | 18005 NE 68th St. (180th Ave.) | 425-556-5972 | www.lisaduparcatering.com

It's pure "dinner theater" at this midpriced Redmond bistro connected to chef Lisa Dupar's catering business, since suppers can "watch" the chefs "at work" "through a large glass window"; the sparse, "kid-friendly" space gets "boisterous", and its "excellent", "definitely different" American fare prompts neighbors to muse "where has this place been all my life?"

Pontevecchio 🗹 *Italian*

23 | 20 | 21 | $36

Fremont | 710 N. 34th St. (bet. Aurora & Fremont Aves.) | 206-633-3989

Located in Fremont, this moderate, "romantic" neighborhood Southern Italian is best known for its live Friday night "opera singers", but also boasts "tasty" old-fashioned standards like mushroom risotto and homemade red sauce; as for the servers, surveyors are severely split: "slow and inattentive" vs. so "great" that "you feel like a guest in their home!"

Ponti Seafood Grill ◗ *Seafood*

22 | 23 | 23 | $46

Fremont | 3014 Third Ave. N. (Nickerson St.) | 206-284-3000 | www.pontiseafoodgrill.com

This "lovely" Fremont stalwart swims with "fresh" Pacific NW seafood, including a "legendary" Thai curry pasta with crab, plus a "deep, reasonable" wine list; though some snipe it's "past its prime" and the service can be "spotty", most are enamored of the "great deck" and its "wonderful, romantic" views of the Lake Washington Ship Canal.

NEW Porcella

Urban Market *French/Mediterranean*

24 | 15 | 18 | $20

Bellevue | 10245 Main St. (bet. 102nd & 103rd Aves.) | 425-286-0080 | www.porcellaurbanmarket.com

"Light lunches" and expensive snacks are on offer at this "real" French-Mediterranean "deli" in the Old Town section of Bellevue where "high-end" cheeses and "housemade" charcuterie are relatively pricey but "treats for the tongue"; while takeout is popular, there's a newly expanded dining area.

NEW Portage *French/Pacific NW*

26 | 20 | 23 | $39

Queen Anne | 2209 Queen Anne Ave. N. (Boston St.) | 206-352-6213 | www.portagerestaurant.com

A "wonderful addition" to Queen Anne's Restaurant Row, this Pacific NW–French bistro "excites taste buds" with "unique" dishes that are "beautifully executed", followed by "grand" desserts, all delivered by "helpful" servers; if its "lovely, quiet" space feels tight, the "intimacy" only "adds to the overall enjoyment."

Portalis 🅼 *American/European*

18 | 23 | 19 | $26

Ballard | 5205 Ballard Ave. NW (20th Ave.) | 206-783-2007 | www.portaliswines.com

At this "very cool" wine bar and shop in Ballard, a "limited menu" of "good" American and European "small bites" are on offer for nibbling alongside the "great" pours; an "incredibly knowledgeable" staff works the "exposed-brick" room, which is "cozy", "comfortable" and ideal for "quiet conversation"; P.S. in warm weather "they throw open the large doors" for an "almost outside" experience.

preet's *Indian*　　▽ 25 | 15 | 14 | $19

Redmond | 8440 160th Ave. NE (bet. 83rd & 85th Sts.) | 425-867-9400 | www.preets.com

"Undeniably enjoyable vegetarian" dishes are the hallmark of this "inviting" Indian eatery in "simple" environs; service is so "slow" that one critic quips it's the "home of the three-hour lunch", so settle in and relax, since "the food is good, once you get it" – all in all, it's "worth the stop in Redmond."

Primo Grill *Mediterranean*　　25 | 20 | 23 | $37

Tacoma | 601 S. Pine St. (6th Ave.) | 253-383-7000 | www.primogrilltacoma.com

Chef-owner Charlie McManus "does wonders" with local ingredients at this midpriced "blue-chip" Mediterranean in Tacoma with "fantastic" wood-fired pizzas purveyed in a "homey, pretty" dining room that's "usually" "crowded"; "friendly" service and a "great" wine list add up to an "outstanding" experience.

☑ Purple Cafe & Wine Bar, The *Pacific NW*　22 | 23 | 21 | $33

NEW **Downtown** | 1225 Fourth Ave. (University St.) | 206-829-2280
Kirkland | Parkplace Ctr. | 323 Park Pl. (NE 85th St.) | 425-828-3772 🅢
Woodinville | 14459 Woodinville-Redmond Rd. (NE 145th St.) | 425-483-7129 Ⓜ
www.thepurplecafe.com

An "extensive" array of "tasty" Pacific NW food and wine (from "a menu you could ski down") wows worshipers at this popular trio of cafe/wine bars where "educated" waiters make choosing easier; "contemporary" dining rooms and an enormous "cylindrical floor-to-ceiling" tower of vino at the newer Downtown location add to the "intrigue", though cynics say the "entrees veer toward the pedestrian."

Purple Dot Café ● *Chinese*　　▽ 18 | 14 | 12 | $18

International District | 515 Maynard Ave. S. (King St.) | 206-622-0288

The huge menu at this ID Chinese eatery includes "good dim sum" early in the day and "typical Hong Kong cafe food" (like 'beef internal delicacies' paired with spaghetti) later on; "trendy" multicolor decor detracts from service that "requires patience", and a 3:30 AM closing time on Friday and Saturday nights "makes for a great way to end a night on the town."

Pyramid Alehouse *Pub Food*　　16 | 16 | 17 | $21

Pioneer Square | 1201 First Ave. S. (Royal Brougham Way) | 206-682-3377 | www.pyramidbrew.com

It's "beer heaven" say sports fans about this casual "microbrew *haus*" across the street from the Mariners' and Seahawks' stadiums; on "game days", crowds descend for the "good" (if "a bit uninspired") "pub food" and "great suds" on tap, so "go early" if you want a table.

	FOOD	DECOR	SERVICE	COST

NEW Qube *Asian/French* 22 | 19 | 22 | $43

Downtown | 1901 Second Ave. (Stewart St.) | 206-770-5888 |
www.quberestaurant.com

"Cubed sets" (three courses, each with an ingredient served three
ways) meet "imaginative" Asian-French alchemy at this "hip"
Downtowner that plays "inventively" with food; the industrial glam
setting is too "austere" for some ("decor distraction dominates"
quips a cubist), but others call the glowing "communal table" "awesome" for "after-work get-togethers" and say the sunken bar serves
"divine drinks"; N.B. the Food score does not reflect a chef change.

Queen City Grill *American* 22 | 19 | 21 | $40

Belltown | 2201 First Ave. (Blanchard St.) | 206-443-0975 |
www.queencitygrill.com

Exuding "cosmopolitan" charm, this "friendly", "lively" 1907 "saloon" turned Belltown American churns out reliably "excellent fish
and shellfish" alongside a "great NW wine list"; a crowd that's
"slightly older" and "more moneyed" than in the neighboring singles
bars fills up the "high-backed" wooden booths, which are especially
"inviting" on a "wet and rainy Seattle night."

Queen Mary Tearoom M *Tearoom* ▽ 19 | 23 | 20 | $27

Ravenna | 2912 NE 55th St. (bet. 29th & 30th Aves.) | 206-527-2770 |
www.queenmarytearoom.com

The "ultimate mother-daughter-granddaughter" gathering spot,
this Ravenna tearoom is like a "trip to Merry Old England" complete
with "Victoriana" decor and more than 60 "delicious" brews, plus
"watercress sandwiches", "scones" and "divine little cakes"; just be
sure to "make reservations for afternoon tea, or risk a reprimand
from the queen herself."

Racha Noodles & 21 | 19 | 19 | $24
Thai Cuisine *Noodle Shop*

Seattle Center | 23 Mercer St. (bet. 1st & Queen Anne Aves.) |
206-281-8883
Olympia | Westfield Shoppingtown | 625 Black Lake Blvd. SW
(9th Ave. SW) | 360-943-8883
Renton | 104 S. Rainier Ave. (Victoria St. SW) | 425-271-4219
Woodinville | 13317 NE 175th St. (133rd Ave.) | 425-481-8833
www.rachathai.com

A "step above" the usual Thai "contenders", this "beautiful, reliable"
mini-chain earns a shout out for its "extensive menu" of "fresh",
"economical" classics and "unique" specialties; the Seattle Center
location is "great" for a bite "before or after" the theater.

R&L Home of Good Bar-B-Q 🅂 M ⊄ *BBQ* ▽ 21 | 5 | 15 | $15

Capitol Hill | 1816 E. Yesler Way (bet. 18th & 19th Aves.) | 206-322-0271
Arguably "the best bone joint in town", this family-run Capitol Hill
old-timer (it's been around since 1952) "smokes the meat on the
premises" for a "taste like home (and that's a good thing)"; expect
cafeteria-style service, and ask to "have the sauce on the side", as it
can be way hot; N.B. no credit cards.

	FOOD	DECOR	SERVICE	COST

🛛 Ray's Boathouse *Pacific NW/Seafood*   24 | 24 | 23 | $44

Shilshole | 6049 Seaview Ave. NW (60th St.) | 206-789-3770 |
www.rays.com

"Classic" Northwest seafood and "breathtaking" views of Shilshole
Bay have Seattleites calling this a "perennial favorite" for "celebratory dinners" and spoiling "out-of-town guests"; the "professional"
service never lags and everything's "always good no matter what
you order", which makes the final bill "easier to digest."

Ray's Cafe *Pacific NW/Seafood*   22 | 22 | 21 | $28

Shilshole | 6049 Seaview Ave. NW (61st St.) | 206-782-0094 |
www.rays.com

A "low-cost alternative" one floor up from brother Ray's Boathouse,
this "casual" seafooder soars with "spectacular views" and "tasty"
fish that's "simpler" than the fine dining downstairs; there's "no better place than their deck on a summer evening", especially "at sunset" when boaters from nearby Shilshole Marina "hit it."

Red Door *Pub Food*   17 | 16 | 16 | $19

Fremont | 3401 Evanston Ave. N. (34th St.) | 206-547-7521 |
www.reddoorseattle.com

"Juicy" burgers are the menu highlight at this Fremont "landmark"
with an eponymous scarlet portal, "reasonably priced" pub grub and
"excellent" selection of "brews"; the "spacious" digs are a "cool
place" to "people-watch", though "on a hot day" the "deck is the
best place" for drinking beer.

Red Fin *Japanese*   23 | 22 | 21 | $34

Downtown | Hotel Max | 612 Stewart St. (6th Ave.) | 206-441-4340 |
www.redfinsushi.com

Stylish travelers and seekers of the "high-end food scene" rave
about the "funky, New York-hip" interior and "clever sushi rolls" at
this Downtown Japanese in the Hotel Max; the "fabulous" cocktails
and "sake tasting flights" sport price tags that are right in line with
the upscale decor.

Red Mill Burgers 🅼⇗ *Burgers*   24 | 10 | 13 | $11

Phinney Ridge | 312 N. 67th St. (Phinney Ave.) | 206-783-6362
Interbay | 1613 W. Dravus St. (15th Ave.) | 206-284-6363
www.redmillburgers.com

Don't miss one of the "best darn burgers in town", plus "great" onion
rings and "outrageously good" shakes at these low-cost Phinney
Ridge-Interbay "guilty pleasures"; the food overshadows the "average" service and crowded quarters where you shouldn't expect "any
elbow room"; N.B. no cell phones allowed.

Red Robin *Burgers*   15 | 14 | 16 | $17

Eastlake | 3272 Fuhrman Ave. E. (Eastlake Ave.) | 206-323-0918
Seattle Waterfront | Pier 55 | 1101 Alaskan Way (Spring St.) |
206-623-1942
Bellevue | 408 Bellevue Sq. (NE 4th St.) | 425-453-9522
Issaquah | 1085 Lake Dr. (11th Ave. NW) | 425-313-0950
Redmond | 2390 148th Ave. NE (bet. 22nd & 24th Sts.) | 425-641-3810

(continued)

Red Robin

Redmond | Redmond Town Ctr. | 7597 170th Ave. NE (NE 76th St.) | 425-895-1870

Des Moines | 22705 Marine View Dr. S. (Kent Des Moines Rd.) | 206-824-2214

Everett | 1305 SE Everett Mall Way (Mall Dr.) | 425-355-7330

Lynnwood | Alderwood Mall | 18410 33rd Ave. W. (184th St.) | 425-771-6492

Woodinville | 18029 Garden Way NE (140th Ave.) | 425-488-6300
www.redrobin.com
Additional locations throughout the Seattle area

In the 1940s, this "solid" national chain was born in a ramshackle dive overlooking Lake Washington – and today the "noisy", "kid-friendly" local outposts still pull in the masses with 22 variations of "huge burgers that drip down your shirt", shakes and "bottomless french fry baskets"; everything is "reasonably priced" and "helpfully" served by a "young and peppy" staff.

NEW Remedy Teas *Tearoom*

∇ 23 | 21 | 25 | $9

Capitol Hill | 345 15th Ave. E. (Harrison St.) | 206-323-4832 | www.remedyteas.com

Nibble on "nice" savory and sweet snacks as you choose from the 150 "interesting" organic loose-leaf teas displayed on the wall of this "marvelously modern" tearoom tucked into an old Capitol Hill building; a "relaxing" vibe and "background" electronica music soothe sippers who "hang out" with "a book, a friend or a laptop."

Restaurant Shilla *Japanese/Korean*

∇ 15 | 11 | 10 | $31

Downtown | 2300 Eighth Ave. (Denny Way) | 206-623-9996

A Seoul food menu shares space with sushi selections at Downtown's "only" Korean-Japanese eatery, situated just across from Denny Park; the grill-your-own BBQ arrives with traditional side dishes in a retro-y setting that's nice enough to be "date-worthy", despite service that jurors judge "not accommodating" and food deemed not always up to par.

☑ Restaurant Zoë *American*

27 | 22 | 25 | $46

Belltown | 2137 Second Ave. (Blanchard St.) | 206-256-2060 | www.restaurantzoe.com

There are "no zzzzzzs" at this zesty restaurant joke reviewers, since it's got a "cool beyond cool" Belltown vibe that's "bustling and fun", and the "flawless" New American cuisine boasts "knock-your-socks-off flavors" from "local, fresh ingredients"; "seating is tight" in the slightly "sterile" space, but "personable" "service makes up for it", as do the bar's "delicious" "twists on classic" cocktails.

Rhodie's Smokin' BBQ ☒ *BBQ*

- | - | - | I

Seattle Center | 351 Broad St. (Denny Way) | 206-448-4080

Sure, this Seattle Center joint is "in a gas station", but that doesn't deter pork cravers who belly up to the utilitarian counter for BBQ ribs, brisket and the usual sides; since it's takeout only, famished 'cuemeisters picnic on the lawn of the Pacific Science Center across the street.

	FOOD	DECOR	SERVICE	COST

Rikki Rikki *Japanese*
19 | **16** | **19** | **$25**

Kirkland | Parkplace Ctr. | 442 Park Pl. (bet. 5th & 6th Sts.) | 425-828-0707 | www.rikkirikki.com

"Yummy yummy" say fans of this modern sushi stop in toney Kirkland serving mucho makimono rolls, plenty of cooked choices for sashimi-phobes, plus a whopping 30 sakes; the service is "friendly", but even the Japanese cartoon art on the walls doesn't win over detractors who call the fare "pedestrian."

Ristorante Italianissimo *Italian*
25 | **20** | **24** | **$33**

Woodinville | 15608 Woodinville-Duvall Pl. (156th Ave.) | 425-485-6888 | www.italianissimoristorante.com

This "little" Northern Italian "jewel" makes Woodinville's A-list thanks to its "outstanding" homemade pastas and "perfectly cooked" meats at prices that "don't require taking out a second mortgage"; regulars who give props to the "pleasant" service recommend "asking for a booth" and saving plenty of room for the "wonderful homemade desserts."

Ristorante Paradiso *Italian*
22 | **19** | **21** | **$31**

Kirkland | 120A Park Ln. (Lake Washington Blvd.) | 425-889-8601 | www.ristoranteparadiso.com

"Hidden" on Kirkland's Restaurant Row, this "unpretentious" Italian has been serving the "same reliable menu for years" to locals who laud the "delicious" veal, "saltimbocca that dances on the tongue" and wine list that's 200 labels strong; the old-world decor makes it a "cozy" retreat, and even better are its "reasonable prices"; P.S. try not to fill up on the "to-die-for" bread.

Romio's Pizza & Pasta *Pizza*
16 | **11** | **14** | **$17**

Downtown | 917 Howell St. (9th Ave.) | 206-622-6878
Eastlake | 3242 Eastlake Ave. E. (bet. Fuhrman & Harvard Aves.) | 206-322-4453
Greenwood | 8523 Greenwood Ave. N. (bet. 85th & 87th Sts.) | 206-782-9005
Magnolia | 2001 W. Dravus St. (20th Ave.) | 206-284-5420
Redmond | 16801 Redmond Way (Avondale Way NE) | 425-702-2466
Edmonds | 630 Edmonds Way (Paradise Ln.) | 425-744-0284
Everett | 11223 19th Ave. SE (Silver Lake Rd.) | 425-316-0305
Everett | 2803 Colby Ave. (California St.) | 425-252-0800
Lynnwood | 4306 228th St. SW (44th Ave.) | 425-673-2187
www.romios-pizza.com

Medium-crust "specialty" pizzas that are "thick, rich and decadent" make these parlors a popular dial-for-dinner option; those who dine in say the service is quick, but there's "not a fancy place" in the whole chain, and complainers cry that it's only "mediocre."

Rosebud Restaurant & Bar *American*
▽ **19** | **17** | **21** | **$27**

Capitol Hill | 719 E. Pike St. (Harvard Ave.) | 206-323-6636 | www.rosebud-restaurant.com

Tucked into an old-fashioned Capitol Hill building, this "jewel in the rough" is abloom with "good" American dinners and a "great" weekend brunch delivered by "accommodating" waiters; though "rarely crowded" and with a decor that some call "dated", the "bar is always lively" and there's a sweet, secret patio out back.

Rose's Bakery Cafe 🅑 *Pacific NW*

— | — | — | I

Eastsound | 382 Prune Alley (Rose St.) | 360-376-4292

On Orcas Island, Eastsound's "renovated" old firehouse is a "fine setting" for this cafe's "simple" Pacific NW cuisine made from isle ingredients, many of them organic; lingerers savor local and French wines by the large windows that look out on a park.

Rosita's Mexican Grill *Mexican*

19 | 13 | 19 | $19

Green Lake | 7210 Woodlawn Ave. NE (bet. 71st & 72nd Sts.) | 206-523-3031 | www.rositasrestaurant.com

This "always busy" Green Lake "typical" Mexican is a "step up from the chains" with "great tortillas" that are "made as you wait"; "take the kids", since the "fun" atmosphere is family-friendly and an "efficient" staff gets the grub out "quick."

Roti Cuisine of India *Indian*

20 | 15 | 16 | $20

Queen Anne | 530 Queen Anne Ave. N. (Mercer St.) | 206-216-7684

"Filling", "fresh and flavorful" Indian that's "spicy if you want it to be" is the specialty at this "lovely" Queen Anne storefront where diners are "treated like family"; naan-believers nag that it's only "standard curry shop stuff."

🆉 Rover's 🅑🅜 *French*

28 | 24 | 27 | $99

Madison Valley | 2808 E. Madison St. (28th Ave.) | 206-325-7442 | www.rovers-seattle.com

Thierry Rautureau's "unparalleled" New French degustation menus (including five- and eight-course options, plus a "stellar" vegetarian version) make this "elegant", "world-class" Madison Valley farmhouse a "haven" for appreciative locals and loads of visiting celebrities; service that "defines perfection" rounds out the "breathtakingly expensive" "experience"; N.B. à la carte options and Friday lunches can soften the wallet impact.

Ruby's *Diner*

16 | 20 | 17 | $15

Redmond | 16501 NE 74th St. (bet. 164th & 165th Aves.) | 425-861-7829 | www.rubys.com

This 1940's, red-and-white formica-ed "classic diner" in Redmond serves "exactly what you would expect": "good burgers", and shakes and sundaes in "generous portions" for the bucks; the "toy train going around the tracks overhead" makes it a "great place" for kids, and the staff is happy to get you "in and out quickly."

Russell's 🅑 *American*

— | — | — | M

Bothell | 3305 Monte Villa Pkwy. (35th Ave. S.) | 425-486-4072 | www.rdlcatering.com

White linens and formal service inside a vintage Bothell barn give an incongruous air to this "great" New American from celebrity caterer Russell Lowell whose client list includes some of the most famous people in the world; with Woodinville wine country as a backdrop, its

| | FOOD | DECOR | SERVICE | COST |

list of pours leans to Northwest and California bottles; breakfast and lunch are very low-key, and some advise going "for the sunsets."

Ruth's Chris Steak House   *Steak*
23 | 20 | 22 | $57

Downtown | Grand Hyatt | 727 Pine St. (bet. 7th & 8th Aves.) | 206-624-8524
Bellevue | 565 Bellevue Sq. (NE 8th St.) | 425-451-1550
www.ruthschris.com

This chain's famous "buttery" "steaks and chops" are on display at Seattle's two outposts, though the local digs are "quieter" and more "modern" than others around the country; the Downtown link, in the Grand Hyatt hotel, offers breakfast with "crabmeat eggs Benedict" that is "worth the trip to Seattle", and in Bellevue fans flock to the "very busy" "happy hour", but call them "overpriced" and "not note-worthy"; N.B. scores do not reflect a post-Survey ownership change.

Saigon Bistro   *Vietnamese*
∇ 23 | 11 | 14 | $20

International District | Asian Plaza | 1032 S. Jackson St. (10th Ave.) | 206-329-4939

"You get your money's worth" at this Vietnamese in the ID's Little Saigon district where behind a plain exterior there's "fresh" food inside, including shrimp rolls "to die for"; around since 1993, some surmise this early entree on the Southeast Asian dining scene is losing ground to the fierce "competition" that's sprung up in the area.

NEW Saint-Germain ⑤ Ⓜ   *French*
21 | 20 | 21 | $22

Madison Valley | 2811A E. Madison St. (bet. 28th & 29th Aves.) | 206-323-9800 | www.saintgermainseattle.com

Madison Valley locals "love" this "quaint" "French snack bar" and its "simple but perfectly done" sandwiches and gratins, plus the "excellent", "inexpensive" wines by the glass; when chef Jean-Michel Omnés is "playing his accordion" in the "crisp white and blue" space, you "feel like you are in Paris."

Saito's Japanese
Cafe & Bar ⑤ Ⓜ   *Japanese*
26 | 18 | 21 | $41

Belltown | 2122 Second Ave. (bet. Blanchard & Lenora Sts.) | 206-728-1333

"Seriously great sushi and sashimi" makes this one of the "best in Seattle", tucked into a vintage "long, narrow" Belltown storefront gussied up with bamboo, blonde and black accents and an S-curved bar; sated surveyors "forget all about" the sushi chef's "cold fish" attitude as soon as the "pristine" pescatorial fare is served, and an "extensive" selection of nearly 50 sakes doesn't hurt either.

⊠ Salish Lodge Dining Room   *French*
24 | 26 | 25 | $60

Snoqualmie | Salish Lodge & Spa | 6501 Railroad Ave. SE (Hwy. 202) | 425-888-2556 | www.salishlodge.com

Perched "at the top" of Snoqualmie Falls with "glorious" views, this New French "destination" is "wonderful" for "celebrating a milestone" or popping the question – it's got "the supreme 'oohhh' factor"; the fare is "inventive" and there's "top notch-service" too, all of which comes at a price nearly as "high" as the falls themselves.

	FOOD	DECOR	SERVICE	COST

Saltoro *American*

FOOD 22 | DECOR 21 | SERVICE 21 | COST $27

North Seattle | 14051 Greenwood Ave. N. (N. 143rd St.) | 206-365-6025
The "charming" "neighborhood joint" for The Highlands' denizens offers a "select" menu of "solid" New American plates, "wonderful" desserts and "great" drinks; "twinkle lights" and "handblown glass" give the "dark" digs a slightly "high-end" vibe, plus there's "a cozy fire" to nuzzle by while the sometimes "slow" service takes its time.

☑ Salty's *Seafood*

FOOD 20 | DECOR 22 | SERVICE 20 | COST $39

West Seattle | 1936 Harbor Ave. SW (Fairmont Ave.) | 206-937-1600
Redondo | 28201 Redondo Beach Dr. S. (282nd St.) | 253-946-0636
www.saltys.com
It's all about the "right on the water" views at these two seafooders that satisfy gawking gazers with "good" fin fare plus a "spectacular Sunday brunch" (on Saturdays too, at Alki Beach) featuring "endless piles of fresh oysters, shrimp and crab"; there's a "crowded", "cruise-like atmosphere" and the final bill can get "a bit pricey", but most say it's "worth it", especially for "impressing" "out-of-town guests."

Salute of Bellevue *Italian*

FOOD 19 | DECOR 17 | SERVICE 19 | COST $32

Bellevue | 10134 Main St. (bet. 101st & 102nd Aves.) | 425-688-7613
Italian food fans *mangia* on "mouthwatering" morsels at this "romantic" trattoria in Bellevue's spiffy Old Main Street area where the "good" eats are a "great value"; its "lovely", rustic room welcomes "don't-miss" flamenco and opera nights, plus there's a see-who's-here patio in front.

Salvatore Ristorante ☑ *Italian*

FOOD 23 | DECOR 16 | SERVICE 21 | COST $28

Ravenna | 6100 Roosevelt Way NE (61st St.) | 206-527-9301
When it's "good, old-fashioned Italian you're after", this rustic Ravenna "faithful" is "the place", serving "creative specials" alongside a list of wines from The Boot – plus there are "personable waiters" to boot; surveyors say it's among the "best" neighborhood spots, with a laid-back vibe dictated by "wonderful" owner-chef Salvatore Anania.

Sam's Sushi *Japanese*

FOOD 18 | DECOR 13 | SERVICE 18 | COST $22

Ballard | 5506 22nd Ave. NW (Market St.) | 206-783-2262
Seattle Center | 521 Queen Anne Ave. N. (bet. Mercer & Republican Sts.) | 206-282-4612
For quick fish, this "real-find" twinset gives Seattle Center and Ballard sushistas "very fresh" Japanese "comfort food", udon and tempura at a "great price"; the service is "basic", and a "lack of ambiance" keeps more decor-obsessed reviewers "from going back."

Sand Point Grill *Eclectic*

FOOD 17 | DECOR 17 | SERVICE 20 | COST $28

Sand Point | 5412 Sand Point Way NE (55th St.) | 206-729-1303
In pretty Sand Point, this "low-key but very hip" restaurant and watering hole attracts a "Wasp-y" clientele with "consistent, if not imaginative" Eclectic plates and a "chummy" vibe; naggers note that service is sometimes "slow" and say it's "fine if you live nearby", but "not worth traveling to."

	FOOD	DECOR	SERVICE	COST

Santa Fe Cafe *New Mexican*   21 | 18 | 21 | $25

Phinney Ridge | 5910 Phinney Ave. N. (bet. 59th & 60th Sts.) | 206-783-9755

This convivial New Mexican in Phinney Ridge has been "waking up" the taste buds for 21 years with "green chiles", "cheesy enchiladas" and a serious level of "spiciness"; add in good service and a "warm" setting with Anasazi colors, and you've got diners who hope this "veteran" "never changes."

Santorini Greek Grill 🅢🈲 *Greek*   23 | 12 | 18 | $18

Kirkland | 106 Central Way (1st St.) | 425-822-0555

For "fast, inexpensive and delicious" Greek goods, Kirklanders head to this "neighborhood favorite" and "load up" on affordable gyros, sandwiches and salads "served with enthusiasm"; be sure to say hi to the "chatty" owner who is often "behind the grill" and, since there are only a "few tables", get your grub to go and eat nearby "at the waterfront."

Sazerac *Southern*   20 | 21 | 19 | $39

Downtown | Hotel Monaco | 1101 Fourth Ave. (Spring St.) | 206-624-7755 | www.sazeracrestaurant.com

Downtown's "trendy" Hotel Monaco hosts this "inventive" Southern-inspired restaurant that boasts an "eclectic", if somewhat "limited" menu", including "catfish to die for", "fantastic" breakfasts and namesake cocktails; the "intensely decorated" "big-ish" dining room attracts a "noisy, young crowd" that congregates for "people-watching" and doesn't seem to mind service that can be "inconsistent."

Scandinavian Cafe at
Scandinavian Specialties 🅢Ⓜ *Scandinavian*   - | - | - | I

Ballard | 6719 15th Ave. NW (bet. 67th & 70th Sts.) | 206-784-7020 | www.scanspecialties.com

In Scandinavian Ballard, this taste of "the northland" serves "great" hard-to-find Scandie "home cooking" – such as "open-face sandwiches" and *beste kake* like Aunt Lina used to make – all at a "reasonable cost"; frequented by expats and their descendants, the "little" cafe is conveniently tucked inside the ScanSelect Scandinavian Specialties import shop.

Sea Garden *Chinese/Seafood*   20 | 14 | 17 | $24

International District | 509 Seventh Ave. S. (King St.) | 206-623-2100 🌙
Bellevue | 200 106th Ave. NE (2nd St.) | 425-450-8833 | www.seagardenofbellevue.com

"Catch the fish" dishes at this Cantonese "old line" seafood duo that "just keeps chugging along" with "always reliable" fin fare, "good dim sum" at the Bellevue branch and "late-night" hours at the more-modern ID outpost (serving till 3 AM on weekends); though the decor is largely "forgettable" and the menu can be a "little pricier" than the competition, even detractors admit it's "ok in a pinch."

Sea Grill *Seafood*

| 22 | 20 | 22 | $45 |

Tacoma | 1498 Pacific Ave. (Commerce St.) | 253-272-5656 | www.the-seagrill.com

"Seafood is the thing" at this Tacoma "gem" where seasonal treats like Copper River and the harder-to-find Yukon salmon are served in a "somewhat cavernous", "nouveau '60s" space that's overseen by "friendly but formal" service; penny-pinchers who find it "pricey" for T-town should try the affordable and "exceptionally good" burger from the bar menu.

⚡ Seastar

| 26 | 24 | 24 | $49 |

Restaurant & Raw Bar *Seafood*

Bellevue | Civica Office Commons | 205 108th Ave. NE (2nd St.) | 425-456-0010 | www.seastarrestaurant.com

This "hot spot" in "upscale" Bellevue entices with "exquisitely prepared" fin fare and "hedonistic" comfort food (think lobster mac 'n' cheese) that's "rather expensive, but worth it"; despite service that can be "cold and aloof", the "airy", "elegant" dining room continually "crackles with fashion and money", so expect a "high-energy" experience.

Señor Moose Café *Mexican*

| 24 | 16 | 21 | $18 |

Ballard | 5242 Leary Ave. NW (bet. Ione Pl. & 20th Ave.) | 206-784-5568 | www.senormoose.com

"Holy guacamole", it's "not your typical border food" at this "hip" Central Mexican cafe on Ballard's Leary Avenue, where the inexpensive "homestyle cooking" consists of "fresh, local" ingredients and "incendiary salsa"; "dinners are just as good" as the buzzed-about breakfasts, though voters are split on the "tongue in cheek" decor – some say it "doesn't get past tacky", while others insist it "adds to the enjoyment."

Sentosa Asian

| ▽ 15 | 16 | 8 | $21 |

Cuisine & Bakery *Chinese*

Kirkland | 107 Lake St. (bet. Central Way & Park Ln.) | 425-889-0689 | www.sentosa-asiancuisine.com

The "good" daily dim sum at this Kirkland Chinese is "freshest" early in the day, so go then and order as the "carts and trays" are conveyed "straight from the oven"; the "white linen" atmo is serene, especially at dinner when "Hong Kong–style" fare is ordered from a menu, though "slow", sometimes "sullen" service has a few voters saying they'd "go more often if it wasn't so frustrating."

Serafina *Italian*

| 24 | 23 | 22 | $38 |

Eastlake | 2043 Eastlake Ave. E. (Boston St.) | 206-323-0807 | www.serafinaseattle.com

"A dream" murmur fans about this "romantic" Eastlaker with "fabulous", "rustic" Italian eats that are "simple", "fresh and seasonal"; "joyfully noisy on most nights", the "delightful", candlelit environs, built circa 1920, have a "neighborhood enoteca"-like feel, and there's "live music" on weekends plus a "garden patio" that's "probably the best reason to come" "on warm summer evenings."

	FOOD	DECOR	SERVICE	COST

NEW Serious Pie *Pizza* `25` `16` `19` `$24`
Downtown | 316 Virginia St. (bet. 3rd & 4th Aves.) | 206-838-7388 | www.tomdouglas.com

At this "chaotic" Downtown rumpus room, the pie-us snack on Tom Douglas' "very tasty" "Northwest pizzas with a smile", topped with the "finest", "foraged" artisan ingredients; "communal tables" "foster multiparty chats" in the "tightly packed", "small" quarters, and the "pricey" costs seems "fairly reasonable" given that "this is seriously some of the best" 'za "you'll ever eat."

74th St. Ale House *Pub Food* `19` `15` `16` `$19`
Phinney Ridge | 7401 Greenwood Ave. N. (74th St.) | 206-784-2955 | www.seattlealehouses.com

Cranked up English "pub grub" that's "prepared with care", an "outstanding" microbrew list and the nightly meet-and-greet crowd make this Phinney Ridge stalwart a "welcoming" and "lively" place; "you won't be drawn in by the decor" warns one local, and some quibble about the "indifferent" staff, but still, it's "always crowded."

Shallots *Pan-Asian* `22` `16` `21` `$24`
Belltown | 2525 Fourth Ave. (Vine St.) | 206-728-1888 | www.shallotsseattle.com

The "awesome smells" emanating from this Belltown Pan-Asian "sleeper" draw in locals for "lovely", "unpretentious" fare that cause some to call it "Wild Ginger" for "half the price and none of the attitude"; the "small" storefront's "boring decor" doesn't scare off "lunch hour" feasters who laud the "fast and friendly service."

Shamiana *Indian/Pakistani* `23` `20` `20` `$27`
Kirkland | Houghton Vill. | 10724 NE 68th St. (108th Ave.) | 425-827-4902

"Interesting flavors" abound at this "quiet, relaxing" Kirklander proffering "well-prepared" Indian and Pakistani dishes, including their "signature" "Major Grey's Chicken Curry"; "good" service and a "lunch buffet" that "isn't your usual" fare make it worth "often returns."

Shanghai Garden *Chinese* `22` `11` `15` `$20`
International District | 524 Sixth Ave. S. (bet. King & Weller Sts.) | 206-625-1689
Issaquah | 80 Front St. N. (Sunset Way) | 425-313-3188 Ⓜ

"A cut above" average in its genre, this "family-run" Issaquah and ID Chinese duet is locally famous for its "hand-shaved noodles" that "rock" and "delicious", "healthy" dumplings; food arrives at the table "faster than you can blink", and to top it off, it's "inexpensive."

Sharp's Roaster & Ale House *American* `-` `-` `-` `|`
SeaTac | 18427 International Blvd. (188th St.) | 206-241-5744

Close to Sea-Tac airport, this casual American "carnivore's heaven" makes layovers less loathsome with "deliciously tender slow-cooked meat", "great salads" and "lots of ales and brews on tap"; the "not fancy, not frilly" decor soars with bent airplane propellers on the ceiling, tap handles on the walls and a wagering wheel for determining beer prices – so "what's not to like?"

	FOOD	DECOR	SERVICE	COST

Shea's Lounge Ⓜ *Pacific NW* ▽ 24 | 21 | 23 | $35

Pike Place Market | Pike Place Mkt. | 94 Pike St. (1st Ave.) | 206-467-9990 | www.chezshea.com

"Lower-key" than the adjoining Chez Shea, this Pike Place Market "lounge/cafe" is a "great way to sample" the parent place's Pacific NW provisions in a less pricey, "more casual manner"; locals relax in the "romantic", "small dining room" over "wonderful appetizers", "imaginative" drinks and a "foie gras crème brûlée" that's "to die for."

Shiki Japanese *Japanese* 24 | 11 | 19 | $28

Queen Anne | 4 W. Roy St. (Queen Anne Ave.) | 206-281-1352 | www.shiki-sushi.com

Owner-chef Ken Yamamoto is "one of a few" sushi chefs in America "qualified" to prepare "blowfish" – and his "less-daring sushi" is "delicious" too, at this "sleepy", midpriced Queen Anne nook; regulars seek out the "seasonal" surprises and "excellent sake selection", and what the space "lacks in ambiance" is made up for "in freshness and style."

🗷 Shiro's Sushi *Japanese* 27 | 15 | 21 | $45

Belltown | 2401 Second Ave. (Battery St.) | 206-443-9844 | www.shiros.com

In a "town filled with sushi joints", this "much-touted", "bustling" Belltowner is among "the best", since Kyoto expat Shiro Kashiba cuts "nothing but the freshest" fish (his "knife work is exceptional"), much of it "local"; a $30 tasting menu is a bargain, though sushistas recommend getting the "spendy" "omakase" for maximum "dazzle"; P.S. "no reservations" mean "be prepared to wait."

Shoalwater *Pacific NW* - | - | - | E

Seaview | Shelburne Inn | 4415 Pacific Hwy. (45th St.) | 360-642-4142 | www.shoalwater.com

Seaview's "destination restaurant" in the Shelburne Inn is a "favorite" for its "great" Pacific NW fare and "outstanding wine list"; the 102-year-old Victorian building sets an upscale tone, and "wonderful owners" Ann and Tony Kischer let diners "relax and enjoy the luxury experience" that's "worth the drive."

Shuckers *Seafood* 25 | 22 | 24 | $45

Downtown | Fairmont Olympic Hotel | 411 University St. (4th Ave.) | 206-621-1984

The fin fare is "stellar" at this "wood-paneled" Downtowner in the "elegant" Fairmont Olympic Hotel where an "efficient" staff serves "dependably fresh" oysters, a "don't-miss" "seafood Caesar" and more; set in an ex-haberdashery, it exudes a "warm" feeling whether dining in a streetside "window" seat or one of the "private alcoves."

Shultzy's *Sandwiches* 20 | 13 | 19 | $13

University District | 4114 University Way NE (bet. 41st & 42nd Sts.) | 206-548-9461 | www.shultzys.com

This "classic student sausage joint" is a University District "standby" for "heartburn favorites" (like "homemade" wursts) accompanied by "good German beers"; its zinc and mahogany bars jam "before and after" "UW Husky games", so though the servers are "friendly", at prime times the food can get "backed up."

Silent Heart Nest *Vegetarian*   ▽ 16 | 16 | 14 | $15

Fremont | 3508 Fremont Pl. N (35th St.) | 206-633-5169
"Peaceful" and low-cost, this vegetarian venue, operated by an East Indian religious group, is known for its "tasty" "neat loaf" (that tastes like meatloaf) and "healthy", "hearty", often-organic lunch and breakfast fare; "multicolor, twirly" artworks and inspirational thoughts decorate the Fremont space, which formerly housed the more swashbuckling (now defunct) The Longshoreman's Daughter cafe; N.B. no dinner.

☑ Sitka & Spruce Ⓜ *Eclectic*   28 | 14 | 18 | $35

Eastlake | 2238 Eastlake Ave. E. (bet. Boston & E. Lynn Sts.) | 206-324-0662 | www.sitkaandspruce.com
This "funky" "strip-mall" storefront in Eastlake is an "unbelievable surprise", turning out "plate-lickingly delicious" food courtesy of chef-owner Matt Dillon, whose "inventive" Eclectic menu features "local" ingredients "you've never tasted" before; the "tiny", "cramped" room "fills up fast", so expect "aggravatingly long waits", plus "shared tables" and service that "could use some polish" – none of which bothers the "haute"-minded foodies who flock here.

611 Supreme Ⓜ *French*   23 | 18 | 18 | $19

Capitol Hill | 611 E. Pine St. (Boylston St.) | 206-328-0292
Bon vivants cheer *"c'est magnifique"* for the "divine", "to-die-for" crêpes rolled at this "hip" French Capitol Hill spot, which also serves other "reasonably priced" Parisian fare; "the "attentive" staff and "intimate" bar make this a prime place "for a date", a "late-night sweets craving" or a drink "before hitting the neighborhood clubs."

☑ 6 · 7 *Pacific NW*   24 | 26 | 24 | $51

Seattle Waterfront | Edgewater Hotel, Pier 67 | 2411 Alaskan Way (bet. Vine & Wall Sts.) | 206-269-4575 | www.edgewaterhotel.com
"Watch the sunset" over the Seattle Waterfront as ships sail "right by" the windows of this Edgewater Hotel restaurant overlooking Elliott Bay and featuring "one of the best decks" in the city; the "seasonal", pricey Pacific NW fare is "excellent", the bar is "laid-back" and the "friendly" staff and "Northwest-chic" decor (including modish fake trees) add to the "warm", "romantic" vibe.

☑ SkyCity at the Needle *Pacific NW*   21 | 26 | 22 | $57

Seattle Center | Space Needle | 400 Broad St. (4th Ave. N.) | 206-905-2111 | www.spaceneedle.com
The "atmosphere is the high point" at this revolving roost at the "top of the Space Needle" with the "most commanding urban view" around; a "celebration" destination and lure for "tourists", it offers "attentive" service and "surprisingly good" (if "expensive") Pacific NW fare, though even admirers admit "ok, no one comes for the food."

	FOOD	DECOR	SERVICE	COST

Smarty Pants ◐ *Sandwiches*
| | − | − | − | I |

Georgetown | 6017 Airport Way S. (Vale St.) | 206-762-4777 |
www.smartypantsseattle.com

This "intentional dive" on the hip strip in Georgetown offers sloppy
sandwiches, beer and locally notorious cocktails like the Bacon
Martini, amid motorcycle-heavy decor; never mind the time of "day
or night", it's "almost always crowded" with a "real interesting mix"
of bikers and imbibers; despite service that's "stretched thin", locals
concur "it's hard to beat."

NEW Sorrentino Ⓜ *Italian*
| | 18 | 18 | 20 | $30 |

Queen Anne | 2128 Queen Anne Ave. N. (Boston St.) | 206-694-0055 |
www.sorrentinoseattle.com

"Mamma Enza" gives a "warm" welcome at her "solid" Queen Anne
Hill trattoria serving "nicely presented" Sicilian specialties that are
"a bit different"; "white tablecloths" spiff up the "small" space
where surveyors say the prices are "reasonable", and service can be
"like a leopard – spotty."

Sostanza Trattoria ⓈⒺ *Italian*
| | 22 | 21 | 23 | $37 |

Madison Park | 1927 43rd Ave. E. (Madison St.) | 206-324-9701 |
www.sostanzaseattle.com

An "intimate" Madison Park "favorite", this sweet spot draws ap-
plause for its "satisfying pastas" and other "reliably good" Northern
Italian fare, plus "delightful" service; the "outdoor patio" "facing
Lake Washington" is "great in summer", and when a breeze blows
there are "blankets in a basket" for huddling under.

NEW Spazzo *Italian*
| | 20 | 20 | 18 | $31 |

Redmond | Redmond Town Ctr. | 16499 NE 74th St. (bet. 164th &
166th Aves.) | 425-881-4400 | www.schwartzbros.com

Once a Bellevue favorite, this "trendy Italian bistro" has been rein-
carnated in Redmond Town Center where its old fans are regrouping
for "very good" pizzas, pastas and grilled meats, and "great" wine
too; the "contemporary", Med-hued digs are "fun", but cynics say the
food "still needs a bit of polish" and "can be on the expensive side."

Spencer's For Steaks & Chops *Steak*
| | − | − | − | E |

SeaTac | Hilton | 17620 Pacific Hwy. S. (176th St.) | 206-248-7153 |
www.spencersforsteaksandchops.com

In the Hilton, this "hotel restaurant" that's "convenient" to Sea-Tac
airport attracts big spenders with "very good" USDA prime bone-in
Spencer steak and a wine list that's nearly 300-bottles strong; a sky-
and-clouds painted ceiling gives out-of-towners a glimpse of things
to come during their visit, though critics call the menu "ho hum."

NEW Spitfire ◐ *Caribbean/Pan-Latin*
| | ▽ 19 | 19 | 16 | $20 |

Belltown | 2219 Fourth Ave. (Blanchard St.) | 206-441-7966 |
www.spitfireseattle.com

Game watchers who want "more than wings and lite beer" tout this
"trendy" Belltown Caribbean–Pan-Latin that offers "great finger-
food for a sports bar", in a "lively" setting; though service can be

"frazzled and forgetful", there are more than 20 plasma-screen TVs to keep fans occupied; N.B. 21-and-over only.

Sport *Eclectic* | 18 | 23 | 16 | $23 |

Seattle Center | Fisher Plaza | 140 Fourth Ave. N. (Broad St.) | 206-404-7767 | www.sportrestaurant.com

Right in the KOMO-TV building facing the Seattle Center, this "gourmet" sports bar is the "place to catch the game no one else is showing", since "plasmas" are "all over the joint" and the front tables have "their own TVs"; the slightly "pricey" Eclectic fare includes Kobe beef burgers ("one of the best around") and "must-have" fries – the main gripe is that even on game nights it can be "too quiet."

St. Clouds ● *Pacific NW* | 21 | 20 | 24 | $27 |

Madrona | 1131 34th Ave. (Union St.) | 206-726-1522 | www.stclouds.com

Madronans munch on a blend of "creative" and "straight-up" Pacific NW noshes at this "home-away-from-home" where "good food for the value" draws families "early in the evening" and "adults" later on (there's live music four nights a week); the "terrific" staff "knows everyone's" name, and its "stark", yet "comfortable" space is enhanced by a "primo" "back garden" on "warm summer nights."

NEW Steelhead Diner Ⓜ *Pacific NW* | 23 | 21 | 22 | $38 |

Pike Place Market | Pike Place Mkt. | 95 Pine St. (1st Ave.) | 206-625-0129 | www.steelheaddiner.com

At this "edgy" year-old Pike Place Market diner, chef-owner Kevin Davis (late of The Oceanaire) crafts "dynamic", midpriced Pacific NW comfort food from fresh ingredients, many plucked "right from" the nearby "market stalls"; some suppers sip "exclusively Northwest" wines in the "laid-back" dining room with sightlines into the "open kitchen", while others "sit at the bar" for its views of Elliott Bay.

Stellar Pizza, Ale & Cocktails ● *Pizza*   ▽ | 21 | 19 | 16 | $22 |

Georgetown | 5513 Airport Way S. (Lucile St.) | 206-763-1660 | www.stellarpizza.com

The "diverse array" of "imaginative" Northwest pizzas entice star-struck locals at this "informal" parlor with an "awesome Georgetown vibe" and more than a dozen microbrews on tap; "tattooed and pierced" servers wait on the equally "eclectic crowd."

Streamliner Diner Ⓕ *Diner* | 16 | 10 | 15 | $14 |

Bainbridge Island | 397 Winslow Way E. (Ericksen Ave.) | 206-842-8595

There's "always a line on weekends" at this "funky" Bainbridge Island "institution" known for its "great homemade biscuits" and "down-home" breakfasts that are "reasonably priced"; "crowded", "unpretentious" and "buzzy", the "diner"-esque space suffers from service that naysayers note "leaves much to be desired."

Stumbling Goat Bistro Ⓜ *Pacific NW* | 24 | 19 | 22 | $39 |

Greenwood | 6722 Greenwood Ave. N. (67th St.) | 206-784-3535 | www.stumblinggoatbistro.com

A "terrific" "change from the mundane", this "quintessential neighborhood bistro" boasts "innovative" Pacific NW fare made with sus-

	FOOD	DECOR	SERVICE	COST

tainable "local ingredients"; its "relaxed, convivial" Greenwood air and prices "low enough" to make it a "regular" "splurge" have surveyors saying it's "simply a delight."

Sunfish ⓜ⌀ *Seafood* — 21 | 10 | 13 | $12

West Seattle | 2800 Alki Ave. SW (62nd Ave.) | 206-938-4112
For some of the "best" "not greasy" fish 'n' chips around, hit this humble West Seattle seafooder with patio seating across from Alki Beach; both "cod and halibut" are on offer, and with a "hard-working" staff and easygoing prices, it's among the "best deals in town."

Sunlight Cafe *Eclectic* — 16 | 9 | 13 | $16

Roosevelt | 6403 Roosevelt Way NE (bet. 64th & 65th Sts.) | 206-522-9060
This "hippie-dippy" vegetarian "landmark" "doesn't seem to have changed" since its birth in the '70s and still serves a "wide variety" of Eclectic meat-free "delights" that can veer toward the "bizarre"; a "cheery" vibe and cheap prices don't do much for critics who are "not impressed."

Sushiman ⓜ *Japanese* — 24 | 17 | 20 | $36

Issaquah | 670 NW Gilman Blvd. (7th Ave.) | 425-391-4295
Ex-sumo wrestler "turned knowledgeable sushi chef" Bobbi Suetsugu puts on "dinner and a show" at this "kid-friendly" Issaquah Japanese with "quality" fin fare and a "friendly greeting when you walk in the door"; despite "high" costs and "nondescript" environs, most say "it is definitely worth it."

Sushiya ⓩ *Japanese* — – | – | – | M

Kirkland | 11451 98th Ave. NE (116th St.) | 425-821-3958
Sushi made with "care and flair" is the hallmark of this "creative" Kirkland Japanese where the chefs are "patient with novices" and "grizzled old veterans" alike; its "quaint" sake collection is just one more reason locals return here "again and again."

ⓩ Szechuan Chef *Chinese* — 27 | 15 | 18 | $19

Bellevue | Kelsey Creek Ctr. | 15015 Main St. (148th Ave.) | 425-746-9008
"So hot but worth the sweat" pant admirers of the "huge selection" of "fantastic", "fiery" Szechuan fare at this "always wonderful" Chinese "hole-in-the-wall"; it's "easy to miss" in a Bellevue "strip mall", so follow your nose toward the "aroma of deliciousness", and expect the "friendly" service to get the food out "fast."

Szmania's ⓜ *German/Pacific NW* — 23 | 21 | 23 | $42

Magnolia | 3321 W. McGraw St. (34th Ave.) | 206-284-7305 | www.szmanias.com
Magnolians call this "classic" "clubhouse" their "special-occasion" "staple" thanks to Austrian-born chef Ludger Szmania's "innovative" Pacific NW–German "specialties" made with "local ingredients" (the "wurst is the best"); with two fireplaces, the "sophisticated" "European setting" is "perfect for that rainy, chilly night", enhanced by an "informed" staff.

	FOOD	DECOR	SERVICE	COST

Tacos Guaymas *Mexican* 20 | 10 | 15 | $12

Capitol Hill | 1415 Broadway E. (bet. Pike & Union Sts.) | 206-860-3871
Fremont | 106 N. 36th St. (1st Ave.) | 206-547-5110
Green Lake | 6808 E. Green Lake Way N. (2nd Ave.) | 206-729-6563
West Seattle | 4719 California Ave. SW (Alaska St.) | 206-935-8970
White Center | 1622 SW Roxbury St. (bet. 16th & 17th Aves.) | 206-767-4026
Everett | 1814 112th St. SE (19th Ave.) | 425-338-7998
Federal Way | 314434 Pacific Hwy. S. (312th St.) | 253-529-5900
Tacoma | 2630 S. 38th St. (Pine St.) | 253-471-2224
Lynnwood | 5919 196th St. SW (58th Pl.) | 425-670-3580
Renton | 530 Rainier Ave. S. (bet. 4th Pl. & 7th St.) | 425-235-2152
"Inexpensive" Mexican that's fast, "fresh" and "flavorful" brings feasters to these "straightforward" taquerias with "salsa bars" that could "make anything taste delicious"; brisk "takeout" and "nice people" add to the experience.

Tai Tung *Chinese* ▽ 20 | 8 | 15 | $16

International District | 655 S. King St. (Maynard Ave.) | 206-622-7372
This "old-school" ID "institution" has been serving "consistently good" Cantonese dishes for 70 years and counting, and still thrives thanks to fans who fawn over "pineapple chicken" that's worth "flying" in for, and specials that are pasted on the mirror; "everything is great" except the "charmless" decor, but "who cares" when the prices are this "cheap"?

Takis Mad Greek ⑤ *Greek* ▽ 18 | 8 | 17 | $15

Ballard | 8539 15th Ave. NW (bet. 85th & 87th Sts.) | 206-297-9200
"Authentic" gyros and other homemade specialties abound at this "very informal", inexpensive Ballard Hellenic with counter service and a few tables and chairs; owner Takis Dotas is a Greek music star, so expect the joint to hop on Saturday nights when he picks up his bouzouki to play.

Tamarind Tree *Vietnamese* 24 | 22 | 19 | $22

International District | 1036 S. Jackson St. (12th Ave.) | 206-860-1404 | www.tamarindtreerestaurant.com
"Tucked" in back of an ID strip mall, this Vietnamese "oasis" is a "culinary surprise", serving "superb bobay mon (beef seven ways)" in a "seriously sexy" "modern" dining room, with "cheap" prices, to boot; though some say the "service is lacking", most counter that it gets "deservedly crowded" and "everyone should go at least once."

Tango *Spanish* 23 | 21 | 22 | $33

Capitol Hill | 1100 Pike St. (Boren Ave.) | 206-583-0382 | www.tangorestaurant.com
"Tapas are tops" at this "colorful" Capitol Hill Spanish salon with bites "so tempting" that enthusiasts "want to try them all"; its "cool", "full-of-energy" dining room is a "pleasant change" from the "high-powered Downtown dining scene" just blocks away, and those in-the-know "eat at the bar" and search out the "amazing happy-hour specials."

| | FOOD | DECOR | SERVICE | COST |

Tap House Grill *Eclectic*
18 | 18 | 17 | $27

NEW **Downtown** | 1506 Sixth Ave. (bet. Pike & Pine Sts.) | 206-816-3314
Bellevue | 550 106th Ave. NE (4th St.) | 425-467-1728
www.taphousegrill.com

The "gravitational pull" of 160 "beers on tap" and "good comfort food" draw a "pretty" crowd of "twenty- and thirtysomething singles" to these Downtown and Bellevue Eclectics; the "lively" digs are "glitzy" enough to earn it the title of "almost the Bellagio of pubs", and service is "quick", except at happy hour when the bar "gets packed."

NEW TASTE M *Pacific NW*
▽ 19 | 14 | 15 | $28

Downtown | Seattle Art Museum | 1300 First Ave. (bet. Union & University Sts.) | 206-903-5291 | www.tastesam.com

In the Seattle Art Museum Downtown, this "imaginative" Pacific NWer hits both "modern" and "traditional" notes with a "sustainable" menu that's "priced well below most" other in-attraction canteens; looking out onto urban First Avenue, the bright, contemporary and "noisy" space is a visual counterpoint to the comforting food.

Taste of India *Indian*
22 | 14 | 18 | $19

University District | 5517 Roosevelt Way NE (56th St.) | 206-528-1575 | www.tasteofindiaseattle.com

Set in a "converted house", this Indian eatery gets "more crowded every year" as University District locals discover its "good, cheap" staples – including "butter chicken" and "palak paneer" – that "dazzle" with their "depth"; service can be a "little rushed", making this "not the place to have a leisurely meal."

NEW Tavolàta ● *Italian*
24 | 20 | 21 | $37

Belltown | 2323 Second Ave. (bet. Battery & Bell Sts.) | 206-838-8008 | www.tavolata.com

Owners Ethan Stowell and Patric Gabre-Kidan put a "fresh spin" on Italian at this latest midpriced "hot spot" for the "young and hip", a sibling to Stowell's esteemed Union – and worlds apart; "interesting" ingredients, homemade mozzarella and "wonderful" "fresh" pastas abound in its "cool, industrial" Belltown space that's "lots of fun", though a few note that the "communal table in the center of the room" is popular for "celebrations", so it can be "noisy."

Taxi Dogs ⊘ *Hot Dogs*
▽ 15 | 6 | 14 | $10

Pike Place Market | Pike Place Mkt. | 1928 Pike Pl. (bet. Stewart & Virginia Sts.) | 206-443-1919

This quintessential Pike Place Market cooked-to-order frankfurter nook offers what fast-foodies call "the best hot dog in the market"; it's "worth standing in line" for one of the many varieties that fans get for "takeout" to eat in Steinbrueck Park.

Tempero do Brasil M *Brazilian*
▽ 24 | 14 | 18 | $25

University District | 5628 University Way NE (bet. 56th St. & Ravenna Blvd.) | 206-523-6229 | www.temperodobrasil.net

"Hidden among homes" just north of the University District, this "lively" Brazilian offers a "to-die-for" feijoada (meat and bean stew), "flavorful" seafood and "very good" caipirinhas (Brazil's version of the mojito"); the dining room is small and simple, making this "unique place" an "intimate hang."

	FOOD	DECOR	SERVICE	COST

Ten Mercer ● American
22 | 22 | 23 | $35

Queen Anne | 10 Mercer St. (bet. 1st & Queen Anne Aves.) | 206-691-3723 | www.tenmercer.com

This "friendly" Queen Anne standby lures Seattle Center opera and theatergoers with an "interesting" menu of "inspired" New American preps; an "efficient" staff works the "crisp", "classy" room in a 1920s-era building where, in the second-floor dining room, "natural light" from the "big front window" is a "nice" touch; P.S. the "jolly" downstairs bar is 21-and-over only.

Texas Smokehouse Bar-B-Q BBQ
20 | 13 | 16 | $16

Woodinville | Hollywood Vineyards | 14455 Woodinville Redmond Rd. (NE 145th St.) | 425-486-1957 | www.texas-smokehouse.com

"Dig in" and "get your fingers dirty" at this Woodinville 'cue pit that's "as close to the real thing" as you'll find in these parts; "excellent" burnt ends, "tender brisket", "real Texas beers" and sides that "remind you that the meal is more than just the meat" are dished out at a counter, so it's "not high-class dining", but you get "good portions for the cost."

Thai Ginger Thai
22 | 16 | 17 | $20

Downtown | Pacific Pl. | 600 Pine St. (bet. 6th & 7th Aves.) | 206-749-9100
Madison Park | 1841 42nd Ave. E. (Madison St.) | 206-324-6467
Bellevue | 3717 Factoria Blvd. SE (bet. I-90 & 38th St.) | 425-641-4008
Issaquah | 4512 Klahanie Dr. SW (Issaquah Fall City Rd.) | 425-369-8233
Redmond | Redmond Town Ctr. | 16480 NE 74th St. (Bear Creek Pkwy.) | 425-558-4044
www.thaiginger.com

Never mind that this "fast, friendly" chain has "even expanded to the ballpark", its "high-quality" Thai food remains "light, fresh and delicious"; the settings fit with the Southeast Asian theme, and prices are "fair", which means, yes, they get "packed."

Thaiku Thai
21 | 22 | 16 | $19

Ballard | 5410 Ballard Ave. NW (22nd Ave.) | 206-706-7807

The "coolest" Thai noodle house in Ballard, this "standard bearer" boasts "unusual dishes" and "three-alarm-fire" spicing, easily extinguished with the "killer" "yohimbe" herb cocktails; "1920s apothecary" meets "opium den" decor, plus a "noisy" "blast" at happy hour, woos even those who lament the "inconsistent" service and slightly "pricey" tabs.

Thai on Mercer Thai
▽ 18 | 15 | 19 | $21

Mercer Island | 7691 SE 27th St. (77th Ave.) | 206-236-9990

A "divine" "tamarind halibut" leads the lineup at this "tasty" Bangkok "gourmet" on Mercer Island; a "good bet" for diners "ready to Thai one on", owner Eddie Khoabtrakool "treats you like family" and offers extras like "no salt/fat" dishes.

	FOOD	DECOR	SERVICE	COST

Thai Siam *Thai*
| | 23 | 16 | 21 | $17 |

Ballard | 8305 15th Ave. NW (83rd St.) | 206-784-5465 |
www.thaisiamrestaurant.com

This "hole-in-the-wall" Ballard Thai stays "busy" cooking up "lots of choices" of inexpensive, "quality" fare, served by a "nice staff"; the modest interior has an old Siam feel, and "tables squished into a small space" mean be prepared to "sit close" or opt for "takeout."

Thai Tom ☞ *Thai*
| | 26 | 9 | 14 | $12 |

University District | 4543 University Way NE (bet. 45th & 47th Sts.) | 206-548-9548

UWers "bow down" to the "gods/chefs" at this "tiny" University District Thai where the "unbeatable bowls of goodness" include plenty of "pure pepper spice" and "incredibly cheap", "addicting" noodles; the lines stretch "out the door on most days", so leave your name, "cruise the avenue" and then take your spot in the "hot", "cramped" room where you can sit "literally a foot" from the "stir-fry" action.

Thanh Vi ☒ *Vietnamese*
| | ▽ 24 | 6 | 19 | $10 |

University District | 4226 University Way NE (bet. 42nd & 43rd Sts.) | 206-633-7867

"Simply delicious" Vietnamese food is the lure at this eatery that may be the "friendliest spot in the University District"; its "fresh", "healthy" banh mi sandwiches, BBQ pork and "large portions" of spring rolls are a "bargain" – you "can't get much cheaper and still have a decent meal."

That's Amore *Italian*
| | - | - | - | M |

Mt. Baker | 1425 31st Ave. S. (Atlantic St.) | 206-322-3677 |
www.thatsamoreseattle.com

From its "window tables", this warm Mount Baker "hidden gem" of a trattoria has what some call the "best view of Downtown Seattle and Elliott Bay"; to boot, the "really good" Italian menu features filet mignon, Neapolitan pizzas and pastas that are "not slathered in tomato sauce", alongside a "very good selection" of vino.

Thin Pan *Thai*
| | ▽ 21 | 20 | 18 | $25 |

Kirkland | 170 Lake St. S. (bet. Kirkland Way & 2nd Ave.) | 425-827-4000

"Fresh, zingy" and "unique" Thai tastes ensure there are "lines out the door" at this stylish, "upscale" Kirkland "favorite" with a "friendly" staff; locals know to settle into the windowside tables to "watch the world drive by" on trendy Lake Street.

Third Floor Fish Cafe *Seafood*
| | 24 | 23 | 22 | $44 |

Kirkland | 205 Lake St. S., 3rd fl. (2nd Ave.) | 425-822-3553 |
www.fishcafe.com

Kirklanders coo over this "very upscale" "standby" with "inventive" seafood and an "incredible" Lake Washington and Seattle view that's visible from every table in the terraced, "lots-of-brass" dining room; drawing an "older crowd", it's a "great place" for "out-of-town guests" and "business dinners" with associates who won't mind the "pricey-but-worth-it" tabs.

	FOOD	DECOR	SERVICE	COST

13 Coins ⚫ *Italian*
18 | 16 | 18 | $31

Downtown | 125 Boren Ave. N. (Denny Way) | 206-682-2513
SeaTac | 18000 Pacific Hwy. S. (opp. Sea-Tac Airport) |
206-243-9500
www.13coins.com

"Minor league pyromaniacs" perch at the counter and watch the
"amazing chefs" put on a "flaming" good show at this "classic"
Downtown–SeaTac Italian duo where "fresh takes" on "old
standards" are served in "beyond huge" portions by a "witty" staff;
reviewers are split on the 1960s "nostalgic-retro" decor – a
"wonderful" "throwback" vs. "shopworn" – but no matter, say
supporters who ask "where else" can you get "eggciting omelets"
and "lobster 24/7"?

35th Street Bistro *French*
24 | 20 | 21 | $33

Fremont | 709 N. 35th St. (Fremont Ave.) | 206-547-9850 |
www.35bistro.com

"What's not to like?" ask admirers of this "very French" gem in
Fremont that delights habitués with its "excellent" Provence-
inspired bistro food, including "high-quality, unusual cheeses"; the
"helpful" staff, "well-priced" wine list and "casually elegant" dining
room add to the charm, though some lament that it tends to be
"noisy" when "busy."

Three Girls Bakery *Bakery*
24 | 9 | 18 | $11

Pike Place Market | Pike Place Mkt. | 1514 Pike Pl. (Pine St.) | 206-622-1045
It's all about the "really wonderful" sandwiches (including possibly
the "best meatloaf in town"), "homemade soups" and "tasty" baked
goods at this "small" "dive" in the Pike Place Market that's been operating since 1912; there's "minimal service" and seating, especially
when "crowded", so consider just "grabbing a loaf of bread" to go.

3 Pigs Bar-B-Que ⊠ *BBQ*
21 | 10 | 14 | $14

Bellevue | 1044 116th Ave. NE (bet. 8th & 12th Sts.) |
425-453-0888

Fans insist that "midnight dreams" are made of the "state-of-the-
art" BBQ dished up at this "down-home" Bellevue pork-eteria across
from Overlake Hospital, and though a few rib raters contend it's
"nothing special", it's hard to argue with "the decent value"; for
those who grumble about the sometimes "inattentive" service and
"cramped" seating, there's always takeout.

NEW Tilth Ⓜ *American*
25 | 18 | 22 | $47

Wallingford | 1411 N. 45th St. (International Ave.) | 206-633-0801 |
www.tilthrestaurant.com

Small-farm fans salute this Wallingford certified-organic New
American, calling chef-owner Maria Hines' "exceptionally refined",
"high-concept" fare a "decadent" "delight"; the "tiny", "lively"
(some say "cramped" and "loud") room is the color of fresh corn and
butter lettuce, and "happy to help" servers guide diners through the
dishes (offered in tasting and full portions) and "small winery"
drinks list; there's a "hearty" weekend brunch too.

	FOOD	DECOR	SERVICE	COST

Tin Room Bar 🄢 *American* — | - | - | I

Burien | 923 SW 152nd St. (bet. 9th & 10th Aves.) | 206-242-8040 |
www.tinroombar.com

In a former 1930s Burien tin shop, this "tiny", "friendly" neighborhood pub beckons to "nostalgia" fans with tables made from ancient workbenches, plus an old sheet-metal roller over the bar; though most come for the decor and drinks (they make their sour mix from scratch), the American fare is "top-notch", served by "friendly" (though "hurried") waiters.

Toi 🄢 *Thai* — | - | - | M

Downtown | 1904 Fourth Ave. (Stewart St.) | 206-267-1017 |
www.toiseattle.com

The East gets a modern treatment at this "swanky" Downtowner where the Thai treats range from "good" to "inspired"; "dark", "glam" Asian environs (the original Dahlia Lounge space) are enlivened by huge graphics projected onto the wall, leading to an "underwater feeling" that some call "clever", but leads others to opine that dinner here is "more about the atmosphere than the food."

Tokyo Garden Teriyaki *Japanese* — | - | - | I

University District | 4337 University Way NE (bet. 43rd & 45th Sts.) |
206-632-2014

"Pretty good" Japanese teriyaki, sushi that "hits the spot" and "generous helpings" of Korean bibimbop are the hallmarks of this University District favorite of UW students, alums, hangers-on and "moviegoers" waiting for the "film to start" at the nearby Varsity or Neptune theaters; the consensus is that it's always "fast and on the cheap."

Top Gun Seafood ➊ *Chinese/Seafood* 21 | 11 | 13 | $21

Bellevue | 12450 SE 38th St. (124th Ave.) | 425-641-3386

There's "always a wait on weekends" at this "good value" Bellevue dim sum "hideaway" where "they keep the carts rolling" with a wide "selection" of "hot and fresh" Chinese bites, skewed toward seafood; "go before 11 AM" to avoid the lines, and steel yourself for "decor and service that are nothing to swoon over."

Tosoni's 🄢 Ⓜ *Continental* 26 | 17 | 24 | $51

Bellevue | 14320 NE 20th St. (bet. 140th & 148th Aves.) | 425-644-1668

Although "often overlooked", this "wonderful" Continental transcends its Bellevue "strip-mall" locale thanks to "lovingly prepared" meat and game dishes that "never disappoint"; with warm colors and "close tables", the quarters feel distinctly "European", and those who find the "expensive" prices worth it can tell chef Walter Walcher himself, since he often joins diners to "sit and chat over a glass of wine."

Toyoda Sushi Ⓜ *Japanese* 23 | 14 | 19 | $29

Lake City | 12543 Lake City Way NE (bet. 125th & 127th Sts.) |
206-367-7972

It's "crowded" like "in Tokyo" at this "off-the-beaten-path" Lake City Japanese joint where sushi sharks feed on "excellent", "affordable" fin fare and "vegetarian items too"; "nonexistent decor" doesn't deter a cadre of regulars who are "treated like royalty", or the more "lowly subjects" who aver that the waits are "worth it."

Trader Vic's *Polynesian* 16 | 23 | 17 | $42
Bellevue | 700 Bellevue Way NE (bet. 6th & 8th Sts.) | 425-455-4483 | www.tradervicsbellevue.com

This "tribute to all things tiki" is Bellevue's go-to spot for Polynesian food (the consensus is the "wood-fired cooked dishes are the best") paired with "exotic" cocktails in kitchy glasses; "eating in the bar is the secret" to skipping the dining room's "long waits", and though the atmosphere is "downright festive", some reviewers say that, given the expense, the experience is "not as good" as it should be.

Trattoria Mitchelli ◐ *Italian* 16 | 16 | 17 | $22
Pioneer Square | 84 Yesler Way (bet. 1st & Western Aves.) | 206-623-3885 | www.mitchellis.com

Though it's "seldom crowded", this "cheerful" 30-year-old standby in Pioneer Square is still a "blast" say boosters who stop in for "generous portions" of "decent Italian food"; it's prime for "splitting a pizza" pre-ferry or grabbing affordable grub "after a night of partying", since its doors stay open until 4 AM on Fridays and Saturdays - except in winter, when it closes earlier.

Troiani ⊠ *Italian* 22 | 20 | 22 | $43
Downtown | 1001 Third Ave. (Madison St.) | 206-624-4060 | www.troianiseattle.com

This "fancy" Downtown Italian is an "ace in the hole" for lawyers and business types wanting "El Gaucho beef" (it shares the same owner), plus seafood and pasta, when they "can't get a table elsewhere"; the sleek setting features "huge windows", "dark woods" and "vivid art", while "free valet parking" helps offset prices that are "a little spendy."

Tropea *Italian* 26 | 20 | 25 | $30
Redmond | 8042 161st Ave. NE (Redmond Way) | 425-867-1082 | www.ristorantetropea.com

A "pleasant surprise" say Redmondites who are "overwhelmed" by this "little" Italian eatery's "authentic" flavors and "incredible" wine list; "lovely" "bistro" atmosphere and "welcoming hospitality" are just two additional reasons that this neighborhood spot leaves fans "extremely pleased."

Tulio Ristorante *Italian* 24 | 20 | 22 | $44
Downtown | Hotel Vintage Park | 1100 Fifth Ave. (Spring St.) | 206-624-5500 | www.tulio.com

"Happy crowds" cram into chef Walter Pisano's "bustling", "classy" restaurant in the Hotel Vintage Park for "sweet potato gnocchi", "rissotti" and other Italian specialties that are "always a treat"; "old-world charm" abounds, as does service that makes you "feel like a king or a queen"; N.B. for wine lovers, the Italian list numbers some 200 labels.

	FOOD	DECOR	SERVICE	COST

Turkish Delight 🍴 *Turkish* ▽ 21 | 8 | 18 | $10
Pike Place Market | Pike Place Mkt. | 1930 Pike Pl. (bet. Stewart & Virginia Sts.) | 206-443-1387

"Inexpensive" Turkish "fast foods" (the baklava wins raves) are the calling card at this no-decor Pike Place Market "ethnic treat"; do like the locals and "eat at the open window", since there's "no better spot" for people-watching.

Tutta Bella Neapolitan Pizzeria *Pizza* 23 | 17 | 20 | $19
Columbia City | 4918 Rainier Ave. S. (Hudson St.) | 206-721-3501
Wallingford | 4411 Stone Way N. (44th St.) | 206-633-3800
www.tuttabella.com

The "real deal" for Naples-style pizza, these Columbia City and Wallingford siblings have the esteemed Verace Pizza Napoletana certification for their "fresh", "fantastic" thin-crust pies made with Italian flour and San Marzano tomatoes; those hoping to relax with a "nice" wine in the "comfortable", "lively" quarters should "show up after 6:30 PM" to avoid the "very noisy" "families" who come to feast; N.B. a Downtown branch, on Westlake Avenue, is in the works.

21 Central Steakhouse 🔒 *Steak* 20 | 19 | 23 | $49
Kirkland | 21 Central Way (First St.) | 425-822-1515 | www.21central.com

This "unpretentious", well-kept Kirkland secret serves some of the "best steaks on the Eastside", delivered by "excellent" waiters in a "dark, quiet", "authentic New York" chophouse setting complete with high-backed mahogany booths and splashes of leopard print cushions; fans say it "deserves more customers."

22 Doors ◑ *American* 19 | 19 | 17 | $26
Capitol Hill | 405 15th Ave. E. (Harrison St.) | 206-324-6406 | www.twentytwodoors.com

Located on 15th Avenue East's Restaurant Row, this "very hip" Capitol Hill boîte offers "good" American small plates, a "rockin' burger" and "excellent" weekend brunch, and if service can be "inconsistent", at least the bartenders "never skimp" on the "creative" cocktails; both the "upscale" interior, sporting 22 vintage doors from the old Camlin Hotel, and the "great patio" are "intimate" enough for a tête-à-tête.

Two Bells Bar & Grill *Pub Food* 19 | 11 | 15 | $15
Belltown | 2313 Fourth Ave. (bet. Battery & Bell Sts.) | 206-441-3050 | www.thetwobells.com

For "messy" burgers on a "baguette bun", Belltowners swear by this "friendly" tavern offering "top-quality pub grub"; the "bartenders are a blast", and warm colors and cool local artwork spruce up the "authentically gritty" digs, making it a "low-key place" to "meet friends."

Typhoon! *Thai* 22 | 19 | 18 | $28
Downtown | 1400 Western Ave. (Union St.) | 206-262-9797
Redmond | Bella Bottega | 8936 161st Ave. NE (90th St.) | 425-558-7666
www.typhoonrestaurants.com

These "always good" Downtown and Redmond siblings (part of a larger chain) turn out the standard Thai dishes plus more "interesting choices" that "you'll never find anywhere else", supplemented by a "vast" selection of teas and wine; the "upscale" bamboo-and-antique Asian-inspired setting is "lovely", though a minority decries the "uneven" service and says there's "more style than substance" here.

Udupi Palace   *Indian* | 20 | 12 | 13 | $17 |

Bellevue | 15600 NE Eighth St. (156th Ave.) | 425-649-0355 | www.udupipalace.net

One of the "best places" for "real" South Indian cuisine, this Bellevue vegetarian with "tasty" dosas, curries and "lassi drinks" caters to a "mostly Indian clientele" who don't mind that the fare "can be very hot"; get recommendations from the "helpful staff" or hit up the inexpensive lunch buffet, a "wonderful way" for newbies to taste the "many options."

NEW Umi Sake House ● *Japanese* | 22 | 24 | 18 | $35 |

Belltown | 2230 First Ave. (Bell St.) | 206-374-8717 | www.umisakehouse.com

At this "fabulous" taste of "Tokyo in Belltown", the "extensive" sushi selection is matched by a list of 70 sakes, causing some to coo it's "an easy choice" for a "dinner before heading out" to the club scene that's right outside the door; "spartan-chic" decor draws the "beautiful people", as does a "best bang-for-the-buck happy hour" that's extended "until 8 PM" for those seated at the front four tables.

☑ Union   *American* | 26 | 21 | 23 | $54 |

Downtown | 1400 First Ave. (Union St.) | 206-838-8000 | www.unionseattle.com

Young chef-owner Ethan Stowell's "spirited" seasonal New American cuisine is "beautifully prepared, presented and served" with "a wine list to match" at this "pricey" Downtown "favorite" where the menu changes daily, so if you see something you like, "order it, because it won't be around for long"; an "attractive crowd" keeps the "elegant" "modernist room" full (and often "noisy"); P.S. the "bar menu is a killer deal."

Union Square Grill   *Pacific NW* | 22 | 21 | 22 | $46 |

Downtown | 621 Union St. (7th Ave.) | 206-224-4321 | www.unionsquaregrill.com

This "respected" (if "a bit pricey") Pacific NW "steak and chop place" is also a "solid choice for seafood" and game, and keeps "very busy" thanks to business bigwigs and theatergoers heading to shows at A.C.T. across the street; the "clubby" art deco space "feels like New York" but with "an air of hospitality instead of haughtiness."

Uptown China   *Chinese* | 18 | 10 | 14 | $21 |

Queen Anne | 200 Queen Anne Ave. N. (John St.) | 206-285-7710 | www.uptown-china.com

"A cut above the average", this lower Queen Anne Chinese lays out "excellent lunch" deals and "chef's specialties" that are the "best things on the menu"; some sigh the decor is "nothing special" and the fare's "a little pricey", but others aver that the quality and location ("convenient to Seattle Center events") make it "worth it."

	FOOD	DECOR	SERVICE	COST

Uptown Espresso *Coffeehouse*

19	14	19	$7

Belltown | 2504 Fourth Ave. (Wall St.) | 206-441-1084
Downtown | 1933 Seventh Ave. (bet. Stewart & Virginia Sts.) |
206-728-8842
Lake Union | 500 Westlake Ave. N. (Republican St.) | 206-621-2045
Queen Anne | 525 Queen Anne Ave. N. (bet. Mercer & Republican Sts.) |
206-285-3757
Seattle Waterfront | Pier 70 | 2801 Alaskan Way (Broad St.) |
206-770-7777
West Seattle | 3845 Delridge Way SW (Andover St.) | 206-933-9497
West Seattle | 4301 SW Edmunds St. (California Ave.) | 206-935-3753
www.uptownespresso.net

"You won't want to drink the foam – it's too pretty" at these "consistently good" coffeehouses (and No. 1 Bang for the Buck) where the
java is "liquid velvet, smooth and sweet"; the pastries are "pretty
good" too say locals who "sit, read and people-watch" from the
"comfy chairs" in the "very chill" shops.

Vegetarian Bistro *Chinese/Vegetarian*

–	–	–	I

International District | 668 S. King St. (bet. 6th & 7th Aves.) |
206-624-8899

Even General Tso goes vegetarian at this "friendly" ID faux-meat
chowhouse serving "light and innovative" updates on Chinese classics; a segment of surveyors says the "quite good" dim sum outranks
its dinners, and vegans should note that "some items contain dairy."

Veil ⊠Ⓜ *American*

23	20	19	$54

Queen Anne | 555 Aloha St. (Taylor Ave.) | 206-216-0600 |
www.veilrestaurant.com

"Miami" mod design meets "posh food and drink" on lower Queen
Anne at this New American from "French Laundry"–trained chef
Shannon Galusha; even quibblers who find the *très chic* interior"
"too full of itself" ("what's with that giant table on a pedestal?")
gush that the "inventive", "serious" food is "terrific", albeit, say
some, "expensive" for such "small" portions.

Via Tribunali Ⓜ *Pizza*

23	22	18	$27

Capitol Hill | 913 E. Pike St. (B'way) | 206-322-9234
NEW **Queen Anne** | 317 W. Galer St. (3rd Ave.) | 206-264-7768
www.viatribunali.com

"Extremely flavorful", "smoky" Neapolitan "thin-crust" pies make this
Capitol Hill–Queen Anne duo a formidable "contender" in the eter-
nal argument over who makes the "best pizza" (acolytes add that its
oven was brought "brick by brick" from Italy); the "medieval-chic"
room is "cramped" and the staff can be "snooty", but hordes of "eye-
candy" types still endure "borderline absurd" waits for a seat.

NEW Vi Bacchus
Sake Bar & Bistro *Japanese*

–	–	–	M

Capitol Hill | 1401 Broadway E. (Union St.) | 206-328-5275 |
www.vibacchus.com

Diners are "warmly greeted and cared for" at this "charming addition
to Broadway" boasting a "diverse" Japanese izakaya and sushi menu

FOOD DECOR SERVICE COST

and a "great" collection of sake; the "elegant" setting emits a Zen "calm" that's rare in such a boisterous, bar-driven neighborhood.

Vios Cafe 🅂 *Greek*   24 | 18 | 20 | $22
Capitol Hill | 903 19th Ave. E. (Aloha St.) | 206-329-3236 |
www.vioscafe.com
"Nice all around" say regulars of this Capitol Hill "neighborhood gathering spot" serving a "limited menu" of "first-rate" Greek fare at "long", wooden "family-style" tables; a large "children's play area" means it's a "dream" for "parents with young kids", and though the prices can add up, "service with a smile" is a bonus.

Voilà! Bistrot 🅜 *French*   22 | 20 | 22 | $34
Madison Valley | 2805 E. Madison St. (28th Ave.) | 206-322-5460 |
www.voilabistrot.com
A "taste of Paris on the cheap" is the verdict on this "fabulous" Madison Valley "comfort"-food bistro (expect "classics" like coq au vin) from French chef-owner Laurent Gabrel, who keeps "wonderful smells coming from the kitchen"; "inexpensive" prices and "cozy" decor make up for the "din" in the "noisy" dining room.

🆉 Volterra ◗ *Italian*   25 | 21 | 22 | $42
Ballard | 5411 Ballard Ave. NW (22nd Ave.) | 206-789-5100 |
www.volterrarestaurant.com
Chef "Don Curtiss is a star" proclaim patrons of this "adventuresome" Northern Italian "favorite" in a "rustic" Ballard storefront offering pasta, "wild boar tenderloin" and "generous wine pours"; service is "courteous" and "knowledgeable" – the main drawback is that it can get "so noisy you have to mime how much you love the food."

NEW Volunteer Park Café & Marketplace 🅜 *American*   ▽ 26 | 22 | 18 | $18
Capitol Hill | 1501 17th Ave. E. (Galer St.) | 206-328-3155 |
www.alwaysfreshgoodness.com
In a century-old corner grocery store on Capitol Hill, this newcomer serves "wonderful" American comfort-food breakfasts, lunches and dinners to "neighborhood" noshers who "flock to it"; it's "always crowded", and the staff, while "extremely helpful", can be "very slow", so selfish sorts hope "no more" customers discover this "real find."

NEW Wann Japanese Izakaya *Japanese*   ▽ 19 | 22 | 20 | $28
Belltown | 2020 Second Ave. (bet. Lenora & Virginia Sts.) | 206-441-5637 |
www.wann-izakaya.com
"Zen-like" decor is the setting for "traditional izakaya fare" (Japanese "tapas") at this moderately priced Belltowner that's popular with groovy salarymen and salarywomen; imbibers come for the sakes, shochu and cocktails, as much as the food, which some call "just ok."

Wasabi Bistro ◗ *Japanese*   22 | 18 | 18 | $32
Belltown | 2311 Second Ave. (bet. Battery & Bell Sts.) | 206-441-6044 |
www.wasabibistro.biz
"Good, fresh" dinners and "affordable" sushi draw a "lively crowd" to this "flashy" Belltown Japanese bistro that's always "bustling"

| | FOOD | DECOR | SERVICE | COST |

with "beautiful people", sports figures and those who love them; a sleek, "fun" look dresses the dining room, though some find it a "little froufrou", and quibble that the staff could be more "knowledgeable" and less "sporadic."

⊠ Waterfront Seafood Grill ◑ *Seafood* | 24 | 25 | 24 | $56 |

Seattle Waterfront | Pier 70 | 2801 Alaskan Way (Broad St.) | 206-956-9171 | www.waterfrontpier70.com

"Stellar" Elliott Bay views only slightly outshine the "spectacular" fish at this "pretty", "glass-walled" Seattle Waterfront seafooder; called an "average" "tourist trap" by jaded sorts, most say it's "great" for "expense-account or milestone" dining, enhanced by a "savvy and attentive" staff; P.S. there's a "fantastic patio for grabbing a sunset drink."

Waters, a Lakeside Bistro *Pacific NW* ▽ | 22 | 24 | 21 | $48 |

Kirkland | Woodmark Hotel | 1200 Carillon Pt. (Lake Washington Blvd.) | 425-803-5595 | www.watersbistro.com

"You can't go wrong" with the New American–Pacific NW cuisine at this "lovely" lair in Kirkland's Woodmark Hotel where the menu is "seasonal" and "well prepared", if slightly spendy; it's ideal for a "quiet business lunch" or in the evening, when the "view of Lake Washington" is especially enticing thanks to "sunsets galore."

NEW Wilde Rover ◑ *Pub Food* | - | - | - | I |

Kirkland | 111 Central Way (bet. 1st & Lake Sts.) | 425-822-8940 | www.wilderover.com

Expect a plethora of "great" beers and whiskies, plus "fish 'n' chips" and "slightly obscure" offerings like black-and-white pudding at this traditional Irish pub in Kirkland; the dark-wood atmo is "authentic" and there's a "good chance your server is from Dublin", but still, some say that the experience is "inconsistent."

⊠ Wild Ginger *Pacific Rim* | 25 | 23 | 22 | $41 |

Downtown | 1401 Third Ave. (Union St.) | 206-623-4450 | www.wildginger.net

It's "come a long way" since its start on Western Avenue 18 years ago say the legions who "love" this still-"buzzy", "beautiful" 350-seat Pacific Rim "hot spot" that's once again Seattle's Most Popular restaurant thanks to anthropologist-turned-restaurateur Rick Yoder's "sumptuous" menu of Asian curries, satays and spicy lahksa soups served by an "accommodating" staff; its Downtown digs are "noisy", "crowded" and "over-the-top" decry objectors, yet still diners can't get enough of it, so the lion's share of voters urges even "if you have to wait for a table, do it."

World Class Chili ⊠⊅ *American* ▽ | 24 | 12 | 16 | $12 |

Pike Place Market | Pike Place Mkt. | 93 Pike St. (1st Ave.) | 206-623-3678 | www.worldclasschili.com

The name says it all at this "hearty" beanateria in the Pike Place Market, which "hits the spot" with chili in "more varieties than you can consider" ("albeit in small portions"); spiceheads say try the

"Cincinnati", which has chocolate in it, and look for owner Joe Canavan, "a legend" in the market.

NEW Yama at The Galleria *Asian Fusion* ∇ 23 | 22 | 18 | $38

Bellevue | Bellevue Galleria | 550 106th Ave. NE, 3rd fl. (bet. 4th & 8th Sts.) | 425-453-4007 | www.yamagalleria.com

"Beautiful", "forward-thinking" sushi and a "vast" Asian fusion menu make this chic yearling a "welcome" Bellevue addition; Japanese tea garden accents, a snazzy raw-fish bar and cool tatami rooms set a scene that's great for a "date", especially since there's a "movie theater" "around the corner."

Yanni's ⑤ *Greek* 22 | 14 | 17 | $24

Phinney Ridge | 7419 Greenwood Ave. N. (75th St.) | 206-783-6945 | www.yannisgreekrestaurant.com

Join the locals at this "does-it-right" Phinney Ridge Greek for "large portions" of "traditional" Hellenic fare, doled out amid hanging grapes and glass-lamp decor; make a "reservation" or "you may not get in", and even acolytes warn that the "snail's-pace" service means "you could ossify by the time your meal arrives."

Yarrow Bay Grill *Eclectic/Seafood* 24 | 24 | 22 | $46

Kirkland | 1270 Carillon Pt. (Lake Washington Blvd.) | 425-889-9052 | www.ybgrill.com

This "fancy" Kirkland seafooder attracts locals and tourists with "surprisingly good" (if "overpriced") Eclectic fare and a "killer location" on Carillon Point, complete with a "marvelous" "view over the lake"; white linen and sparkling lights add "romance" to the "mellow interior" where service is "johnny-on-the-spot."

Zaina Food, Drink & Friends ❶ *Mideastern* 22 | 13 | 17 | $15

Pioneer Square | 108 Cherry St. (1st Ave.) | 206-624-5687

"Simple", "expertly prepared" Middle Eastern faves like falafel and schwarma provide meal appeal to Pioneer Square workers and night owls who haunt this "authentic" aerie; it's "hidden" in plain sight on Cherry Street, so just "look for the overhead sign with the camels", and don't be deterred by the "sometimes-curt" service.

Zao Noodle Bar *Noodle Shop* 16 | 15 | 15 | $17

University Village | University Vill. | 2590 NE University Vill. (bet. 25th Ave. & 45th St.) | 206-529-8278 | www.zao.com

University Village shoppers refuel at this "tasty" Pan-Asian "noodle shop" offering "quick" bites in a "fun" atmosphere; though many marvel over the "inexpensive" tabs, others opine the food's only "ok" and "not worth" it.

Zeeks Pizza *Pizza* 18 | 11 | 15 | $14

Belltown | 419 Denny Way (5th Ave.) | 206-285-8646
Green Lake | 7900 E. Green Lake Dr. N. (79th St.) | 206-285-8646
Phinney Ridge | 6000 Phinney Ave. N. (60th St.) | 206-286-8646
Queen Anne | 41 Dravus St. (Nickerson St.) | 206-285-8646
Ravenna | 2108 NE 65th St. (bet. Ravenna Blvd. & 21st St.) | 206-285-8646

(continued)

Zeeks Pizza

Kirkland | 124 Park Ln. (Lake St. S.) | 425-893-8626
www.zeekspizza.com

"Unique" Northwest pizzas – check out the "tree hugger" and a "Puget pounder" – are made with "fresh" ingredients and a "thin crust" at this "well-priced" chainlet that's "very family-friendly"; those scared off by the "noisy" kids inside may be happy to hear that they have "reliable" delivery.

Zephyr Grill & Bar *American*   19 | 18 | 18 | $33

Kent | Kent Station | 240 W. Kent Station St. (bet. 1st Ave. & 2nd Pl.) | 253-854-5050 | www.zephyrgrill.com

A "nice addition" in Kent Station, this American eating depot goes the added mile, serving an "extra pot" of *fromage* with its "cheesiest" mac 'n' cheese, and "ice tea" accompanied by a "pitcher" of "sugared lemon water"; the Northwest-y atmosphere is "smart", though some patrons wish they could say the same of the fairly "inexperienced", "inconsistent" staff.

Zinnia *American*   ∇ 23 | 22 | 22 | $39

Mill Creek | Mill Creek Town Ctr. | 15130 Main St. (bet. 151st & 153rd Sts.) | 425-357-0512 | www.zinniawa.com

Planted in the "trendy" Mill Creek Town Center, this "flower is worth the drive to the suburbs" for a whiff of its "careful" New American fare that's crafted with "super-fresh, local ingredients"; the "pretty", bud-filled dining room feels genteel, and there's a "great, affordable wine list" – though some surveyors find the experience "rather pricey."

Z'Tejas *Southwestern*   18 | 17 | 19 | $26

Bellevue | Bellevue Sq. | 535 Bellevue Sq. (NE 8th St.) | 425-467-5911 | www.ztejas.com

"Newfangled" Southwestern eats are the hallmark of this "crowded" chainster in upscale Bellevue Square where pretty power-shoppers "get off their feet" and rest over "sinfully good" mac 'n' cheese and "mushroom enchiladas" – or just grab a margarita at the "lively bar"; grudging graders rate the fare just "passable", and pass on the "slow service" during "peak shopping hours."

INDEXES

Cuisines 126
Locations 137
Special Features 147

Cuisines

Includes restaurant names, locations and Food ratings. ⚡ indicates places with the highest ratings, popularity and importance.

AFGHAN

Kabul Afghan | **Wallingford** — 25

AFRICAN

Pan-Africa Cafe | **Pike Pl Mkt** — 21

AMERICAN (NEW)

NEW Bennett's Pure Food | **Mercer Is**	22
NEW Betty | **Queen Anne**	22
Bick's Broadview | **Greenwood**	21
Bis on Main | **Bellevue**	24
Blackbird Bistro | **W Seattle**	19
Cafe Nola | **Bainbridge Is**	21
Café Septieme | **Capitol Hill**	16
Calcutta Grill | **Newcastle**	20
⚡ Cascadia | **Belltown**	25
Crave | **Capitol Hill**	20
Crow | **Queen Anne**	23
⚡ Crush | **Madison Vly**	26
NEW Dish D'Lish | **Ballard**	18
Earth & Ocean | **Downtown**	22
⚡ Eva | **Green Lk**	26
Fox Sports Grill | **Downtown**	12
Garage | **Capitol Hill**	13
Hi Life | **Ballard**	18
Jones, The | **Maple Leaf**	20
Lampreia | **Belltown**	25
⚡ Lark | **Capitol Hill**	27
Market St. Grill | **Ballard**	25
⚡ Mistral | **Belltown**	28
Moxie | **Queen Anne**	21
Nell's | **Green Lk**	25
94 Stewart | **Pike Pl Mkt**	21
Pair | **Ravenna**	25
⚡ Palace Kitchen | **Downtown**	24
Persimmon | **Fremont**	22
Pomegranate Bistro | **Redmond**	25
Portalis | **Ballard**	18
Queen City Grill | **Belltown**	22
⚡ Rest. Zoë | **Belltown**	27
Rosebud | **Capitol Hill**	19
Russell's | **Bothell**	–
Saltoro | **N Seattle**	22
Ten Mercer | **Queen Anne**	22
NEW Tilth | **Wallingford**	25
22 Doors | **Capitol Hill**	19
⚡ Union | **Downtown**	26
Veil | **Queen Anne**	23
Waters Lakeside | **Kirkland**	22
Zinnia | **Mill Creek**	23

AMERICAN (TRADITIONAL)

Alki Bakery | **multi.**	21
Alki Homestead | **W Seattle**	20
Athenian Inn | **Pike Pl Mkt**	16
Atlas Foods | **Univ Vill**	16
Bad Albert's Tap | **Ballard**	16
Barking Dog | **Ballard**	17
Beecher's Cheese | **Pike Pl Mkt**	24
Belltown Bistro | **Belltown**	18
Bing's Burgers | **Madison Pk**	16
Blue Onion | **Univ Dist**	17
BluWater | **multi.**	16
NEW Bottle Rocket | **Wallingford**	–
Broadway Grill | **Capitol Hill**	16
Buckley's | **Seattle Ctr**	19
Café Soleil | **Madrona**	20
Caffé Minnie's | **Queen Anne**	12
⚡ Cheesecake Factory | **multi.**	17
Coastal Kitchen | **Capitol Hill**	20
Columbia City Ale | **Columbia City**	18
Deluxe B&G | **Capitol Hill**	16
Dish, The | **Fremont**	23
Eats Mkt. Café | **W Seattle**	20
Eggs Cetera's | **Wallingford**	15
Elliott Bay Brewery | **W Seattle**	20
Endolyne Joe's | **W Seattle**	19

Ezell's | **multi.**	24
5 Point Café | **Belltown**	19
5 Spot | **Queen Anne**	20
14 Carrot Cafe | **Eastlake**	18
Geraldine's | **Columbia City**	20
Glo's | **Capitol Hill**	26
Gordon Biersch | **Downtown**	14
Greenlake B&G | **Green Lk**	16
Hattie's Hat | **Ballard**	16
Hilltop Ale Hse. | **Queen Anne**	22
Hi Spot Cafe | **Madrona**	23
Honey Bear | **Lake Forest Pk**	21
NEW Hot Dish | **Ravenna**	-
icon grill | **Downtown**	20
Julia's | **multi.**	16
Kidd Valley | **multi.**	18
Lockspot Cafe | **Ballard**	18
Louisa's Cafe | **Eastlake**	21
Lowell's | **Pike Pl Mkt**	17
Luna Park Cafe | **W Seattle**	15
Mae's | **Phinney Ridge**	18
Maggie Bluff's | **Magnolia**	18
Z Maltby Cafe | **Maltby**	26
Matts' Rotisserie | **Redmond**	20
Original Pancake | **multi.**	21
Pike Pub | **Pike Pl Mkt**	16
Pyramid Ale | **Pioneer Sq**	16
Red Door | **Fremont**	17
Red Robin | **multi.**	15
Ruby's | **Redmond**	16
Sharp's Roaster | **SeaTac**	-
Streamliner | **Bainbridge Is**	16
Tin Room Bar | **Burien**	-
NEW Volunteer Pk. Café | **Capitol Hill**	26
World Class Chili | **Pike Pl Mkt**	24
Zephyr Grill | **Kent**	19

ARGENTINEAN

Buenos Aires Grill | **Downtown**	23

ASIAN

Z Flying Fish | **Belltown**	25
NEW Qube | **Downtown**	22

ASIAN FUSION

Z Indochine Asian | **Tacoma**	23
Z Lynn's Bistro | **Kirkland**	26
NEW Yama/Galleria | **Bellevue**	23

BAKERIES

Alki Bakery | **multi.**	21
NEW Z Bakery Nouveau | **W Seattle**	28
Belle Epicurean | **Downtown**	26
Z Belle Pastry | **Bellevue**	27
Z Cafe Besalu | **Ballard**	27
Crumpet Shop | **Pike Pl Mkt**	24
Essential Baking | **multi.**	23
Le Fournil | **Eastlake**	21
Le Panier | **Pike Pl Mkt**	23
Louisa's Cafe | **Eastlake**	21
Macrina | **multi.**	25
Noah's Bagels | **multi.**	17
Sentosa Asian | **Kirkland**	15
Three Girls Bakery | **Pike Pl Mkt**	24

BARBECUE

Dixie's BBQ | **Bellevue**	22
Frontier Room | **Belltown**	19
Jones BBQ | **multi.**	22
Pecos Pit BBQ | **SODO**	25
Pig Iron Bar-B-Q | **S Seattle**	22
R&L Good BBQ | **Capitol Hill**	21
Rhodie's Smokin' | **Seattle Ctr**	-
Texas Smokehse. | **Woodinville**	20
3 Pigs BBQ | **Bellevue**	21

BELGIAN

Brouwer's | **Fremont**	20

BRAZILIAN

Tempero/Brasil | **Univ Dist**	24

BRITISH

Neville's/British | **Redmond**	20
Queen Mary Tea | **Ravenna**	19
74th St. Ale Hse. | **Phinney Ridge**	19

CAJUN

Bayou on First | **Pike Pl Mkt**	-
New Orl. Creole | **Pioneer Sq**	14

CAMBODIAN

Phnom Penh | Intl Dist | - |

CARIBBEAN

Kallaloo | Columbia City | - |
☑ Paseo | Fremont | 27 |
NEW Spitfire | Belltown | 19 |

CHEESE SPECIALISTS

Beecher's Cheese | Pike Pl Mkt | 24 |

CHEESE STEAKS

Phila. Fevre | Madison Vly | 23 |

CHINESE

(* dim sum specialist)
Bamboo Gdn. Szechuan | Bellevue | - |
Bamboo Gdn. Veg. | Queen Anne | 18 |
Black Pearl | multi. | 15 |
Café Ori | Bellevue | 21 |
China Gate* | Intl Dist | 20 |
Four Seas* | Intl Dist | 17 |
Fu Man Dumpling | Greenwood | 19 |
Ho Ho Seafood | Intl Dist | 21 |
Honey Court | Intl Dist | 23 |
House of Hong* | Intl Dist | 21 |
Hunan Garden | Bellevue | 18 |
NEW Inchin's Bamboo | Redmond | - |
Jade Garden* | Intl Dist | 23 |
Judy Fu's | Maple Leaf | 19 |
Kau Kau BBQ | Intl Dist | 24 |
Louie's Cuisine | Ballard | 15 |
Mee Sum Pastries | Pike Pl Mkt | 21 |
Noble Court* | Bellevue | 21 |
NEW O'Asian* | Downtown | 20 |
P.F. Chang's | multi. | 19 |
Purple Dot Café* | Intl Dist | 18 |
Sea Garden* | multi. | 20 |
Sentosa Asian* | Kirkland | 15 |
Shanghai Gdn. | multi. | 22 |
☑ Szechuan Chef | Bellevue | 27 |
Tai Tung | Intl Dist | 20 |
Top Gun Seafood* | Bellevue | 21 |
Uptown China | Queen Anne | 18 |
Veg. Bistro | Intl Dist | - |

COFFEEHOUSES

B&O Espresso | Capitol Hill | 20 |
☑ Cafe Besalu | Ballard | 27 |
Dilettante Chocolates | multi. | 23 |
Uptown Espresso | multi. | 19 |

COFFEE SHOPS/DINERS

CJ's Eatery | Belltown | 21 |
Hattie's Hat | Ballard | 16 |
Luna Park Cafe | W Seattle | 15 |
Mae's | Phinney Ridge | 18 |
Original Pancake | multi. | 21 |
Ruby's | Redmond | 16 |

CONTINENTAL

Geneva | First Hill | 25 |
Tosoni's | Bellevue | 26 |

CREOLE

Kallaloo | Columbia City | - |
New Orl. Creole | Pioneer Sq | 14 |

CROATIAN

Pogacha | multi. | 18 |

DELIS

Bagel Oasis | Ravenna | 21 |
Bakeman's | Downtown | 22 |
Buffalo Deli | Belltown | 23 |
FareStart/2100 | S Seattle | - |
From Russia/Love | Bellevue | - |
Gilbert's Main St. Bagel | Bellevue | 22 |
Goldbergs' Deli | Bellevue | 17 |
Noosh Café | Queen Anne | - |
Phila. Fevre | Madison Vly | 23 |
Three Girls Bakery | Pike Pl Mkt | 24 |

DESSERT

NEW ☑ Bakery Nouveau | W Seattle | 28 |
B&O Espresso | Capitol Hill | 20 |
Belle Epicurean | Downtown | 26 |
☑ Belle Pastry | Bellevue | 27 |
☑ Cafe Besalu | Ballard | 27 |
☑ Cheesecake Factory | multi. | 17 |
Dilettante Chocolates | multi. | 23 |
Essential Baking | multi. | 23 |

Gelatiamo	**Downtown**	24
Le Fournil	**Eastlake**	21
Macrina	**multi.**	25
Three Girls Bakery	**Pike Pl Mkt**	24

ECLECTIC

Alibi Room	**Pike Pl Mkt**	19
Atlas Foods	**Univ Vill**	16
Beach Cafe/Point	**Kirkland**	18
Black Bottle	**Belltown**	22
Chanterelle	**Edmonds**	19
Circa	**W Seattle**	23
Coastal Kitchen	**Capitol Hill**	20
Crocodile Cafe	**Belltown**	14
Cyclops	**Belltown**	17
Dulces Latin	**Madrona**	21
☑ Elemental	**Lake Union**	26
Joeys	**multi.**	19
NEW Local Vine	**Belltown**	-
Maple Leaf Grill	**Maple Leaf**	18
Marco's Supperclub	**Belltown**	21
Marjorie	**Belltown**	22
NEW Poco Wine	**Capitol Hill**	-
Sand Point Grill	**Sand Point**	17
☑ Sitka & Spruce	**Eastlake**	28
Sport	**Seattle Ctr**	18
Sunlight Cafe	**Roosevelt**	16
Tap House Grill	**multi.**	18
Yarrow Bay Grill	**Kirkland**	24

ERITREAN

| Dahlak Eritrean | **S Seattle** | - |

ETHIOPIAN

| Assimba Ethiopian | **Capitol Hill** | 22 |
| Café Soleil | **Madrona** | 20 |

EUROPEAN

| Dinette | **Capitol Hill** | 24 |
| Portalis | **Ballard** | 18 |

FILIPINO

| Kusina Filipina | **Beacon Hill** | - |

FONDUE

| Melting Pot | **multi.** | 19 |

FRENCH

Andre's Eurasian	**Bellevue**	19
NEW ☑ Bakery Nouveau	**W Seattle**	28
Belle Epicurean	**Downtown**	26
☑ Belle Pastry	**Bellevue**	27
Brass. Margaux	**Downtown**	19
Café Darclée	**Belltown**	-
☑ Campagne	**Pike Pl Mkt**	26
Carnegie's	**Ballard**	21
Chez Shea	**Pike Pl Mkt**	26
NEW Coupage	**Madrona**	23
NEW Entre Nous	**Downtown**	-
☑ Georgian	**Downtown**	26
Le Fournil	**Eastlake**	21
☑ Le Gourmand	**Ballard**	27
Le Panier	**Pike Pl Mkt**	23
☑ Lynn's Bistro	**Kirkland**	26
Maximilien	**Pike Pl Mkt**	21
NEW Porcélla	**Bellevue**	24
NEW Portage	**Queen Anne**	26
NEW Qube	**Downtown**	22
NEW Saint-Germain	**Madison Vly**	21
611 Supreme	**Capitol Hill**	23

FRENCH (BISTRO)

Boat St. Cafe	**Queen Anne**	25
☑ Cafe Campagne	**Pike Pl Mkt**	25
NEW Café Presse	**Capitol Hill**	-
Crémant	**Madrona**	24
Crepe de France	**Pike Pl Mkt**	23
☑ Le Pichet	**Pike Pl Mkt**	24
Madison Pk. Cafe	**Madison Pk**	22
35th St. Bistro	**Fremont**	24
Voilà! Bistrot	**Madison Vly**	22

FRENCH (NEW)

☑ Mistral	**Belltown**	28
☑ Rover's	**Madison Vly**	28
☑ Salish Lodge	**Snoqualmie**	24

GERMAN

Die BierStube	**Roosevelt**	-
Feierabend	**Lake Union**	18
Szmania's	**Magnolia**	23

GREEK

Costas Greek	**Univ Dist**	17
Costas Opa	**Fremont**	19
NEW Divine	**Maple Leaf**	–
Z Lola	**Downtown**	24
Panos Kleftiko	**Queen Anne**	23
Santorini Greek	**Kirkland**	23
Takis Mad Greek	**Ballard**	18
Vios Cafe	**Capitol Hill**	24
Yanni's	**Phinney Ridge**	22

HAMBURGERS

Cyclops	**Belltown**	17
Deluxe B&G	**Capitol Hill**	16
Dick's Drive-In	**multi.**	19
Elliott Bay Brewery	**W Seattle**	20
Endolyne Joe's	**W Seattle**	19
Kidd Valley	**multi.**	18
Luna Park Cafe	**W Seattle**	15
Maggie Bluff's	**Magnolia**	18
Red Mill Burgers	**multi.**	24
Red Robin	**multi.**	15
Shultzy's	**Univ Dist**	20
Sport	**Seattle Ctr**	18
Two Bells B&G	**Belltown**	19

HAWAIIAN

Kauai Family Rest.	**Georgetown**	21
'Ohana	**Belltown**	21

HEALTH FOOD

(See also Vegetarian)

14 Carrot Cafe	**Eastlake**	18

HOT DOGS

Diggity Dog's	**Wallingford**	19
Matt's Gourmet Dogs	**multi.**	18
Taxi Dogs	**Pike Pl Mkt**	15

INDIAN

NEW Inchin's Bamboo	**Redmond**	–
India Bistro	**Ballard**	23
Kabob House	**Greenwood**	23
Mayuri	**Bellevue**	25
Moghul Palace	**Bellevue**	22
Pabla Indian	**Downtown**	20
preet's	**Redmond**	25
Roti Cuisine	**Queen Anne**	20
Shamiana	**Kirkland**	23
Taste of India	**Univ Dist**	22
Udupi Palace	**Bellevue**	20

IRISH

Fado Irish	**Pioneer Sq**	14
Kells Irish	**Pike Pl Mkt**	17
Paddy Coynes	**Downtown**	18
NEW Wilde Rover	**Kirkland**	–

ITALIAN

(N=Northern; S=Southern)

Abbondanza Pizzeria	**W Seattle**	18
Acorn Eatery	**Crown Hill**	17
Al Boccalino	**Pioneer Sq**	22
Z Armandino's Salumi	**Pioneer Sq**	28
Assaggio	N	**Downtown**	23
Asteroid	**Fremont**	25
NEW Barolo	N	**Downtown**	22
NEW Beàto	**W Seattle**	23
Brad's Swingside	**Fremont**	24
Bricco/Regina	**Queen Anne**	22
Buca di Beppo	S	**multi.**	14
Cafe Bengodi	**Pioneer Sq**	19
Café Darclée	**Belltown**	–
Z Cafe Juanita	N	**Kirkland**	28
Cafe Lago	**Montlake**	23
Cafe Veloce	**Kirkland**	21
Calabria	S	**Kirkland**	17
Cellar Bistro	N	**Capitol Hill**	–
Ciao Bella	**Univ Vill**	21
Cucina De-Ra	N	**Belltown**	21
De Nunzio's	**Pioneer Sq**	16
NEW DiVino	N	**Ballard**	22
Firenze	N	**Bellevue**	22
Four Swallows	**Bainbridge Is**	25
Frankie's Pizza	**Redmond**	20
Fremont Classic	**Fremont**	19
Gelatiamo	**Downtown**	24
Grazie	**multi.**	20
Il Bistro	**Pike Pl Mkt**	23
Il Fornaio	**Downtown**	20
Z Il Terrazzo	**Pioneer Sq**	27

La Fontana Siciliana | S | Belltown — 24
La Medusa | Columbia City — 25
La Rustica | S | W Seattle — 25
La Vita É Bella | Belltown — 22
Luigi's Pizza | Magnolia — 16
Machiavelli | N | Capitol Hill — 21
Madame K's Pizza | Ballard — 21
Mamma Melina | Univ Dist — 21
Mioposto | Mt. Baker — -
Mondello | S | Magnolia — 23
Northlake Tav. | Univ Dist — 21
Olympia Pizza | multi. — 18
Osteria La Spiga | Capitol Hill — 24
Palomino | Downtown — 21
Pasta & Co. | multi. — 22
Pasta Bella | multi. — 19
NEW Perché/Pasta | Green Lk — 22
Pink Door | Pike Pl Mkt — 22
Pontevecchio | S | Fremont — 23
Rist. Italianissimo | N | Woodinville — 25
Rist. Paradiso | Kirkland — 22
Romio's Pizza/Pasta | multi. — 16
Salute/Bellevue | Bellevue — 19
Salvatore | Ravenna — 23
Serafina | Eastlake — 24
NEW Sorrentino | S | Queen Anne — 18
Sostanza | N | Madison Pk — 22
NEW Spazzo | Redmond — 20
NEW Tavolàta | Belltown — 24
That's Amore | Mt. Baker — -
13 Coins | multi. — 18
Tratt. Mitchelli | N | Pioneer Sq — 16
Troiani | Downtown — 22
Tropea | Redmond — 26
Tulio | Downtown — 24
Z Volterra | N | Ballard — 25

JAPANESE
(* sushi specialist)
Aoki Grill/Sushi* | Capitol Hill — 19
Benihana | Downtown — 18
Blue C Sushi* | multi. — 15
Bush Garden* | Intl Dist — 19
Z Chiso* | Fremont — 26

Flo* | Bellevue — 25
Fort St. George | Intl Dist — -
Fuji Sushi* | Intl Dist — 25
I Love Sushi* | multi. — 23
Izumi* | Kirkland — 25
Kikuya | Redmond — 22
Z Kisaku Sushi* | Green Lk — 27
Z Maneki | Intl Dist — 27
Mashiko* | W Seattle — 25
Musashi's* | Wallingford — 21
Z Nishino* | Madison Pk — 27
Ototo Sushi* | Queen Anne — 24
Red Fin* | Downtown — 23
Rest. Shilla | Downtown — 15
Rikki Rikki* | Kirkland — 19
Saito's Japanese* | Belltown — 26
Sam's Sushi* | multi. — 18
Shiki* | Queen Anne — 24
Z Shiro's Sushi* | Belltown — 27
Sushiman* | Issaquah — 24
Sushiya* | Kirkland — -
Tokyo Garden | Univ Dist — -
Toyoda Sushi* | Lake City — 23
NEW Umi Sake Hse.* | Belltown — 22
NEW Vi Bacchus* | Capitol Hill — -
NEW Wann Izakaya | Belltown — 19
Wasabi Bistro* | Belltown — 22
NEW Yama/Galleria* | Bellevue — 23

KOREAN
NEW Coupage | Madrona — 23
Hosoonyi | Lynnwood — 24
Kimchi Bistro | Capitol Hill — -
Rest. Shilla | Downtown — 15
Tokyo Garden | Univ Dist — -

LEBANESE
Karam's Lebanese | Capitol Hill — 19
Medit. Kitchen | Bellevue — 22

MALAYSIAN
Malay Satay Hut | multi. — 24

MEDITERRANEAN
Andaluca | Downtown — 24
Z Brasa | Belltown — 25

CUISINES

Capitol Club | **Capitol Hill**	19
☑ Carmelita | **Greenwood**	26
El Greco | **Capitol Hill**	23
Fish Club | **Seattle Waterfront**	22
La Medusa | **Columbia City**	25
Medit. Kitchen | **Bellevue**	22
Mona's Bistro | **Green Lk**	23
Mor Mor Bistro | **Poulsbo**	18
Olives Cafe | **Edmonds**	23
☑ Phoenecia/Alki | **W Seattle**	27
NEW Porcella | **Bellevue**	24
Primo Grill | **Tacoma**	25

MEXICAN

Agua Verde | **Univ Dist**	22
Azteca | **multi.**	14
Burrito Loco | **Crown Hill**	22
Coliman | **Georgetown**	-
El Camino | **Fremont**	21
El Chupacabra | **Greenwood**	14
El Gallito | **Capitol Hill**	18
El Puerco Lloron | **Pike Pl Mkt**	21
Galerias | **Capitol Hill**	22
Gordito's Mex. | **Greenwood**	22
Jalisco Mex. | **multi.**	17
☑ La Carta/Oaxaca | **Ballard**	26
La Cocina/Puerco | **Bellevue**	20
Luisa's Mex. | **Greenwood**	16
Malena's Taco | **multi.**	20
Mama's Mexican | **Belltown**	17
Mexico Cantina | **Downtown**	20
MuyMacho | **S Park**	-
Ooba's Mex. Grill | **multi.**	24
Peso's Kitchen | **Queen Anne**	23
Rosita's Mex. | **Green Lk**	19
Señor Moose | **Ballard**	24
Tacos Guaymas | **multi.**	20

MIDDLE EASTERN

Zaina Food | **Pioneer Sq**	22

MOROCCAN

Kasbah | **Ballard**	-
Marrakesh | **Belltown**	21

NEW MEXICAN

Santa Fe Cafe | **Phinney Ridge**	21

NOODLE SHOPS

Krittika Noodles | **Green Lk**	22
Mike's Noodle Hse. | **Intl Dist**	25
Noodle Ranch | **Belltown**	17
Pho Bac | **Intl Dist**	21
Pho Thân Bros. | **multi.**	22
Racha Noodles | **multi.**	21
Zao Noodle Bar | **Univ Vill**	16

PACIFIC NORTHWEST

Alibi Room | **Pike Pl Mkt**	19
☑ Anthony's HomePort | **multi.**	20
Anthony's Pier 66 | **Seattle Waterfront**	21
Barking Frog | **Woodinville**	24
NEW Boka Kitchen | **Downtown**	22
Brass. Margaux | **Downtown**	19
☑ Canlis | **Lake Union**	27
Chez Shea | **Pike Pl Mkt**	26
Christina's | **Eastsound**	26
Coho Cafe | **multi.**	18
Coldwater | **Downtown**	20
Cutters Bayhse. | **Pike Pl Mkt**	19
☑ Dahlia Lounge | **Downtown**	25
☑ Etta's Seafood | **Pike Pl Mkt**	24
FareStart | **Downtown**	22
Four Swallows | **Bainbridge Is**	25
Friday Harbor Hse. | **Friday Harbor**	-
☑ Georgian | **Downtown**	26
☑ Herbfarm, The | **Woodinville**	29
NEW Hills' Food/Wine | **Shoreline**	23
Hunt Club | **First Hill**	22
☑ Inn at Langley | **Langley**	27
Ivar Acres of Clams | **Seattle Waterfront**	20
Ivar Salmon Hse. | **Lake Union**	19
Lampreia | **Belltown**	25
Matt's/Mkt. | **Pike Pl Mkt**	-
NEW O/8 | **Bellevue**	21
NEW Oliver's Twist | **Phinney Ridge**	25
NEW Opal | **Queen Anne**	25
Paragon | **Queen Anne**	19
Place Pigalle | **Pike Pl Mkt**	23

subscribe to zagat.com

Pogacha	**multi.**	18
Ponti Seafood	**Fremont**	22
NEW Portage	**Queen Anne**	26
Z Purple Cafe	**multi.**	22
Z Ray's Boathse.	**Shilshole**	24
Ray's Cafe	**Shilshole**	22
Rose's Bakery	**Eastsound**	–
Shea's Lounge	**Pike Pl Mkt**	24
Shoalwater	**Seaview**	–
Z 6 · 7	**Seattle Waterfront**	24
Z SkyCity/Needle	**Seattle Ctr**	21
St. Clouds	**Madrona**	21
NEW Steelhead	**Pike Pl Mkt**	23
Streamliner	**Bainbridge Is**	16
Stumbling Goat	**Greenwood**	24
Szmania's	**Magnolia**	23
NEW TASTE	**Downtown**	19
Union Sq. Grill	**Downtown**	22
Waters Lakeside	**Kirkland**	22

PACIFIC RIM

Madoka	**Bainbridge Is**	20
Z Wild Ginger	**Downtown**	25

PAKISTANI

Kabob House	**Greenwood**	23
Shamiana	**Kirkland**	23

PAN-ASIAN

Chinoise	**multi.**	19
NEW Coupage	**Madrona**	23
Dragonfish	**Downtown**	20
Lee's	**W Seattle**	23
NEW Made/Kitchen	**Intl Dist**	21
Noodle Ranch	**Belltown**	17
Shallots	**Belltown**	22
Zao Noodle Bar	**Univ Vill**	16

PAN-LATIN

Azul	**Mill Creek**	23
La Casa/Mojito	**multi.**	21
Mission	**W Seattle**	20
NEW Spitfire	**Belltown**	19

PERSIAN

Alborz	**Redmond**	23
Caspian Grill	**Univ Dist**	–

PERUVIAN

Mixtura	**Kirkland**	24

PIZZA

Abbondanza Pizzeria	**W Seattle**	18
All-Purpose Pizza	**Capitol Hill**	16
NEW Bambino's Pizzeria	**Belltown**	19
Belltown Pizza	**Belltown**	20
Cafe Lago	**Montlake**	23
Cafe Veloce	**Kirkland**	21
Coyote Creek Pizza	**multi.**	20
Crash Landing Pizza	**Ballard**	18
Delfino's Pizza	**Univ Vill**	17
Fremont Classic	**Fremont**	19
La Vita É Bella	**Belltown**	22
Luigi's Pizza	**Magnolia**	16
Madame K's Pizza	**Ballard**	21
Mioposto	**Mt. Baker**	–
Northlake Tav.	**Univ Dist**	21
Olympia Pizza	**multi.**	18
Pagliacci Pizza	**multi.**	22
Palomino	**Downtown**	21
Pegasus Pizza	**W Seattle**	20
Piecora's Pizza	**Capitol Hill**	21
Primo Grill	**Tacoma**	25
Romio's Pizza/Pasta	**multi.**	16
NEW Serious Pie	**Downtown**	25
Stellar Pizza	**Georgetown**	21
Tutta Bella	**multi.**	23
Via Tribunali	**multi.**	23
Zeeks Pizza	**multi.**	18

POLYNESIAN

Luau Polynesian	**Green Lk**	15
Trader Vic's	**Bellevue**	16

PUB FOOD

Bad Albert's Tap	**Ballard**	16
Barking Dog	**Ballard**	17
Brouwer's	**Fremont**	20
Buckley's	**Seattle Ctr**	19
Circa	**W Seattle**	23
Columbia City Ale	**Columbia City**	18
Cyclops	**Belltown**	17

CUISINES

Deluxe B&G | **Capitol Hill**	16
Elliott Bay Brewery | **W Seattle**	20
Fado Irish | **Pioneer Sq**	14
Gordon Biersch | **Downtown**	14
Hale's Ales | **Fremont**	17
Kells Irish | **Pike Pl Mkt**	17
Paddy Coynes | **Downtown**	18
Pike Pub | **Pike Pl Mkt**	16
Pyramid Ale | **Pioneer Sq**	16
Red Door | **Fremont**	17
74th St. Ale Hse. | **Phinney Ridge**	19
Two Bells B&G | **Belltown**	19
NEW Wilde Rover | **Kirkland**	-

PUERTO RICAN

La Isla | **Ballard**	25

RUSSIAN

Café Yarmarka | **Pike Pl Mkt**	-
From Russia/Love | **Bellevue**	-
Piroshky Piroshky | **Pike Pl Mkt**	23

SANDWICHES

☑ Armandino's Salumi | **Pioneer Sq**	28
Baguette Box | **multi.**	23
Goldbergs' Deli | **Bellevue**	17
Noosh Café | **Queen Anne**	-
Other Coast Cafe | **multi.**	25
NEW Saint-Germain | **Madison Vly**	21
Shultzy's | **Univ Dist**	20
Smarty Pants | **Georgetown**	-

SCANDINAVIAN

Scandinavian Cafe | **Ballard**	-

SEAFOOD

☑ Anthony's HomePort | **multi.**	20
Anthony's Pier 66 | **Seattle Waterfront**	21
Athenian Inn | **Pike Pl Mkt**	16
Beach Cafe/Point | **Kirkland**	18
Bell St. Diner | **Seattle Waterfront**	18
Bonefish Grill | **multi.**	19
☑ Brooklyn Sea/Steak | **Downtown**	23
Chandler's Crab | **Lake Union**	22
Chinook's/Salmon Bay | **Magnolia**	21
Coho Cafe | **multi.**	18
Coldwater | **Downtown**	20
Cutters Bayhse. | **Pike Pl Mkt**	19
Dash Point Lobster | **Tacoma**	21
Duke's Chowder | **multi.**	18
☑ Elliott's Oyster | **Seattle Waterfront**	23
Emmett Watson's | **Pike Pl Mkt**	22
☑ Etta's Seafood | **Pike Pl Mkt**	24
Fish Club | **Seattle Waterfront**	22
☑ Flying Fish | **Belltown**	25
Friday Harbor Hse. | **Friday Harbor**	-
F.X. McRory's | **Pioneer Sq**	17
Ho Ho Seafood | **Intl Dist**	21
Ivar Acres of Clams | **Seattle Waterfront**	20
Ivar Mukilteo | **Mukilteo**	21
Ivar Salmon Hse. | **Lake Union**	19
Jack's Fish Spot | **Pike Pl Mkt**	20
Lockspot Cafe | **Ballard**	18
Marina Park Grill | **Kirkland**	22
Matt's/Mkt. | **Pike Pl Mkt**	-
Matts' Rotisserie | **Redmond**	20
☑ McCormick & Schmick's | **multi.**	21
McCorm./Schm. Harbor | **Lake Union**	21
McCormick's Fish | **Downtown**	21
☑ Oceanaire | **Downtown**	23
NEW O/8 | **Bellevue**	21
Oyster Bar/Chuckanut | **Bow**	24
Pacific Grill | **Tacoma**	-
☑ Palisade | **Magnolia**	23
Ponti Seafood | **Fremont**	22
Queen City Grill | **Belltown**	22
☑ Ray's Boathse. | **Shilshole**	24
Ray's Cafe | **Shilshole**	22
☑ Salty's | **multi.**	20
Sea Garden | **multi.**	20
Sea Grill | **Tacoma**	22
☑ Seastar | **Bellevue**	26

Shoalwater | **Seaview**	–
Shuckers | **Downtown**	25
Sunfish | **W Seattle**	21
Third Floor Fish | **Kirkland**	24
Top Gun Seafood | **Bellevue**	21
☒ Waterfront Seafood | **Seattle Waterfront**	24
Yarrow Bay Grill | **Kirkland**	24

SMALL PLATES

(See also Spanish tapas specialist)

Black Bottle | Eclectic | **Belltown**	22
☒ Lark | Amer. | **Capitol Hill**	27
NEW Local Vine | Eclectic | **Belltown**	–
NEW Oliver's Twist | Pac. NW | **Phinney Ridge**	25
Olives Cafe | Med. | **Edmonds**	23
Pair | Amer. | **Ravenna**	25
Portalis | Amer./Euro. | **Ballard**	18
NEW Umi Sake Hse. | Japanese | **Belltown**	22
NEW Vi Bacchus | Japanese | **Capitol Hill**	–

SOUL FOOD

Catfish Corner | **Capitol Hill**	21
Kingfish | **Capitol Hill**	23

SOUTH AMERICAN

Copacabana Cafe | **Pike Pl Mkt**	20

SOUTHERN

Ezell's | **multi.**	24
Kingfish | **Capitol Hill**	23
Sazerac | **Downtown**	20

SOUTHWESTERN

Cactus | **multi.**	22
Desert Fire | **Redmond**	16
Santa Fe Cafe | **Phinney Ridge**	21
Z'Tejas | **Bellevue**	18

SPANISH

(* tapas specialist)

NEW Gaudi | **Ravenna**	–
☒ Harvest Vine* | **Madison Vly**	26
Ibiza | **Pioneer Sq**	19
Tango* | **Capitol Hill**	23

STEAKHOUSES

Buenos Aires Grill | **Downtown**	23
☒ Daniel's Broiler | **multi.**	25
DC's Steakhouse | **Sammamish**	15
☒ El Gaucho | **multi.**	25
F.X. McRory's | **Pioneer Sq**	17
☒ JaK's Grill | **multi.**	26
Melrose Grill | **Renton**	27
☒ Metro. Grill | **Downtown**	26
Morton's | **Downtown**	24
Outback Steak | **multi.**	15
Pacific Grill | **Tacoma**	–
Ruth's Chris | **multi.**	23
Spencer's Steaks | **SeaTac**	–
21 Central Steak | **Kirkland**	20
Union Sq. Grill | **Downtown**	22

TAIWANESE

NEW Facing East | **Bellevue**	–

TEAROOMS

Queen Mary Tea | **Ravenna**	19
NEW Remedy Teas | **Capitol Hill**	23

TEX-MEX

NEW Austin | **Ballard**	–
Jalisco Mex. | **multi.**	17

THAI

Ayutthaya | **Capitol Hill**	22
Bahn Thai | **Queen Anne**	20
☒ Bai Pai Fine Thai | **Roosevelt**	22
Galanga Thai | **Tacoma**	24
Kaosamai | **Fremont**	–
Krittika Noodles | **Green Lk**	22
Mae Phim Thai | **Downtown**	21
May | **Wallingford**	20
Racha Noodles | **multi.**	21
Thai Ginger | **multi.**	22
Thaiku | **Ballard**	21
Thai on Mercer | **Mercer Is**	18
Thai Siam | **Ballard**	23
Thai Tom | **Univ Dist**	26
Thin Pan | **Kirkland**	21
Toi | **Downtown**	–
Typhoon! | **multi.**	22

TURKISH

Turkish Delight | **Pike Pl Mkt** 21

VEGETARIAN

(* vegan)

Bamboo Gdn. Veg. | **Queen Anne** 18

Cafe Flora | **Madison Pk** 22

🟥 Carmelita | **Greenwood** 26

Chaco Canyon* | **Univ Dist** ‐

preet's | **Redmond** 25

Silent Heart Nest | **Fremont** 16

Sunlight Cafe | **Roosevelt** 16

Udupi Palace | **Bellevue** 20

Veg. Bistro | **Intl Dist** ‐

VIETNAMESE

Andre's Eurasian | **Bellevue** 19

Bambuza | **Downtown** 19

Green Leaf | **Intl Dist** 25

Lemon Grass | **Intl Dist** 20

🟥 Monsoon | **Capitol Hill** 27

Pho Bac | **Intl Dist** 21

Pho Cyclo | **multi.** 20

Pho Thân Bros. | **multi.** 22

Saigon Bistro | **Intl Dist** 23

Tamarind Tree | **Intl Dist** 24

Thanh Vi | **Univ Dist** 24

Locations

Includes restaurant names, cuisines and Food ratings. ☑ indicates places with the highest ratings, popularity and importance.

Seattle

BALLARD/SHILSHOLE

☑ Anthony's HomePort | Pac. NW/Seafood	20
NEW Austin | Tex-Mex	-
Bad Albert's Tap | Pub	16
Barking Dog | Pub	17
☑ Cafe Besalu | Bakery	27
Carnegie's | French	21
Crash Landing Pizza | Pizza	18
NEW Dish D'Lish | Amer.	18
NEW DiVino | Italian	22
Hattie's Hat | Diner	16
Hi Life | Amer.	18
India Bistro | Indian	23
Kasbah | Moroccan	-
☑ La Carta/Oaxaca | Mex.	26
La Isla | Puerto Rican	25
☑ Le Gourmand | French	27
Lockspot Cafe | Amer./Seafood	18
Louie's Cuisine | Chinese	15
Madame K's Pizza | Pizza	21
Malena's Taco | Mex.	20
Market St. Grill | Amer.	25
Original Pancake | Diner	21
Other Coast Cafe | Sandwiches	25
Pasta Bella | Italian	19
Pho Thân Bros. | Viet.	22
Portalis | Amer./Euro.	18
☑ Ray's Boathse. | Pac. NW/Seafood	24
Ray's Cafe | Pac. NW/Seafood	22
Sam's Sushi | Japanese	18
Scandinavian Cafe | Scan.	-
Señor Moose | Mex.	24
Takis Mad Greek | Greek	18
Thaiku | Thai	21
Thai Siam | Thai	23
☑ Volterra | Italian	25

BEACON HILL/ MT. BAKER

Kusina Filipina | Filipino	-
Mioposto | Italian	-
That's Amore | Italian	-

BELLTOWN

NEW Bambino's Pizzeria | Pizza	19
Belltown Bistro | Amer.	18
Belltown Pizza | Pizza	20
Black Bottle | Eclectic	22
☑ Brasa | Med.	25
Buffalo Deli | Deli	23
Café Darclée | French	-
☑ Cascadia | Amer.	25
CJ's Eatery | Diner	21
Crocodile Cafe | Eclectic	14
Cucina De-Ra | Italian	21
Cyclops | Eclectic	17
☑ El Gaucho | Steak	25
5 Point Café | Amer.	19
☑ Flying Fish | Asian/Seafood	25
Frontier Room | BBQ	19
La Fontana Siciliana | Italian	24
Lampreia | Pac. NW	25
La Vita É Bella | Italian	22
NEW Local Vine | Eclectic	-
Macrina | Bakery/Dessert	25
Mama's Mexican | Mex.	17
Marco's Supperclub | Eclectic	21
Marjorie | Eclectic	22
Marrakesh | Moroccan	21
☑ Mistral | Amer./French	28
Noodle Ranch | Noodles	17
'Ohana | Hawaiian	21
Queen City Grill | Amer.	22
☑ Rest. Zoë | Amer.	27
Saito's Japanese | Japanese	26
Shallots | Pan-Asian	22
☑ Shiro's Sushi | Japanese	27
NEW Spitfire | Carib./Pan-Latin	19

LOCATIONS

NEW Tavolàta | *Italian*	24
Two Bells B&G | *Pub*	19
NEW Umi Sake Hse. | *Japanese*	22
Uptown Espresso | *Coffee*	19
NEW Wann Izakaya | *Japanese*	19
Wasabi Bistro | *Japanese*	22
Zeeks Pizza | *Pizza*	18

CAPITOL HILL

All-Purpose Pizza | *Pizza*	16
Aoki Grill/Sushi | *Japanese*	19
Assimba Ethiopian | *Ethiopian*	22
Ayutthaya | *Thai*	22
Baguette Box | *Sandwiches*	23
B&O Espresso | *Coffee*	20
Broadway Grill | *Amer.*	16
NEW Café Presse | *French*	–
Café Septieme | *Amer.*	16
Capitol Club | *Med.*	19
Catfish Corner | *Soul*	21
Cellar Bistro | *Italian*	–
Coastal Kitchen | *Amer./Eclectic*	20
Crave | *Amer.*	20
Deluxe B&G | *Burgers*	16
Dick's Drive-In | *Burgers*	19
Dilettante Chocolates | *Dessert*	23
Dinette | *Euro.*	24
El Gallito | *Mex.*	18
El Greco | *Med.*	23
Ezell's | *Amer.*	24
Galerias | *Mex.*	22
Garage | *Amer.*	13
Glo's | *Amer.*	26
Jalisco Mex. | *Tex-Mex*	17
Julia's | *Amer.*	16
Karam's Lebanese | *Lebanese*	19
Kimchi Bistro | *Korean*	–
Kingfish | *Soul*	23
Z Lark | *Amer.*	27
Machiavelli | *Italian*	21
Z Monsoon | *Viet.*	27
Noah's Bagels | *Bakery*	17
Olympia Pizza | *Pizza*	18
Osteria La Spiga | *Italian*	24
Pagliacci Pizza | *Pizza*	22

Pho Cyclo | *Viet.*	20
Pho Thân Bros. | *Viet.*	22
Piecora's Pizza | *Pizza*	21
NEW Poco Wine | *Eclectic*	–
R&L Good BBQ | *BBQ*	21
NEW Remedy Teas | *Tea*	23
Rosebud | *Amer.*	19
611 Supreme | *French*	23
Tacos Guaymas | *Mex.*	20
Tango | *Spanish*	23
22 Doors | *Amer.*	19
Via Tribunali | *Pizza*	23
NEW Vi Bacchus | *Japanese*	–
Vios Cafe | *Greek*	24
NEW Volunteer Pk. Café | *Amer.*	26

COLUMBIA CITY/ SEWARD PARK

Columbia City Ale | *Pub*	18
Geraldine's | *Amer.*	20
Jones BBQ | *BBQ*	22
Kallaloo | *Carib./Creole*	–
La Medusa | *Italian/Med.*	25
Tutta Bella | *Pizza*	23

CROWN HILL

Acorn Eatery | *Italian*	17
Burrito Loco | *Mex.*	22
Dick's Drive-In | *Burgers*	19

DOWNTOWN

Andaluca | *Med.*	24
Assaggio | *Italian*	23
Bakeman's | *Deli*	22
Bambuza | *Viet.*	19
NEW Barolo | *Italian*	22
Belle Epicurean | *Bakery/French*	26
Benihana | *Japanese*	18
NEW Boka Kitchen | *Pac. NW*	22
Brass. Margaux | *French/Pac. NW*	19
Z Brooklyn Sea/Steak | *Seafood*	23
Buenos Aires Grill | *Argent.*	23
Z Cheesecake Factory | *Amer.*	17
Coldwater | *Pac. NW/Seafood*	20
Z Dahlia Lounge | *Pac. NW*	25

Dilettante Chocolates	*Dessert*	23
Dragonfish	*Pan-Asian*	20
Earth & Ocean	*Amer.*	22
NEW Entre Nous	*French*	-
FareStart	*Pac. NW*	22
Fox Sports Grill	*Amer.*	12
Gelatiamo	*Dessert*	24
☐ Georgian	*French/Pac. NW*	26
Gordon Biersch	*Amer.*	14
icon Grill	*Amer.*	20
Il Fornaio	*Italian*	20
☐ Lola	*Greek*	24
Mae Phim Thai	*Thai*	21
☐ McCormick & Schmick's	*Seafood*	21
McCormick's Fish	*Seafood*	21
☐ Metro. Grill	*Steak*	26
Mexico Cantina	*Mex.*	20
Morton's	*Steak*	24
NEW O'Asian	*Chinese*	20
☐ Oceanaire	*Seafood*	23
Other Coast Cafe	*Sandwiches*	25
Pabla Indian	*Indian*	20
Paddy Coynes	*Pub*	18
☐ Palace Kitchen	*Amer.*	24
Palomino	*Italian*	21
P.F. Chang's	*Chinese*	19
☐ Purple Cafe	*Pac. NW*	22
NEW Qube	*Asian/French*	22
Red Fin	*Japanese*	23
Rest. Shilla	*Japanese/Korean*	15
Romio's Pizza/Pasta	*Pizza*	16
Ruth's Chris	*Steak*	23
Sazerac	*Southern*	20
NEW Serious Pie	*Pizza*	25
Shuckers	*Seafood*	25
Tap House Grill	*Eclectic*	18
NEW TASTE	*Pac. NW*	19
Thai Ginger	*Thai*	22
13 Coins	*Italian*	18
Toi	*Thai*	-
Troiani	*Italian*	22
Tulio	*Italian*	24
Typhoon!	*Thai*	22

☐ Union	*Amer.*	26
Union Sq. Grill	*Pac. NW*	22
Uptown Espresso	*Coffee*	19
☐ Wild Ginger	*Pac. Rim*	25

EASTLAKE/LAKE UNION

Azteca	*Mex.*	14
BluWater	*Amer.*	16
Bonefish Grill	*Seafood*	19
☐ Canlis	*Pac. NW*	27
Chandler's Crab	*Seafood*	22
☐ Daniel's Broiler	*Steak*	25
Duke's Chowder	*Seafood*	18
☐ Elemental	*Eclectic*	26
Feierabend	*German*	18
14 Carrot Cafe	*Amer.*	18
I Love Sushi	*Japanese*	23
Ivar Salmon Hse.	*Pac. NW/Seafood*	19
Joeys	*Eclectic*	19
Le Fournil	*Bakery/French*	21
Louisa's Cafe	*Amer.*	21
McCorm./Schm. Harbor	*Seafood*	21
Outback Steak	*Steak*	15
Red Robin	*Burgers*	15
Romio's Pizza/Pasta	*Pizza*	16
Serafina	*Italian*	24
☐ Sitka & Spruce	*Eclectic*	28
Uptown Espresso	*Coffee*	19

FIRST HILL

Geneva	*Continental*	25
Hunt Club	*Pac. NW*	22

FREMONT/WALLINGFORD

Asteroid	*Italian*	25
Baguette Box	*Sandwiches*	23
Blue C Sushi	*Japanese*	15
NEW Bottle Rocket	*Amer.*	-
Brad's Swingside	*Italian*	24
Brouwer's	*Belgian*	20
Chinoise	*Pan-Asian*	19
☐ Chiso	*Japanese*	26
Costas Opa	*Greek*	19
Dick's Drive-In	*Burgers*	19

LOCATIONS

Diggity Dog's	Hot Dogs	19	☑ Eva	Amer.	26
Dish, The	Amer.	23	Fu Man Dumpling	Chinese	19
Eggs Cetera's	Amer.	15	Gordito's Mex.	Mex.	22
El Camino	Mex.	21	Greenlake B&G	Amer.	16
Essential Baking	Bakery	23	Jalisco Mex.	Tex-Mex	17
Fremont Classic	Italian	19	Kabob House	Pakistani	23
Hale's Ales	Pub	17	Kidd Valley	Burgers	18
Julia's	Amer.	16	☑ Kisaku Sushi	Japanese	27
Kabul Afghan	Afghan	25	Krittika Noodles	Noodles	22
Kaosamai	Thai	–	Luau Polynesian	Polynesian	15
May	Thai	20	Luisa's Mex.	Mex.	16
Musashi's	Japanese	21	Mae's	Amer.	18
Olympia Pizza	Pizza	18	Mona's Bistro	Med.	23
☑ Paseo	Carib.	27	Nell's	Amer.	25
Persimmon	Amer.	22	NEW Oliver's Twist	Pac. NW	25
Pontevecchio	Italian	23	NEW Perché/Pasta	Italian	22
Ponti Seafood	Seafood	22	Pho Thân Bros.	Viet.	22
Red Door	Pub	17	Red Mill Burgers	Burgers	24
Silent Heart Nest	Veg.	16	Romio's Pizza/Pasta	Pizza	16
Tacos Guaymas	Mex.	20	Rosita's Mex.	Mex.	19
35th St. Bistro	French	24	Santa Fe Cafe	New Mex.	21
NEW Tilth	Amer.	25	74th St. Ale Hse.	Pub	19
Tutta Bella	Pizza	23	Stumbling Goat	Pac. NW	24
			Tacos Guaymas	Mex.	20
			Yanni's	Greek	22
			Zeeks Pizza	Pizza	18

GEORGETOWN/ SOUTH PARK/ SOUTH SEATTLE

Alki Bakery	Bakery	21
Coliman	Mex.	–
Dahlak Eritrean	Eritrean	–
Ezell's	Amer.	24
FareStart/2100	Deli	–
Jalisco Mex.	Tex-Mex	17
Kauai Family Rest.	Hawaiian	21
MuyMacho	Mex.	–
Pig Iron Bar-B-Q	BBQ	22
Smarty Pants	Sandwiches	–
Stellar Pizza	Pizza	21

GREEN LAKE/ GREENWOOD/ PHINNEY RIDGE

Bick's Broadview	Amer.	21
BluWater	Amer.	16
☑ Carmelita	Med.	26
Duke's Chowder	Seafood	18
El Chupacabra	Mex.	14

INTERBAY/MAGNOLIA

Chinook's/Salmon Bay	Seafood	21
El Ranchon Mexican	Mex.	15
Luigi's Pizza	Italian	16
Maggie Bluff's	Burgers	18
Mondello	Italian	23
☑ Palisade	Seafood	23
Red Mill Burgers	Burgers	24
Romio's Pizza/Pasta	Pizza	16
Szmania's	German/Pac. NW	23

INTERNATIONAL DISTRICT

Bush Garden	Japanese	19
China Gate	Chinese	20
Fort St. George	Japanese	–
Four Seas	Chinese	17
Fuji Sushi	Japanese	25
Green Leaf	Viet.	25

Ho Ho Seafood	*Chinese/Seafood*	21
Honey Court	*Chinese*	23
House of Hong	*Chinese*	21
Jade Garden	*Chinese*	23
Kau Kau BBQ	*Chinese*	24
Lemon Grass	*Viet.*	20
NEW Made/Kitchen	*Pan-Asian*	21
Malay Satay Hut	*Malaysian*	24
Z Maneki	*Japanese*	27
Mike's Noodle Hse.	*Noodles*	25
Phnom Penh	*Cambodian*	-
Pho Bac	*Viet.*	21
Purple Dot Café	*Chinese*	18
Saigon Bistro	*Viet.*	23
Sea Garden	*Chinese/Seafood*	20
Shanghai Gdn.	*Chinese*	22
Tai Tung	*Chinese*	20
Tamarind Tree	*Viet.*	24
Veg. Bistro	*Chinese/Veg.*	-

LAKE CITY/ NORTHGATE/ NORTH SEATTLE

Azteca	*Mex.*	14
Dick's Drive-In	*Burgers*	19
Jalisco Mex.	*Tex-Mex*	17
Kidd Valley	*Burgers*	18
La Casa/Mojito	*Pan-Latin*	21
Outback Steak	*Steak*	15
Saltoro	*Amer.*	22
Toyoda Sushi	*Japanese*	23

LAURELHURST/ SAND POINT

Z JaK's Grill	*Steak*	26
Sand Point Grill	*Eclectic*	17

LESCHI/MADRONA

BluWater	*Amer.*	16
Café Soleil	*Amer./Ethiopian*	20
NEW Coupage	*French/Pan-Asian*	23
Crémant	*French*	24
Z Daniel's Broiler	*Steak*	25
Dulces Latin	*Eclectic*	21
Hi Spot Cafe	*Amer.*	23
St. Clouds	*Pac. NW*	21

MADISON PARK/ MADISON VALLEY

Bing's Burgers	*Amer.*	16
Cactus	*SW*	22
Cafe Flora	*Veg.*	22
Chinoise	*Pan-Asian*	19
Z Crush	*Amer.*	26
Essential Baking	*Bakery*	23
Z Harvest Vine	*Spanish*	26
Madison Pk. Cafe	*French*	22
Z Nishino	*Japanese*	27
Phila. Fevre	*Deli*	23
Z Rover's	*French*	28
NEW Saint-Germain	*French*	21
Sostanza	*Italian*	22
Thai Ginger	*Thai*	22
Voilà! Bistrot	*French*	22

MAPLE LEAF/ ROOSEVELT

Z Bai Pai Fine Thai	*Thai*	22
Die BierStube	*German*	-
NEW Divine	*Greek*	-
Jones, The	*Amer.*	20
Judy Fu's	*Chinese*	19
Maple Leaf Grill	*Eclectic*	18
NY Pizza Place	*Pizza*	25
Sunlight Cafe	*Eclectic*	16

MONTLAKE

Cafe Lago	*Italian*	23

PIKE PLACE MARKET

Alibi Room	*Pac. NW*	19
Athenian Inn	*Amer./Seafood*	16
Bayou on First	*Cajun*	-
Beecher's Cheese	*Cheese*	24
Z Cafe Campagne	*French*	25
Café Yarmarka	*Russian*	-
Z Campagne	*French*	26
Chez Shea	*French/Pac. NW*	26
Copacabana Cafe	*S Amer.*	20
Crepe de France	*French*	23
Crumpet Shop	*Bakery*	24
Cutters Bayhse.	*Pac. NW/Seafood*	19
El Puerco Lloron	*Mex.*	21

Emmett Watson's | *Seafood*		22
☑ Etta's Seafood |		24
Pac. NW/Seafood		
Il Bistro | *Italian*		23
Jack's Fish Spot | *Seafood*		20
Kells Irish | *Irish*		17
Le Panier | *Bakery/French*		23
☑ Le Pichet | *French*		24
Lowell's | *Amer.*		17
Matt's/Mkt. | *Pac. NW/Seafood*		–
Maximilien | *French*		21
Mee Sum Pastries |		21
Chinese/Dessert		
94 Stewart | *Amer.*		21
Pan-Africa Cafe | *African*		21
Pike Pub | *Pub*		16
Pink Door | *Italian*		22
Piroshky Piroshky | *Russian*		23
Place Pigalle | *Pac. NW*		23
Shea's Lounge | *Pac. NW*		24
NEW Steelhead | *Pac. NW*		23
Taxi Dogs | *Hot Dogs*		15
Three Girls Bakery | *Bakery*		24
Turkish Delight | *Turkish*		21
World Class Chili | *Amer.*		24

PIONEER SQUARE/SODO

Al Boccalino | *Italian*		22
☑ Armandino's Salumi |		28
Italian/Sandwiches		
Cafe Bengodi | *Italian*		19
De Nunzio's | *Italian*		16
Fado Irish | *Irish*		14
F.X. McRory's | *Seafood/Steak*		17
Ibiza | *Spanish*		19
☑ Il Terrazzo | *Italian*		27
Jones BBQ | *BBQ*		22
Matt's Gourmet Dogs |		18
Hot Dogs		
New Orl. Creole | *Cajun/Creole*		14
Pecos Pit BBQ | *BBQ*		25
Pho Cyclo | *Viet.*		20
Pyramid Ale | *Pub*		16
Tratt. Mitchelli | *Italian*		16
Zaina Food | *Mideast.*		22

QUEEN ANNE/ SEATTLE CENTER

Bahn Thai | *Thai*		20
Bamboo Gdn. Veg. | *Chinese*		18
NEW Betty | *Amer.*		22
Boat St. Cafe | *French*		25
Bricco/Regina | *Italian*		22
Buca di Beppo | *Italian*		14
Buckley's | *Amer.*		19
Caffé Minnie's | *Amer.*		12
Chinoise | *Pan-Asian*		19
Crow | *Amer.*		23
Dick's Drive-In | *Burgers*		19
5 Spot | *Amer.*		20
Hilltop Ale Hse. | *Amer.*		22
Jalisco Mex. | *Tex-Mex*		17
Julia's | *Amer.*		16
Kidd Valley | *Burgers*		18
Macrina | *Bakery/Dessert*		25
Malena's Taco | *Mex.*		20
Melting Pot | *Fondue*		19
Moxie | *Amer.*		21
Noah's Bagels | *Bakery*		17
Noosh Café | *Deli*		–
Olympia Pizza | *Pizza*		18
NEW Opal | *Pac. NW*		25
Ototo Sushi | *Japanese*		24
Pagliacci Pizza | *Pizza*		22
Panos Kleftiko | *Greek*		23
Paragon | *Pac. NW*		19
Pasta & Co. | *Italian*		22
Pasta Bella | *Italian*		19
Peso's Kitchen | *Mex.*		23
NEW Portage | *French/Pac. NW*		26
Racha Noodles | *Noodles*		21
Rhodie's Smokin' | *BBQ*		–
Roti Cuisine | *Indian*		20
Sam's Sushi | *Japanese*		18
Shiki | *Japanese*		24
☑ SkyCity/Needle | *Pac. NW*		21
NEW Sorrentino | *Italian*		18
Sport | *Eclectic*		18
Ten Mercer | *Amer.*		22
Uptown China | *Chinese*		18

Uptown Espresso	Coffee	19
Veil	Amer.	23
Via Tribunali	Pizza	23
Zeeks Pizza	Pizza	18

RAVENNA/WEDGWOOD

Bagel Oasis	Deli	21
Black Pearl	Chinese	15
NEW Gaudi	Spanish	–
NEW Hot Dish	Amer.	–
Kidd Valley	Burgers	18
Pair	Amer.	25
Queen Mary Tea	Tea	19
Salvatore	Italian	23
Zeeks Pizza	Pizza	18

SEATTLE WATERFRONT

Anthony's Pier 66	Pac. NW/Seafood	21
Bell St. Diner	Seafood	18
Z Elliott's Oyster	Seafood	23
Fish Club	Med.	22
Ivar Acres of Clams	Seafood	20
Matt's Gourmet Dogs	Hot Dogs	18
Red Robin	Burgers	15
Z 6·7	Pac. NW	24
Uptown Espresso	Coffee	19
Z Waterfront Seafood	Seafood	24

UNIVERSITY DISTRICT/ UNIVERSITY VILLAGE

Agua Verde	Mex.	22
Atlas Foods	Amer./Eclectic	16
Blue C Sushi	Japanese	15
Blue Onion	Amer.	17
Caspian Grill	Persian	–
Chaco Canyon	Vegan	–
Ciao Bella	Italian	21
Costas Greek	Greek	17
Delfino's Pizza	Pizza	17
La Casa/Mojito	Pan-Latin	21
Mamma Melina	Italian	21
Matt's Gourmet Dogs	Hot Dogs	18
Northlake Tav.	Pizza	21
Pagliacci Pizza	Pizza	22
Pasta & Co.	Italian	22

Pho Thân Bros.	Viet.	22
Shultzy's	Sandwiches	20
Taste of India	Indian	22
Tempero/Brasil	Brazilian	24
Thai Tom	Thai	26
Thanh Vi	Viet.	24
Tokyo Garden	Japanese	–
Zao Noodle Bar	Noodles	16

WEST SEATTLE

Abbondanza Pizzeria	Pizza	18
Alki Bakery	Bakery	21
Alki Homestead	Amer.	20
NEW Z Bakery Nouveau	Bakery/French	28
NEW Beàto	Italian	23
Blackbird Bistro	Amer.	19
Cactus	SW	22
Circa	Eclectic	23
Duke's Chowder	Seafood	18
Eats Mkt. Café	Amer.	20
Elliott Bay Brewery	Pub	20
Endolyne Joe's	Amer.	19
Z JaK's Grill	Steak	26
La Rustica	Italian	25
Lee's	Pan-Asian	23
Luna Park Cafe	Amer.	15
Mashiko	Japanese	25
Mission	Pan-Latin	20
Pegasus Pizza	Pizza	20
Z Phoenecia/Alki	Med.	27
Pho Thân Bros.	Viet.	22
Z Salty's	Seafood	20
Sunfish	Seafood	21
Tacos Guaymas	Mex.	20
Uptown Espresso	Coffee	19

WHITE CENTER

| Tacos Guaymas | Mex. | 20 |

Eastside

BELLEVUE

Andre's Eurasian	French/Viet.	19
Azteca	Mex.	14
Bamboo Gdn. Szechuan	Chinese	–

☑ Belle Pastry	*Bakery/Dessert*	27
Bis on Main	*Amer.*	24
Café Ori	*Chinese*	21
Calcutta Grill	*Amer.*	20
☑ Cheesecake Factory	*Amer.*	17
☑ Daniel's Broiler	*Steak*	25
Dixie's BBQ	*BBQ*	22
NEW Facing East	*Chinese*	–
Firenze	*Italian*	22
Flo	*Japanese*	25
From Russia/Love	*Russian*	–
Gilbert's Main St. Bagel	*Deli*	22
Goldbergs' Deli	*Deli*	17
Grazie	*Italian*	20
Hunan Garden	*Chinese*	18
I Love Sushi	*Japanese*	23
Joeys	*Eclectic*	19
Jones BBQ	*BBQ*	22
Kidd Valley	*Burgers*	18
La Cocina/Puerco	*Mex.*	20
Mayuri	*Indian*	25
☑ McCormick & Schmick's	*Seafood*	21
Medit. Kitchen	*Lebanese/Med.*	22
Melting Pot	*Fondue*	19
Moghul Palace	*Indian*	22
Noble Court	*Chinese*	21
NEW O/8	*Pac. NW*	21
Ooba's Mex. Grill	*Mex.*	24
Outback Steak	*Steak*	15
Pagliacci Pizza	*Pizza*	22
Pasta & Co.	*Italian*	22
P.F. Chang's	*Chinese*	19
Pho Thân Bros.	*Viet.*	22
Pogacha	*Croatian/Pac. NW*	18
NEW Porcella	*French/Med.*	24
Red Robin	*Burgers*	15
Ruth's Chris	*Steak*	23
Salute/Bellevue	*Italian*	19
Sea Garden	*Chinese/Seafood*	20
☑ Seastar	*Seafood*	26
☑ Szechuan Chef	*Chinese*	27
Tap House Grill	*Eclectic*	18
Thai Ginger	*Thai*	22

3 Pigs BBQ	*BBQ*	21
Top Gun Seafood	*Chinese/Seafood*	21
Tosoni's	*Continental*	26
Trader Vic's	*Polynesian*	16
Udupi Palace	*Indian*	20
NEW Yama/Galleria	*Asian Fusion*	23
Z'Tejas	*SW*	18

ISSAQUAH/
SAMMAMISH

Coho Cafe	*Pac. NW/Seafood*	18
DC's Steakhouse	*Steak*	15
☑ JaK's Grill	*Steak*	26
Julia's	*Amer.*	16
Pogacha	*Croatian/Pac. NW*	18
Red Robin	*Burgers*	15
☑ Salish Lodge	*French*	24
Shanghai Gdn.	*Chinese*	22
Sushiman	*Japanese*	24
Thai Ginger	*Thai*	22

KIRKLAND

☑ Anthony's HomePort	*Pac. NW/Seafood*	20
Azteca	*Mex.*	14
Beach Cafe/Point	*Eclectic/Seafood*	18
BluWater	*Amer.*	16
Cactus	*SW*	22
☑ Cafe Juanita	*Italian*	28
Cafe Veloce	*Italian*	21
Calabria	*Italian*	17
Coyote Creek Pizza	*Pizza*	20
Izumi	*Japanese*	25
Jalisco Mex.	*Tex-Mex*	17
Kidd Valley	*Burgers*	18
☑ Lynn's Bistro	*Asian Fusion/French*	26
Marina Park Grill	*Seafood*	22
Matt's Gourmet Dogs	*Hot Dogs*	18
Mixtura	*Peruvian*	24
Original Pancake	*Diner*	21
Outback Steak	*Steak*	15
☑ Purple Cafe	*Pac. NW*	22

Rikki Rikki | *Japanese* 19

Rist. Paradiso | *Italian* 22

Santorini Greek | *Greek* 23

Sentosa Asian | *Chinese* 15

Shamiana | *Indian/Pakistani* 23

Sushiya | *Japanese* -

Thin Pan | *Thai* 21

Third Floor Fish | *Seafood* 24

21 Central Steak | *Steak* 20

Waters Lakeside | *Pac. NW* 22

NEW Wilde Rover | *Pub* -

Yarrow Bay Grill | 24
Eclectic/Seafood

Zeeks Pizza | *Pizza* 18

MERCER ISLAND

NEW Bennett's Pure Food | 22
Amer.

Noah's Bagels | *Bakery* 17

Thai on Mercer | *Thai* 18

REDMOND

Alborz | *Persian* 23

Coho Cafe | *Pac. NW/Seafood* 18

Coyote Creek Pizza | *Pizza* 20

Desert Fire | *SW* 16

Frankie's Pizza | *Italian* 20

NEW Inchin's Bamboo | -
Chinese/Indian

Kikuya | *Japanese* 22

Malay Satay Hut | *Malaysian* 24

Matts' Rotisserie | *Amer.* 20

Neville's/British | *British* 20

Ooba's Mex. Grill | *Mex.* 24

Pasta & Co. | *Italian* 22

Pho Thân Bros. | *Viet.* 22

Pomegranate Bistro | *Amer.* 25

preet's | *Indian* 25

Red Robin | *Burgers* 15

Romio's Pizza/Pasta | *Pizza* 16

Ruby's | *Diner* 16

NEW Spazzo | *Italian* 20

Thai Ginger | *Thai* 22

Tropea | *Italian* 26

Typhoon! | *Thai* 22

Outlying Areas

BAINBRIDGE ISLAND

Cafe Nola | *Amer.* 21

Four Swallows | *Italian/Pac. NW* 25

Madoka | *Pac. Rim* 20

Streamliner | *Diner* 16

BOTHELL/KENMORE/ MALTBY

Bonefish Grill | *Seafood* 19

Grazie | *Italian* 20

Jalisco Mex. | *Tex-Mex* 17

Kidd Valley | *Burgers* 18

☑ Maltby Cafe | *Amer.* 26

Outback Steak | *Steak* 15

Russell's | *Amer.* -

BURIEN/DES MOINES/ KENT

☑ Anthony's HomePort | 20
Pac. NW/Seafood

Azteca | *Mex.* 14

Duke's Chowder | *Seafood* 18

Red Robin | *Burgers* 15

Tin Room Bar | *Amer.* -

Zephyr Grill | *Amer.* 19

EDMONDS/SHORELINE

☑ Anthony's HomePort | 20
Pac. NW/Seafood

Black Pearl | *Chinese* 15

Chanterelle | *Eclectic* 19

NEW Hills' Food/Wine | 23
Pac. NW

Olives Cafe | *Med.* 23

Pho Thân Bros. | *Viet.* 22

Romio's Pizza/Pasta | *Pizza* 16

EVERETT/MUKILTEO

☑ Anthony's HomePort | 20
Pac. NW/Seafood

Ivar Mukilteo | *Seafood* 21

Outback Steak | *Steak* 15

Pho Thân Bros. | *Viet.* 22

Red Robin | *Burgers* 15

Romio's Pizza/Pasta | *Pizza* 16

Tacos Guaymas | *Mex.* 20

LOCATIONS

FEDERAL WAY/TACOMA

Ⓩ Anthony's HomePort | Pac. NW/Seafood	20
Azteca | Mex.	14
Dash Point Lobster | Seafood	21
Duke's Chowder | Seafood	18
Ⓩ El Gaucho | Steak	25
Galanga Thai | Thai	24
Ⓩ Indochine Asian | Asian Fusion	23
Melting Pot | Fondue	19
Outback Steak | Steak	15
Pacific Grill | Seafood/Steak	–
Pho Thân Bros. | Viet.	22
Primo Grill | Med.	25
Sea Grill | Seafood	22
Tacos Guaymas | Mex.	20

GIG HARBOR

Ⓩ Anthony's HomePort | Pac. NW/Seafood	20

LAKE FOREST PARK/ MOUNTLAKE TERRACE

Honey Bear | Amer.	21

LYNNWOOD

Buca di Beppo | Italian	14
Ezell's | Amer.	24
Hosoonyi | Korean	24
Kidd Valley | Burgers	18
Red Robin | Burgers	15
Romio's Pizza/Pasta | Pizza	16
Tacos Guaymas | Mex.	20

MILL CREEK/ SNOHOMISH

Azteca | Mex.	14
Azul | Pan-Latin	23
Zinnia | Amer.	23

NW WASHINGTON

Ⓩ Anthony's HomePort | Pac. NW/Seafood	20
Oyster Bar/Chuckanut | Seafood	24

OLYMPIA

Ⓩ Anthony's HomePort | Pac. NW/Seafood	20
Racha Noodles | Noodle	21

POULSBO

Mor Mor Bistro | Med.	18

REDONDO

Ⓩ Salty's | Seafood	20

RENTON

Kidd Valley | Burgers	18
Matt's Gourmet Dogs | Hot Dogs	18
Melrose Grill | Steak	27
Racha Noodles | Noodle	21
Tacos Guaymas | Mex.	20

SAN JUAN ISLANDS

Christina's | Pac. NW	26
Friday Harbor Hse. | Pac. NW/Seafood	–
Rose's Bakery | Pac. NW	–

SEATAC/TUKWILA

Azteca | Mex.	14
Grazie | Italian	20
Outback Steak | Steak	15
Sharp's Roaster | Amer.	–
Spencer's Steaks | Steak	–
13 Coins | Italian	18

SW WASHINGTON COAST

Shoalwater | Pac. NW	–

WHIDBEY ISLAND

Ⓩ Inn at Langley | Pac. NW	27

WOODINVILLE

Barking Frog | Pac. NW	24
Ⓩ Herbfarm, The | Pac. NW	29
Ooba's Mex. Grill | Mex.	24
Ⓩ Purple Cafe | Pac. NW	22
Racha Noodles | Noodles	21
Red Robin | Burgers	15
Rist. Italianissimo | Italian	25
Texas Smokehse. | BBQ	20

Special Features

Listings cover the best in each category and include names, locations and Food ratings. Multi-location restaurants' features may vary by branch. Ⓩ indicates places with the highest ratings, popularity and importance.

BREAKFAST

(See also Hotel Dining)

Athenian Inn	**Pike Pl Mkt**	16
Bad Albert's Tap	**Ballard**	16
NEW Bottle Rocket	**Wallingford**	-
Dish, The	**Fremont**	23
Endolyne Joe's	**W Seattle**	19
5 Point Café	**Belltown**	19
5 Spot	**Queen Anne**	20
14 Carrot Cafe	**Eastlake**	18
Geraldine's	**Columbia City**	20
Glo's	**Capitol Hill**	26
Hi Spot Cafe	**Madrona**	23
Julia's	**multi.**	16
Macrina	**multi.**	25
Original Pancake	**multi.**	21
Ruby's	**Redmond**	16

BRUNCH

Alki Bakery	**Georgetown**	21
Ⓩ Anthony's HomePort	**multi.**	20
Azul	**Mill Creek**	23
B&O Espresso	**Capitol Hill**	20
Barking Dog	**Ballard**	17
Barking Frog	**Woodinville**	24
NEW Bennett's Pure Food	**Mercer Is**	22
Blackbird Bistro	**W Seattle**	19
Blue Onion	**Univ Dist**	17
BluWater	**multi.**	16
Boat St. Cafe	**Queen Anne**	25
NEW Boka Kitchen	**Downtown**	22
Brass. Margaux	**Downtown**	19
Broadway Grill	**Capitol Hill**	16
Buckley's	**Seattle Ctr**	19
Ⓩ Cafe Campagne	**Pike Pl Mkt**	25
Cafe Flora	**Madison Pk**	22
Cafe Nola	**Bainbridge Is**	21
Café Soleil	**Madrona**	20
Calcutta Grill	**Newcastle**	20
Chandler's Crab	**Lake Union**	22

Chanterelle	**Edmonds**	19
Ⓩ Cheesecake Factory	**multi.**	17
Circa	**W Seattle**	23
Coastal Kitchen	**Capitol Hill**	20
Coho Cafe	**multi.**	18
NEW Coupage	**Madrona**	23
Crave	**Capitol Hill**	20
Crocodile Cafe	**Belltown**	14
Deluxe B&G	**Capitol Hill**	16
NEW Divine	**Maple Leaf**	-
Dragonfish	**Downtown**	20
Earth & Ocean	**Downtown**	22
Eats Mkt. Café	**W Seattle**	20
El Camino	**Fremont**	21
El Greco	**Capitol Hill**	23
El Puerco Lloron	**Pike Pl Mkt**	21
Ⓩ Etta's Seafood	**Pike Pl Mkt**	24
Fish Club	**Seattle Waterfront**	22
5 Spot	**Queen Anne**	20
Galerias	**Capitol Hill**	22
NEW Gaudi	**Ravenna**	-
Geraldine's	**Columbia City**	20
Gordon Biersch	**Downtown**	14
Hale's Ales	**Fremont**	17
Hattie's Hat	**Ballard**	16
NEW Hills' Food/Wine	**Shoreline**	23
Hunt Club	**First Hill**	22
Ivar Acres of Clams	**Seattle Waterfront**	20
Ivar Salmon Hse.	**Lake Union**	19
Kells Irish	**Pike Pl Mkt**	17
Kingfish	**Capitol Hill**	23
Ⓩ Lola	**Downtown**	24
Ⓩ Lynn's Bistro	**Kirkland**	26
Macrina	**multi.**	25
Madison Pk. Cafe	**Madison Pk**	22
Maximilien	**Pike Pl Mkt**	21
McCorm./Schm. Harbor	**Lake Union**	21

Mona's Bistro | **Green Lk**	23
Mondello | **Magnolia**	23
⊠ Monsoon | **Capitol Hill**	27
NEW O/8 | **Bellevue**	21
⊠ Palisade | **Magnolia**	23
Paragon | **Queen Anne**	19
Persimmon | **Fremont**	22
Pomegranate Bistro | **Redmond**	25
Red Fin | **Downtown**	23
Rosebud | **Capitol Hill**	19
⊠ Salty's | **multi.**	20
Sazerac | **Downtown**	20
Señor Moose | **Ballard**	24
Serafina | **Eastlake**	24
⊠ Sitka & Spruce | **Eastlake**	28
⊠ 6 · 7 | **Seattle Waterfront**	24
611 Supreme | **Capitol Hill**	23
⊠ SkyCity/Needle | **Seattle Ctr**	21
Smarty Pants | **Georgetown**	-
NEW Sorrentino | **Queen Anne**	18
St. Clouds | **Madrona**	21
NEW Steelhead | **Pike Pl Mkt**	23
Sunlight Cafe | **Roosevelt**	16
That's Amore | **Mt. Baker**	-
13 Coins | **Downtown**	18
35th St. Bistro | **Fremont**	24
NEW Tilth | **Wallingford**	25
Tratt. Mitchelli | **Pioneer Sq**	16
Tulio | **Downtown**	24
Two Bells B&G | **Belltown**	19
Udupi Palace | **Bellevue**	20
⊠ Volterra | **Ballard**	25
Waters Lakeside | **Kirkland**	22
Zephyr Grill | **Kent**	19

BUFFET

(Check availability)

Brass. Margaux | **Downtown**	19
Calcutta Grill | **Newcastle**	20
Coldwater | **Downtown**	20
Dash Point Lobster | **Tacoma**	21
Fish Club | **Seattle Waterfront**	22
India Bistro | **Ballard**	23
Ivar Salmon Hse. | **Lake Union**	19
Mayuri | **Bellevue**	25

Moghul Palace | **Bellevue**	22
Pabla Indian | **Downtown**	20
Roti Cuisine | **Queen Anne**	20
Shamiana | **Kirkland**	23
Udupi Palace | **Bellevue**	20

BUSINESS DINING

Andaluca | **Downtown**	24
⊠ Brooklyn Sea/Steak | **Downtown**	23
Calcutta Grill | **Newcastle**	20
⊠ Canlis | **Lake Union**	27
⊠ Daniel's Broiler | **multi.**	25
Earth & Ocean | **Downtown**	22
⊠ El Gaucho | **multi.**	25
⊠ Elliott's Oyster | **Seattle Waterfront**	23
Fish Club | **Seattle Waterfront**	22
Fox Sports Grill | **Downtown**	12
⊠ Georgian | **Downtown**	26
Lampreia | **Belltown**	25
⊠ Lola | **Downtown**	24
NEW Made/Kitchen | **Intl Dist**	21
⊠ Metro. Grill | **Downtown**	26
Morton's | **Downtown**	24
⊠ Nishino | **Madison Pk**	27
Pacific Grill | **Tacoma**	-
Ruth's Chris | **multi.**	23
⊠ Salish Lodge | **Snoqualmie**	24
⊠ Seastar | **Bellevue**	26
Shuckers | **Downtown**	25
Spencer's Steaks | **SeaTac**	-
NEW Tavolàta | **Belltown**	24
21 Central Steak | **Kirkland**	20
⊠ Union | **Downtown**	26
Union Sq. Grill | **Downtown**	22
⊠ Volterra | **Ballard**	25
⊠ Waterfront Seafood | **Seattle Waterfront**	24
⊠ Wild Ginger | **Downtown**	25
Yarrow Bay Grill | **Kirkland**	24

CATERING

Alki Bakery | **multi.**	21
Alki Homestead | **W Seattle**	20
Andre's Eurasian | **Bellevue**	19

Assimba Ethiopian | **Capitol Hill**	22
Baguette Box | **Fremont**	23
Bakeman's | **Downtown**	22
NEW Z Bakery Nouveau | **W Seattle**	28
NEW Bambino's Pizzeria | **Belltown**	19
Bambuza | **Downtown**	19
Beecher's Cheese | **Pike Pl Mkt**	24
Belle Epicurean | **Downtown**	26
Z Belle Pastry | **Bellevue**	27
Bis on Main | **Bellevue**	24
BluWater | **multi.**	16
Boat St. Cafe | **Queen Anne**	25
Z Brasa | **Belltown**	25
Buffalo Deli | **Belltown**	23
Cactus | **Madison Pk**	22
Z Carmelita | **Greenwood**	26
Z Cascadia | **Belltown**	25
Catfish Corner | **Capitol Hill**	21
Chaco Canyon | **Univ Dist**	-
Chandler's Crab | **Lake Union**	22
Z Chiso | **Fremont**	26
Z Crush | **Madison Vly**	26
Z Dahlia Lounge | **Downtown**	25
Z Daniel's Broiler | **multi.**	25
Desert Fire | **Redmond**	16
NEW Dish D'Lish | **Ballard**	18
Eats Mkt. Café | **W Seattle**	20
Z Elliott's Oyster | **Seattle Waterfront**	23
Emmett Watson's | **Pike Pl Mkt**	22
From Russia/Love | **Bellevue**	-
Fuji Sushi | **Intl Dist**	25
Galerias | **Capitol Hill**	22
NEW Gaudi | **Ravenna**	-
Z Harvest Vine | **Madison Vly**	26
House of Hong | **Intl Dist**	21
Il Fornaio | **Downtown**	20
I Love Sushi | **multi.**	23
Z Il Terrazzo | **Pioneer Sq**	27
NEW Inchin's Bamboo | **Redmond**	-
India Bistro | **Ballard**	23
Z Indochine Asian | **Tacoma**	23
Jones BBQ | **multi.**	22
Kabul Afghan | **Wallingford**	25
Kallaloo | **Columbia City**	-
Kasbah | **Ballard**	-
Kauai Family Rest. | **Georgetown**	21
Kau Kau BBQ | **Intl Dist**	24
Kikuya | **Redmond**	22
Z La Carta/Oaxaca | **Ballard**	26
Z Lark | **Capitol Hill**	27
La Rustica | **W Seattle**	25
Lee's | **W Seattle**	23
Lemon Grass | **Intl Dist**	20
Z Lola | **Downtown**	24
Z Lynn's Bistro | **Kirkland**	26
Macrina | **multi.**	25
Madison Pk. Cafe | **Madison Pk**	22
Malay Satay Hut | **multi.**	24
Marjorie | **Belltown**	22
Marrakesh | **Belltown**	21
Mashiko | **W Seattle**	25
Mayuri | **Bellevue**	25
Z McCormick & Schmick's | **Downtown**	21
McCorm./Schm. Harbor | **Lake Union**	21
McCormick's Fish | **Downtown**	21
Medit. Kitchen | **Bellevue**	22
Z Metro. Grill | **Downtown**	26
Z Mistral | **Belltown**	28
Mixtura | **Kirkland**	24
Moghul Palace | **Bellevue**	22
Mondello | **Magnolia**	23
Moxie | **Queen Anne**	21
Nell's | **Green Lk**	25
Z Nishino | **Madison Pk**	27
NEW O/8 | **Bellevue**	21
'Ohana | **Belltown**	21
Olives Cafe | **Edmonds**	23
Z Palace Kitchen | **Downtown**	24
NEW Perché/Pasta | **Green Lk**	22
Phila. Fevre | **Madison Vly**	23
Z Phoenecia/Alki | **W Seattle**	27
Pomegranate Bistro | **Redmond**	25
NEW Porcella | **Bellevue**	24

SPECIAL FEATURES

preet's | **Redmond**	25
Primo Grill | **Tacoma**	25
☑ Ray's Boathse. | **Shilshole**	24
Red Fin | **Downtown**	23
☑ Rest. Zoë | **Belltown**	27
Rist. Italianissimo | **Woodinville**	25
☑ Rover's | **Madison Vly**	28
Russell's | **Bothell**	–
Saito's Japanese | **Belltown**	26
☑ Seastar | **Bellevue**	26
NEW Serious Pie | **Downtown**	25
Shallots | **Belltown**	22
Shanghai Gdn. | **Issaquah**	22
Shiki | **Queen Anne**	24
☑ Shiro's Sushi | **Belltown**	27
Shoalwater | **Seaview**	–
☑ Sitka & Spruce | **Eastlake**	28
NEW Sorrentino | **Queen Anne**	18
NEW Spazzo | **Redmond**	20
NEW Spitfire | **Belltown**	19
Szmania's | **Magnolia**	23
Tamarind Tree | **Intl Dist**	24
Tango | **Capitol Hill**	23
Taste of India | **Univ Dist**	22
Texas Smokehse. | **Woodinville**	20
Thai Ginger | **multi.**	22
Thai on Mercer | **Mercer Is**	18
That's Amore | **Mt. Baker**	–
Third Floor Fish | **Kirkland**	24
35th St. Bistro | **Fremont**	24
Tin Room Bar | **Burien**	–
Typhoon! | **multi.**	22
Udupi Palace | **Bellevue**	20
Uptown China | **Queen Anne**	18
Veil | **Queen Anne**	23
☑ Volterra | **Ballard**	25
☑ Wild Ginger | **Downtown**	25

CELEBRITY CHEFS

NEW ☑ Bakery Nouveau | *William Leaman* | **W Seattle**	28
☑ Brasa | *Tamara Murphy* | **Belltown**	25
☑ Crush | *Jason Wilson* | **Madison Vly**	26
☑ Dahlia Lounge | *Tom Douglas* | **Downtown**	25
☑ Etta's Seafood | *Tom Douglas* | **Pike Pl Mkt**	24
Fish Club | *Todd English* | **Seattle Waterfront**	22
Lampreia | *Scott Carsberg* | **Belltown**	25
☑ Lark | *Johnathan Sundstrom* | **Capitol Hill**	27
☑ Lola | *Tom Douglas* | **Downtown**	24
☑ Mistral | *William Belickis* | **Belltown**	28
Pacific Grill | *Gordon Naccarato* | **Tacoma**	–
☑ Palace Kitchen | *Tom Douglas* | **Downtown**	24
☑ Rover's | *Thierry Rautureau* | **Madison Vly**	28
NEW Serious Pie | *Tom Douglas* | **Downtown**	25
☑ Shiro's Sushi | *Shiro Kashiba* | **Belltown**	27
NEW Tavolàta | *Ethan Stowell* | **Belltown**	24
NEW Tilth | *Maria Hines* | **Wallingford**	25
Troiani | *Walter Pisano* | **Downtown**	22
☑ Union | *Ethan Stowell* | **Downtown**	26
☑ Volterra | *Don Curtiss* | **Ballard**	25

CHILD-FRIENDLY
(Alternatives to the usual fast-food
places; * children's menu available)

Andre's Eurasian* | **Bellevue**	19
☑ Anthony's HomePort* | **multi.**	20
Anthony's Pier 66* | **Seattle Waterfront**	21
Beach Cafe/Point* | **Kirkland**	18
Bell St. Diner* | **Seattle Waterfront**	18
Bonefish Grill* | **Lake Union**	19
☑ Carmelita* | **Greenwood**	26
☑ Cascadia* | **Belltown**	25

Catfish Corner* | **Capitol Hill**	21
Chandler's Crab* | **Lake Union**	22
Chanterelle* | **Edmonds**	19
Chinook's/Salmon Bay* | **Magnolia**	21
Circa* | **W Seattle**	23
Earth & Ocean* | **Downtown**	22
☑ Elliott's Oyster* | **Seattle Waterfront**	23
Endolyne Joe's* | **W Seattle**	19
☑ Etta's Seafood* | **Pike Pl Mkt**	24
5 Spot* | **Queen Anne**	20
☑ Georgian* | **Downtown**	26
Gordito's Mex.* | **Greenwood**	22
☑ Maltby Cafe* | **Maltby**	26
Marina Park Grill* | **Kirkland**	22
Matts' Rotisserie* | **Redmond**	20
☑ McCormick & Schmick's* | **Downtown**	21
McCorm./Schm. Harbor* | **Lake Union**	21
McCormick's Fish* | **Downtown**	21
Original Pancake* | **Kirkland**	21
Pagliacci Pizza* | **Bellevue**	22
Palomino* | **Downtown**	21
Pasta Bella* | **multi.**	19
Pegasus Pizza* | **W Seattle**	20
Piecora's Pizza* | **Capitol Hill**	21
Ponti Seafood* | **Fremont**	22
Primo Grill* | **Tacoma**	25
☑ Ray's Boathse.* | **Shilshole**	24
Ray's Cafe* | **Shilshole**	22
☑ Salty's* | **multi.**	20
Santa Fe Cafe* | **Phinney Ridge**	21
Sazerac* | **Downtown**	20
☑ 6 · 7* | **Seattle Waterfront**	24
Spencer's Steaks* | **SeaTac**	-
Szmania's* | **Magnolia**	23
Tacos Guaymas* | **multi.**	20
Third Floor Fish* | **Kirkland**	24
Tutta Bella* | **Columbia City**	23
Vios Cafe* | **Capitol Hill**	24
Waters Lakeside* | **Kirkland**	22
☑ Wild Ginger* | **Downtown**	25

DANCING

☑ El Gaucho | **Belltown**	25
Ibiza | **Pioneer Sq**	19
☑ Indochine Asian | **Tacoma**	23
Kells Irish | **Pike Pl Mkt**	17
New Orl. Creole | **Pioneer Sq**	14

DELIVERY/TAKEOUT

(D=delivery, T=takeout)

Agua Verde | T | **Univ Dist**	22
Alki Bakery | T | **multi.**	21
All-Purpose Pizza | D | **Capitol Hill**	16
☑ Anthony's HomePort | T | **Gig Harbor**	20
☑ Armandino's Salumi | T | **Pioneer Sq**	28
Assimba Ethiopian | T | **Capitol Hill**	22
Asteroid | T | **Fremont**	25
Baguette Box | D, T | **multi.**	23
Bakeman's | D, T | **Downtown**	22
NEW ☑ Bakery Nouveau | T | **W Seattle**	28
Barking Frog | T | **Woodinville**	24
NEW Barolo | T | **Downtown**	22
Bayou on First | T | **Pike Pl Mkt**	-
Beach Cafe/Point | T | **Kirkland**	18
Beecher's Cheese | T | **Pike Pl Mkt**	24
Belle Epicurean | T | **Downtown**	26
☑ Belle Pastry | T | **Bellevue**	27
NEW Bennett's Pure Food | T | **Mercer Is**	22
Bis on Main | T | **Bellevue**	24
Black Bottle | T | **Belltown**	22
Black Pearl | D, T | **multi.**	15
BluWater | D, T | **multi.**	16
NEW Bottle Rocket | D, T | **Wallingford**	-
Buffalo Deli | D, T | **Belltown**	23
Burrito Loco | T | **Crown Hill**	22
☑ Cafe Besalu | T | **Ballard**	27
Cafe Flora | T | **Madison Pk**	22
Cafe Veloce | D, T | **Kirkland**	21
Catfish Corner | T | **Capitol Hill**	21

SPECIAL FEATURE

Chaco Canyon | T | **Univ Dist**	—
Chanterelle | T | **Edmonds**	19
Chinoise | D, T | **multi.**	19
☑ Chiso | T | **Fremont**	26
Christina's | T | **Eastsound**	26
CJ's Eatery | T | **Belltown**	21
Copacabana Cafe | T | **Pike Pl Mkt**	20
Crumpet Shop | T | **Pike Pl Mkt**	24
☑ Dahlia Lounge | T | **Downtown**	25
Desert Fire | T | **Redmond**	16
Diggity Dog's | T | **Wallingford**	19
NEW Dish D'Lish | T | **Ballard**	18
Dixie's BBQ | T | **Bellevue**	22
Eats Mkt. Café | T | **W Seattle**	20
El Camino | T | **Fremont**	21
Elliott Bay Brewery | T | **W Seattle**	20
El Puerco Lloron | T | **Pike Pl Mkt**	21
Essential Baking | T | **multi.**	23
Ezell's | T | **multi.**	24
FareStart/2100 | T | **S Seattle**	—
☑ Flying Fish | T | **Belltown**	25
Four Seas | D, T | **Intl Dist**	17
From Russia/Love | T | **Bellevue**	—
Frontier Room | T | **Belltown**	19
Fuji Sushi | T | **Intl Dist**	25
Galanga Thai | D, T | **Tacoma**	24
Galerias | T | **Capitol Hill**	22
Gelatiamo | D, T | **Downtown**	24
Geraldine's | T | **Columbia City**	20
Gilbert's Main St. Bagel | T | **Bellevue**	22
Goldbergs' Deli | T | **Bellevue**	17
Gordito's Mex. | T | **Greenwood**	22
Green Leaf | T | **Intl Dist**	25
☑ Harvest Vine | T | **Madison Vly**	26
NEW Hills' Food/Wine | T | **Shoreline**	23
Ho Ho Seafood | T | **Intl Dist**	21
Honey Bear | T | **Lake Forest Pk**	21
Honey Court | T | **Intl Dist**	23
Hunan Garden | T | **Bellevue**	18
Il Fornaio | T | **Downtown**	20
NEW Inchin's Bamboo | T | **Redmond**	—
☑ Indochine Asian | T | **Tacoma**	23
Ivar Acres of Clams | T | **Seattle Waterfront**	20
Ivar Mukilteo | T | **Mukilteo**	21
Ivar Salmon Hse. | T | **Lake Union**	19
Jack's Fish Spot | T | **Pike Pl Mkt**	20
Jade Garden | T | **Intl Dist**	23
☑ JaK's Grill | T | **multi.**	26
Jones BBQ | T | **multi.**	22
Judy Fu's | D, T | **Maple Leaf**	19
Kabob House | T | **Greenwood**	23
Kaosamai | D | **Fremont**	—
Karam's Lebanese | T | **Capitol Hill**	19
Kasbah | T | **Ballard**	—
Kauai Family Rest. | T | **Georgetown**	21
Kau Kau BBQ | T | **Intl Dist**	24
Kells Irish | T | **Pike Pl Mkt**	17
Kikuya | T | **Redmond**	22
Kimchi Bistro | T | **Capitol Hill**	—
Kingfish | T | **Capitol Hill**	23
☑ Kisaku Sushi | T | **Green Lk**	27
Krittika Noodles | T | **Green Lk**	22
Kusina Filipina | T | **Beacon Hill**	—
☑ La Carta/Oaxaca | T | **Ballard**	26
La Casa/Mojito | T | **Lake City**	21
La Vita É Bella | T | **Belltown**	22
Lee's | T | **W Seattle**	23
Le Fournil | T | **Eastlake**	21
Le Panier | T | **Pike Pl Mkt**	23
Louie's Cuisine | T | **Ballard**	15
Louisa's Cafe | T | **Eastlake**	21
Luigi's Pizza | T | **Magnolia**	16
Luisa's Mex. | T | **Greenwood**	16
Machiavelli | T | **Capitol Hill**	21
Macrina | T | **multi.**	25
NEW Made/Kitchen | T | **Intl Dist**	21
Mae Phim Thai | T | **Downtown**	21
Malay Satay Hut | D, T | **multi.**	24
Malena's Taco | T | **multi.**	20

Mama's Mexican | D, T | **Belltown** — 17

Matts' Rotisserie | T | **Redmond** — 20

Mayuri | T | **Bellevue** — 25

Medit. Kitchen | D, T | **Bellevue** — 22

Mike's Noodle Hse. | D, T | **Intl Dist** — 25

Mioposto | T | **Mt. Baker** — -

Moghul Palace | T | **Bellevue** — 22

☑ Monsoon | T | **Capitol Hill** — 27

Musashi's | T | **Wallingford** — 21

Neville's/British | T | **Redmond** — 20

☑ Nishino | T | **Madison Pk** — 27

Noah's Bagels | D, T | **Queen Anne** — 17

Noble Court | T | **Bellevue** — 21

Noodle Ranch | T | **Belltown** — 17

Noosh Café | D, T | **Queen Anne** — -

Northlake Tav. | T | **Univ Dist** — 21

NEW O'Asian | D, T | **Downtown** — 20

☑ Oceanaire | T | **Downtown** — 23

Olives Cafe | T | **Edmonds** — 23

Olympia Pizza | D, T | **multi.** — 18

Ooba's Mex. Grill | D, T | **multi.** — 24

Other Coast Cafe | D, T | **multi.** — 25

Outback Steak | D | **Lake Union** — 15

Pabla Indian | T | **Downtown** — 20

Pagliacci Pizza | D, T | **multi.** — 22

☑ Palace Kitchen | T | **Downtown** — 24

Palomino | D, T | **Downtown** — 21

Pan-Africa Cafe | T | **Pike Pl Mkt** — 21

☑ Paseo | T | **Fremont** — 27

Pecos Pit BBQ | T | **SODO** — 25

Pegasus Pizza | T | **W Seattle** — 20

Phila. Fevre | T | **Madison Vly** — 23

Piecora's Pizza | D, T | **Capitol Hill** — 21

Pig Iron Bar-B-Q | T | **S Seattle** — 22

NEW Poco Wine | T | **Capitol Hill** — -

Pomegranate Bistro | T | **Redmond** — 25

NEW Porcella | T | **Bellevue** — 24

preet's | T | **Redmond** — 25

Racha Noodles | D, T | **multi.** — 21

R&L Good BBQ | T | **Capitol Hill** — 21

Red Fin | T | **Downtown** — 23

☑ Rest. Zoë | T | **Belltown** — 27

Rhodie's Smokin' | T | **Seattle Ctr** — -

Rist. Paradiso | D, T | **Kirkland** — 22

Romio's Pizza/Pasta | D | **multi.** — 16

Rose's Bakery | T | **Eastsound** — -

Saigon Bistro | T | **Intl Dist** — 23

NEW Saint-Germain | T | **Madison Vly** — 21

Saito's Japanese | T | **Belltown** — 26

Santorini Greek | T | **Kirkland** — 23

NEW Serious Pie | T | **Downtown** — 25

Shallots | D, T | **Belltown** — 22

Shamiana | D, T | **Kirkland** — 23

Shanghai Gdn. | T | **multi.** — 22

Shultzy's | T | **Univ Dist** — 20

611 Supreme | T | **Capitol Hill** — 23

Smarty Pants | T | **Georgetown** — -

Sostanza | T | **Madison Pk** — 22

NEW Spitfire | T | **Belltown** — 19

Stellar Pizza | T | **Georgetown** — 21

Streamliner | D, T | **Bainbridge Is** — 16

Sunfish | T | **W Seattle** — 21

☑ Szechuan Chef | T | **Bellevue** — 27

Szmania's | T | **Magnolia** — 23

Tai Tung | T | **Intl Dist** — 20

Takis Mad Greek | T | **Ballard** — 18

NEW TASTE | T | **Downtown** — 19

Taste of India | T | **Univ Dist** — 22

Taxi Dogs | T | **Pike Pl Mkt** — 15

Texas Smokehse. | T | **Woodinville** — 20

Thai on Mercer | T | **Mercer Is** — 18

Thai Siam | T | **Ballard** — 23

Thai Tom | T | **Univ Dist** — 26

Thanh Vi | T | **Univ Dist** — 24

13 Coins | T | **multi.** — 18

3 Pigs BBQ | D, T | **Bellevue** — 21

Tokyo Garden | T | **Univ Dist** — -

Top Gun Seafood | T | **Bellevue** — 21

Turkish Delight | T | **Pike Pl Mkt**	21
Tutta Bella | T | **multi.**	23
Uptown China | D, T | **Queen Anne**	18
Veg. Bistro | T | **Intl Dist**	–
NEW Volunteer Pk. Café | T | **Capitol Hill**	26
World Class Chili | T | **Pike Pl Mkt**	24
Zaina Food | T | **Pioneer Sq**	22
Zao Noodle Bar | D, T | **Univ Vill**	16
Zeeks Pizza | D, T | **multi.**	18

DESSERT

Alki Bakery | **multi.**	21
B&O Espresso | **Capitol Hill**	20
Belle Epicurean | **Downtown**	26
☑ Belle Pastry | **Bellevue**	27
☑ Cafe Besalu | **Ballard**	27
Café Septieme | **Capitol Hill**	16
☑ Cheesecake Factory | **multi.**	17
☑ Dahlia Lounge | **Downtown**	25
Dilettante Chocolates | **Capitol Hill**	23
Earth & Ocean | **Downtown**	22
☑ Etta's Seafood | **Pike Pl Mkt**	24
Gelatiamo | **Downtown**	24
Kingfish | **Capitol Hill**	23
Macrina | **multi.**	25
Queen Mary Tea | **Ravenna**	19
Uptown Espresso | **multi.**	19

DINING ALONE

(Other than hotels and places with counter service)

☑ Armandino's Salumi | **Pioneer Sq**	28
Baguette Box | **Fremont**	23
Bakeman's | **Downtown**	22
Blue C Sushi | **Fremont**	15
☑ Brooklyn Sea/Steak | **Downtown**	23
☑ Cafe Campagne | **Pike Pl Mkt**	25
Cafe Flora | **Madison Pk**	22
Café Septieme | **Capitol Hill**	16
Coastal Kitchen | **Capitol Hill**	20
Crave | **Capitol Hill**	20

☑ Elliott's Oyster | **Seattle Waterfront**	23
☑ Etta's Seafood | **Pike Pl Mkt**	24
5 Spot | **Queen Anne**	20
14 Carrot Cafe | **Eastlake**	18
Gilbert's Main St. Bagel | **Bellevue**	22
Greenlake B&G | **Green Lk**	16
☑ Harvest Vine | **Madison Vly**	26
Hattie's Hat | **Ballard**	16
Il Fornaio | **Downtown**	20
☑ Le Pichet | **Pike Pl Mkt**	24
Macrina | **multi.**	25
Mae's | **Phinney Ridge**	18
Malay Satay Hut | **multi.**	24
Marco's Supperclub | **Belltown**	21
Matt's/Mkt. | **Pike Pl Mkt**	–
Mona's Bistro | **Green Lk**	23
Noodle Ranch | **Belltown**	17
☑ Palace Kitchen | **Downtown**	24
Persimmon | **Fremont**	22
Saito's Japanese | **Belltown**	26
St. Clouds | **Madrona**	21
Thaiku | **Ballard**	21
22 Doors | **Capitol Hill**	19
Two Bells B&G | **Belltown**	19
☑ Volterra | **Ballard**	25

DRAMATIC INTERIORS

Andaluca | **Downtown**	24
Assaggio | **Downtown**	23
Bambuza | **Downtown**	19
Barking Frog | **Woodinville**	24
Brouwer's | **Fremont**	20
NEW Café Presse | **Capitol Hill**	–
☑ Canlis | **Lake Union**	27
Capitol Club | **Capitol Hill**	19
☑ Cascadia | **Belltown**	25
☑ Dahlia Lounge | **Downtown**	25
☑ Georgian | **Downtown**	26
☑ Herbfarm, The | **Woodinville**	29
icon Grill | **Downtown**	20
☑ Lola | **Downtown**	24
Luau Polynesian | **Green Lk**	15
Maximilien | **Pike Pl Mkt**	21

🅩 Oceanaire | **Downtown** — 23

🅩 Palisade | **Magnolia** — 23

Pink Door | **Pike Pl Mkt** — 22

NEW Qube | **Downtown** — 22

🅩 6·7 | **Seattle Waterfront** — 24

Trader Vic's | **Bellevue** — 16

🅩 Union | **Downtown** — 26

🅩 Waterfront Seafood | **Seattle Waterfront** — 24

NEW Yama/Galleria | **Bellevue** — 23

ENTERTAINMENT

(Call for days and times of performances)

Asteroid | jazz | **Fremont** — 25

Brad's Swingside | varies | **Fremont** — 24

Buenos Aires Grill | tango | **Downtown** — 23

Café Septieme | jazz | **Capitol Hill** — 16

Calabria | piano | **Kirkland** — 17

Capitol Club | DJs | **Capitol Hill** — 19

Caspian Grill | belly dancing | **Univ Dist** — –

Costas Opa | belly dancing | **Fremont** — 19

Crocodile Cafe | rock | **Belltown** — 14

🅩 Daniel's Broiler | piano | **multi.** — 25

Dulces Latin | piano | **Madrona** — 21

Earth & Ocean | DJ | **Downtown** — 22

🅩 El Gaucho | piano | **multi.** — 25

🅩 Georgian | jazz | **Downtown** — 26

Grazie | jazz | **Bothell** — 20

Hunt Club | piano | **First Hill** — 22

Ibiza | flamenco/samba | **Pioneer Sq** — 19

🅩 Il Terrazzo | guitar | **Pioneer Sq** — 27

🅩 Indochine Asian | DJ | **Tacoma** — 23

Jalisco Mex. | karaoke | **Queen Anne** — 17

Julia's | varies | **multi.** — 16

Kabul Afghan | sitar | **Wallingford** — 25

Kasbah | belly dancing | **Ballard** — –

Kells Irish | Irish folk | **Pike Pl Mkt** — 17

La Casa/Mojito | varies | **Lake City** — 21

La Fontana Siciliana | piano | **Belltown** — 24

La Vita É Bella | accordion | **Belltown** — 22

🅩 Le Pichet | varies | **Pike Pl Mkt** — 24

Mama's Mexican | mariachi band | **Belltown** — 17

Mamma Melina | opera/piano | **Univ Dist** — 21

Maple Leaf Grill | varies | **Maple Leaf** — 18

Marrakesh | belly dancing | **Belltown** — 21

Matt's/Mkt. | jazz | **Pike Pl Mkt** — –

May | DJ/jazz | **Wallingford** — 20

Mayuri | guitar/jazz | **Bellevue** — 25

Mixtura | varies | **Kirkland** — 24

Mona's Bistro | DJ/jazz | **Green Lk** — 23

New Orl. Creole | blues/jazz | **Pioneer Sq** — 14

NEW O'Asian | jazz | **Downtown** — 20

NEW O/8 | varies | **Bellevue** — 21

'Ohana | DJ/island | **Belltown** — 21

Osteria La Spiga | jazz | **Capitol Hill** — 24

Paragon | varies | **Queen Anne** — 19

Pink Door | varies | **Pike Pl Mkt** — 22

Pontevecchio | opera | **Fremont** — 23

Pyramid Ale | blues | **Pioneer Sq** — 16

Racha Noodles | karaoke | **Seattle Ctr** — 21

Serafina | jazz/Latin | **Eastlake** — 24

🅩 6·7 | band/DJ | **Seattle Waterfront** — 24

St. Clouds | blues/jazz/Latin | **Madrona** — 21

Stumbling Goat | guitar | **Greenwood** — 24

Tacos Guaymas | mariachi band | **Green Lk** — 20

Takis Mad Greek | belly dancing | **Ballard** — 18

Tempero/Brasil | Brazilian | **Univ Dist** 24

Toi | DJs | **Downtown** -

Tutta Bella | jazz | **Columbia City** 23

Wasabi Bistro | jazz/Latin | **Belltown** 22

🗹 Waterfront Seafood | piano | **Seattle Waterfront** 24

NEW Wilde Rover | bands/trivia | **Kirkland** -

Yanni's | belly dancing | **Phinney Ridge** 22

FIREPLACES

Alki Homestead | **W Seattle** 20

🗹 Anthony's HomePort | **multi.** 20

BluWater | **multi.** 16

Cactus | **W Seattle** 22

Cafe Veloce | **Kirkland** 21

🗹 Canlis | **Lake Union** 27

🗹 Cascadia | **Belltown** 25

Chandler's Crab | **Lake Union** 22

Christina's | **Eastsound** 26

Cutters Bayhse. | **Pike Pl Mkt** 19

🗹 Daniel's Broiler | **Lake Union** 25

Deluxe B&G | **Capitol Hill** 16

Desert Fire | **Redmond** 16

Duke's Chowder | **multi.** 18

El Chupacabra | **Greenwood** 14

Elliott Bay Brewery | **W Seattle** 20

Friday Harbor Hse. | **Friday Harbor** -

Gordito's Mex. | **Greenwood** 22

Hilltop Ale Hse. | **Queen Anne** 22

Hunt Club | **First Hill** 22

Il Fornaio | **Downtown** 20

🗹 Inn at Langley | **Langley** 27

Ivar Mukilteo | **Mukilteo** 21

Jones BBQ | **Columbia City** 22

Julia's | **Queen Anne** 16

NEW Local Vine | **Belltown** -

Louie's Cuisine | **Ballard** 15

Madison Pk. Cafe | **Madison Pk** 22

Maple Leaf Grill | **Maple Leaf** 18

Mexico Cantina | **Downtown** 20

Mixtura | **Kirkland** 24

Oyster Bar/Chuckanut | **Bow** 24

Paddy Coynes | **Downtown** 18

Paragon | **Queen Anne** 19

Pasta Bella | **Queen Anne** 19

P.F. Chang's | **Bellevue** 19

Pig Iron Bar-B-Q | **S Seattle** 22

Pogacha | **multi.** 18

Ponti Seafood | **Fremont** 22

Ray's Cafe | **Shilshole** 22

Rist. Italianissimo | **Woodinville** 25

Russell's | **Bothell** -

🗹 Salish Lodge | **Snoqualmie** 24

Saltoro | **N Seattle** 22

🗹 Salty's | **W Seattle** 20

Salute/Bellevue | **Bellevue** 19

Sazerac | **Downtown** 20

Shultzy's | **Univ Dist** 20

🗹 6 · 7 | **Seattle Waterfront** 24

Sostanza | **Madison Pk** 22

NEW Spazzo | **Redmond** 20

Szmania's | **Magnolia** 23

NEW Wilde Rover | **Kirkland** -

Yarrow Bay Grill | **Kirkland** 24

GAME IN SEASON

NEW Beàto | **W Seattle** 23

Bis on Main | **Bellevue** 24

NEW Boka Kitchen | **Downtown** 22

Brad's Swingside | **Fremont** 24

🗹 Brasa | **Belltown** 25

🗹 Cafe Campagne | **Pike Pl Mkt** 25

🗹 Cafe Juanita | **Kirkland** 28

🗹 Canlis | **Lake Union** 27

Carnegie's | **Ballard** 21

🗹 Cascadia | **Belltown** 25

Crémant | **Madrona** 24

🗹 Crush | **Madison Vly** 26

🗹 Dahlia Lounge | **Downtown** 25

NEW DiVino | **Ballard** 22

🗹 Elemental | **Lake Union** 26

🗹 El Gaucho | **multi.** 25

NEW Entre Nous | **Downtown** -

🗹 Eva | **Green Lk** 26

Four Swallows | **Bainbridge Is** 25

Geneva | **First Hill**	25
Hunt Club | **First Hill**	22
Il Bistro | **Pike Pl Mkt**	23
☑ Il Terrazzo | **Pioneer Sq**	27
☑ Lark | **Capitol Hill**	27
☑ Le Gourmand | **Ballard**	27
☑ Lola | **Downtown**	24
Market St. Grill | **Ballard**	25
Matt's/Mkt. | **Pike Pl Mkt**	-
☑ Mistral | **Belltown**	28
☑ Monsoon | **Capitol Hill**	27
Moxie | **Queen Anne**	21
Nell's | **Green Lk**	25
NEW O/8 | **Bellevue**	21
Osteria La Spiga | **Capitol Hill**	24
☑ Palace Kitchen | **Downtown**	24
Place Pigalle | **Pike Pl Mkt**	23
NEW Portage | **Queen Anne**	26
☑ Rest. Zoë | **Belltown**	27
Rist. Italianissimo | **Woodinville**	25
Rose's Bakery | **Eastsound**	-
☑ Rover's | **Madison Vly**	28
☑ Salish Lodge | **Snoqualmie**	24
Salvatore | **Ravenna**	23
Serafina | **Eastlake**	24
Shea's Lounge | **Pike Pl Mkt**	24
☑ Sitka & Spruce | **Eastlake**	28
Stumbling Goat | **Greenwood**	24
Szmania's | **Magnolia**	23
Tosoni's | **Bellevue**	26
☑ Union | **Downtown**	26
Veil | **Queen Anne**	23
Voilà! Bistrot | **Madison Vly**	22
☑ Volterra | **Ballard**	25

HISTORIC PLACES

(Year opened; * building)

1800 | Madame K's Pizza* | **Ballard**	21
1889 | Cascadia* | **Belltown**	25
1890 | Brooklyn Sea/Steak* | **Downtown**	23
1890 | Essential Baking* | **Wallingford**	23
1896 | Shoalwater* | **Seaview**	-
1900 | Armandino's Salumi* | **Pioneer Sq**	28
1900 | Metro. Grill* | **Downtown**	26
1900 | Wild Ginger* | **Downtown**	25
1902 | Alki Homestead* | **W Seattle**	20
1902 | That's Amore* | **Mt. Baker**	-
1903 | Crush* | **Madison Vly**	26
1905 | Volunteer Pk. Café* | **Capitol Hill**	26
1907 | Carnegie's* | **Ballard**	21
1907 | Dash Point Lobster* | **Tacoma**	21
1908 | Tutta Bella* | **Columbia City**	23
1909 | Athenian Inn | **Pike Pl Mkt**	16
1909 | Hunt Club* | **First Hill**	22
1910 | China Gate* | **Intl Dist**	20
1910 | Julia's* | **Queen Anne**	16
1910 | Tai Tung* | **Intl Dist**	20
1912 | Three Girls Bakery | **Pike Pl Mkt**	24
1916 | Salish Lodge* | **Snoqualmie**	24
1917 | Matt's/Mkt.* | **Pike Pl Mkt**	-
1917 | Shea's Lounge* | **Pike Pl Mkt**	24
1920 | Cyclops* | **Belltown**	17
1920 | Lockspot Cafe | **Ballard**	18
1920 | Salty's* | **W Seattle**	20
1920 | Serafina* | **Eastlake**	24
1920 | Shuckers* | **Downtown**	25
1920 | Sostanza* | **Madison Pk**	22
1923 | La Carta/Oaxaca | **Ballard**	26
1924 | Georgian | **Downtown**	26
1926 | Madison Pk. Cafe* | **Madison Pk**	22
1926 | Shultzy's* | **Univ Dist**	20
1927 | Oyster Bar/Chuckanut | **Bow**	24
1929 | 5 Point Café | **Belltown**	19
1929 | Queen City Grill* | **Belltown**	22
1930 | Blue Onion* | **Univ Dist**	17

SPECIAL FEATURES

1930 | Union* | **Downtown** 26

1937 | Maltby Cafe* | **Maltby** 26

1938 | Ivar Acres of Clams | 20
Seattle Waterfront

1939 | Marjorie* | **Belltown** 22

1940 | Szmania's* | **Magnolia** 23

1950 | Canlis | **Lake Union** 27

1952 | R&L Good BBQ | 21
Capitol Hill

1953 | Bush Garden | **Intl Dist** 19

1954 | Dick's Drive-In | 19
Wallingford

1954 | Hattie's Hat | **Ballard** 16

1954 | Northlake Tav. | 21
Univ Dist

1957 | Lowell's | **Pike Pl Mkt** 17

HOTEL DINING

Andra, Hotel

☑ Lola | **Downtown** 24

Edgewater Hotel, Pier 67

☑ 6·7 | **Seattle Waterfront** 24

Fairmont Olympic Hotel

Belle Epicurean | **Downtown** 26

☑ Georgian | **Downtown** 26

Shuckers | **Downtown** 25

Friday Harbor House Inn

Friday Harbor Hse. | –
Friday Harbor

Grand Hyatt

Ruth's Chris | **Downtown** 23

Hilton

Spencer's Steaks | **SeaTac** –

Hyatt Regency

NEW O/8 | **Bellevue** 21

Inn at Langley

☑ Inn at Langley | **Langley** 27

Max, Hotel

Red Fin | **Downtown** 23

Mayflower Park Hotel

Andaluca | **Downtown** 24

Monaco, Hotel

Sazerac | **Downtown** 20

Paramount Hotel

Dragonfish | **Downtown** 20

Salish Lodge & Spa

☑ Salish Lodge | **Snoqualmie** 24

Seattle Marriott Waterfront

Fish Club | 22
Seattle Waterfront

Shelburne Inn

Shoalwater | **Seaview** –

Sorrento Hotel

Hunt Club | **First Hill** 22

Vintage Park, Hotel

Tulio | **Downtown** 24

Warwick Seattle Hotel

Brass. Margaux | **Downtown** 19

Westin Hotel

Coldwater | **Downtown** 20

W Hotel

Earth & Ocean | **Downtown** 22

Willows Lodge

Barking Frog | **Woodinville** 24

Woodmark Hotel

Waters Lakeside | **Kirkland** 22

LATE DINING

(Weekday closing hour)

Azul | 12 AM | **Mill Creek** 23

B&O Espresso | 12 AM | 20
Capitol Hill

Belltown Bistro | 1 AM | **Belltown** 18

Black Bottle | 1:30 AM | **Belltown** 22

BluWater | 1 AM | **multi.** 16

Bricco/Regina | 1 AM | 22
Queen Anne

Broadway Grill | 3 AM | 16
Capitol Hill

Buckley's | 1 AM | **Seattle Ctr** 19

NEW Café Presse | 2 AM | –
Capitol Hill

Caffé Minnie's | 24 hrs. | 12
Queen Anne

China Gate | 1:30 AM | **Intl Dist** 20

Deluxe B&G | 12 AM | 16
Capitol Hill

Dick's Drive-In | 2 AM | **multi.** 19

Dilettante Chocolates | 12 AM | 23
Capitol Hill

Dragonfish | 1 AM | **Downtown** 20

Duke's Chowder | 12 AM | multi. 18

☑ Elemental | 12 AM | Lake Union 26

☑ El Gaucho | 1 AM | multi. 25

5 Point Café | 24 hrs. | Belltown 19

5 Spot | 12 AM | Queen Anne 20

☑ Flying Fish | 1 AM | Belltown 25

Frontier Room | 12 AM | Belltown 19

Garage | 12 AM | Capitol Hill 13

Ho Ho Seafood | 1 AM | Intl Dist 21

Honey Court | 2 AM | Intl Dist 23

Ibiza | varies | Pioneer Sq 19

Il Bistro | 1 AM | Pike Pl Mkt 23

Jade Garden | 2:30 AM | Intl Dist 23

Jalisco Mex. | 12 AM | Queen Anne 17

Joeys | 2 AM | multi. 19

La Isla | 12 AM | Ballard 25

NEW Local Vine | 2 AM | Belltown –

☑ Lola | 12 AM | Downtown 24

Louie's Cuisine | 12 AM | Ballard 15

May | 1 AM | Wallingford 20

Paddy Coynes | 12 AM | Downtown 18

☑ Palace Kitchen | 1 AM | Downtown 24

NEW Perché/Pasta | 12 AM | Green Lk 22

Peso's Kitchen | 1 AM | Queen Anne 23

NEW Poco Wine | 12 AM | Capitol Hill –

Purple Dot Café | varies | Intl Dist 18

Sea Garden | 2 AM | Intl Dist 20

Smarty Pants | 12 AM | Georgetown –

NEW Spitfire | 12 AM | Belltown 19

St. Clouds | 12 AM | Madrona 21

Stellar Pizza | 12 AM | Georgetown 21

NEW Tavolàta | 1 AM | Belltown 24

Ten Mercer | 12 AM | Queen Anne 22

13 Coins | 24 hrs. | multi. 18

Top Gun Seafood | 12 AM | Bellevue 21

NEW Umi Sake Hse. | 1 AM | Belltown 22

Via Tribunali | 12 AM | Capitol Hill 23

☑ Volterra | 1 AM | Ballard 25

Wasabi Bistro | 1 AM | Belltown 22

☑ Waterfront Seafood | 12 AM | Seattle Waterfront 24

NEW Wilde Rover | 12 AM | Kirkland –

Zaina Food | 12 AM | Pioneer Sq 22

MEET FOR A DRINK

Alibi Room | Pike Pl Mkt 19

☑ Anthony's HomePort | multi. 20

Azul | Mill Creek 23

Beach Cafe/Point | Kirkland 18

BluWater | multi. 16

☑ Brasa | Belltown 25

☑ Brooklyn Sea/Steak | Downtown 23

Cactus | multi. 22

☑ Campagne | Pike Pl Mkt 26

Capitol Club | Capitol Hill 19

Chandler's Crab | Lake Union 22

Columbia City Ale | Columbia City 18

Crow | Queen Anne 23

Cutters Bayhse. | Pike Pl Mkt 19

☑ Daniel's Broiler | multi. 25

Dragonfish | Downtown 20

El Camino | Fremont 21

☑ El Gaucho | Belltown 25

Elliott Bay Brewery | W Seattle 20

☑ Elliott's Oyster | Seattle Waterfront 23

Four Swallows | Bainbridge Is 25

Fox Sports Grill | Downtown 12

Frontier Room | Belltown 19

F.X. McRory's | Pioneer Sq 17

Garage | **Capitol Hill**	13
Gordon Biersch | **Downtown**	14
Greenlake B&G | **Green Lk**	16
Hale's Ales | **Fremont**	17
Hilltop Ale Hse. | **Queen Anne**	22
Il Bistro | **Pike Pl Mkt**	23
Kells Irish | **Pike Pl Mkt**	17
NEW Local Vine | **Belltown**	-
☑ Lola | **Downtown**	24
Luau Polynesian | **Green Lk**	15
NEW Made/Kitchen | **Intl Dist**	21
Mama's Mexican | **Belltown**	17
☑ Metro. Grill | **Downtown**	26
New Orl. Creole | **Pioneer Sq**	14
'Ohana | **Belltown**	21
Pacific Grill | **Tacoma**	-
☑ Palace Kitchen | **Downtown**	24
Peso's Kitchen | **Queen Anne**	23
Pink Door | **Pike Pl Mkt**	22
NEW Qube | **Downtown**	22
Ray's Cafe | **Shilshole**	22
Ruth's Chris | **multi.**	23
Sazerac | **Downtown**	20
NEW Serious Pie | **Downtown**	25
74th St. Ale Hse. | **Phinney Ridge**	19
☑ 6·7 | **Seattle Waterfront**	24
Tango | **Capitol Hill**	23
NEW Tavolàta | **Belltown**	24
Toi | **Downtown**	-
Troiani | **Downtown**	22
22 Doors | **Capitol Hill**	19
Typhoon! | **multi.**	22
Union Sq. Grill | **Downtown**	22
☑ Volterra | **Ballard**	25
☑ Waterfront Seafood | **Seattle Waterfront**	24

NATURAL/ORGANIC

(These restaurants often or always use organic, local ingredients)

NEW Bennett's Pure Food | **Mercer Is**	22
Blackbird Bistro | **W Seattle**	19
Boat St. Cafe | **Queen Anne**	25
Brad's Swingside | **Fremont**	24
Cafe Flora | **Madison Pk**	22

☑ Cafe Juanita | **Kirkland**	28
Capitol Club | **Capitol Hill**	19
☑ Carmelita | **Greenwood**	26
☑ Cascadia | **Belltown**	25
Chaco Canyon | **Univ Dist**	-
Crave | **Capitol Hill**	20
☑ Crush | **Madison Vly**	26
Cyclops | **Belltown**	17
Desert Fire | **Redmond**	16
Dish, The | **Fremont**	23
NEW Dish D'Lish | **Ballard**	18
NEW Divine | **Maple Leaf**	-
NEW DiVino | **Ballard**	22
El Camino | **Fremont**	21
Elliott Bay Brewery | **W Seattle**	20
Essential Baking | **multi.**	23
☑ Flying Fish | **Belltown**	25
Gordito's Mex. | **Greenwood**	22
☑ Harvest Vine | **Madison Vly**	26
☑ Herbfarm, The | **Woodinville**	29
Hunt Club | **First Hill**	22
Ibiza | **Pioneer Sq**	19
I Love Sushi | **multi.**	23
Jones, The | **Maple Leaf**	20
Julia's | **multi.**	16
La Medusa | **Columbia City**	25
Lampreia | **Belltown**	25
☑ Lark | **Capitol Hill**	27
☑ Le Gourmand | **Ballard**	27
☑ Lola | **Downtown**	24
Macrina | **multi.**	25
Madoka | **Bainbridge Is**	20
☑ Mistral | **Belltown**	28
Moxie | **Queen Anne**	21
94 Stewart | **Pike Pl Mkt**	21
NEW Perché/Pasta | **Green Lk**	22
Persimmon | **Fremont**	22
Pike Pub | **Pike Pl Mkt**	16
NEW Portage | **Queen Anne**	26
☑ Ray's Boathse. | **Shilshole**	24
NEW Remedy Teas | **Capitol Hill**	23
Rose's Bakery | **Eastsound**	-
NEW Serious Pie | **Downtown**	25
Shea's Lounge | **Pike Pl Mkt**	24

☑ Sitka & Spruce | **Eastlake**	28
Stumbling Goat | **Greenwood**	24
Sunlight Cafe | **Roosevelt**	16
NEW TASTE | **Downtown**	19
Thai Siam | **Ballard**	23
Third Floor Fish | **Kirkland**	24
NEW Tilth | **Wallingford**	25
☑ Union | **Downtown**	26
Veil | **Queen Anne**	23
☑ Volterra | **Ballard**	25

NOTEWORTHY NEWCOMERS

Austin | **Ballard**	-
☑ Bakery Nouveau | **W Seattle**	28
Bambino's Pizzeria | **Belltown**	19
Barolo | **Downtown**	22
Beàto | **W Seattle**	23
Bennett's Pure Food | **Mercer Is**	22
Betty | **Queen Anne**	22
Boka Kitchen | **Downtown**	22
Bottle Rocket | **Wallingford**	-
Café Presse | **Capitol Hill**	-
Coupage | **Madrona**	23
Dish D'Lish | **Ballard**	18
Divine | **Maple Leaf**	-
DiVino | **Ballard**	22
Entre Nous | **Downtown**	-
Facing East | **Bellevue**	-
Gaudi | **Ravenna**	-
Hills' Food/Wine | **Shoreline**	23
Hot Dish | **Ravenna**	-
Inchin's Bamboo | **Redmond**	-
Local Vine | **Belltown**	-
Made/Kitchen | **Intl Dist**	21
O'Asian | **Downtown**	20
O/8 | **Bellevue**	21
Oliver's Twist | **Phinney Ridge**	25
Opal | **Queen Anne**	25
Perché/Pasta | **Green Lk**	22
Poco Wine | **Capitol Hill**	-
Porcella | **Bellevue**	24
Portage | **Queen Anne**	26
Qube | **Downtown**	22
Remedy Teas | **Capitol Hill**	23

Saint-Germain | **Madison Vly**	21
Serious Pie | **Downtown**	25
Sorrentino | **Queen Anne**	18
Spazzo | **Redmond**	20
Spitfire | **Belltown**	19
Steelhead | **Pike Pl Mkt**	23
TASTE | **Downtown**	19
Tavolàta | **Belltown**	24
Tilth | **Wallingford**	25
Umi Sake Hse. | **Belltown**	22
Vi Bacchus | **Capitol Hill**	-
Volunteer Pk. Café | **Capitol Hill**	26
Wann Izakaya | **Belltown**	19
Wilde Rover | **Kirkland**	-
Yama/Galleria | **Bellevue**	23

OFFBEAT

Agua Verde | **Univ Dist**	22
Benihana | **Downtown**	18
Blue C Sushi | **Fremont**	15
Buca di Beppo | **multi.**	14
Chaco Canyon | **Univ Dist**	-
Crave | **Capitol Hill**	20
Dixie's BBQ | **Bellevue**	22
5 Point Café | **Belltown**	19
5 Spot | **Queen Anne**	20
Luna Park Cafe | **W Seattle**	15
Madame K's Pizza | **Ballard**	21
Mae's | **Phinney Ridge**	18
Mama's Mexican | **Belltown**	17
Mashiko | **W Seattle**	25
New Orl. Creole | **Pioneer Sq**	14
'Ohana | **Belltown**	21
Pink Door | **Pike Pl Mkt**	22

OUTDOOR DINING

(G=garden; P=patio; S=sidewalk; T=terrace)

Acorn Eatery | T | **Crown Hill**	17
Agua Verde | T | **Univ Dist**	22
Alki Bakery | S | **W Seattle**	21
☑ Anthony's HomePort | P, T | **multi.**	20
Anthony's Pier 66 | T | **Seattle Waterfront**	21
Assaggio | P | **Downtown**	23

SPECIAL FEATURES

B&O Espresso | S | **Capitol Hill** 20

Barking Dog | P | **Ballard** 17

Barking Frog | P | **Woodinville** 24

Beach Cafe/Point | P | **Kirkland** 18

Belltown Bistro | P | **Belltown** 18

Boat St. Cafe | P | **Queen Anne** 25

Brad's Swingside | T | **Fremont** 24

☑ Brooklyn Sea/Steak | P | 23
Downtown

Buffalo Deli | S | **Belltown** 23

Cactus | P | **multi.** 22

☑ Cafe Besalu | S | **Ballard** 27

☑ Cafe Campagne | S | 25
Pike Pl Mkt

☑ Cafe Juanita | G, P | **Kirkland** 28

Cafe Nola | P | **Bainbridge Is** 21

Calabria | P | **Kirkland** 17

☑ Campagne | **Pike Pl Mkt** 26

☑ Carmelita | G | **Greenwood** 26

☑ Cascadia | P | **Belltown** 25

Chandler's Crab | T | **Lake Union** 22

Chinoise | S | **multi.** 19

Chinook's/Salmon Bay | T | 21
Magnolia

Christina's | T | **Eastsound** 26

Coastal Kitchen | P | **Capitol Hill** 20

Copacabana Cafe | T | 20
Pike Pl Mkt

Crave | P | **Capitol Hill** 20

☑ Daniel's Broiler | T | **multi.** 25

Dish, The | P | **Fremont** 23

Dragonfish | P | **Downtown** 20

El Camino | P | **Fremont** 21

El Greco | S | **Capitol Hill** 23

☑ Elliott's Oyster | T | 23
Seattle Waterfront

Emmett Watson's | P | 22
Pike Pl Mkt

Firenze | S | **Bellevue** 22

Fish Club | P | **Seattle Waterfront** 22

☑ Flying Fish | P | **Belltown** 25

Friday Harbor Hse. | P | −
Friday Harbor

Galanga Thai | S | **Tacoma** 24

Gelatiamo | P | **Downtown** 24

Geneva | P | **First Hill** 25

Gordito's Mex. | P | **Greenwood** 22

Hunt Club | S | **First Hill** 22

Il Bistro | T | **Pike Pl Mkt** 23

☑ Il Terrazzo | T | **Pioneer Sq** 27

India Bistro | S | **Ballard** 23

Karam's Lebanese | S | 19
Capitol Hill

La Fontana Siciliana | G | **Belltown** 24

La Rustica | P | **W Seattle** 25

☑ Le Pichet | S | **Pike Pl Mkt** 24

Macrina | S | **multi.** 25

Madison Pk. Cafe | P | 22
Madison Pk

Maggie Bluff's | P | **Magnolia** 18

Marco's Supperclub | P | 21
Belltown

Marina Park Grill | P | **Kirkland** 22

Marjorie | G, P | **Belltown** 22

Matt's Gourmet Dogs | P | 18
Pioneer Sq

Matts' Rotisserie | P | **Redmond** 20

Maximilien | P | **Pike Pl Mkt** 21

McCorm./Schm. Harbor | P | 21
Lake Union

McCormick's Fish | P | 21
Downtown

Nell's | S | **Green Lk** 25

New Orl. Creole | P | **Pioneer Sq** 14

☑ Nishino | T | **Madison Pk** 27

Noodle Ranch | S | **Belltown** 17

Ototo Sushi | P | **Queen Anne** 24

Oyster Bar/Chuckanut | P | **Bow** 24

Pagliacci Pizza | P | **multi.** 22

☑ Palisade | T | **Magnolia** 23

☑ Paseo | S | **Fremont** 27

Pasta & Co. | P, S | **multi.** 22

Pasta Bella | T | **Queen Anne** 19

Pegasus Pizza | P | **W Seattle** 20

Pink Door | T | **Pike Pl Mkt** 22

Place Pigalle | P | **Pike Pl Mkt** 23

Ponti Seafood | P | **Fremont** 22

☑ Purple Cafe | P | **multi.** 22

Ray's Cafe | P | **Shilshole** 22

Red Mill Burgers | P | **multi.** 24

Rist. Italianissimo | P | **Woodinville**	25
Rist. Paradiso | S | **Kirkland**	22
Z Salty's | P, T | **multi.**	20
Santa Fe Cafe | S | **Phinney Ridge**	21
Sazerac | P | **Downtown**	20
Serafina | P, S | **Eastlake**	24
Shallots | P | **Belltown**	22
Shoalwater | T | **Seaview**	-
Shuckers | P | **Downtown**	25
Shultzy's | P | **Univ Dist**	20
Z 6·7 | T | **Seattle Waterfront**	24
Sostanza | P | **Madison Pk**	22
St. Clouds | G, P | **Madrona**	21
Tacos Guaymas | P, S | **multi.**	20
Tap House Grill | P | **Bellevue**	18
Tulio | P | **Downtown**	24
Tutta Bella | S | **multi.**	23
Two Bells B&G | G | **Belltown**	19
Typhoon! | P | **Redmond**	22
Voilà! Bistrot | P | **Madison Vly**	22
Wasabi Bistro | S | **Belltown**	22
Z Waterfront Seafood | P | **Seattle Waterfront**	24
Waters Lakeside | T | **Kirkland**	22
Yarrow Bay Grill | P | **Kirkland**	24
Zeeks Pizza | P | **multi.**	18

PARKING

(V=valet, *=validated)

Andaluca | V | **Downtown**	24
Z Anthony's HomePort | V | **Kirkland**	20
Anthony's Pier 66 | V* | **Seattle Waterfront**	21
Assaggio | V | **Downtown**	23
Asteroid* | **Fremont**	25
NEW Barolo | V | **Downtown**	22
Beach Cafe/Point | V* | **Kirkland**	18
Bell St. Diner | V | **Seattle Waterfront**	18
Benihana* | **Downtown**	18
BluWater | V* | **multi.**	16
NEW Boka Kitchen | V | **Downtown**	22
Z Brasa | V | **Belltown**	25

Brass. Margaux | V | **Downtown**	19
Z Brooklyn Sea/Steak | V | **Downtown**	23
Z Canlis | V | **Lake Union**	27
Chandler's Crab | V* | **Lake Union**	22
Chez Shea* | **Pike Pl Mkt**	26
China Gate | V | **Intl Dist**	20
Costas Opa* | **Fremont**	19
Z Daniel's Broiler | V* | **multi.**	25
Duke's Chowder | V* | **Lake Union**	18
Earth & Ocean | V | **Downtown**	22
Z El Gaucho | V | **multi.**	25
Z Elliott's Oyster | V* | **Seattle Waterfront**	23
Fish Club | V | **Seattle Waterfront**	22
Z Georgian | V* | **Downtown**	26
House of Hong* | **Intl Dist**	21
Hunt Club | V | **First Hill**	22
Z Il Terrazzo | V* | **Pioneer Sq**	27
Z Lola | V | **Downtown**	24
Matt's/Mkt.* | **Pike Pl Mkt**	-
Maximilien* | **Pike Pl Mkt**	21
Z McCormick & Schmick's | V* | **Downtown**	21
McCorm./Schm. Harbor* | **Lake Union**	21
Melting Pot | V | **multi.**	19
Z Metro. Grill | V* | **Downtown**	26
Mission* | **W Seattle**	20
Morton's | V | **Downtown**	24
94 Stewart | V | **Pike Pl Mkt**	21
Z Oceanaire | V | **Downtown**	23
NEW O/8 | V* | **Bellevue**	21
Ooba's Mex. Grill* | **Bellevue**	24
Outback Steak | V | **Lake Union**	15
Z Palisade | V | **Magnolia**	23
Palomino* | **Downtown**	21
P.F. Chang's | V | **Bellevue**	19
Pike Pub* | **Pike Pl Mkt**	16
Pink Door* | **Pike Pl Mkt**	22
Place Pigalle* | **Pike Pl Mkt**	23
Ponti Seafood | V | **Fremont**	22
Z Purple Cafe* | **Downtown**	22

Pyramid Ale* | **Pioneer Sq**	16
☑ Ray's Boathse. | V | **Shilshole**	24
Ray's Cafe | V | **Shilshole**	22
Ruth's Chris | V | **Downtown**	23
☑ Salish Lodge | V | **Snoqualmie**	24
☑ Salty's | V | **W Seattle**	20
Sazerac | V | **Downtown**	20
Sea Grill* | **Tacoma**	22
☑ Seastar | V* | **Bellevue**	26
Shea's Lounge | V* | **Pike Pl Mkt**	
Shuckers | V | **Downtown**	25
☑ 6·7 | V | **Seattle Waterfront**	24
☑ SkyCity/Needle | V | **Seattle Ctr**	21
Spencer's Steaks | V | **SeaTac**	–
Tap House Grill* | **Bellevue**	18
Ten Mercer | V | **Queen Anne**	22
Third Floor Fish | V | **Kirkland**	24
Trader Vic's | V | **Bellevue**	16
Troiani | V* | **Downtown**	22
Tulio | V | **Downtown**	24
21 Central Steak | V | **Kirkland**	20
Union Sq. Grill | V* | **Downtown**	22
NEW Vi Bacchus* | **Capitol Hill**	–
☑ Waterfront Seafood | V* | **Seattle Waterfront**	24
Waters Lakeside | V | **Kirkland**	22
☑ Wild Ginger | V | **Downtown**	25
NEW Yama/Galleria* | **Bellevue**	23
Yarrow Bay Grill | V* | **Kirkland**	24

PEOPLE-WATCHING

Athenian Inn | **Pike Pl Mkt**	16
Bis on Main | **Bellevue**	24
Black Bottle | **Belltown**	22
BluWater | **multi.**	16
Bricco/Regina | **Queen Anne**	22
Broadway Grill | **Capitol Hill**	16
NEW Café Presse | **Capitol Hill**	–
Capitol Club | **Capitol Hill**	19
Crémant | **Madrona**	24
☑ Crush | **Madison Vly**	26
Cutters Bayhse. | **Pike Pl Mkt**	19
Dick's Drive-In | **multi.**	19

NEW Entre Nous | **Downtown**	–
Essential Baking | **Wallingford**	23
☑ Etta's Seafood | **Pike Pl Mkt**	24
☑ Flying Fish | **Belltown**	25
Frontier Room | **Belltown**	19
Garage | **Capitol Hill**	13
Geraldine's | **Columbia City**	20
Gilbert's Main St. Bagel | **Bellevue**	22
Goldbergs' Deli | **Bellevue**	17
Ibiza | **Pioneer Sq**	19
Jack's Fish Spot | **Pike Pl Mkt**	20
Jade Garden | **Intl Dist**	23
Joeys | **multi.**	19
Julia's | **Capitol Hill**	16
Kells Irish | **Pike Pl Mkt**	17
NEW Local Vine | **Belltown**	–
Machiavelli | **Capitol Hill**	21
NEW Made/Kitchen | **Intl Dist**	21
Mama's Mexican | **Belltown**	17
Marina Park Grill | **Kirkland**	22
Noodle Ranch | **Belltown**	17
☑ Oceanaire | **Downtown**	23
'Ohana | **Belltown**	21
Osteria La Spiga | **Capitol Hill**	24
Ototo Sushi | **Queen Anne**	24
Pacific Grill | **Tacoma**	–
P.F. Chang's | **Bellevue**	19
☑ Purple Cafe | **Downtown**	22
☑ Rest. Zoë | **Belltown**	27
Rikki Rikki | **Kirkland**	19
Ruth's Chris | **Downtown**	23
NEW Saint-Germain | **Madison Vly**	21
☑ Seastar | **Bellevue**	26
NEW Serious Pie | **Downtown**	25
Shea's Lounge | **Pike Pl Mkt**	24
NEW Steelhead | **Pike Pl Mkt**	23
NEW TASTE | **Downtown**	19
NEW Tavolàta | **Belltown**	24
13 Coins | **multi.**	18
Trader Vic's | **Bellevue**	16
NEW Umi Sake Hse. | **Belltown**	22
Union Sq. Grill | **Downtown**	22

Via Tribunali | **Capitol Hill** 23

☑ Volterra | **Ballard** 25

Wasabi Bistro | **Belltown** 22

POWER SCENES

Alibi Room | **Pike Pl Mkt** 19

Calcutta Grill | **Newcastle** 20

☑ Canlis | **Lake Union** 27

☑ Crush | **Madison Vly** 26

☑ Daniel's Broiler | **multi.** 25

☑ El Gaucho | **Belltown** 25

☑ Georgian | **Downtown** 26

Lampreia | **Belltown** 25

NEW Local Vine | **Belltown** –

☑ Lola | **Downtown** 24

☑ Metro. Grill | **Downtown** 26

Morton's | **Downtown** 24

☑ Oceanaire | **Downtown** 23

Pacific Grill | **Tacoma** –

☑ Rover's | **Madison Vly** 28

Ruth's Chris | **Downtown** 23

☑ Seastar | **Bellevue** 26

Troiani | **Downtown** 22

Union Sq. Grill | **Downtown** 22

☑ Wild Ginger | **Downtown** 25

Yarrow Bay Grill | **Kirkland** 24

PRIVATE ROOMS

(Restaurants charge less at off times; call for capacity)

Acorn Eatery | **Crown Hill** 17

Al Boccalino | **Pioneer Sq** 22

Andre's Eurasian | **Bellevue** 19

☑ Anthony's HomePort | **multi.** 20

Bambuza | **Downtown** 19

Bick's Broadview | **Greenwood** 21

Brad's Swingside | **Fremont** 24

Buenos Aires Grill | **Downtown** 23

☑ Cafe Juanita | **Kirkland** 28

Calabria | **Kirkland** 17

☑ Canlis | **Lake Union** 27

☑ Carmelita | **Greenwood** 26

☑ Cascadia | **Belltown** 25

Christina's | **Eastsound** 26

Coastal Kitchen | **Capitol Hill** 20

Crow | **Queen Anne** 23

☑ Dahlia Lounge | **Downtown** 25

☑ Daniel's Broiler | **multi.** 25

Dash Point Lobster | **Tacoma** 21

☑ El Gaucho | **multi.** 25

☑ Elliott's Oyster | **Seattle Waterfront** 23

Firenze | **Bellevue** 22

Fish Club | **Seattle Waterfront** 22

☑ Flying Fish | **Belltown** 25

☑ Georgian | **Downtown** 26

☑ Herbfarm, The | **Woodinville** 29

☑ Oceanaire | **Downtown** 23

☑ Ray's Boathse. | **Shilshole** 24

☑ Rover's | **Madison Vly** 28

☑ Salish Lodge | **Snoqualmie** 24

☑ 6 · 7 | **Seattle Waterfront** 24

Troiani | **Downtown** 22

☑ Wild Ginger | **Downtown** 25

Yarrow Bay Grill | **Kirkland** 24

QUIET CONVERSATION

Andaluca | **Downtown** 24

NEW ☑ Bakery Nouveau | **W Seattle** 28

B&O Espresso | **Capitol Hill** 20

☑ Cafe Campagne | **Pike Pl Mkt** 25

☑ Cafe Juanita | **Kirkland** 28

Chaco Canyon | **Univ Dist** –

Chez Shea | **Pike Pl Mkt** 26

Ciao Bella | **Univ Vill** 21

Cucina De-Ra | **Belltown** 21

☑ Daniel's Broiler | **multi.** 25

De Nunzio's | **Pioneer Sq** 16

Dinette | **Capitol Hill** 24

NEW DiVino | **Ballard** 22

Dulces Latin | **Madrona** 21

Earth & Ocean | **Downtown** 22

Eats Mkt. Café | **W Seattle** 20

El Greco | **Capitol Hill** 23

NEW Entre Nous | **Downtown** –

Essential Baking | **Wallingford** 23

☑ Eva | **Green Lk** 26

Four Swallows | **Bainbridge Is** 25

Geraldine's | **Columbia City** 20

Greenlake B&G | Green Lk	16	
Hunt Club | First Hill	22	
☑ Il Terrazzo | Pioneer Sq	27	
☑ Inn at Langley | Langley	27	
☑ Lynn's Bistro | Kirkland	26	
Madison Pk. Cafe | Madison Pk	22	
Marco's Supperclub | Belltown	21	
☑ Mistral | Belltown	28	
Nell's | Green Lk	25	
Pacific Grill | Tacoma	–	
Pair | Ravenna	25	
NEW Portage | Queen Anne	26	
Primo Grill | Tacoma	25	
NEW Qube | Downtown	22	
☑ Rover's | Madison Vly	28	
Russell's | Bothell	–	
Saltoro | N Seattle	22	
Shea's Lounge | Pike Pl Mkt	24	
611 Supreme | Capitol Hill	23	
NEW Tavolàta | Belltown	24	
21 Central Steak | Kirkland	20	
22 Doors | Capitol Hill	19	
☑ Union | Downtown	26	
NEW Yama/Galleria | Bellevue	23	
Zinnia | Mill Creek	23	

RAW BARS

☑ Anthony's HomePort | multi.	20
Anthony's Pier 66 | Seattle Waterfront	21
☑ Brooklyn Sea/Steak | Downtown	23
Chinook's/Salmon Bay | Magnolia	21
Cutters Bayhse. | Pike Pl Mkt	19
☑ Elliott's Oyster | Seattle Waterfront	23
F.X. McRory's | Pioneer Sq	17
Izumi | Kirkland	25
Matts' Rotisserie | Redmond	20
McCorm./Schm. Harbor | Lake Union	21
McCormick's Fish | Downtown	21
☑ Oceanaire | Downtown	23
Sea Grill | Tacoma	22
☑ Seastar | Bellevue	26

Shuckers | Downtown	25
☑ Waterfront Seafood | Seattle Waterfront	24

ROMANTIC PLACES

Bis on Main | Bellevue	24
Boat St. Cafe | Queen Anne	25
☑ Cafe Campagne | Pike Pl Mkt	25
☑ Cafe Juanita | Kirkland	28
☑ Campagne | Pike Pl Mkt	26
☑ Canlis | Lake Union	27
Capitol Club | Capitol Hill	19
Chez Shea | Pike Pl Mkt	26
Christina's | Eastsound	26
Ciao Bella | Univ Vill	21
Crémant | Madrona	24
NEW DiVino | Ballard	22
☑ Elemental | Lake Union	26
NEW Entre Nous | Downtown	–
Four Swallows | Bainbridge Is	25
Geneva | First Hill	25
☑ Harvest Vine | Madison Vly	26
☑ Herbfarm, The | Woodinville	29
Hunt Club | First Hill	22
Il Bistro | Pike Pl Mkt	23
Kasbah | Ballard	–
La Fontana Siciliana | Belltown	24
Lampreia | Belltown	25
☑ Lark | Capitol Hill	27
La Rustica | W Seattle	25
☑ Le Gourmand | Ballard	27
Madison Pk. Cafe | Madison Pk	22
Maximilien | Pike Pl Mkt	21
☑ Mistral | Belltown	28
NEW Oliver's Twist | Phinney Ridge	25
Pacific Grill | Tacoma	–
Pair | Ravenna	25
Pink Door | Pike Pl Mkt	22
Place Pigalle | Pike Pl Mkt	23
Pontevecchio | Fremont	23
NEW Portage | Queen Anne	26
☑ Rover's | Madison Vly	28
☑ Salish Lodge | Snoqualmie	24
Saltoro | N Seattle	22

Serafina	**Eastlake**	24
Shea's Lounge	**Pike Pl Mkt**	24
Szmania's	**Magnolia**	23
NEW Tavolàta	**Belltown**	24
35th St. Bistro	**Fremont**	24
21 Central Steak	**Kirkland**	20
Voilà! Bistrot	**Madison Vly**	22
Z Volterra	**Ballard**	25
Zinnia	**Mill Creek**	23

SENIOR APPEAL

Alki Homestead	**W Seattle**	20
Z Anthony's HomePort	**multi.**	20
NEW Z Bakery Nouveau	**W Seattle**	28
Bonefish Grill	**Lake Union**	19
Calcutta Grill	**Newcastle**	20
Chanterelle	**Edmonds**	19
Chinook's/Salmon Bay	**Magnolia**	21
Dash Point Lobster	**Tacoma**	21
Eats Mkt. Café	**W Seattle**	20
Essential Baking	**Wallingford**	23
Four Swallows	**Bainbridge Is**	25
Geneva	**First Hill**	25
Z Georgian	**Downtown**	26
Geraldine's	**Columbia City**	20
Goldbergs' Deli	**Bellevue**	17
Hunt Club	**First Hill**	22
Ivar Acres of Clams	**Seattle Waterfront**	20
Ivar Mukilteo	**Mukilteo**	21
Ivar Salmon Hse.	**Lake Union**	19
Z Maneki	**Intl Dist**	27
Z McCormick & Schmick's	**Downtown**	21
Northlake Tav.	**Univ Dist**	21
Pacific Grill	**Tacoma**	-
Z Palisade	**Magnolia**	23
Queen Mary Tea	**Ravenna**	19
Z Ray's Boathse.	**Shilshole**	24
NEW Remedy Teas	**Capitol Hill**	23
Russell's	**Bothell**	-
Z Salish Lodge	**Snoqualmie**	24
Saltoro	**N Seattle**	22

NEW TASTE	**Downtown**	19
13 Coins	**multi.**	18
Zinnia	**Mill Creek**	23

SINGLES SCENES

Beach Cafe/Point	**Kirkland**	18
BluWater	**multi.**	16
Capitol Club	**Capitol Hill**	19
Crocodile Cafe	**Belltown**	14
Crow	**Queen Anne**	23
Cutters Bayhse.	**Pike Pl Mkt**	19
Cyclops	**Belltown**	17
Z Daniel's Broiler	**multi.**	25
Fox Sports Grill	**Downtown**	12
F.X. McRory's	**Pioneer Sq**	17
Garage	**Capitol Hill**	13
Gordon Biersch	**Downtown**	14
Hale's Ales	**Fremont**	17
Hattie's Hat	**Ballard**	16
Il Bistro	**Pike Pl Mkt**	23
Joeys	**multi.**	19
Kells Irish	**Pike Pl Mkt**	17
Z Le Pichet	**Pike Pl Mkt**	24
Z Lola	**Downtown**	24
Luau Polynesian	**Green Lk**	15
Machiavelli	**Capitol Hill**	21
Mama's Mexican	**Belltown**	17
Z Metro. Grill	**Downtown**	26
New Orl. Creole	**Pioneer Sq**	14
Z Oceanaire	**Downtown**	23
'Ohana	**Belltown**	21
Z Palace Kitchen	**Downtown**	24
Paragon	**Queen Anne**	19
Peso's Kitchen	**Queen Anne**	23
Pike Pub	**Pike Pl Mkt**	16
Pink Door	**Pike Pl Mkt**	22
Z Purple Cafe	**multi.**	22
Pyramid Ale	**Pioneer Sq**	16
Ray's Cafe	**Shilshole**	22
Z Rest. Zoë	**Belltown**	27
Rosebud	**Capitol Hill**	19
Ruth's Chris	**multi.**	23
Z Salty's	**multi.**	20
Toi	**Downtown**	-
Two Bells B&G	**Belltown**	19

SPECIAL FEATURES

Wasabi Bistro | **Belltown** 22

Ⓩ Wild Ginger | **Downtown** 25

Yarrow Bay Grill | **Kirkland** 24

THEME RESTAURANTS

Buca di Beppo | **multi.** 14

Cafe Veloce | **Kirkland** 21

Luna Park Cafe | **W Seattle** 15

Trader Vic's | **Bellevue** 16

NEW Wilde Rover | **Kirkland** –

TRENDY

Ⓩ Armandino's Salumi | 28
Pioneer Sq

Baguette Box | **multi.** 23

NEW⒵ Bakery Nouveau | 28
W Seattle

Black Bottle | **Belltown** 22

Blue C Sushi | **multi.** 15

NEW Boka Kitchen | **Downtown** 22

Bricco/Regina | **Queen Anne** 22

Buenos Aires Grill | **Downtown** 23

Cactus | **Kirkland** 22

Ⓩ Cafe Besalu | **Ballard** 27

NEW Café Presse | **Capitol Hill** –

Capitol Club | **Capitol Hill** 19

Ⓩ Chiso | **Fremont** 26

NEW Coupage | **Madrona** 23

Crave | **Capitol Hill** 20

Crémant | **Madrona** 24

Crow | **Queen Anne** 23

Ⓩ Crush | **Madison Vly** 26

Dinette | **Capitol Hill** 24

Earth & Ocean | **Downtown** 22

Ⓩ Elemental | **Lake Union** 26

Essential Baking | **Wallingford** 23

Ⓩ Eva | **Green Lk** 26

Fort St. George | **Intl Dist** –

Frontier Room | **Belltown** 19

Garage | **Capitol Hill** 13

Ⓩ Harvest Vine | **Madison Vly** 26

Ibiza | **Pioneer Sq** 19

Ⓩ JaK's Grill | **W Seattle** 26

Joeys | **multi.** 19

Ⓩ La Carta/Oaxaca | **Ballard** 26

Ⓩ Lark | **Capitol Hill** 27

Ⓩ Le Pichet | **Pike Pl Mkt** 24

NEW Local Vine | **Belltown** –

Ⓩ Lola | **Downtown** 24

Macrina | **multi.** 25

Matt's/Mkt. | **Pike Pl Mkt** –

Ⓩ Oceanaire | **Downtown** 23

NEW O/8 | **Bellevue** 21

NEW Oliver's Twist | 25
Phinney Ridge

NEW Opal | **Queen Anne** 25

Osteria La Spiga | **Capitol Hill** 24

Pacific Grill | **Tacoma** –

Ⓩ Palace Kitchen | **Downtown** 24

Persimmon | **Fremont** 22

NEW Porcella | **Bellevue** 24

Ⓩ Purple Cafe | **Downtown** 22

Purple Dot Café | **Intl Dist** 18

Red Fin | **Downtown** 23

NEW Remedy Teas | **Capitol Hill** 23

Ⓩ Rest. Zoë | **Belltown** 27

Ⓩ Seastar | **Bellevue** 26

NEW Serious Pie | **Downtown** 25

Ⓩ Sitka & Spruce | **Eastlake** 28

NEW TASTE | **Downtown** 19

NEW Tavolàta | **Belltown** 24

NEW Tilth | **Wallingford** 25

NEW Umi Sake Hse. | **Belltown** 22

Ⓩ Union | **Downtown** 26

Veil | **Queen Anne** 23

Via Tribunali | **multi.** 23

Ⓩ Volterra | **Ballard** 25

NEW Yama/Galleria | **Bellevue** 23

VIEWS

Agua Verde | **Univ Dist** 22

Ⓩ Anthony's HomePort | **multi.** 20

Anthony's Pier 66 | 21
Seattle Waterfront

Athenian Inn | **Pike Pl Mkt** 16

Beach Cafe/Point | **Kirkland** 18

BluWater | **multi.** 16

Cactus | **multi.** 22

Calcutta Grill | **Newcastle** 20

Ⓩ Canlis | **Lake Union** 27

Chandler's Crab | **Lake Union** 22

Chez Shea	**Pike Pl Mkt**	26
Chinook's/Salmon Bay	**Magnolia**	21
Christina's	**Eastsound**	26
Cutters Bayhse.	**Pike Pl Mkt**	19
☑ Daniel's Broiler	**multi.**	25
Dash Point Lobster	**Tacoma**	21
☑ Elliott's Oyster	**Seattle Waterfront**	23
Fish Club	**Seattle Waterfront**	22
Friday Harbor Hse.	**Friday Harbor**	–
I Love Sushi	**Lake Union**	23
☑ Il Terrazzo	**Pioneer Sq**	27
Ivar Acres of Clams	**Seattle Waterfront**	20
Ivar Salmon Hse.	**Lake Union**	19
Kells Irish	**Pike Pl Mkt**	17
Maggie Bluff's	**Magnolia**	18
Marina Park Grill	**Kirkland**	22
Matt's Gourmet Dogs	**Pioneer Sq**	18
Maximilien	**Pike Pl Mkt**	21
McCorm./Schm. Harbor	**Lake Union**	21
Oyster Bar/Chuckanut	**Bow**	24
☑ Palace Kitchen	**Downtown**	24
☑ Palisade	**Magnolia**	23
Pink Door	**Pike Pl Mkt**	22
Place Pigalle	**Pike Pl Mkt**	23
Pontevecchio	**Fremont**	23
Ponti Seafood	**Fremont**	22
NEW Porcella	**Bellevue**	24
☑ Ray's Boathse.	**Shilshole**	24
Ray's Cafe	**Shilshole**	22
Red Door	**Fremont**	17
Red Robin	**Issaquah**	15
Rose's Bakery	**Eastsound**	–
☑ Salish Lodge	**Snoqualmie**	24
☑ Salty's	**multi.**	20
Shea's Lounge	**Pike Pl Mkt**	24
☑ 6 · 7	**Seattle Waterfront**	24
☑ SkyCity/Needle	**Seattle Ctr**	21
Sostanza	**Madison Pk**	22
Sunfish	**W Seattle**	21

Tacos Guaymas	**Green Lk**	20
That's Amore	**Mt. Baker**	–
Third Floor Fish	**Kirkland**	24
Three Girls Bakery	**Pike Pl Mkt**	24
Tratt. Mitchelli	**Pioneer Sq**	16
Troiani	**Downtown**	22
Turkish Delight	**Pike Pl Mkt**	21
Union Sq. Grill	**Downtown**	22
☑ Waterfront Seafood	**Seattle Waterfront**	24
Waters Lakeside	**Kirkland**	22
Yarrow Bay Grill	**Kirkland**	24

VISITORS ON EXPENSE ACCOUNT

Barking Frog	**Woodinville**	24
☑ Brasa	**Belltown**	25
☑ Canlis	**Lake Union**	27
☑ Cascadia	**Belltown**	25
Chandler's Crab	**Lake Union**	22
☑ Crush	**Madison Vly**	26
☑ Dahlia Lounge	**Downtown**	25
☑ Daniel's Broiler	**multi.**	25
☑ El Gaucho	**Belltown**	25
☑ Georgian	**Downtown**	26
☑ Herbfarm, The	**Woodinville**	29
Hunt Club	**First Hill**	22
Lampreia	**Belltown**	25
NEW Local Vine	**Belltown**	–
☑ Metro. Grill	**Downtown**	26
☑ Mistral	**Belltown**	28
Morton's	**Downtown**	24
☑ Oceanaire	**Downtown**	23
☑ Ray's Boathse.	**Shilshole**	24
☑ Rover's	**Madison Vly**	28
Ruth's Chris	**Downtown**	23
☑ Salish Lodge	**Snoqualmie**	24
☑ Seastar	**Bellevue**	26
Troiani	**Downtown**	22
☑ Union	**Downtown**	26
☑ Volterra	**Ballard**	25

WATERSIDE

Agua Verde	**Univ Dist**	22
☑ Anthony's HomePort	**multi.**	20

SPECIAL FEATURES

Anthony's Pier 66 | **Seattle Waterfront**	21
Beach Cafe/Point | **Kirkland**	18
Bell St. Diner | **Seattle Waterfront**	18
BluWater | **multi.**	16
Chandler's Crab | **Lake Union**	22
Chinook's/Salmon Bay | **Magnolia**	21
Christina's | **Eastsound**	26
☑ Daniel's Broiler | **multi.**	25
Dash Point Lobster | **Tacoma**	21
Duke's Chowder | **multi.**	18
☑ Elliott's Oyster | **Seattle Waterfront**	23
Friday Harbor Hse. | **Friday Harbor**	-
I Love Sushi | **Lake Union**	23
Ivar Acres of Clams | **Seattle Waterfront**	20
Ivar Mukilteo | **Mukilteo**	21
Ivar Salmon Hse. | **Lake Union**	19
Maggie Bluff's | **Magnolia**	18
McCorm./Schm. Harbor | **Lake Union**	21
Oyster Bar/Chuckanut | **Bow**	24
☑ Palisade | **Magnolia**	23
Ponti Seafood | **Fremont**	22
☑ Ray's Boathse. | **Shilshole**	24
Ray's Cafe | **Shilshole**	22
Red Robin | **Issaquah**	15
☑ Salty's | **multi.**	20
☑ 6 · 7 | **Seattle Waterfront**	24
Sostanza | **Madison Pk**	22
Third Floor Fish | **Kirkland**	24
21 Central Steak | **Kirkland**	20
☑ Waterfront Seafood | **Seattle Waterfront**	24
Waters Lakeside | **Kirkland**	22
Yarrow Bay Grill | **Kirkland**	24

WINNING WINE LISTS

☑ Anthony's HomePort | **multi.**	20
Anthony's Pier 66 | **Seattle Waterfront**	21
Barking Frog | **Woodinville**	24
NEW Barolo | **Downtown**	22
NEW Beàto | **W Seattle**	23
Bis on Main | **Bellevue**	24
Brad's Swingside | **Fremont**	24
☑ Brasa | **Belltown**	25
Brass. Margaux | **Downtown**	19
Bricco/Regina | **Queen Anne**	22
☑ Cafe Campagne | **Pike Pl Mkt**	25
☑ Cafe Juanita | **Kirkland**	28
☑ Campagne | **Pike Pl Mkt**	26
☑ Canlis | **Lake Union**	27
☑ Cascadia | **Belltown**	25
Chez Shea | **Pike Pl Mkt**	26
Christina's | **Eastsound**	26
NEW Coupage | **Madrona**	23
Crémant | **Madrona**	24
☑ Crush | **Madison Vly**	26
☑ Dahlia Lounge | **Downtown**	25
☑ Daniel's Broiler | **multi.**	25
De Nunzio's | **Pioneer Sq**	16
NEW DiVino | **Ballard**	22
Dulces Latin | **Madrona**	21
Earth & Ocean | **Downtown**	22
☑ Elemental | **Lake Union**	26
☑ Eva | **Green Lk**	26
☑ Flying Fish | **Belltown**	25
Four Swallows | **Bainbridge Is**	25
Garage | **Capitol Hill**	13
☑ Georgian | **Downtown**	26
Grazie | **multi.**	20
☑ Harvest Vine | **Madison Vly**	26
☑ Herbfarm, The | **Woodinville**	29
NEW Hills' Food/Wine | **Shoreline**	23
Hunt Club | **First Hill**	22
Ibiza | **Pioneer Sq**	19
Il Bistro | **Pike Pl Mkt**	23
Julia's | **Queen Anne**	16
Lampreia | **Belltown**	25
☑ Le Gourmand | **Ballard**	27
☑ Le Pichet | **Pike Pl Mkt**	24
NEW Local Vine | **Belltown**	-
☑ Lola | **Downtown**	24
Madison Pk. Cafe | **Madison Pk**	22

Mamma Melina | **Univ Dist**	21
Marjorie | **Belltown**	22
Market St. Grill | **Ballard**	25
☑ Metro. Grill | **Downtown**	26
☑ Mistral | **Belltown**	28
Mixtura | **Kirkland**	24
☑ Monsoon | **Capitol Hill**	27
Morton's | **Downtown**	24
Nell's | **Green Lk**	25
94 Stewart | **Pike Pl Mkt**	21
NEW O/8 | **Bellevue**	21
Olives Cafe | **Edmonds**	23
Osteria La Spiga | **Capitol Hill**	24
NEW Poco Wine | **Capitol Hill**	–
Portalis | **Ballard**	18
☑ Purple Cafe | **Downtown**	22
Queen City Grill | **Belltown**	22
☑ Ray's Boathse. | **Shilshole**	24
☑ Rover's | **Madison Vly**	28
Russell's | **Bothell**	–
Ruth's Chris | **Downtown**	23
☑ Salish Lodge | **Snoqualmie**	24
☑ Seastar | **Bellevue**	26
Shea's Lounge | **Pike Pl Mkt**	24
Tango | **Capitol Hill**	23
NEW Tavolàta | **Belltown**	24
Troiani | **Downtown**	22
Voilà! Bistrot | **Madison Vly**	22
☑ Volterra | **Ballard**	25
☑ Wild Ginger | **Downtown**	25
Yarrow Bay Grill | **Kirkland**	24

WORTH A TRIP

Bainbridge Island	
Four Swallows	25
Bow	
Oyster Bar/Chuckanut	24
Eastsound, Orcas Island	
Christina's	26
Friday Harbor, San Juan Island	
Friday Harbor Hse.	–
Langley, Whidbey Island	
☑ Inn at Langley	27
Seaview	
Shoalwater	–
Snoqualmie	
☑ Salish Lodge	24
Woodinville	
☑ Herbfarm, The	29

Wine Vintage Chart

This chart, based on our 0 to 30 scale, is designed to help you select wine. The ratings (by **Howard Stravitz,** a law professor at the University of South Carolina) reflect the vintage quality and the wine's readiness to drink. We exclude the 1991–1993 vintages because they are not that good. A dash indicates the wine is either past its peak or too young to rate. Loire ratings are for dry white wines.

Whites	88	89	90	94	95	96	97	98	99	00	01	02	03	04	05	06
French:																
Alsace	-	25	25	24	23	23	22	25	23	25	27	25	22	24	25	-
Burgundy	-	23	22	-	28	27	24	22	26	25	24	27	23	27	26	24
Loire Valley	-	-	-	-	-	-	-	-	-	24	25	26	23	24	27	24
Champagne	24	26	29	-	26	27	24	23	24	24	22	26	-	-	-	-
Sauternes	29	25	28	-	21	23	25	23	24	24	28	25	26	21	26	23
California:																
Chardonnay	-	-	-	-	-	-	-	-	24	23	26	26	25	27	29	25
Sauvignon Blanc	-	-	-	-	-	-	-	-	-	-	27	28	26	27	26	27
Austrian:																
Grüner Velt./Riesling	-	-	-	-	25	21	26	26	25	22	23	25	26	25	26	-
German:	25	26	27	24	23	26	25	26	23	21	29	27	24	26	28	-

Reds	88	89	90	94	95	96	97	98	99	00	01	02	03	04	05	06
French:																
Bordeaux	23	25	29	22	26	25	23	25	24	29	26	24	25	24	27	25
Burgundy	-	24	26	-	26	27	25	22	27	22	24	27	25	25	27	25
Rhône	26	28	28	24	26	22	25	27	26	27	26	-	25	24	25	-
Beaujolais	-	-	-	-	-	-	-	-	-	24	-	23	25	22	28	26
California:																
Cab./Merlot	-	-	28	29	27	25	28	23	26	22	27	26	25	24	24	23
Pinot Noir	-	-	-	-	-	-	24	23	24	23	27	28	26	25	24	-
Zinfandel	-	-	-	-	-	-	-	-	-	-	25	23	27	24	23	-
Oregon:																
Pinot Noir	-	-	-	-	-	-	-	-	-	-	-	27	25	26	27	-
Italian:																
Tuscany	-	-	25	22	24	20	29	24	27	24	27	20	25	25	22	24
Piedmont	-	27	27	-	23	26	27	26	25	28	27	20	24	25	26	-
Spanish:																
Rioja	-	-	-	26	26	24	25	22	25	24	27	20	24	25	26	24
Ribera del Duero/Priorat	-	-	-	26	26	27	25	24	25	24	27	20	24	26	26	24
Australian:																
Shiraz/Cab.	-	-	-	24	26	23	26	28	24	24	27	27	25	26	24	-
Chilean:	-	-	-	-	-	-	24	-	25	23	26	24	25	24	26	-

subscribe to zagat.com